PENGUIN BOOKS

THE PRIVATE WORLD OF BALLET

John Gruen was born in France in 1926 and educated in Berlin, in Milan, and in America (at the City College of New York and the University of Iowa). His varied career has included work as a bookstore salesclerk, composer, publisher's publicity director, photographer's agent, and art gallery director. From 1960 to 1967 he was art and music critic for the New York *Herald Tribune,* and he has been art critic of *New York* magazine and a feature writer for *Vogue.* He is now a contributing editor to *Dance* magazine, frequent contributor to the Sunday entertainment pages of *The New York Times,* and the host of a weekly radio program on the dance. Mr. Gruen, who is also currently writing a biography of Gian-Carlo Menotti, lives in New York with his wife, the painter Jane Wilson, and their daughter.

John Gruen THE PRIVATE
WORLD OF

PENGUIN BOOKS

BALLET

Penguin Books Ltd, Harmondsworth, Middlesex, England
Penguin Books, 625 Madison Avenue, New York, New York 10022, U.S.A.
Penguin Books Australia Ltd, Ringwood, Victoria, Australia
Penguin Books Canada Ltd, 41 Steelcase Road West, Markham, Ontario, Canada
Penguin Books (N.Z.) Ltd, 182–190 Wairau Road, Auckland 10, New Zealand

First published by The Viking Press 1975
Published in Penguin Books 1976

Copyright © John Gruen, 1970, 1971, 1972, 1974, 1975
All rights reserved

LIBRARY OF CONGRESS CATALOGING IN PUBLICATION DATA
Gruen, John
The private world of ballet
(A Penguin Book)
Reprint of the 1975 ed. published by The Viking Press, New York.
Includes index.
1. Ballet–Biography. 2. Ballet–History.
I. Title
[GV1785.A1G78 1976]   792.8′092′2 [B] 76-24890
ISBN 0 14 00.4343 8 (pbk.)

The article "George Balanchine" originally appeared in Vogue.

Printed in the United States of America by
The Murray Printing Company, Forge Village, Massachusetts
Set in Linotype Times Roman

There are those who claim that ballet dancers cannot possibly express in words what they articulate so eloquently with their bodies. This book will, I hope, prove them wrong—or, at least, give them pause.

I have not set out to write a historical tract on classical dance and dancers. This book is an encounter with individuals who inhabit a heretofore circumscribed world—a world that has in recent years roused the imagination and curiosity of an international public.

In speaking with more than seventy figures in the dance, over a period of nearly two years, I was amazed, delighted, and moved to find them possessed of remarkable lucidity, and complexity, as well as unique talent and artistry. Dancers feel passionately and fervently about their art and the lives they devote to it.

Because dancers have not traditionally been thought of as articulate, and because their art is devoted to physical rather than to verbal expression, the general public seldom knows what they are about. Unlike film and television actors, theater people, sports figures, or politicians, dancers are seldom interviewed and revealed as personalities or as human beings. For a ballet dancer to receive wide public attention, he must either make a dramatic leap from an Iron Curtain country, or become the object of national pride and recognition. Today's outstanding examples are, of course, Rudolf Nureyev and Dame Margot Fonteyn.

This book does not claim to offer full-length portraits of its subjects but hopes to break through the anonymity of artists practicing a noble, yet "silent" art. It hopes to make clear the fact that there are lives at work before the curtain goes up and after it comes down.

To my knowledge, this may be the first book in which a large segment of the classical dance world speaks for itself.

Where to begin and where to end the survey became the chief problem. Clearly, I could not speak with every major or representative figure in the world of ballet. Because of timing, geographical limitations, and a publication deadline, there are certain glaring omissions. I was unable, for example, to speak to some of the illustrious Soviet dancers, or to members of the great Danish, Swedish, and Dutch companies. At the time of my visit to London, Madame Tamara Karsavina, one of the legendary dancers of Diaghilev's Ballets Russes, was unavailable. Sir Frederick Ashton, the great British choreographer, was ill.

Some celebrated figures in the dance, such as Jerome Robbins and Nora Kaye (to mention but two), declined to be interviewed. However, most of the dancers and choreographers not personally interviewed are discussed from varying points of view by the artists here represented.

Obviously, in a work of this kind, personal preferences take precedence over encyclopedic coverage. Even so, not every dancer represented is my special favorite. By the same token, many of my favorite dancers are not included. Ultimately, the choices were chosen to be a fair representation of the varied strata of the ballet world.

What remains to be said is that dancers as people and as artists change, evolve, and mature with the years. What they strongly felt and believed during these interviews (done mainly between 1972 and 1974) may not be representative of what they feel and believe today—or may feel and believe tomorrow.

What is constant, however, is that dancing has been their life, and the moments shared here offer personal, often poignant glimpses and insights into the private world of ballet.

JOHN GRUEN

New York City
February 1974

ACKNOWLEDGMENTS

I have received generous and unstinting help from many individuals in the writing of this book. First and foremost, I wish to thank the dancers, choreographers, and teachers of the dance who have not only allowed me to interview them but who have permitted me to witness their working methods in the classroom, during rehearsals, and in performance.

I am grateful to Genevieve Oswald, Curator of the Dance Collection, The New York Public Library, and for the cooperation of her staff.

For their help in putting me in touch with the artists represented, I am most grateful to Vivien Wallace, press officer, The Royal Ballet, Covent Garden, London; Rosella Hightower, ballerina and head of Le Centre de Danse International, Cannes; Virginia Hymes and Irene Shaw of the American Ballet Theatre; Virginia Donaldson, Marie Gutscher, and Barbara Horgan of the New York City Ballet; Rima Corben and Robert Larkin of the Joffrey Ballet; Sheila Porter and Lillian Libman of Hurok Concerts, Inc. My thanks also to the late Christopher Allen and to Marit Gentele for introducing me to Erik Bruhn.

For his extraordinary diligence and patience in the transcription of some eighty taped interviews, for his scholarly acumen on the history of dance and dancers, and for his good humor and wit during long months of work, I am particularly grateful to Andrew M. Wentink of the Dance Collection, Performing Arts Research Center of the Library and Museum of Performing Arts, Lincoln Center, New York.

My very special thanks, also, to Joan Ungaro, who has assisted me in the preparation of the manuscript, and to Louis Peres, who photocopied early photographs of Serge Lifar, Igor Markevitch, Léonide Massine, Alexandra Danilova, Alicia Markova, Anton Dolin, John Gilpin, Vera Zorina, Sono Osato, and Rosella Hightower, the originals of which are in the collection of The New York Public Library at Lincoln Center Astor, Lenox, and Tilden Foundations.

No book on the dance can be written without the invaluable aid of *The Dance Encyclopedia*, compiled and edited by Anatole Chujoy and P. W. Manchester (New York: Simon and Schuster, 1967). My thanks to *The New York Times* for permission to reprint my interviews with Rudolf Nureyev, Dame Margot Fonteyn, Marcia Haydée, and Natalia Makarova, and to *Vogue* magazine for permission to reprint portions of my interview with George Balanchine.

Finally, for their unfailing support, I am deeply indebted to my former editor, Ann Hancock, and to my present editor, Barbara Burn.

CONTENTS

Che Current Scene

CITY CENTER JOFFREY BALLET ———————————————

Looking Ahead

Looking
Back

Anthony

SERGE LIFAR

August in Cannes is hell. It's National Vacation time in France, and the citizens flee the cities and swarm over the countryside. They rush to the South of France like lemmings drawn to the sea. In August 1972, I went in search of dancers who no longer dance—the retired *étoiles* with fabulous pasts. The Côte d'Azur is their turf. It is, after all, where it all started: Monte Carlo—the ravishing Riviera spot where Sergei Diaghilev brought the classical dance to Europe.

That summer in Cannes, large posters announced a gala in homage to

Diaghilev, presented and conceived by Serge Lifar. The occasion was Diaghilev's centennial. The event would take place at the Palm Beach Casino, and *toute la Côte d'Azur* would be there. Upon closer examination of the posters, one noted that *le spectacle* honoring Diaghilev was in reality centered on M. Serge Lifar. Four of Lifar's own ballets would be danced on the Casino's open terrace. A mammoth exhibition of Lifar's own paintings would be on view in one of the Casino's large *salons*.

As luck would have it, the *mistral*, a high Mediterranean wind, made its appearance on the very evening of the gala. I walked the long stretch of the Croisette leading to the Palm Beach Casino, wondering how the *mistral* would affect the outdoor festivities. I arrived at the Palm Beach somewhat early, in the hope of meeting with Serge Lifar and obtaining an appointment from him for an interview.

The Casino was astir with activity as I entered its elegant foyer. The *mistral* was in fairly high gear. I noted workmen vainly trying to bind an enormous Picasso backdrop to poles erected on the outdoor stage. It was a losing battle. Finally, fearing damage to the Picasso, the idea was abandoned. The stage remained bare throughout the evening. Meanwhile, the terrace was aglitter with nearly a hundred tables holding floral centerpieces, expensive silver, chinaware, and glasses, which rattled and shook with the assault of the unabating wind. Waiters stood in clusters at various points of the terrace, clearly aghast at the prospect of serving food in such weather.

The *salon* began to fill. Women in elaborate coiffures eyed each other in distress. What havoc would the *mistral* wreak on their hairdos? Most of them wore décolleté gowns, and only a few carried evening wraps or fur pieces to protect them from the high-blown chill.

At last, Serge Lifar, in white tie and tails, made his appearance. To his left was his constant companion, the Comtesse Lela d'Anlefeldt. To his right were the conductor Igor Markevitch and Count Serge Tolstoy. The look on Lifar's face was one of total dismay. We were introduced, but his thoughts were clearly elsewhere. His eyes turned in the direction of the open terrace, with its tables, its stage, and orchestra stand. "*Quel désastre!* What a moment for the *mistral* to come! My poor dancers will freeze to death! The musicians will be unable to play! Everyone will go home! What shall we do?" The Countess, a small-boned, blue-eyed, blond woman of great charm and liveliness, was all solicitude. "Stop worrying, Serge, my darling. The winds will subside, you'll see." But Lifar was inconsolable. "*Quel désastre!*" he kept repeating.

Serge Lifar is now a man in his late sixties with a careworn face. His features, with their Oriental cast, still reflect the intensity and slight mystery seen in photographs of the days when he was Diaghilev's last *premier danseur* with the Ballets Russes. The trim, taut body has, of course, altered through the years. But in his walk, and in his gestures, Lifar continues to bear the elegant mark of the dancer. Lifar's hands are particularly beautiful, and he uses them with special grace. Most notable is his voice. It is something of a foghorn. Gravelly, and without the slightest variance in pitch, it is a continuous drone of Russian and French.

Lifar stood in the center of the foyer, greeting arriving dignitaries, some of whom had come from many parts of Europe. He was apologetic to one and all, practically taking the blame for nature's whims. Some three hundred guests had arrived. Outside, the wind had grown more fierce. People were milling in the foyer, not at all anxious to take their seats on the open terrace. They chatted, consuming a great deal of superb champagne. They knew the dinner would last for nearly three hours.

Finally, guests and dignitaries reluctantly began to brave the terrace. A swarm of waiters began serving the appetizer—*Le Caviar de la Volga*. As it was being consumed, a spotlight suddenly illuminated an especially erected platform in one corner of the *salon*, high above the guests. A staircase led up to it, reminiscent of the simple set of Balanchine's *Apollo*. Upon the platform stood a lone chair. In a moment, a tall gentleman slowly ascended the stairs. He was dressed in tails and top hat. He wore white gloves, a monocle, and held a cane. He sat in the chair, to thunderous applause. Clearly, the figure was the living representation of Sergei Diaghilev.

The Comtesse d'Anlefeldt, my dinner companion, was ecstatic. "Isn't it wonderful!" she exclaimed. "Lifar found this fellow in the kitchens of the Casino. He couldn't believe his eyes when he saw the resemblance to Diaghilev. It was Lifar's idea to get him all dressed up like that. He will be sitting there all evening, as a symbol!" Serge Lifar was all smiles, accepting the compliments of his astonished guests.

Somehow, the Lifar ballets failed to evoke the grandeur or glamour or artistic achievement of the golden days of Diaghilev's Ballets Russes. Danced indifferently, and choreographed more or less predictably, Lifar's works received the warm applause of friends. When it was over—it had gotten quite late, and quite cold—the speeches began. Robert Manuel of the Comédie Française lauded Diaghilev, as well as Lifar. Poems were recited, and other speeches came in lengthy succession. At my side, Lifar's Countess often had tears in her eyes. At times, she would turn to me and say, "Just look at my Serge! Is he not the most beautiful man you have ever seen in your life? You know, half the people here were responsible for his dismissal in 1959 as director of the Paris Opera. Now they kiss him on the cheeks, and consider him a monument. Poor Serge, he has suffered so much, and he is so selfless and good. One day, the whole world will know what Lifar has done for French ballet!"

Toward the end of the evening, I secured an appointment to interview Lifar. We would meet in a few days at the bar of the Hotel Majestic, in Cannes.

Serge Lifar's testament to his own greatness, his autobiography, *My Life*, published in 1965, recalls his childhood in pre-Revolutionary Russia (he was born in Kiev, in 1905) and charts the course of a life spent in the service of the dance. It was Nijinsky's sister, Bronislava, who discovered the young dancer at the Kiev Conservatory of Music. She brought him to Paris to join Diaghilev's Ballets Russes in 1923. Two years later, he became the company's *premier danseur*. In 1929, he scored an immense personal success dancing the title role in George Balanchine's *Le Fils Prodigue*, to a score by Prokofiev and décor by Rouault. (Felia Doubrovska danced the Siren, and the young Anton Dolin danced one of the Prodigal Son's companions.)

Fascinating are Lifar's chapters dealing with his years as head of the Paris Opera Ballet during the German occupation of World War II, and the political enmeshments which resulted in his abrupt dismissal and a trial condemning him never to appear again on any French stage. Lifar had danced before Goebbels, Goering, and had met Adolph Hitler. As Lifar put it, he had consorted with the Germans not for personal gain or safety, but in the name of French culture. Ultimately, the dancer was exonerated by the French government, and in 1947 was reinstated as director of the Paris Opera Ballet, serving until 1959, when he was once again curtly dismissed.

On the appointed day, Lifar and I met at the Hotel Majestic. He was sun-tanned, wore a blue-and-white flowered shirt, blue slacks. A bright red sweater was tied casually around his shoulders. Lifar ordered drinks, and in his low-pitched drone, told me something of his present life.

"I no longer dance. I retired from the dance in 1956. My last appearance was at the Paris Opera as Albrecht in *Giselle*, partnering Yvette Chauviré. I am seldom asked to choreograph. I live here in Cannes and lead a very quiet life. I would say, however, that my life is in the past, in the present, and also in the future. The past is easy. The present is easy. But the future is difficult.

"You wish to hear about Diaghilev? Diaghilev was a Don Juan of the arts. He was eternally dissatisfied. He smelled out genius. He made use of it. Once having made use of it, he searched out the next genius. Take his discovery of Stravinsky. Stravinsky was an unknown composer in Saint Petersburg. Diaghilev heard his 'Feu d'Artifice,' and understood there was something extraordinary in Stravinsky. But then Diaghilev discovered Prokofiev, and Stravinsky lost his first place. He was no longer Diaghilev's 'first son.' And so it went. After Prokofiev, he found Dukelsky, Nabokov, Rieti . . . it was like that with everyone—with Benois, with Bakst, with Nijinsky, with Massine, with me. Diaghilev thirsted after the new. We are all his spiritual sons. One could go on. First, he loved Fokine; then Nijinsky replaced him as choreographer. Then Massine choreographed. Then

Bronislava Nijinska. Finally, there was Balanchine, and then I, myself, as choreographer. When he died, two of his discoveries were at his side— Lifar and Markevitch, a mere boy of sixteen when Diaghilev found him.

"You ask what Diaghilev was to Lifar. Even when I was still in Russia, Diaghilev was a god for me. When I went to Paris to join him, it seemed like a miracle. To us Russians in Europe, he was a kind of tsar—he was a link to all that Russia stood for before the Revolution. Diaghilev was a Grand Duke in exile. Remember, that when I was a young boy in Kiev, I watched the aristocracy crumble around me. Somehow, I could never shake my duty toward my country and my Emperor. And so, when at the age of seventeen I was brought to Diaghilev in Paris, *he* became my Emperor.

"In those days the Ballets Russes were a total hierarchy. Talent did not count for much. Seniority counted. We young people were treated like errand boys. We had to run out and buy cigarettes for aging dancers who no longer knew how to dance. At any rate, Diaghilev soon discovered that I possessed special qualities. He saw that I had the line that he had seen in Nijinsky, in Massine. I was his third great discovery. What was so ironic is that, at that time, I knew nothing of the history of ballet. I was always a poor student. In school, I was always the last. Diaghilev became my mentor. He introduced me to painting, to music, to the ways of the world. We traveled together, as he and Nijinsky had traveled together. We were always together. And I learned so much!

"But to tell you the truth, I was not a happy boy when I first arrived in Paris to join the company. I felt myself lacking in the great art of the ballet. Consider the male dancers around me: Vilzak, Vladimirov, Idzikowski, Woizikowski. I suffered tremendously. I wanted to pack up all my things and enter a Greek monastery. But I stayed. I kept myself apart, thinking and trying to solve my moral and philosophical dilemmas.

"I survived my early unhappiness because of Diaghilev. He saved me. Once, I overheard him say, 'This boy *will* be a dancer.' Well, in two years, I became equal to the greatest dancers. This shows you the faith Diaghilev had in me. Because of my fantastic progress, I became privileged, and Diaghilev saw to it that I was treated with respect. Of course, I was totally under his influence.

"Sergei Diaghilev was a marvelous man. And how complex! He could be very shy, very sentimental. The impression he made was one of total sophistication. And yet, there was something primitive about him as well —almost to a point of repulsiveness. Strangely enough, when I knew him, he preferred living in shabby hotel rooms. He liked to wear seedy clothes. He would walk around in the same moth-eaten fur coat, and he was careless of his personal appearance. And yet he radiated incredible vitality and drive."

Lifar sipped his drink, and the years seemed to fall off as he recounted his past life with the man who gave him identity, fame, and notoriety. I asked Lifar whether Diaghilev had ever spoken to him about Nijinsky.

"The subject was too painful for Diaghilev to discuss. He seemed reluctant to disclose certain things about Vaslav. But many years later, I realized that there was something about Nijinsky's madness that no one had ever dared speak about. I can only tell you that Nijinsky's sister, Bronislava, wrote a memoir just prior to her death in Los Angeles in 1972. This memoir is now in the possession of Nijinsky's daughter, Kyra. If it were ever published, the book would become one of the greatest documents of the twentieth century! I can assure you, the real truth about Nijinsky is to be found in this memoir—not in the books written by Nijinsky's widow, Romola, nor in the recently published Nijinsky biography by Richard Buckle. Bronislava had the answers! Remember, she was my teacher in Kiev. I was like her son. She told me things about Vaslav that were absolutely stupefying. Once the truth comes to light, there will be no more hypotheses possible about him. I have taken a vow of silence. But, believe me, his story is far more tragic than anyone knows."

At this moment, Lifar's Countess joined us. Once more, Lela d'Anlefeldt cast adoring eyes on her beloved Serge. She said that they must soon drive to Antibes for a dinner party, and then on to another soiree. But the Countess was willing to sit awhile and recount her meeting with Lifar:

"We met in Paris in 1958. I was a house guest of the Grand Duke André Romanov, the last cousin of the Tsar. Every Wednesday, the Grand Duke held a soiree for all the Paris arists and intellectuals. The Duke was an aristocrat who had fallen on hard times, but still, his *salon* was of the highest standards. One Wednesday, I was told that Lifar would appear. I had never met him before. When he walked into the room, he wore a flowing cape. His beautiful dark eyes scanned the room. He looked mysterious. There was something of Rasputin about him. The Duke whispered to me, 'Serge is the most unusual man in Europe—even for us Russians. He is the greatest of artists, and he has a heart of gold.'

"I learned that Lifar was one of the Duke's most intimate friends. I looked at Serge, and I felt a little sorry for him. I was told he was penniless, that he rode the Métro. He was still working at the Paris Opera, but they paid him next to nothing. Of course, Serge never worked for money. He lived for art. He gave his life, his soul, and all of his talent to the Opera. When I realized all that, I felt I could help him. It was my greatest privilege. I am not as wealthy as some people think. I remember millionaires coming up to me in later months, saying, 'Oh, Countess, thank you for all you are doing for our god!' This made me so angry. Why didn't these millionaires help Lifar—their god? I haven't any power, really. They needn't have thanked little me. I have a heart. That is all."

The Countess, often introduced as Madame Lifar, has been Lifar's constant companion for some fifteen years. It was the Countess who touched on Lifar's dismissal from the Paris Opera in 1959.

"It was terrible for poor Serge. He went to the Opera one day and was simply told that his services would no longer be needed. He collapsed. He had to be taken out of the opera house on a stretcher and placed in a hospital."

"Let's not talk about that, I beg you," said Lifar. "I know perfectly well why I was dismissed. The fact is, I was a man who knew too much. The new administration exercised a kind of revenge upon me, but I was exonerated years ago! I have lived through the Third Republic, and the Fourth, and the Fifth. I was an honored man. De Gaulle himself wanted to bestow a title upon me. I refused, because I need no titles. God gave me my talent, my work, my inspiration. That was all I ever needed!"

Brushing aside a few tears, the Countess added, "This giant of the dance has yet to be offered another position. He is like a man without a country, and this breeds illness and unhappiness. My heart breaks when I watch Serge sitting in his room surrounded by the great souvenirs of his past. He has no money. He is like a lost child."

Lifar smiled at his Countess, then rose, saying they were expected in Antibes. The two slowly walked through the imposing lobby of the Hotel Majestic. Their life these days is little more than a series of luncheons, teas, cocktails, dinners, and soirees given by the French aristocracy who live along the Côte d'Azur. As he wanders from party to party, Lifar seems a sad and lonely figure whose world has collapsed. His only reality is embedded in his memory. His triumphs and the great figures of his past trail behind him like so many ghosts.

IGOR MARKEVITCH

During the Diaghilev Gala at the Palm Beach Casino in Cannes, Serge Lifar introduced me to the conductor Igor Markevitch. A man of aristocratic bearing, with an iconlike face, he exuded elegance and refinement. Known internationally as a major musical figure, his connection with the world of ballet is equally renowned. As Diaghilev's last discovery, and as Nijinsky's son-in-law, he holds a unique place in the history of the Ballets Russes.

Markevitch invited me to his villa in Saint-Césaire, some miles above the town of Grasse. Contrasting dramatically with the run-down buildings of the minuscule village, Markevitch's villa was a study in architectural grandeur and elegance. I was ushered into a large foyer by a young secretary. She asked me to wait and disappeared. I found myself surrounded by a superb collection of paintings by Picasso, Miró, and Matisse, as well as a large number of photographs showing Markevitch with notables in the world of music and dance. From a distant room came the sounds of a piano. Someone was practicing passages from Brahms's Second Piano Concerto. I later learned that the person at the piano was Markevitch's sixteen-year-old son, Oleg (his other son, Vaslav, appears in the photograph). In a few minutes, the secretary reappeared, asking me to follow her to a large living room, where the Maestro would receive me.

Igor Markevitch greeted me cordially. Wearing a summer suit of subdued color, he asked me to sit with him near a large terrace overlooking a verdant whirlpool of treetops. The conductor's heavy-lidded Slavic eyes were melancholic.

"But what do you want with me? I conduct very little these days. I am not in the public eye. I devote all my time to writing books on conducting. Now and then, I make some recordings. What could I possibly tell you?"

I explained that his contact with the legendary figures of Diaghilev's Ballets Russes prompted my visit—I was writing a book on the ballet.

"Ah, the Ballets Russes! I will tell you what I can. As you probably know, I made the acquaintance of Diaghilev when I was sixteen years old. That was in 1928. I was extremely close to him until his death the following year. Do you remember that famous photograph taken on the stage of the Paris Opera of Nijinsky, Lifar, and Karsavina? Well, I assisted in the taking of that photograph. At the time, I was studying piano with Alfred Cortot, and composition with Nadia Boulanger, at the Paris Conservatory. I wanted to become a composer. A few months after my meeting with Diaghilev, I composed a piano concerto. I showed it to him. He was most impressed. Of course, I wanted to write a ballet score for him. But Diaghilev thought I was too young to entrust me with such a responsibility. However, he did arrange for my concerto to be performed during a Ballets Russes performance. This was in 1929. My concerto was premiered during the company's last season at Covent Garden, London. It was programmed between Nijinsky's *L'Après-Midi d'un Faune*, and *Le Renard*, which was Serge Lifar's first choreographic effort for Diaghilev. I was of course terribly excited to be so honored."

Markevitch recalled his brief friendship with Diaghilev:

"We had so many projects together—so many ideas. But he died. We discussed a ballet based on Andersen's *The Emperor's New Clothes*. I was to compose the score, Lifar would choreograph, Picasso would do the décor. We discussed the idea of a ballet based on music by Hindemith, and even went so far as to visit Hindemith in Baden-Baden in the summer of

1929. Boris Kochno, Diaghilev's secretary, Lifar, and I were to have met Diaghilev in Venice to discuss this ballet when word came that Diaghilev was dying. The three of us rushed to his side. And that is how it all ended.

"It was a terrible blow to me, personally. Remember, I was his last discovery—his last protégé. To put it simply, Diaghilev was a colossus. He revolutionized the art of choreography, and he did this without sacrificing the language of the classical ballet. Today, unfortunately, too many choreographers want to destroy the concepts of classical ballet. Diaghilev created revolution after revolution. For example, in earlier times, it was the ballerina who held center stage. Men were merely cavaliers. Diaghilev was the first to give importance to the male dancer—to the male *corps de ballet*. Think how this has enriched the possibilities of choreography. I seriously doubt whether we would have had a Nijinsky, a Lifar, a Massine, or a Dolin, without Diaghilev.

"*Au fond*, and perhaps because Diaghilev was homosexual, he needed a man to create for. He had a very singular character. There was in him a strong feminine streak. More than anything else, however, he was a perfectionist. I remember so well, when I showed him my piano concerto, his telling me how this and that had to be changed. At times, this was infuriating. There are many such instances. One day, I visited Diaghilev in his hotel. As I entered the lobby, I met a man who had just been to see him. The man was in tears. When I saw Diaghilev minutes later, I asked him who that poor fellow was. He smiled diabolically, and said, 'Oh, that was Prokofiev. He burst into tears because I asked him to change the finale of his score for *Le Fils Prodigue*. It was the third time I requested the change.' Diaghilev seemed to take a sadistic pleasure in making his artists suffer.

"Boris Kochno related to me that when Picasso brought his sketches for *Pulcinella* to Diaghilev, he was told that this costume must be red and not green, that this dress must be longer, and that one shorter. Picasso was so enraged that he tore up every single sketch. He told Diaghilev that he would rather start all over again than make changes. Picasso was never inclined to correct anything. Ultimately, however, all of Diaghilev's discoveries produced their very best for him."

Igor Markevitch married Kyra Nijinsky in 1936. They have a son, Vaslav. The marriage lasted ten years. In 1946, the conductor married his present wife, Topazia Caetani. They have three children, Allegra, Nathalie, and Oleg. At the time of my visit, Mme Markevitch was traveling in Italy. Of his children, only young Oleg was still at home. Markevitch spoke of his relationship with Nijinsky:

"I never saw Nijinsky dance. I was far too young. I only came to know him in 1936, when he became my father-in-law. It was then that I married his daughter, Kyra, who, at the time, was a very gifted dancer. You see, all the Nijinskys were very gifted, but they needed direction and guidance.

Kyra needed a Diaghilev. In truth, I am convinced that without a Diaghilev, Nijinsky might not have been Nijinsky. Moreover, Nijinsky would not have been an innovative choreographer without Diaghilev's encouragement.

"You surely know how everyone around Diaghilev predicted disaster when Nijinsky embarked on choreographing *L'Après-Midi d'un Faune*. When it was finally danced, everyone hated it. The main problem with Nijinsky was his inability to communicate ideas. He had extreme difficulty in expressing himself verbally. I will illustrate. Jean Cocteau once told me that he was at a dinner with Nijinsky and others. Throughout the evening, Nijinsky would keep his head lowered, and would move it very slowly from side to side. Cocteau asked him, 'Why are you doing that with your head?' And Nijinsky answered, 'I am getting into the habit of behaving like a faun, with its horns.' It shows you how deeply he felt about the act of creation. It shows how he wanted to get to the truth of it. We all know that Debussy's score is not very long, but I am told that Diaghilev allowed Nijinsky to rehearse *Faune* two hundred times. I suspect it was in order to permit Nijinsky to sufficiently focus his ideas and make them clear to himself, the dancers, and, of course, the audience. I would be willing to swear that one of the principal causes of Nijinsky's madness was his overwhelming inability to express those things which he himself felt so strongly. Cocteau told me as much, many times. Cocteau said that when Nijinsky choreographed Stravinsky's *Le Sacre du Printemps* and invented the steps for the sacrificial dance, it seemed like an upheaval of nature—it was like watching a forest gone mad."

In a voice tinged with sadness, Markevitch continued to relate how Nijinsky had married, against everyone's advice; how it produced a radical change in his relationship with Diaghilev; and how, having married Romola, Nijinsky was suddenly obliged to become a family man, a role he was ill-suited for.

"You see, my father-in-law never had to worry about anything while he was under the wing of Diaghilev. Before his marriage, he knew nothing about paying bills, purchasing clothes, acquiring a passport. The fact is, Diaghilev knew how to deal with Nijinsky's character. Diaghilev knew all of Nijinsky's shortcomings—his lack of education, his temperament. I am certain that if Nijinsky hadn't married, he would have been able to continue to dance much longer. Finally, there was the breakdown.

"During his madness, Nijinsky was deeply influenced by mysticism and religion, subjects he barely understood. You have only to read his diary to know what I mean. Also, for years and years, Nijinsky searched for ways to notate dance. Romola told me that he finally found a way, but his papers on the subject are practically undecipherable. It was perhaps a great loss for the dance.

"But an even greater loss was Nijinsky's breakup with Diaghilev. We all know that Diaghilev was extremely taken with male beauty—with male genius. I would say that the greatest works created by the Ballets Russes were a direct result of love affairs. I remember Misia Sert, that wonderfully gifted friend of the dance, telling me, 'But you know, Igor, Diaghilev had something very rare. He knew how to love.' And this was so true. In my case . . . when I brought him my first compositions, his emotions spilled over. He had found another young man of talent. There is no question that Diaghilev was the greatest *agent provocateur* that ever existed.

"As for Nijinsky, his genius permitted him to do extraordinary things. For example, those enormous leaps. I am told that when he jumped, he would empty his lungs of air, breathing in at the height of the jump, so as to prolong his suspension. It was an immense discovery. But he was incapable of explaining it. The moment he would begin to explain anything, he would be at a loss for words. He had, of course, always been rather bizarre. There was something savage about him.

"When I knew him, he had already been ill a long time. When I married Kyra, she had been seeing very little of her father; he had been committed to a sanitorium. He was there for nearly twenty years. It was I who brought Kyra together with her father. It was a very emotional reunion. It was also I who decided, with the approval of Romola, to have him treated with insulin injections, which had just then come into use. The results were interesting, because Nijinsky no longer raved after the insulin shock.

"My son, Vaslav, named after his grandfather, could at times be left alone with him. Nijinsky was charming with his little grandson. I am proud to say that insofar as he could, Nijinsky loved me very much. I spent whole days together with him. I would feed him, dress him, shave him. It was all very strange to be sitting with this great man—surely the most astonishing innovator of the new ballet. I feel strongly that his concepts of choreography have never been fully understood, nor fully developed."

Igor Markevitch paused. He seemed spent, exhausted by the sudden and vivid recollection of Nijinsky. A look of sadness came over his face. For a moment he closed his eyes. What images, I wondered, were hidden behind the closed lids? Opening his eyes, he said, "Nijinsky died in 1950. His memory haunts me."

I. Momauw

LÉONIDE MASSINE

One of the great figures of twentieth-century choreography, Léonide Massine was in New York in September 1972. He had come at the invitation of Robert Joffrey to help restage the revival of his ballet *Le Beau Danube*, which Joffrey and his company presented that season. Standing in the rehearsal room, wearing matador pants, Massine seemed at first glance the quick, meteoric figure that had excited the ballet public for some forty years. There he stood, nearly seventy-seven, putting the dancers through their paces, imbuing them with the dancing technique that he had made his own. Still agile and possessed of that terse, clipped, staccato sense of movement that has come to be identified with the name Massine, he demonstrated the sequences of variations that gave *Le Beau Danube* its particular essence and quality. With the help of an assistant, working very quickly, he brought to life a ballet noted for its charm, its wit, and its bravura passages.

The young dancers responded to the instructions that would ultimately transform them into engagingly abandoned characters of Old Vienna. It was Massine's task to make this abandonment as clear as possible to young American dancers unfamiliar with this style. At one point, Massine called in Alexandra Danilova, who years earlier had scored a triumph in the role of the Street Dancer. It was a strange and moving experience to observe Massine and Danilova momentarily re-creating the movements that so precisely reflected the spirit and the atmosphere of the work.

Massine was a study in alertness during rehearsal, but the energy seemed to drain from him once it was over. I offered to postpone our interview, but he would not hear of it. "Let's go up to the office," he said. "The only thing you must understand is that I will have to lie down." I followed Massine into a small, dark office at the Joffrey School, where the rehearsal had been held, and he instantly lay down on a cot. He had picked up a large handkerchief, and unfolded it and placed it over his face. I was about to interview a faceless, prone figure. There were many moments of silence. I thought he had fallen asleep. But from beneath the handkerchief he slowly said, "You can start asking some questions."

Having read his book *My Life in Ballet*, and having found it somewhat dry and devoid of personal information, I thought I would begin by questioning him about his relationship with Sergei Diaghilev. It was Diaghilev who had taken the young dancer into his company in 1914 and who had encouraged him to choreograph. Massine remained with the great impresario for six years before launching himself on an independent career.

"Diaghilev was a man with whom it was extremely difficult to argue," Massine began. "He always knew exactly what he wanted, and his judgment was final—not just with dancers and choreographers but with composers and with painters. Everyone listened to him. Everyone followed his suggestions. Now I can say that I was too young to have understood the value of this great man. I should have listened to every word he said, because he was so right, so to the point. You don't find that kind of judgment anywhere any more. From where I sit now, I would not repeat my mistakes. I would listen to every word he had to say."

I asked Massine to describe his meeting with Nijinsky, whom he had in fact replaced in the Diaghilev company.

"I saw Nijinsky rehearsing his *L'Après-Midi d'un Faune* in Madrid, and I was so very amazed by his remarks and by his gifts as a choreographer. In that little piece, which is rather emotionless, Nijinsky could get big emotions out of it. It was amazing to see him show the dancers what to do—how the nymph walks, how she reacts to the faun, the way she must run away from him. Nijinsky had the gift of a creator. Every time I hear that his choreography for *Le Sacre du Printemps* was terrible, I get furious. It's simply not true. Nijinsky may not have had knowledge on a big scale, but he had the ingredients to feel the elements of archaic Russia."

Turning to his own choreography, and speaking very slowly and with a certain diffidence, Massine said that of all the ballets he had choreographed *Le Tricorne* would most likely become a classic. ("Without flattering myself, I can say that it stands in the front line of my works.") It seemed to me that Massine was not inclined to talk at greater length either about his life or about his ballets. Instead, he seemed to want to talk about an entirely different aspect of his creativity.

"I'm about to bring into the world something that in my estimation is the capital work of my entire career. For several years, I have been writing a book that will probably be called 'Massine on Choreography.' The book deals with the full understanding of the harmony of the human body. Through all these years of dancing and creating dances, I discovered that everything we have been taught in dance was devoid of any true harmony. The classical school is devoid of a sense of harmony. What classical dancing possesses is a kind of artificial harmony. I mean, classical dance has created long lines, and one or two outstanding positions that we all know. But beyond that, we are in the dark as to the matter of what true harmony consists of. How does true harmony relate to the human body—relate one part of the body to another?"

Massine spoke as though he had finally come to understand the mysteries inherent in movement. He kept referring to the physiology of dance.

"The trunk, the torso, is the master of all good and bad postures. Unfortunately, in academic dancing this focal point is sort of camouflaged by the gift of technique. A dancer stands on one leg . . . applause. A dancer jumps higher than anyone else . . . applause. But, you see, that sort of thing is against the very essence of natural harmony. . . . Negation of harmony is a straight line. Deviating from a straight, vertical line brings you into the field of harmony. I have established this theory, and it holds true of all works of culture and civilization. It is a truth in art. Academic techniques lead us to believe that dancing is a special art. That's nonsense. The aesthetics of art and harmony can't be divided into various parts. There is only one that exists. But what I am looking for is something else—the eternal principle of harmonic value in the human being. All my present choreography is done according to these new principles. And, of course, I give instruction on these theories. The trouble with my new discoveries is that there are no ABC's to work with or to impart. But I travel all over in order to teach these theories to students of dance-theory courses—courses that I established myself three years ago. I have devised

THE PRIVATE WORLD OF BALLET   18

formulas, and they are all written down, because without writing you can talk your tongue off and people will not understand."

Massine continued to elaborate on his theories of the basic harmony of movement, although I must admit that his explanations were not clear. I tried to get at the root of his theories—attempted to make Massine elucidate his concepts so that they could be easily understood by both dancer and layman. I asked Massine to explain how the theories could be applied to the art of choreography. I wondered whether he had put them to use in his previous choreographic works.

"Oh no, not at all. The difference between my previous works and what I am doing now is like day and night. Only now can I see how childish, how helpless I was at the time that I started. Only now, when I am equipped with all these things with which I can compose, can I *really* see the capabilities of the human body. I don't have to think any longer of the academic schools at all. Of course, I don't think academicism should be forgotten."

Try as hard as I might, I was unable to extricate from Massine the basic premise of his theories. His book, when it is finally published, may offer the clarity that seemed missing in his own conversation with me. Still, I wanted to get closer to his aesthetic and physiological discoveries, so I made an appointment with his daughter, Tatiana, who has assisted her father in remounting his various ballets throughout the years. Tatiana Massine was willing to augment Massine's theories:

"Father's theories will open up a lot of doors to aspiring choreographers. It will help them to avoid making mistakes that are fatal. But let me give you an example. You have a dancer, say Gary Chryst, dancing in *Parade*. At one point in the ballet, he just stands on one foot, and nothing else moves on his body. Only his other foot flexes and goes up, flexes and goes up—nothing else moves. If at that same time he had been doing other movements, the focus would have been taken off his foot and it would have given an entirely different dimension to what he was doing. That movement could be accentuated by a movement of the head or the arms. But then, the movement of the ankle, which has something slightly comical about it, would be completely destroyed. There would be too much going on.

"What it all boils down to is that the body is an extraordinarily rich instrument. I don't think that every choreographer starting out knows how powerful even just a finger movement is. What Father has done is to make a study of the various possibilities of every part of the body. He has made a study of the relationship between the parts of the body and this he has analyzed by way of angles. It is through angles that he divides possibilities of movement. Take the arm. If you are just standing with your arms just along the side of your body, you can lift an arm twenty-two and a half degrees, and then forty-five, ninety, and a one hundred and eighty. This all sounds like mathematics, but when Father has his students before him, he'll say, 'Turn your torso in direction D, which will be the right-hand side of the stage, forty-five degrees,' and the student will do exactly that. In other words, he won't, as other choreographers might, tell dancers to move a little less, a little more. By employing numerals and degrees, the dancer will know *exactly* where and how to move. His head will be inclined to twenty-two and a half degrees and no more. His bodily movements will be divided and analyzed. It's a dissection. And, it's worked out with geometry and mathematics. Once you've learned the process of this dissection, you can show a student, choreographer, or dancer exactly what you want from them. You won't need to say, 'Throw your head back.' You'll say, 'Incline your head twenty-two and a half degrees, and turn your torso *x* number of degrees, and open your arm in direction F, again *x* number of degrees, and everything will come out with tremendous precision."

Tatiana Massine informed me that her father had been teaching this method at the Royal Ballet School in England for four years and with extraordinary results. Clearly then, Massine's theories on choreography deal with the elimination of accidental gesture and movement. It is an efficient system designed to make choreography into a science broaching no improvisation. As Tatiana put it, this system is an analysis of the value of movement—its weight, richness, or poverty. According to her father's principles, everything can be analyzed.

"Of course, Father cannot teach a choreographer to do good choreography. The talent and inspiration has to be there to begin with. But he can teach him that there are other ways of moving . . . that he can go beyond the strictures laid down by classical ballet.

"Now, Father believes very much in ballet classes because he's been taking them all his life, and he does what everyone does, even today at the age of seventy-seven. What he feels, I think, is that the academic study of ballet isn't complete enough. It doesn't teach a dancer a rich enough language. Many dancers are limited by it—unless they have this very extraordinary spark and genius for understanding that there are other ways of moving beyond the pirouette and the arabesque."

Sometime earlier, Eugenia Delarova Doll, once married to Massine, had consented to talk to me about her life in the Ballets Russes as Massine's second wife. A lively, highly articulate woman, Mrs. Doll has been a friend of the ballet all her life. She is known for her extreme generosity, as well as for her acute and sensitive eye in spotting dancers of potential greatness. Full of humor and gaiety, she told me that I must never refer to her as a ballerina.

"I was a solo dancer, a character dancer, a *comédienne*," she explained, in her explosive Russian way. "I was born in Saint Petersburg, and I started to study ballet after the Revolution. I was in the same class as Sergeiev and

Balanchine. George was already starting to do choreography. Later, George, Geva, and Danilova left for Europe. I stayed and studied for another four years. After that, I went to Paris. It was in Paris I met Lèonide Massine. I met him in a class. Egorova was teaching. It was during the exercises that I saw before me a beautiful young man. He looked at me all the time. He was watching every step I did. Then, after the class, he followed me down the stairs and said, 'I heard you just came from Russia.' We started talking. Then he said, 'Where are you going?' I said, 'To the right.' He went to the left. And that was all.

"But he found out that I was dancing at the Folies-Bergère. Massine came to see me. I almost fainted, because I didn't know who he was. Then I received a note from him saying, 'I would love to meet you again.' That's how we met. While I was with the Folies-Bergère, I was also rehearsing with the Nemtchinova-Dolin Company. All of a sudden, Massine appeared again. He said, 'Could I correct you a little bit?' So he corrected me, and then asked me again if we could meet. He was really following me. Three months later we were married.

"At first, he was a little bit too gloomy for me. I thought he was too serious. But slowly I changed him. I glamorized his clothes and started much more of a social life. We had musicales and parties at the homes of Etienne de Beaumont and Misia Sert. Cocteau was there, and Kochno and Picasso, and the whole ballet crowd. At the restaurants, I remember Picasso making drawings on menus for me. I left them there. I just couldn't be bothered. Anyway, Massine and I were married just before we went to America. We started working together at the Roxy Theatre in New York. At that time, I was asked to be in one of the first talking pictures made in Hollywood—*Broadway Melody*. Massine didn't want me to go, but I talked him into it. You see, he was a very jealous man. Unbelievably jealous. That was his sickness."

Massine was working at the Roxy when he received word that Diaghilev, with whom he had broken in 1920, had died. Talk began of starting a new Russian company. Massine and Delarova returned to Europe, and in Monte Carlo, where Colonel de Basil was just starting a new Ballets Russes, Massine was hired as principal choreographer. They worked at the Monte Carlo Opera, staging ballets, including several by Massine himself. Delarova danced character roles in several of her husband's productions and became a kind of mediator when things became tense with the company. By then Massine was already noted for his incredibly disciplined working methods.

"He was a very, very hard worker. He never changed. He is exactly the same today at seventy-seven as when I met him. He just worked everybody to death. Everybody fainted, and still he kept on working us. I did a lot of work too, but my work was unnoticed. I would get advice from people. I would consult. Later, the company came to America. I remember that we toured in a big trailer. Of course, we picked up dancers everywhere in America. I remember, in Kansas City, we auditioned a young girl who just didn't look the way a ballerina should look. Somehow, I talked Massine into taking her. The girl was Rosella Hightower.

"Once we took a boat going to Europe with the company. One time, I was walking my little dog on the top deck and I called to him in Russian. Suddenly a man stopped me and said, 'Are you Russian?' I said, 'Yes.' He said, 'Are you with the ballet?' I said, 'Yes.' He said, 'My name is Serge Denham. I am a banker, and I am in love with the ballet. Can I meet you all?' I said, 'I will arrange it.' And that's how we met Denham—through my little dog. Then, afterward, we met his wife, his daughters, and he gave parties, and he met all of us, and he became interested. The next thing we knew, we started a new company, headed by Denham."

It was in 1938 that Massine left the de Basil company to join forces with Denham in the formation of yet another Ballet Russe. Delarova and several other dancers from the de Basil company followed him to Denham.

In rather haphazard fashion, Eugenia Delarova Doll continued relating her life and travels with Massine:

"We traveled and we worked. At one point, Vera Zorina was in our company and she started flirting with Massine. She flirted like mad. I didn't like it. I got mad and I cried and everything started to go wrong. It was pretty much the beginning of the end between me and Massine. And there was Zorina always sitting on the top deck reading a book. We would be walking around, Massine and I, and she would give him these looks. Of course, she was a gorgeous-looking girl. I got more and more nervous. But Zorina married Balanchine. She did not break up our marriage. There was another woman, a dancer, whom he eventually married. She was Tatiana Orlova. She was beautiful. She is the mother of Tatiana and Lorca.

"But my ten years with Massine were good, most of the time. Now, I would say that I was too young, but I learned an awful lot from him. I didn't know very much. He took me to every museum all over the world. . . . He wanted his children to become dancers, but he started them too early. When the children came to America, I was something of a mother to them. Today, Massine is still fantastic. He looks after himself very well. You know, he doesn't eat in restaurants. He brings his own lunch and cooks soup. That was always what he did. With Massine, it is always work, work, work. We are divorced, but now we are friends. I don't think he remembers how I suffered."

While the Massine family is no longer the closed unit it once was, it is still involved in the dance. Massine himself travels to many parts of the world to remount his ballets and to instruct companies on his new choreographic theories. His wife Tatiana Orlova heads a ballet school in Paris. His son, Lorca Massine, choreographed and danced for Béjart's Ballets of the Twentieth Century, and was connected for several seasons with the New York City Ballet. He is currently choreographing throughout Europe. Massine's daughter, Tatiana, while presently an art dealer in New York, occasionally joins her father, helping him to restage his own works.

Louis Peres

FELIA DOUBROVSKA

In a large, airy dance studio of the School of American Ballet in New York City, a toe class is in progress. The teacher, this afternoon, is demonstrating a complex combination of steps to some twenty young students. Delicately lifting her dark blue chiffon overskirt, the teacher exposes long and slender legs in pink tights. The pianist begins a slow Chopin waltz. Her body lifts effortlessly on half *pointe*. Her head turns slightly. Her large, deep-set eyes gaze into the distance—a distance that seems to extend far beyond the studio walls. For a fraction of a moment, she seems a young girl again, on the stage of the Maryinsky Theatre in Saint Petersburg. She might be gazing at the shadowy figures of Karsavina and Nijinsky dancing in *Le Pavillon d'Armide*. She begins to move, and slowly her arms rise. The girls at the *barre* seem transfixed by the beauty and serenity of her momentary return to the past . . . they are in the presence of their beloved teacher, Felia Doubrovska.

Madame Doubrovska had allowed me to watch her class. When I entered the studio, she said, "Sit on the side, in the middle. You will see better. And don't look at me. Look only at these beautiful girls. They are all virgins."

When class was over, she invited me to pay her a visit at her apartment. A date was set for the following day.

Doubrovska lives in a large apartment on Broadway at Seventy-ninth Street. When I rang the doorbell, sharp and piercing barks greeted my ears. In a moment, the door opened, and there stood Doubrovska holding a tiny, very noisy Yorkshire terrier sporting a pink ribbon on its head. "Stop that barking, Lila. We have a guest!" She led me into a simply furnished living room and offered tea. "I live alone in this large apartment. Only two years ago, Pierre, my husband, was here with me. Now, he has passed away. I have no relatives. I live here alone with my little Lila. What will happen to my little Lila when I die?"

Madame Doubrovska, wearing a blue silk dress, speaks quickly and melodiously. Her English is heavily flavored with a curious mixture of Russian and French. We sit together on a couch. She pours some tea. I look at her interesting, aristocratic face—the eyes large and luminous; the nose, aquiline; the chin, gently curved. Her fading features are carefully accented by rouge, eye shadow, and lipstick. Though seated, she is a figure in constant motion. Her hands move in rapid succession to her throat, to her face, to her lap.

"My life has been so long. I am seventy-seven years old. But I will try to answer your questions.

"When I was seven, my parents took me to a Christmas party, and someone gave me a toy ballerina. I was so excited. This was in Saint Petersburg, where I was born. A gracious gentleman was there—Mr. Andryanov. He was premier danseur of the Maryinsky Ballet. He introduced himself to my mother, and, looking at me, told her that I would make a nice dancer. My mother said I was very frail. He said dancing would be good for my health. Three years later, I began my studies at the Maryinsky. My closest friend at the school was Olga Spessivtzeva. She was so beautiful. Our ideals were Pavlova and Karsavina. Spessivtzeva liked Karsavina. I liked Pavlova. We constantly tried to imitate them. We took part in many of the ballets at the Maryinsky. We were little swans, and we were in *The Sleeping Beauty*. Fokine was one of our teachers. Olga advanced very rapidly. She worked very hard. I was very lazy. When I saw

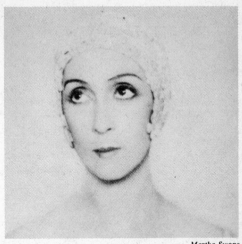

Martha Swope

Olga working so hard, I, too, worked hard. When we graduated, I danced the Black Swan *pas de deux*. I thought I would die, but I didn't. In Russia, I only reached the rank of soloist."

Felia Doubrovska remained at the Maryinsky Theatre until 1920. She lived through three years of the Revolution, before escaping to France. In Paris, she appeared at the Théâtre des Champs-Elysées as featured dancer in a theatrical revue.

"The critics said that I would become the peer of Pavlova. I don't lie. It's the truth. Mr. Diaghilev saw my reviews. He found me through Pierre Vladimirov, who was not yet my husband. Diaghilev came to my home and asked me to show him what I did at the Champs-Elysées. I danced to some music of Drigo. Diaghilev said he would put me in his *Sleeping Beauty*. I joined his company. It was not easy for me. Then, I began to be given more roles.

"One day, Diaghilev came to my Paris apartment and brought me a cake. Balanchine also came. He went to the kitchen and cooked the dinner. Diaghilev began to drink a little. He was in a very good mood. He said, 'Are you sure Balanchine will not poison me with the dinner he is making?' He was a little drunk. The dinner was very good."

Doubrovska remained with the Diaghilev company until 1929. During that period, she created the role of the Bride in Nijinska's *Les Noces*, the Film Star in Balanchine's *Pastorale*, Calliope in *Apollon Musagète*, and, her most famous role, the Siren in *The Prodigal Son*.

"I also danced in Nijinska's *Les Biches*. Mr. Diaghilev did not like the costume I was wearing. He told me to go to Coco Chanel and choose a dress in which I could move. And so, I went, and she designed a dress for me.

"At the beginning, I was not happy with the company. My contract said I was a soloist, but too often I was given roles that were very, very small. I decided to leave. I went to America. Pavlova was dancing in America, and I joined her company. I danced the Queen of the Wilis in *Giselle*. It was the time when my future husband, Pierre Vladimirov, also danced with Pavlova. I stayed with her for six weeks. Then I received a letter from Boris Kochno, saying that they missed me in Paris—that I should return to Diaghilev. So, I went back. I was given much more to dance. It was then I danced in *The Prodigal Son*. Lifar danced with me. He was marvelous. Serge was such a nice boy. He didn't realize that he was such a big success. Balanchine did everything for him. Later, Lifar was very mean to Balanchine. In those years, Lifar was the love of Diaghilev. He took the place of Nijinsky, and he was sweet to everybody.

"Alexandra Danilova—Choura—was also in the company. She was taken with Lifar. When I danced with him, she was jealous. When she danced with him, I was jealous. I have so many little letters from him. I danced many roles. But you must not say that I was a great ballerina, because I was not. I could do everything, but because I was so tall, I was not able to dance in many ballets. But I danced *Firebird*. That was the time they brought Nijinsky on stage. He was already very sick. Diaghilev called all of us together, trying to revive Nijinsky's memory. Karsavina was there, and Lifar. Diaghilev told Nijinsky, 'Look at Karsavina. She danced with you in *Petrouchka*.' He asked him to look and to look, but Nijinsky did not respond. His wife, Romola, was with him, too. She said to him, 'Smile, Vaslav. Smile.' Vaslav smiled automatically. It was very sad and pathetic.

"I only saw Nijinsky dance once. It was at the Maryinsky. They were giving *Le Pavillon d'Armide*. I was onstage. I fanned the Princess. When Nijinsky came out, it was like somebody flying. The Maryinsky stage is very big. But he leaped from one side of the stage to the other. He just seemed to fly. He was a beautiful, beautiful dancer. His face was not beautiful, however—just pleasant. My husband, Pierre, was a very good friend of his. Vaslav could dance without ever getting tired. In one night, he would dance *Le Spectre de la Rose, Les Sylphides*, and *Schéhérazade*. In every one of these ballets, he was completely different. It was the same when he danced *Petrouchka* and the *Faune*. His sister, Bronislava, also danced in *Faune*. She was the First Nymph. She was a very good dancer, but she was not pretty. When we did *Sleeping Beauty* in 1921, Diaghilev gave her a role to dance. But he took her out on the second day, because she was not pretty. I remember the last performance Olga Spessivtzeva ever danced. It was *Swan Lake*. Anton Dolin, Danilova, and I danced the *pas de trois* in that performance."

Felia Doubrovska's memory darts quickly from remembrance to remembrance. With eyes flashing, she fixes on moments—sudden recollections fly into her mind. She spoke again of Diaghilev:

"He was always very nice to me. I will tell you a little story. My husband once gave me some perfume in a beautiful atomizer. He gave it to me on the occasion of his leaving to tour and dance with Pavlova. I kept this atomizer in my dressing room. One day, during a rehearsal, Danilova came to the theater some hours before the rest of us. She had a little cold. She wanted to feel better, and so she looked for some perfume. She didn't have her own with her. So, she saw my little atomizer on my dressing table, and probably said to herself, Well, Doubrovska is not here. She will not mind if I use some of her perfume. As she was applying it, the bottle fell out of her hand, and it broke on the floor. She ran to Diaghilev, and told him what she had done. He said not to worry—that he would take care of it. By that time, I had arrived for a rehearsal, and was working on the stage. After an hour, Diaghilev called me. 'Doubrovska! You did the rehearsal very well. I want to give you a little present.' He gave me a lovely bottle of perfume. I was so surprised. I said, 'Thank you. Now I will have a memento of you.' But the Russian word I used implied a memory of one who is dead. Diaghilev became furious. He stormed off the stage. I later found out that Diaghilev was very superstitious. Any mention of death upset him terribly. Nobody ever mentioned the word death to him. But I was so excited, I didn't realize what I was saying. Later, he forgave me."

Doubrovska married Pierre Vladimirov in 1922. She had met him during her school days at the Maryinsky. Vladimirov became *premier danseur* with the Imperial Ballet in 1915, dancing leading roles in *Le Carnaval, Giselle, Raymonda*, among others. In 1918, he left Russia and danced with the Diaghilev company. In 1928, Vladimirov joined the Anna Pavlova company, partnering Pavlova until her death in 1931. Some years later, he came to New York and joined the faculty of the School of American Ballet, where he taught, on and off, until his death in 1970. Felia Doubrovska spoke poignantly about her late husband:

"I was in love with Pierre when we were both very young, at the Maryinsky Theatre. I was younger than he. Pierre had already finished his studies. I was *so* in love with him! He was very temperamental. He wanted to do things *his* way. In *Swan Lake*, for example, he wanted to do his own Coda in the Black Swan *pas de deux*. Legat and Oboukhov had done it before him, and in a manner that was very *distingué*. Their variation in the Coda was *sissonne sissonne, sous-sus, double tour*. But Vladimirov didn't do it that way. He did not come to the middle of the stage to do his Coda. He started from the side. Now, everybody does it that way.

"Pierre never paid any attention to me. But Oboukhov was his friend. Anatole Oboukhov was a wonderful dancer, and later taught here in

America at Balanchine's school. Anyway, Anatole helped me to make the acquaintance of Pierre. I remember, one day, overhearing Pierre say that the next day would be his birthday. I rushed up to him and said that it was my birthday, too. Of course, it was not really my birthday. But I invited him to my house for a little party. Still, he did not pay any attention to me. A few days later, we danced in *Swan Lake* together. He was the Prince, and he danced with Karsavina. I danced the Spanish Variation. After the performance, we all stood in front of the curtain to take our bows. Everybody was brought flowers—everybody except me. Pierre noticed this. He took some flowers from his own bouquet, and handed them to Karsavina, asking her to pass them on to me. When that happened, I lost my heart to him completely. Finally, we were married. It was in 1922, in London.

"We were married a very long time. Of course, he traveled very much, and had many affairs. My mother never wanted me to marry him. She did not come to our wedding. But later, before she died, my mother told me that Pierre was a good husband. She told me that no matter how many affairs he had, I was still the wife, and if anything became serious he would want to divorce me. Well, he never wanted a divorce. Nothing became serious."

In 1938, the Vladimirovs came to live in America. Doubrovska became prima ballerina of the Metropolitan Opera Ballet, but the following year she retired from the stage. Some years later, she joined the faculty of the School of American Ballet, at the invitation of George Balanchine.

"I went to teach at the Balanchine school when it was still located on Madison Avenue. I was so nervous. When I walked into my first class, it was worse than performing on the stage. My knees were shaking. The students were already in the room. But what was really terrifying was the fact that, leaning against the windows, were Tamara Geva, Danilova, Zorina, and Maria Tallchief. All of Mr. Balanchine's wives were standing there!

"I have never stopped teaching. At the beginning, Mr. Balanchine wanted me to dance in a revival of *The Prodigal Son*. I told him I would never dance again. I decided not to be on the stage any more. I wanted the memory of my dancing to remain as pleasant as possible."

Felia Doubrovska rose and went to a table on which lay several scrapbooks. She brought them over, and we began looking at the yellowing, crumbling pages on which images of Doubrovska at her height passed before our eyes. Doubrovska silently and slowly and lovingly turned each page. "You see, everything I have told you is the truth. I had a beautiful life. Now, my life is coming to an end. I will not be teaching much longer. I am still not over the shock of my Pierre's death. I still remember so vividly the day when he was not feeling well. I called the doctor. He said that Pierre should go into the hospital. Then, at midnight, they called me. Pierre had died. I did not even have a chance to say good-by to him. . . ."

ALEXANDRA DANILOVA

She is without question the most glamorous former prima ballerina extant—and the most amusing. Alexandra Danilova is no sufferer, at least not on the surface. Cheerful, gay, spontaneous, and full of surprising and remarkable energy, she projects an intoxicating *joie de vivre*. Seeing her, one is struck by her trim and svelte figure, her *au courant* fashions, her splendid, shapely legs, and by a face that continues to have the unmistakable look of the Star. Whether attending a party, a performance, or teaching class at the School of American Ballet, Danilova's presence is all-pervasive. Whether sitting in a room teeming with people or sipping champagne at intermission on the Grand Promenade of the New York State Theater, Danilova attracts fascinated attention.

Other dancers of her vintage may have had supreme acclaim, but none have had the unique éclat of Danilova. She was born in Peterhof, Russia, in a year carefully guarded, even from *The Dance Encyclopedia*, but most likely in the middle of the first decade of this century. Her life and triumphs are a matter of record. But to meet Danilova in person is always an event.

Madame Danilova invited me to visit her in her New York City apartment on West Fifty-seventh Street. She lives there alone, surrounded by paintings and drawings given to her by admirers the world over. That afternoon, Danilova wore a dark red dress, red tights, red shoes. We sat on a velvet-upholstered chaise flanked by a small round table, upon which stood a single photograph—of Sergei Diaghilev. I admired Danilova's collection of prints, drawings, and paintings. At that, she sprang up and said, "Come! We will make a tour!"

"This, Bérard made for me. This sketch Mr. Denham gave to me. This, somebody gave to me when I taught in Berlin. Look what Berman writes on this painting: '*À la chère et grande Danilova, son ami et admirateur.*' This, somebody did of me in *Gaîté Parisienne*. I think it's particularly beautiful. This, is painted on silk. I was teaching in Düsseldorf. And this is my beloved Leningrad. When people come here, they always say it's an exhibition, because I have always new things."

In her heavy, Russian-accented English, Danilova cheerfully recounted impressions of her childhood—impressions that were far from gay. When she was two years old, her well-to-do aristocratic father died. Shortly thereafter, Danilova lost her mother. She and her sister Helen, three years her senior, were sent to live with their grandmother. Within a year, this relative also died, and the sisters were separated. Helen remained with Alexandra's godmother. Three-year-old Alexandra went to live with a certain Madame Lydia Golovzeva. The child regarded this wealthy woman as her aunt, and lived quite happily with her for several years.

At the age of seven, Alexandra—Choura, as everyone called her—was enrolled in a preparatory school, where she showed a particular aptitude for dancing. By eight, she was accepted at the Imperial Ballet School in Petrograd.

"I had to go through medical examinations. They wanted to find out whether you are bowlegged or not, or have heart trouble. After all, I always say that nobody wants to see a ballet dancer drop dead in the middle of a variation. Anyway, I passed. The first year, I didn't understand anything. Later, I was considered a very capable and talented pupil. You know, even before ballet school, I spent hours before the mirror and did all sorts of movements that drove my governess and aunt absolutely crazy.

I used to go up on toe. I never saw ballet. It was just inspiration. . . . Then came the Revolution. I stayed at the Imperial School, but there was terrible hunger, and the school changed names to Russian State Ballet School. I was making excellent progress, and I was given many little parts. My very first solo at the Maryinsky was in *Coppélia.*

"At the Maryinsky, I met George Balanchine. He was my schoolmate. We were counted as very good students—interesting and talented. George did his first choreography when he was sixteen. He wanted to form a little company for modern ballets. Then he had this idea that he wanted to go to Germany with me, Tamara Geva, and some others. It was Vladimir Dimitriev who took us to Germany. We went to Berlin, and performed with success. We were called 'The Russian State Dancers.' Then we performed in London. Again, big success. We stayed in Europe a long time. We did not go back to the Maryinsky Theatre. Besides, I wanted to see Paris first. We all arrived in Paris. It was 1925.

"Diaghilev heard about us. He gave us audition. I was so fresh, you know. Tamara and George showed what they could do to Mr. Diaghilev. Then, Diaghilev turned to me and said, 'And so, what can you do, Danilova?' I said to him, 'Mr. Diaghilev, if I am good enough for the Maryinsky Theatre, I am good enough for you!' He was so amazed. He laughed. He said, 'But show me *something*!' So, I did a little hopping around. We joined the company. Bronislava Nijinska was just then choreographing *Les Biches*. From the beginning, Madame Nijinska resented us very much. Then, when Diaghilev wanted Balanchine to do some choreography, she left the company and Balanchine took over."

Alexandra Danilova, Tamara Geva, and George Balanchine joined Diaghilev's Ballets Russes at its height. Dancing in the company at that time were such luminaries as Spessivtzeva, Karsavina, Lopoukhova, Vera Nemtchinova, Alice Nikitina, Ludmilla Shollar, Alicia Markova, Felia Doubrovska, Anton Dolin, Serge Lifar, Léonide Massine, and Léon Woizikowski. Chief choreographers were Nijinska, Massine, and Lifar. Danilova took part in ballets that have become landmarks in twentieth-century dance. When, in 1926, Balanchine choreographed *The Triumph of Neptune*, she scored her first great personal triumph in the Diaghilev Company. Her success was so dazzling that Diaghilev appointed her prima ballerina of the Ballets Russes. Other roles included Firebird, a Can-Can Dancer in Massine's *La Boutique Fantasque*, Terpsichore in Balanchine's *Apollon Musagète*.

"Everybody said I was too young, that I would be unable to do big parts. But Diaghilev did not listen. At the beginning, I was a little bit afraid of him. You know, he was sort of untouchable to me. Such a great man! He was always surrounded by young composers and painters. We met Stravinsky, Picasso—everybody. I was so very young. I was so busy, trying to catch up, and learning what the company was doing, because, don't forget, I was brought up on a strictly classical tradition of the Maryinsky. Little by little, I took over the repertoire of the company. Then, Diaghilev died, in 1929. The company broke up. I went with Colonel de Basil's company. I was prima ballerina, and Massine was chief choreographer."

Danilova was willing to speak of her long liaison with George Balanchine:

"People think I was married to George. I was not. But we lived together as man and wife in Paris. He was very young, and also very old for his age. He was a sort of philosopher in dancing. He loved music. I was just a silly girl. I always wanted to go to the night clubs and dance. George would say, 'What?! You want to go to those dark rooms?!' I don't think I was good companion for him, intellectually. He was very fond of me because we had been together in school. We had many things in common, but it was all ballet. Don't forget, we knew each other since we were nine years old. Then, when Diaghilev died, life separated us. George went to London. I went to Monte Carlo. To many people, my relationship with George seemed strange. They tell many stories. But it wasn't big drama. After we separated, we continued to see each other. We have big understanding, and big tenderness. Of course, now, we work again together. I teach in his school."

Danilova joined Colonel de Basil's Ballets Russes in 1933, after serving for one year as soloist with the Monte Carlo Opera Ballet, and dancing for a short period in London. With de Basil, she scored great personal success in ballets created for her by Massine, Nijinska, and Balanchine. She danced leading roles in Massine's *Le Beau Danube* and *Gaîté Parisienne;* in Nijinska's *Les Biches* and *Bolero*; and in Balanchine's *Jack in the Box*, *Le Baiser de la Fée, Serenade, The Card Party*; and scores of other ballets, including such classics as *Swan Lake, Coppélia*, and *Les Sylphides.*

Danilova spoke of working with Léonide Massine:

"Well, he was a terrifically dedicated man. He adored the art. But, as a person, he was very difficult. He was very dry. All he could think about was ballet. He had no rapport with dancers. He prepared everything at home, before coming to rehearsal. I don't mean to be disrespectful, but with him, everything was always strictly art. He is not very friendly . . . nice, you know. For instance, we danced together many, many years. Then, I came to America—to New York. When he came also, he didn't even call me to say hello. Dolin, and even great ballerinas, when they come, they call me, because, we always say, ballet is a big family.

"Even when he was with Diaghilev, Massine was very dry. This was not the case with somebody like Anton Dolin. I danced with him very often. We still see each other, even today. He helped so many dancers. He is a good person. But when you do something good, people don't talk about it. They only talk if you do something bad. I liked Alicia Markova. You know, Balanchine found her in London. She was a pupil of Astafieva; then her father committed suicide because he lost a lot of money. Astafieva called Diaghilev about Alicia. Diaghilev and Balanchine went to see her. She was twelve years old. George thought she was very talented. That is how he chose her to dance *Le Chant du Rossignol*. That's how Alicia started.

"Alicia and I have drifted apart, but she always has a tender spot for me. She never forgets my birthday. Wherever she is in the world, she sends me card. Of course, she was very temperamental. Don't forget, Alicia was Irish and Jewish. That's a fantastic combination! She was very attached to Diaghilev. He was like a father to her. Then, when he died, she was still a very young girl, and she fell deeply in love with Anton Dolin. Everybody knows that. It was very difficult for Dolin . . . you know, to keep the borders defined. They danced beautifully together. Alicia tried all kinds of tricks to make Dolin fall in love with her. It didn't happen, and it left a little bitter in her. I think Dolin put her on the map, because, at the time, he was big star. But Alicia was a real ballerina.

"Like every human being, Alicia had all kinds of emotions. She wouldn't be a big ballerina if she didn't have big emotions. At the time, when she was young, she had to fight for her place. Now, she has quieted down. Alicia danced so often Giselle. I remember, I was a little bit hurt when she would tell me that *Giselle* was *her* ballet. I wanted to dance Giselle, too. I went to Balanchine. I cried to him about it. He told me that the world is big. That I could dance Giselle in South Africa, and other places. Also, George always told me to remember that there would always be better dancers and worse dancers. Look at today. Some people say Fracci is the great Giselle. Others prefer Natalia Makarova. George was right. There is room for everybody."

Although Alexandra Danilova never married George Balanchine, she did marry twice.

"I decided that I should marry somebody who had nothing to do with the ballet, and so I married an industrial man, Giuseppe Massara. He was Italian. We met in London. He was one of the engineers who did the first air conditioning in South African gold mines. But this being married didn't work at all. He hated the ballet. I hated air conditioning. He didn't want me to be in the theater. I stayed with him one year only. Then, he was sick, and he died. That didn't work at all. I joined the Ballet Russe de Monte Carlo and came to America.

"Then, after years and years, I married again—a ballet dancer. That didn't work out, either. I was prima ballerina, and he was not first dancer. He was very capable boy, and he was a wonderful soloist, but I'm afraid that there was a little bit jealousy there. He started to drink, and that finished that. We divorced. From that time on, I decided to stay free lance."

Madame Danilova carefully avoided any mention of dates. Her marriages and their time sequence remained a vague quantity. What is known is that Danilova's career spanned from 1922, when she began as soloist with the Maryinsky Theatre, through her farewell New York appearance as guest ballerina with the Ballet Russe de Monte Carlo at the Metropolitan Opera in New York in 1957. It was a career studded with triumphs and legendary acclaim.

Several days after my visit with the ballerina, I went to watch her teach a variations class at the School of America Ballet. We had a little time together before the class began. Danilova is as conscientious about her classroom attire as she is for a gala. She wore pink tights, pink slippers, a peach-colored leotard, over which she tied a rose-colored chiffon overskirt. Around her head, she wore a peach-colored scarf tied under her chin. Her make-up had been carefully applied. As we talked, she proceeded to remove her rings and bracelets, placing them in a small jewel case she carries for that purpose. "In ballet, hands and arms must be free of all jewelry," she announced.

"Is the life of a dancer full of sacrifices?" I asked.

"Well, I think it's a wonderful life," Danilova answered. "You work hard, and you sacrifice. But you meet everybody, from the leaders of the world to the carpenter of the theater. Of course, you have to keep your head on the shoulder. I remember, a friend of mine said, 'Well, Choura, you work so hard! I'm not surprised that you went on the top.' I told her that it was quite easy to get on the top, but to *stay* there is very slippery. You see, a lot of young dancers think that once you are there, you don't have to work. Just the opposite is true."

It was time to enter the classroom. With a flamboyant whoosh of her chiffon skirt, she strode into the studio where the girls were already gathered. Danilova moved to the *barre*, motioned to the pianist, and began to demonstrate the first exercise. With amazing dexterity, the ballerina executed the entire class as though she were herself a student. Her understanding of technique and style was made tangible at every turn. Every so often, she would stop and say, "Expression in movement must not be done with the face, but with the body. . . . Be careful with your arms! Your arms are your violins. . . . Listen to the music! The music must inspire you."

Class over, we chatted another few minutes in the empty studio.

"I teach them soul," Danilova said, clasping her hands to her abdomen, in a gesture suggesting a feeling too visceral to verbalize. "Today, young dancers always know everything. Generally, they don't ask you advice. However, when I teach, I look for the language of a pupil. If it is not there—if there is no rapport—then, I look elsewhere. George always tells me not to pay too much attention to pupils who are not talented. Of course, to start with, I love all my pupils. Then I find the talented ones. They are always the most arrogant. They are not very *simpático* to work with, but I just ignore this. Later they will find out, because art is very cruel."

Danilova and I then walked out of the classroom. As she led me down the hall of the School of American Ballet toward her dressing room, she said, "I think people who are connected with art are very lucky people. We can always sort of forget our sorrow in art. The French say, '*Tout passe*. . . .' But if you're honest with your art, it always stays with you. Love seldom stays with you. Love is never permanent, but art is permanent."

MURIEL STUART

uriel Stuart is unalterably British. Her tall, proud stature has the regality of one raised and bred among aristocrats. Her speech reflects the forthright British crispness and eloquence, and her humor has a mischievous snap to it. Yet, this thoroughly Shavian woman spent her youngest years in the ballet company of the goddess of Russian dance—Anna Pavlova. From 1916 to 1926, Miss Stuart studied and danced in the Pavlova company. It was her only period of professional performing.

Today, Muriel Stuart teaches at the School of American Ballet, where she has been on the faculty for thirty years.

Students who thrill to the romantic aura of the Maryinsky tradition embodied by Muriel Stuart's fellow teachers, Danilova and Doubrovska, are exposed to a far more austere teaching method in Miss Stuart's classes. Hers is a lean and measured approach. In the classroom, she is the essence of cordiality. Her instructions, demonstrations, and corrections are given with the benign despotism of a Mary Poppins—"a spoonful of sugar helps the medicine go down." She insists on a quiet atmosphere even during the most strenuous exercises. Her innate musicality, lyricism, and splendid posture set the students an example of restraint and control. Miss Stuart imparts the elegance, breeding, and poetry of self-containment.

There are no sartorial eccentricities in Miss Stuart's classroom garb. Her long legs do not shimmer through chiffon skirts. She wears an ankle-length overskirt and a plain leotard top. Her white hair is cropped close to her head. When she demonstrates, everything reflects the Pavlovian tradition. She represents the contrast and variety in teaching methods available to students at the School of American Ballet.

My interview with Miss Stuart was scheduled for teatime. She lives in a modest, handsomely furnished apartment boasting some particularly choice American primitive paintings—a passion of Miss Stuart's. That afternoon she wore a rose-and-white-checked Irish linen dress. "We must let the tea brew before drinking it," she said. "But do help yourself to these little cakes." We sat at her dining-room table in straight-backed chairs. An atmosphere of calm pervaded the room. But Miss Stuart was in splendid good humor, recalling her childhood in her native London:

"Actually," she said, "I was born in South Norwood, which is a suburb of London. Like most small girls in England, I went to a dancing class— fancy dancing class, they used to call it. Once a year, the students each had a solo which they did at a sort of dancing teachers' convention in London. I remember doing a dance called the Folly Dance. I wore a little cap and bells and I held a stick from which a Pulcinella dangled. The dance was extremely simple, but I suppose I was all right in it. I was about six or seven. Afterward, someone told my parents, 'This child should be trained for classical dancing.' Well, this excited my parents to a rather big degree. They had never thought of my being a dancer in any shape or form. But very shortly after this event, Anna Pavlova announced that she wanted to choose eight children whom she wished to teach herself. She preferred them to be previously untrained in classical ballet. She wanted to do this herself. You can imagine the effect this had on my parents! They quickly prepared for my application as one of these eight children."

"I went to Ivy House, which was Pavlova's beautiful London residence. There were sloping lawns down to a pond with swans on it. There was a hall, and in this hall were many gifts in big cases. The children were kept in that hall. One by one, we went in to dance for her. I'll never forget it. When it came to be my turn, I was of course terribly nervous. Pavlova was sitting there on a chair, with this marvelous hair, two pearl earrings, and the simplest gown you could possibly imagine. It was long—almost like an Isadora Duncan gown. She told me to come in. She spoke English extremely well. She turned to her pianist and said, 'Play a waltz.' Then she turned to me and said, 'Now, darling, move.' And I started to move. Then she signaled the pianist to change the tempo—and he played a polka. I immediately changed the rhythm of my dancing. You see, she wanted to see if I had rhythm. Then she asked me to come and sit beside her. She looked at me most carefully. She wanted to see if the proportions of my body were right. This was terribly important to her."

Miss Stuart recounted this initial meeting with Pavlova as though relating a fairy tale. She spoke slowly, distinctly, and securely, as though the impressions were as recent as yesterday. She told how Pavlova kept her next to her, as other children came in to dance, some doing imitations of the Dying Swan on *pointe*. When all the children had danced for Pavlova, someone came to take down addresses. Everyone was told that a letter would be sent to those who would be accepted.

"After several weeks of anxious waiting," Miss Stuart continued, "a letter came. It said, 'Muriel has been selected as one of Madame Pavlova's students,' and it went on to give us the date and hour when the lessons would begin. I can honestly tell you, looking back, that Pavlova's patience was fantastic. First of all, she had not taught anyone ever, let alone eight little girls that had never had any training. Of course, there wasn't a morning that we weren't in tears. Not a morning! Pavlova wanted us to do the simplest thing thousands of times. We had to do very unexciting things, like *demi-pliés, tendus*, and *ronds de jambe*—and all this, endlessly. It was most frustrating—especially for the mothers, who wanted to see quick results.

"Anyway, after having taught all these years, I will never understand how Pavlova steeled herself to put up with us. When I went into Pavlova's company, I was really very poorly equipped—certainly when compared to the girls who prepare today to go into companies. Of course, at the time, the classic ballets were very simple, and if you had the gift, the strength, and some technique, you got someplace. I spent one entire year *not* appearing on the stage at all—just learning and looking. I was fifteen, and I learned how to put my make-up on, and how to walk on stage. It was an apprenticeship of the old days, something we don't have today, unfortunately. Now, you either sink or swim."

Muriel Stuart interrupted her account. Like any meticulous British hostess, she applied herself exclusively to the "pouring" ceremony. With quick, neat gestures, she helped us to our various teatime preferences. This ac-

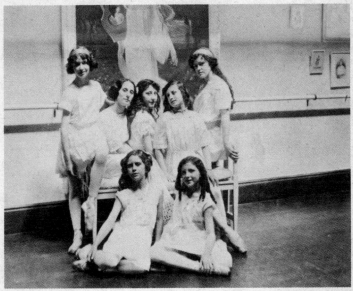

Miss Stuart is on the far left, standing next to Pavlova.

complished, she willingly answered more questions about Pavlova: What were Pavlova's teaching methods? What was her teaching philosophy?

"What she imparted to us was a philosophy of life. She would give us a class in the morning, and then, afterward, she would gather us around her chair. She would say, 'Look, you're going to take a bus or a train to get home. You'll see lots of people when you're in this bus or train. Well, I want you to look at all the faces around you, and you'll see someone who is sad or angry. You must feed yourself through your eyes as well as your ears. If you're going to be an artist, you must do this. This is just as important as the exercises you did with me this morning. You must try to understand people. You must try to understand *why* they behave as they do. One day, you *will* dance on the stage, and then you must think that if you can make one sad person in the audience happy, even for a moment, you'll begin to be a little bit of an artist.' She said these things to us very often. Of course, we didn't really understand all this at the time. I mean, we used to think how strange she was. When I joined the company, we made many tours and we would travel by train. I remember Pavlova walking into our train compartment and getting very irritated when she saw us looking at magazines—film magazines, or something stupid like that. She would collect them and throw them all out of the window. Instead, we would receive from her all sorts of books. I have some of them here in my library—books like *The Life of Napoleon* or *The Life of Duse*. You see, she realized that she had disrupted our education to a certain extent—none of us were able to go to college. She wanted to give us a different view of life. For example, when we traveled to the Orient, we all had to go see the museums and then write little résumés of what we felt when we looked at such-and-such a picture. When we went to Egypt—we did a dreadful Egyptian ballet there which I loathed . . . but never mind—she wanted us to go to the temples and the tombs. We were so very young and it was difficult to take all that in."

Pavlova seemed, according to Miss Stuart, a model of eventemperedness. Patient to an uncommon degree, Pavlova seldom flared into anger. Only once did she lose her temper.

"I'll never forget the one time she did. She rehearsed us in two ballets over and over again. One was *The Blue Danube divertissement*, which I think she had arranged, and the other was a ballet which she created, and was a masterpiece of its kind, called *Autumn Leaves*. Well, she wanted very much for this work to be very flowing, and she became very, very angry because she couldn't get some of the girls' bodies to move a certain way. One of these girls suddenly stopped and said to Pavlova, 'I don't know what you're talking about!' At that, Pavlova burst into tears, then lifted a chair from the floor, crashed it down with enormous anger, and left the rehearsal. It was the first time I saw her really very angry."

Miss Stuart now turned to the Pavlova repertory, which, for the most part, consisted of mediocre ballets created primarily to show Pavlova at her most exalted. They were simplistic in subject matter, but obviously pleased audiences everywhere. The fact was, the public came to see Pavlova—not her vehicles. Some of her works—*The Dying Swan, California Poppy*, among a handful of others—have achieved a certain immortality, but the general run of the repertory, fostered by Pavlova's husband and manager Victor E. Dandré, seemed to have bordered on the banal. Pavlova was fully aware of the limited scope of these ballets. Often, she strived to enlarge and deepen their aesthetic content, but Dandré, knowing that the public was satisfied, insisted on a repertorial *status quo*. Muriel Stuart elaborated: "Throughout my years with Pavlova, I knew perfectly well she was not enjoying the ballets she was doing. She wanted to go further—to do things that were more creative. But Dandré would not let her do this. He knew that the people came to see Pavlova in *The Dying Swan, Die Puppenfee*, and *Giselle*, and these were the things that kept the company together and in business. When we did an experiment one time—it happened to be a very costly one—it was not a success at all. I can't think of the name of it. But, you see, Dandré was really saving her, in a sense, and delivering to the public what they wanted to see."

What did Pavlova look like? What was she like in performance? What was her effect on her public? Miss Stuart lifted her head and clasped her hands.

"Oh, she was extraordinary looking. She had an ivory complexion. I wouldn't say she was a beautiful woman, but she transcended beauty. She had those dark, piercing eyes. She was the sort of person who could, as they say, see from the back of her head. And, she had the uncanny ability of sensing what was right and what was wrong. . . . In performance, I've never seen anything greater in my life. When she danced Giselle, we were almost terrified of her in the first act, because we used to so *believe* her madness, that she might catch us by the throat, that we were lucky if we got away. It was extraordinary! I would say that basically, Pavlova was a lyrical poetess in her movements. Of course, today, dancers are much more prepared technically. Pavlova never did *fouettés*—she didn't have the strength for them. She was simply an artist. That's what she wanted us to be—musical, alive, and all the things we probably *couldn't* be for her. . . . When I was with the company, there were, I think, eight tall girls, eight short girls, and some fine Russian and Polish male dancers. Later, there were some American men like Edward Caton and Aubrey Hitchins. The point is, it was never a large company. We never did whole classical ballets like, say, *Sleeping Beauty*. I mean, Pavlova did her *pas de deux* from it, and we did several little dances. And so it was with other classics. . . .

"As for her effect on the people, I don't think I can remember any other artist being loved and adored the way this woman was. It was always a mystical experience that they went through. It was almost a religious thing when she danced the Dying Swan or the Dying Rose. It was an experience that doesn't happen today because we don't do these things any more, and I don't think we need to do them. But people at that time had seen very little ballet, and it was the day of the Great Artist. She mesmerized her audience. She had a quality that enraptured them. When this woman came out to make her *révérence*—to thank the people—this was a moment as great as the dancing itself. It was like a benediction—a blessing. This was not a conscious thing. She did it unconsciously."

Miss Stuart commented on her personal relationship with Pavlova. The legendary ballerina had taken a special interest in Muriel Stuart. She wanted her to work much harder, to study much longer. But this gifted pupil, by her own admission, lacked ambition:

"I was simply happy to be with Pavlova," she said, "to be her soloist. And I could have been happy like that forever . . . or until I fell in love. Pavlova never wanted me to be married; but I did fall in love, and I did want to be married and be with the man I fell in love with. He was the violinist with the company—a Russian, Julian Brudetzky. He left the company to become a concert master of the San Francisco Symphony. I followed him against Pavlova's wishes. Finally, she said, 'Muriel, I am sad that you won't remain with me. But if you must go, take this envelope. It

contains some money with which you can return to me at any time. . . .'
Then, Pavlova looked at me and said, 'If you insist upon marriage, please
have a child . . . because I never did.' "

When Muriel Stuart followed Julian Brudetzky to San Francisco, her
professional dancing career came to an end, but it was the beginning of her
teaching career, which continues to this day. Very early in her marriage,
she danced briefly with the Chicago Civic Opera Company, and choreographed two ballets for them. She was also engaged to teach the Opera's
ballet corps. Eager to expand her knowledge of dance, she began to study
modern dance techniques with Harald Kreutzberg. In the meantime, her
marriage to Julian Brudetzky began to flounder.

"My husband was a great musician and he taught me a great deal about
music—about listening. There wasn't a night that we didn't have chamber
music in the house. As for our having a child as Pavlova had hoped, it did
not happen. My husband didn't want a child. *He* was the child. To be
completely honest with you, that was why I left."

Miss Stuart came to New York and studied with Martha Graham for
two years. It was through Graham and Agnes de Mille that her New York
teaching career began. The two dancer-choreographers had talked to Lincoln Kirstein, who invited Miss Stuart to join the faculty at the School of
American Ballet. The year was 1937. It was around that time that Muriel
Stuart remarried. "I met and married a lovely, sweet person by the name
of James Warrick. He was a playwright who wrote *Blind Alley*. With him,
I had a child, our son Peter. Today, he is married to someone else—to a
sweet and lovely person. We are all quite friendly. Anyway, I was married
seven years to my first husband and seven years to my second husband.
I've only been married twice. That isn't too bad, is it? Let's say that marriage, for me, is a very difficult thing. I am a career woman. A teacher is a
career person. An artist is a career person. It is not enough for such people
to just make a home. I've had a career since the age of thirteen."

Living alone and clearly liking it, Miss Stuart is not given to sentimen-
talizing over the past. She has a youth and vigor that is altogether of the
moment. Basically, she is forward-looking and retains the British trait of
positive thinking. Teaching is her life and she approaches it with high
purpose.

"All teachers who are successful must love people," she said. "I think
teaching is a dedication. I think there are lots of people who teach with
knowledge—but without love. If you love what you're doing, you are
going to be successful. What's so exciting about teaching is that you never
know what will happen—what students may cross your path. Because of
my life with Pavlova, I tend to like a lyric dancer best. I want a lyric
poetess. Technique today is all over the place. I look for the artist—for the
exciting personality. When I find it, and I have found a few, then I am
fulfilled."

ALICIA MARKOVA

The most difficult people to write about are the ones who are legends in their own time. Yet Dame Alicia Markova, née Lilian Alicia Marks, is only a mortal after all, but an enchanting one. As she told me during our interview in London in the summer of 1972, "My elders always spoke about ballerinas not being human—that they were unreal. Why, it's not true at all." Markova is anything but unreal; the trouble begins when one tries to separate the legend from the person.

It seems, of course, unreal that she was a pupil of Enrico Cecchetti, of

Nicholas Legat, of Serafina Astafieva, and of Vincenzo Celli; that Diaghilev found her when she was but ten years old and that at the age of
fourteen she entered his Ballets Russes; that at the age of sixteen she
danced the leading role in Balanchine's first choreographic effort for the
Ballets Russes, *Le Chant du Rossignol*; that she helped spearhead the entire school of British ballet with performances of ballets by Frederick
Ashton, Antony Tudor, Ninette de Valois; that she was the first English
dancer to dance Giselle as well as Odette-Odile in the full-length *Swan Lake*.

Markova's history, highlighted by continuous triumph, continues to
amaze when one thinks of her unsurpassed artistry, of her supreme performances in partnership with Anton Dolin—a partnership which brought
the art of ballet to a world-wide public. As has so often been said before,
Markova belongs to that unique and small number of dancers, who, like
Nijinsky and Pavlova, influenced and heightened the appeal of classical
dance in their own time.

This monument—this fabled figure—is today a gracious, modest
woman in her sixties, looking far younger than her years, and retaining
that delicacy and brightness which ignited the stages of the world. Absent
from the stage for only a little over a decade (she formally retired in
1963), Markova can, by no stretch of the imagination, be considered a
historic relic. When she invited me to her apartment in Knightsbridge,
London, she was as charming as any titled hostess of British society. We
sat in a lonely gray and white parlor, right out of Cecil Beaton. Markova
wore a lounging suit—a silk floral print. Her jet-black hair was *en bouffant*,
crowning the perfect oval of her face. The dark-brown eyes were sparkling, her skin, soft and roseate. As she sat, feet crossed, she was a study
in delicate repose. The sound of her voice, with its British accent, was
nothing if not musical. The aura of her presence was one of larklike
alertness, and everything she told was said with a smile.

I commented on a ravishing topaz ring she was wearing. "It was a gift I
received in Brazil," she said. "And this," she continued pointing to a
necklace, "was given to me by members of an American symphony orchestra." Looking about the room, I noticed a delicate pitcher decorated with a
portrait of Taglioni and a Scotsman in *La Sylphide*. "It's cracked, alas, but
someone found it for me, and it's one of my most cherished possessions."

Dame Alicia then told me that her London schedule had been very
busy: "I have been quite involved this year. I have promised to give
master classes for the Royal Academy of Dancing. Also, I'm giving the
address tomorrow for the Imperial Society Congress. I've just given my
annual award to the Arts Educational School. Last March I flew to Glas-
gow to do an hour's television program with the Scottish Theatre Ballet.
We taped a master class devoted exclusively to my interpretation of Giselle.
Things have been most hectic for me. Of course, each year I fly to
America. I'm professor of dance at the University of Cincinnati. That's

always such a pleasure because then I can visit all my many American friends."

I asked Markova how it all began for her. Did she know from the very first that her life would be dedicated to the dance?

"I don't think it entered my head that I wanted to be a dancer. Even when my parents took me to see Pavlova, it never entered my head. Of course, I was deeply impressed. I thought Pavlova was absolutely out of this world! I thought she was *so* beautiful, but I was merely an admirer and I was only nine years old. Pavlova danced at the Queen's Hall, which now of course is gone. I remember it was a *divertissement* program. I think she danced *California Poppy* and *Christmas*. After the performance I was brought backstage to meet her. I was already spinning like a top, having been enrolled in Astafieva's class. Well, Pavlova told my father that I might come and visit her the following morning. Naturally, I was thrilled. And so, I went to Ivy House. She started putting me to work in her studio by giving me a *barre*. She advised me on certain technical things. I was most impressed and learned so much. You see, I was only a little English girl, not brought up in the great tradition of the Russians. Here in London, we had no one to set us an example.

"After the *barre*, Pavlova told me something amazing. She said that the most important thing for me to remember was to take very good care of my teeth. I've never forgotten that. She was so right because bad teeth can affect your whole body. After she told me that, she asked me to get out of my work clothes and rub myself down with alcohol or eau de cologne. Well, I hadn't brought anything like that along. I said to her 'But I had my bath this morning, Madame Pavlova.' She disappeared, and in two minutes came back with a beautiful towel and a flask with cologne which had her initials on it, painted in gold. 'Here,' she said. 'Rub yourself down, because after working, your pores are open and it is dangerous to rush out without first having a thorough rubdown.' I did as she told me. All the while, I was eying the cologne flask she had left with me with the initials 'A.P.' on it. For the first time in my life I was tempted to steal. But I didn't. She might never have asked me back. But it was such a temptation!"

Markova went on to relate that Pavlova came to see her in the class she was taking with Astafieva, how she had been looking for some girls for her company. By then, however, Diaghilev had already seen Alicia Marks in Astafieva's class. Eventually, after the death of her father, the young girl was invited to join the Diaghilev company. Sometime later, Pavlova came to see Markova in a performance with the Diaghilev company in Paris. There was great excitement when word came that Pavlova was viewing the performance from a box. Markova was in the *corps de ballet*. When the great ballerina went backstage to greet young Markova, she expressed her dismay over the evening's program which consisted of the kind of modern works which had initially caused her to leave the Diaghilev company, sometime before World War I. Pavlova felt that the classics were the essence of ballet. When Diaghilev died in 1929, word came to Markova from Pavlova inviting the young dancer to join her company. She wrote saying that Markova could enter the *corps de ballet*, but would also be given solo roles. Instead, however, Alicia Markova returned to her native England and in London joined the Vic-Wells company.

Dame Alicia's recollections of her period with Diaghilev were most vivid:

"Mr. Diaghilev and his company came to London in 1921. They were going to stage *The Sleeping Princess* at the Alhambra. He went around one day looking for extra dancers in their teens. At the time, I was studying with Astafieva. I was only ten years old and a funny-looking thing, with this Buster Brown hairdo and socks. And that was the very first time that Mr. Diaghilev saw me. He asked me do a little dance. I danced a solo I was doing at the time, to a Rubinstein waltz. He said he would take me. . . . He spoke to Nijinska, and they thought of putting me in *The Sleeping Princess* and giving me a special variation as the Fairy Dewdrop. When everything was set, Mr. Diaghilev discovered that children were not allowed to dance onstage. One had to get a special license. But apparently he cleared all of that with the London County Council and got a special license for me. Then came the first great disappointment of my life. I came down with diphtheria. Can you imagine?! It was really awful, because in those days, one had to spend three months in an isolation ward. I never appeared as the Fairy Dewdrop. But when I got out of the hospital, Mr. Diaghilev took me to see the performances at the Alhambra. That was so fortunate because I saw all the great dancers." (Young Alicia saw in that historic production such celebrated dancers as Olga Spessivtzeva, Pierre Vladimirov, Lydia Lopoukhova, Felia Doubrovska, Lubov Egorova, Bronislava Nijinska, Vera Nemtchinova, and Léon Woizikowski.) "Those dancers set a standard for me for life."

Ultimately, Markova entered the company and remained with it for four years. She recalled her close relationship with Diaghilev:

"My father died just about the time I went with Mr. Diaghilev. He took over as a father for me. He was my spiritual and artistic father. . . . He arranged for my governess to come with me. She and I went to live with Madame Nijinska, who had a daughter more or less my age. But my staying with Madame Nijinska was short-lived because Balanchine soon after entered the company as dancer and choreographer. Bronislava Nijinska had a terrible row with Diaghilev and suddenly she was out. Mr. Balanchine became very intrigued with me. One day, he asked me to do some steps for him. I was still very small, but I could do anything he asked me to do . . . thirty-two *fouettés, double tours* in the air, all kinds of things. Well, Mr. Balanchine chose me to appear in the revival of Stravinsky's *Le Chant du Rossignol*. I was sixteen. Until that point, I had been dancing

small roles such as Riding Hood in *The Sleeping Princess* and other roles suitable for me. All the while I was taking class with Cecchetti and learning his method. When I danced the *Nightingale*, I of course came into contact with Mr. Igor Stravinsky. He took over my musical education. . . .

"The regimen of the company was very strict. We always had class at nine o'clock every morning, regardless of how late we had worked the night before. Sometimes, in those days, when Balanchine or Massine were choreographing, we might work until two o'clock in the morning. When they were inspired, no one stopped them. We just worked. Today, of course, we no longer do that. The unions would not allow it. . . . But that's how we worked on the *Nightingale*. I must say it was very difficult for me. Stravinsky would come to the rehearsals and play the score on the piano. During that first rehearsal, I was almost in tears. I thought, I'll never be able to do this. Stravinsky was so sweet. He took me aside and said, 'Little bird' (that's what he used to call me), don't worry. I will tell you what to do. Listen to the music and learn it by ear. If you learn the music by ear, you will never have to worry.' I will always be grateful to Mr. Stravinsky for having told me that, because from that time on, every score, every orchestration, I've learned by ear. Mr. Grigoriev, the *régisseur* of the company, would always say, 'Count!' But from that moment on, I stopped counting because counting was no good for me. Many, many years later, when I danced in America and Mr. Billy Rose asked me to dance in his spectacle *The Seven Lively Arts*, he asked who the greatest composer might be from whom to commission a work for me. Without hesitation, I said 'Stravinsky.' And that's how *Scènes de Ballet* was commissioned."

Markova was the most protected member of the Diaghilev company. When she did not perform, she went to bed at 6:30. She was not permitted to accept invitations of any sort. It was only when the ballerina reached her eighteenth birthday that Diaghilev permitted her to socialize.

"On my eighteenth birthday," Dame Alicia recalled, "we danced a charity performance in Monte Carlo at the Hôtel de Paris. After the performance, I was told I could stay up for supper. I was allowed to purchase my first evening dress and my first pair of party shoes. Mr. Diaghilev ordered champagne. It was like my coming-out party. In later years, I was grateful that Mr. Diaghilev was so protective of me. But then, being the baby of the company, everybody protected me—Danilova, Massine, Balanchine. . . . I had to be seen, not heard, and I had to be protected. But I'll never forget that lovely party."

These early years provided Markova with firsthand knowledge of the working methods of choreographers who were to influence twentieth-century dance. She told of her part in the creative process of the young Léonide Massine. While Massine had already produced his masterpiece *Le Tricorne* (Markova appeared in the *corps de ballet* of this production), he took advantage of Markova's youthful eagerness to help him create subsequent works for Diaghilev's Ballets Russes.

"When Massine began choreographing his ballet *Ode*," Markova said, "he mounted on me the steps that would eventually be danced by the principals of the company. I would learn the steps that Danilova, Nikitina, and Doubrovska would dance. You see, these dancers were so busy performing that their time with Massine was limited. And so, after I had learned the steps, it fell to me to teach them to the ballerinas. In that way, I acquired so much knowledge and learned so many things about roles that I never danced. I don't think it is generally known that the role Felia Doubrovska danced in *Ode* was intended for me. Unfortunately, I became ill with pneumonia and had to be out of the company for two months. Anyway, Massine knew I loved to work, and he would experiment with me. All the choreographers knew that I adored to work with them in new things even if I didn't dance the roles myself."

Dame Alicia was eighteen years old when Sergei Diaghilev died in Venice. The year was 1929. The ballerina had proven herself. She was becoming a major talent in the Diaghilev company. Important roles were planned for her. Markova recalled her last year with the company:

"From the age of fourteen to eighteen, I had worked terribly hard," she said, her voice turning somber. "I had done everything I was told. I'd been terribly obedient. I had achieved everything Mr. Diaghilev had wanted me to achieve. He said that I was now ready to *really* work on my own. For the first time I was being given more money and some wonderful roles were being scheduled for me for the next season. There would be a new ballet created by Lifar. I was to be his partner. I was to be in Nijinska's *Les Biches* and dance in a revival of Fokine's *Firebird*. My greatest opportunity was to 'cover' for Spessivtzeva in *Giselle*. You can imagine how happy I was! I thought, Now all my hard work has been worth it. It was the summer of 1929, and we all went on holiday. I returned to England. Then the news of Diaghilev's death came . . . the second biggest disappointment of my life. We tried to keep the company together. Actually, we went back for the opera season the following year at Monte Carlo. We all tried our best. Mr. Grigoriev, Madame Danilova, Tchernicheva, and all the rest were there. But it wasn't the same. For myself, I didn't want to continue. I think I felt quite ill for a few months. I felt I wanted to give up dancing."

The Diaghilev Ballets Russes ultimately disbanded. Dancers left for many different parts of the world, some centering in Paris, others in London, some in New York. Alicia Markova's fate altered with the arrival of a letter, "A letter from a young man named Frederick Ashton." Its postmark was London. The letter proposed that she dance in a number of incidental dances choreographed by Ashton for the Dryden play, *Mariage à la Mode*, produced by Sir Nigel Playfair at the Lyric Theatre, Hammersmith. It went on to express that it might possibly be beneath her to appear in incidental dances after having performed with the Ballets Russes. Young Ashton went on to praise the ballerina, saying he had watched her from the gallery every night. He added that he had been studying dance with Massine and Marie Rambert. Markova accepted the invitation forthwith.

And so began her British career, dancing first in the Dryden play, then with the Ballet Club, just established by Marie Rambert, then moving to the Vic-Wells Ballet company founded by Ninette de Valois, a former colleague in the Diaghilev company.

"We alternated between two theaters," Markova recalled, "spending two weeks each at the Old Vic and at the Sadler's Wells. In those days, the Shakespeare people were at the Old Vic, while the opera and the ballet were at the Sadler's Wells. Eventually, we stayed at the Sadler's Wells. I became prima ballerina of the Vic-Wells. My first important role was created for me by Ashton. It was *La Péri* with music by Dukas, which I first danced with Ballet Rambert. At the Vic-Wells, I danced in Ashton's *Les Rendezvous*, *The Haunted Ballroom*, and *The Rake's Progress*. This all happened in the mid-Thirties."

Through their close association, Markova and Ashton brought acclaim for themselves and helped to establish a British ballet tradition. During this period, Markova achieved her most singular success. She became the first British ballerina to dance Giselle, the role with which she is most frequently associated. She has danced this role countless times, and with each performance seemed to have given it increasing depth and luminosity. When Markova danced *Giselle*, with the Ballet Theatre at the Metropolitan Opera in 1944, critic Edwin Denby wrote: "Alicia Markova in *Giselle* is Ballet Theatre's greatest glory. . . . There is no other dancer whose movement is so perfectly centered, and who controls so exactly the full continuity of a motion. From the center to the extremities. . . . All her qualities, of dancing, of mime, of presence, find a perfect use in the part of Giselle; the extraordinary effect Miss Markova creates in this part is obvious to the thousands who watch her, whether they are familiar with ballet or not. Last night again she received a unanimous ovation."

Throughout her long career, Markova's most famous partner was Anton Dolin. I asked Dame Alicia to comment on their long and complex association.

"It's very difficult to talk about. It was a matter of having great confidence in each other. Remember, I was only ten when we first met. He was already a *premier danseur* with the Diaghilev company. We would work together before the morning class and after the morning class. He would partner me. He was in *The Sleeping Princess* and he would watch what the great dancers were doing during the performance. Then, he would come to class the next day and ask me to try out what Spessivtzeva had been dancing to perfection the night before. I was a very obedient child, and whatever he asked me to do, I did." (It is said that Markova developed a lasting infatuation with her partner—an infatuation and a love that Dame Alicia did not care to disclose during our talk. She simply said, "I have never married.")

Entering the fourth decade of her ballet career, Markova formed, with Dolin, the London Festival Ballet in 1950. This was the culmination of what had been on two previous occasions the Markova-Dolin Ballet company, the first of which was formed in 1935. Markova appeared with the London Festival Ballet until 1951, when she began a series of guest appearances with companies throughout the world. With her retirement in 1963, Markova accepted an invitation from Rudolf Bing to be the director of the Metropolitan Opera Ballet, a post she held for two years.

I urged Dame Alicia to speak about her approach to the various interpretations of ballets she had danced.

"Whenever a choreographer told me he was going to do a ballet on me, I would always do research. First, I would go to the music. I would research the composer so I'd know what I was working with. Second, I would work on the character I was to portray. Then, I'd research the period in which the ballet might be set. This was so important. And in that way, you learn so much. Today, I hate to say, young dancers don't read enough. They don't do their 'homework.' I feel that young dancers must gather all the information they can and put all the information together like a puzzle. They must not copy dancers. They must merely take what is good for *them*. They must also say, 'That was good in *that* period. We are now in *this* period. We've moved ahead.' To bring life to the classics, you must do a bit of updating—otherwise, they just become museum pieces. And that's no good. Of course, you must preserve the line, the tradition. But the outlook must be fresh. This helped me so much during my whole career. I ran two tracks. All the romantic, classical ballets, I liked to do straight. Then when I did the modern works, I felt that they fed each other. The new things kept the classical things vital and alive."

In 1960, Alicia Markova was created a Commander of the Order of the British Empire by Her Majesty Queen Elizabeth II. In 1963, she was made Dame of the Order of the British Empire. "During my investiture before the Queen, the small orchestra played the pizzicato from Delibes's *Sylvia*. I thought this was most appropriate."

Dame Markova bade me farewell, saying, "A ballerina's life can be glorious. But it does not get any easier. I don't think anyone must ever think about it getting easier. I think you must try to enjoy what you are doing. It is the most important thing. Somehow, looking back, I can honestly say I enjoyed dancing."

Maurice Seymour

ANTON DOLIN

When, in the summer of 1973, Jerome Robbins conceived his *Celebration: The Art of the Pas de Deux* for the Spoleto Festival of Two Worlds, he invited the great British dancer Anton Dolin to introduce the spectacle. It was Robbins' thought that the legendary dancer might begin the evening by demonstrating, with the aid of two young Italian dancers, what a *pas de deux* was all about. Dolin, who danced with the Diaghilev company, had partnered some of the world's greatest ballerinas. He would be eminently qualified to present an evening of *pas de deux'*, and would

Julian Braunsweg

. . . and JOHN GILPIN

lend a historic touch to the occasion. As it turned out, this charming idea of his participating was ultimately dropped, with everyone agreeing that it would in some way burden the evening.

Being in Spoleto that summer, it was my pleasure to meet Anton Dolin and his friend and long-time companion, the British dancer John Gilpin. The two could be seen walking in the Piazza del Duomo, always immaculately dressed, or sitting at one of the outdoor cafés sipping an *apéritif*. The handsome older man, white-haired, straight-backed, shed an aura of romance. Dolin! The first English dancer to have won international recognition. The legendary partner of Karsavina, Spessivtzeva, Nemtchinova, Doubrovska, Danilova—and, of course, Alicia Markova—the ballerina with whose name his will be eternally linked. Dolin! For whom Bronislava Nijinska created *Le Train Bleu* in 1924 for the Diaghilev company, who created one of the Evil Companions in Balanchine's *Le Fils Prodigue*, who danced in Balanchine's *Le Bal*, and in countless classical productions, setting the standard for such roles as Albrecht in *Giselle*, the Fairy Prince in *The Nutcracker*, and the male leads in *The Sleeping Beauty* and *Swan Lake*. There he sat—the man everyone calls Pat (for Anton Dolin is not really his name). Born Sydney Francis Patrick Chippendall Healey-Kay in Sinfold, Sussex, in 1904, Dolin wore a blue summer suit, a purple tie, over which hung a chain bearing a cross. Next to him sat John Gilpin, born in 1930, a former member of Ballet Rambert, of the Ballets de Paris de Roland Petit, of the London Festival Ballet. A man of extraordinary charm, he was a virtuoso dancer as well as a *danseur noble*. A guest artist with such companies as the Royal Ballet and the American Ballet Theatre, Gilpin now devotes most of his time to teaching and coaching. Both men were sun-tanned and exuded health and vitality. This summer, they were sharing a villa in Capri. Despite the disappointment of not partaking in the Robbins Spoleto presentation, they seemed in excellent spirits.

Dolin explained what had happened:

"Well, I tell you. I felt it was wrong. When Menotti and Jerry called me and asked me to come here to do this introduction, I was, of course, delighted. But then, when I realized that Jerry had gotten together five of the greatest dancing couples doing these *pas de deux*, I felt it was incongruous to show the right and the wrong way to do the *pas de deux*. Anyhow, I couldn't be more pleased to be here and be part of all this."

I asked Dolin to tell me what his life was like at the moment.

"What I'm doing now is taking a really long and complete holiday. I rented a very old villa in Capri, and I've decided to write a new book. It will be called 'My Friends!' "

With a broad grin, Gilpin added, "Yes, it will be five pages long."

"It will *not* be five pages long," said Dolin. "I have a lot of friends. It's going to be a very *long* book. I'm going to write about people that I have known. It's a name-dropping book, and I don't care. I've written long chapters about Diaghilev, Cocteau, Stravinsky, Picasso, Braque, Tallulah Bankhead, Gracie Fields, Beatrice Lillie, Jack Buchanan, Galina Ulanova, Noël Coward. The book will be stories about these people—some very short, some not so short. All will be very kind, but all, I hope, will tell the truth."

Will Dolin not write about Alicia Markova?

"That goes without saying. I *have* to write about Markova. Otherwise, she'll put a dagger in my back. But when I'm not writing and not taking time off, I spend a few weeks in Bloomington, at Indiana University, where I am the chairman of the Dance Faculty. I work there with my cochairman, Marina Svetlova. I shall be going there at the end of October to set up the fall program. I've gotten to the time in my life where I want to be active in my own way."

Dolin reminisced about his first great mentor, Sergei Diaghilev:

"Some people have said that Diaghilev was a monster. Well, he was not a monster. He was a jealous person. He hated anything that was not one-hundred-per-cent real and genuine. When I first met him, I was terrified of him. He was in London in 1921 reviving *Sleeping Beauty* at the Alhambra Theatre. I was studying with the great teacher Serafina Astafieva. Diaghilev came around because he wanted some extras for the production. I was chosen, and even had a chance to dance in the *corps de ballet*. Then, the Diaghilev company left London, and I remained behind making my career in England. A year later, Diaghilev had heard about me and wrote to Astafieva asking, 'Who is this young Russian boy that you're hiding from me?' She wrote back to him, 'It's not a Russian boy. It's an English boy who was with you a year and a half ago in *Sleeping Beauty*.'

"Well, I auditioned for Diaghilev in Paris three months later, and made my debut in Monte Carlo on January 1, 1924, dancing in *Daphnis and Chloë*. But Diaghilev was a great man. I was so very proud that he took an interest in the rather stupid, ignorant young English boy that I was. I wish I had realized more what this man was. I wish I had taken more advantage of him. At the time, I got bored being taken to museums. Diaghilev took me everywhere. But, my God! What he did for my career! Everything that I owe, and have learned, and have done, in my lifetime, is due principally to this man."

Dolin recalled his meeting with Alicia Markova, who was a child of fourteen when she danced with the Diaghilev company, and who, it is said, fell passionately in love with him:

"Markova was always like a little sister to me—always. I think she was in love with me. I hope she still is."

I told Dolin that when I interviewed Markova, she hesitated to speak of her true feelings about him.

"I'm not hesitant," said Dolin.

"But you're Irish. You're not English," said Gilpin.

"That's right. The worst side of me is Irish, and that's the side of me I like best. I have a vile temper, but I've learned to cope with it. Anyway— Markova. Markova will go down in history as one of the sweetest persons in the world. I loathe the word 'sweet.' I don't want any artist to be described as a sweet person. Those who really know her will tell you that Markova had one hell of a bad temper. She danced like a will-o'-the-wisp, yet she had the strength of an ox. She could be terribly difficult at times. She detested rehearsals. I remember one time when we first started Festival

Ballet, saying to her, 'Alicia, I'm not going to go on dancing the Fairy Prince in *Nutcracker* any more. I'm ten years older than you, and I don't feel like a fairy prince. I want you to dance with a new, younger Fairy Prince—John Gilpin.' Well, she didn't want to do it with him. She had known she would be dancing with John weeks in advance, but she would never rehearse. It came, literally, to the day of the performance. Finally I said, 'Alicia, are you going to rehearse, or not? Because if you're not going to rehearse, I'm going to announce to the audience that you are sick and Nathalie Krassovska will take your place.' Well, Alicia condescended to rehearse at last. She rehearsed in high heels. Of course, John Gilpin was terribly nervous. He was dancing the whole of *Nutcracker* for the first time in London. He was terrified. He didn't want to do it. He came to me and said, 'Mr. Dolin, I can't dance under these conditions. It's just not fair to me.' I told Gilpin he *must* dance, because I knew instinctively that nothing would go wrong. I knew Markova well enough to know that whatever happened, nothing would go wrong—for her sake. Of course, they danced brilliantly.

"John Gilpin, whom I met in 1949, was a dancer whom I had first considered a conceited little boy. I remember he was rehearsing with John Taras—doing the ballet *Design for Strings*."

"Yes," John Gilpin continued. "I remember Mr. Dolin coming into the rehearsal studio, and going up to Mr. Taras, saying, 'Is John Gilpin here?' And Mr. Dolin came up to me. He said he had a message from Marie Rambert. He said, 'Marie Rambert wants me to give you a kiss.' I was stunned."

Dolin laughed, and said, "Yes, I had that message from Marie Rambert, but after giving John Gilpin that message, I added, 'I'm not going to give you a kiss. I'm going to shake your hand.' And that's how Gilpin and I met. At the time, he was dancing with the Marquis de Cuevas's Grand Ballet de Monte Carlo. Then he left, and came back to London. Actually, John was very shy and very nervous. I ultimately gave him those roles in the Festival Ballet that I no longer wished to dance, such as the Man in *Les Sylphides*, and the Fairy Prince in *Nutcracker*."

John Gilpin remained with the London Festival Ballet from 1950 through 1962 as principal dancer, and from 1962 to 1965 as artistic director.

"I did my first *Giselle* with Markova when I was twenty," said Gilpin. "Then, in the next two years, with Festival, I hit the 'right moment,' and danced with everyone—Danilova, Slavenska, Chauviré, Krassovska. When I first did *Le Beau Danube* with Danilova, I danced the Hussar. I remember being so very amused. When I appeared on stage, there was Danilova in her red dress, looking absolutely wonderful. She looked at me and said, 'You know, John, I think maybe you must put on a mustache. Otherwise people will think I'm your grandmother.' I loved dancing with her. She was a wonderful artist. I've been very lucky through the whole of my career. I danced with Antoinette Sibley in her first performance of *Sleeping Beauty*. I danced with Carla Fracci in her first *Giselle*.

It was Anton Dolin who had invited Carla Fracci to come from Milan and dance her very first Giselle at London's Royal Festival Hall. The year was 1959. Dolin recalled the occasion:

"We gave three performances of *Giselle*—Thursday, Friday, and Saturday. The first was Markova and myself. The second was Yvette Chauviré and myself, which was, incidentally, my last performance of Albrecht in London. I danced my last *Giselle* with her. On Saturday, it was Carla Fracci with John Gilpin. On Monday morning, the papers came out in London. The *Daily Mail* had a big headline saying, 'The third *Giselle* was best of all.' That Monday, when Carla came to the theater, Markova didn't say a word to her. I thought her eyes were going to kill Fracci. That's Markova. Yvette Chauviré came to the theater, and she went up to Carla Fracci and said, 'You were marvelous! I am so happy for you.' Yvette was always very warm.

"When Gilpin danced a beautiful *Spectre de la Rose* with Anita Lander in Paris, Yvette was there. Everyone knew Yvette Chauviré in Paris. She was the queen of ballet in Paris, as Markova was the queen of ballet in London. Well, afterward, Yvette rose from her box. She screamed, she bravoed! That's the greatness of Yvette Chauviré."

Dolin then spoke to me briefly about Olga Spessivtzeva:

"She danced like every dream that one will always want to dream. She was the most gorgeous dancer in the world. No one has ever surpassed her technically. No one has ever equaled her purity of line. It was like an Ingres painting. She was beautiful to look at. The most wonderful *pointes*, feet, legs, arms. She may not always have been the most musical dancer, but when she had to follow music that was completely wrong from the point of view of tempo, she would follow it. She had three great roles: Giselle, Princess Aurora in *The Sleeping Beauty*, and Odette–Odile in *Swan Lake*. She was not good, funnily enough, in *Les Sylphides*. When she danced *Les Sylphides* in Monte Carlo, it was not one of her great roles. I described her strangeness, her panics, her near madness in my book. But there were so many more things I could have said. I wouldn't dare say them, and wouldn't want to say them while she's alive. She's in America now, living on the Tolstoy Farm."

"The last time I danced in New York," said John Gilpin, "was on the Twenty-fifth Anniversary of Ballet Theatre. I danced *Giselle*. And Spessivtzeva was brought to see it. I danced with Ruth Ann Koesun. Spessivtzeva came backstage. She seemed very moved. She still had those marvelous black eyes. I was so in awe of her. I had never seen her before."

John Gilpin has not danced in two years.

"I had three very bad operations on both legs," he said. "I had two on my right leg for massive blood clots, and one on my left leg. After the third operation my doctor said, 'John, I think it's dangerous now for you to perform.' But I can still move. I can teach."

"Move?!" exclaimed Dolin. "You should see him coaching young dancers. It is marvelous to see him showing, and dancing, after nearly two years. He can still get up and do it!"

Anton Dolin looked admiringly at John Gilpin. Asked what he would say to a young male dancer wishing to make the ballet his career, Dolin paused, mused, then said:

"I would say, first, look at yourself. Look at yourself in the mirror. Do you have the physique? Not necessarily the beauty—but the physique. Do you have the legs, the body, the arms, and above all, the *intelligence* to be a dancer? Because, to be a dancer, you need all. Also, dancers must know about life. A dancer has got to think about other things besides just dancing—putting on his damn tights, and his shoes, and his costume and his make-up. Let him go to the theater, look at paintings, read. Don't just live in a world of ballet."

"Yes," added Gilpin. "When I first started dancing, I was told it would be a very hard life, and a very short career. I would not advise anybody, girl or boy, to become a dancer—unless he had talent and intelligence. Because, no matter how much technical ability you have, on stage, you must go beyond technique. The fireworks of technicality are not enough. You must have other qualities—those that will eventually make you an artist. Those qualities are hard to define."

Anton Dolin then answered a question regarding his own particular qualities as a dancer:

"It's terribly difficult to describe oneself. But you've asked the question, and I'll answer it, and be perfectly honest. I think I had great showmanship. I could walk onto a stage, and it would mean something. I remember once in London, a critic came to see a performance of *Giselle*. I was dancing with Toumanova. I had smashed up my knee, and could not dance full out. Anyway, the next morning, the critic said: 'To see Dolin just walk onto the stage and almost walk through the role of Albrecht is, to me, just as great as seeing the greatest dancer dance the role.' I've always remembered that. I learned to walk on the stage. That is one thing that I also admire about Rudolf Nureyev. Nureyev walks on the stage with such beauty, and he can stand still so marvelously. I think I did the same, in my time. Maybe less arrogantly, less flamboyantly. That, I think, was a little of my quality."

VERA ZORINA

Imagine a beautiful seven-year-old German girl walking with an older woman, a Russian friend of her mother's, to a ballet teacher's studio in Berlin in the 1920s. The child is about to be looked at by the Russian dancer Eugenia Eduardova. The girl and her companion are admitted to the studio. In a moment, Eduardova appears. She exchanges some brief remarks with the woman. They speak in Russian. The aristocratic teacher looks at the child, turns, and walks out of the room, slamming the door behind her. Stunned, the two are left in an awful silence. The child looks questioningly at her friend. "What happened?" the child asks tremulously. "You are too young to study with Eduardova," is the reply. "You must wait two years. Eduardova does not accept children until they are nine years old." This news is Eva Brigitta Hartwig's first great tragedy.

Thus did *not* begin the dancing career of the ravishing and memorable Vera Zorina. This small drama was related to me by Zorina, the second Mrs. George Balanchine and now Mrs. Goddard Lieberson, when I visited her in her New York town house on New York's East Side. Brigitta, as her friends call her, entered the small and elegantly austere sitting room to greet me. She wore severely tailored black and white-pin-striped slacks and a blue turtleneck sweater that complemented her large gray eyes. Everything about her suggested an intense and terse intelligence. The face no longer bears the exquisite and aristocratic line and smoothness that movie fans adored. Instead, the years have deepened and intensified the striking symmetry of her features. Character, sophistication, and a kind of Nordic vitality contrive to give her face extraordinary nobility. When she speaks, Zorina projects a voice accented with a subtle German emphasis. The small room in which we sat suddenly became curiously claustrophobic with her commanding presence. A maid entered carrying a tray with coffee and cake. As we sat, Zorina started the story of How it all began:

"I can say very honestly that nobody really told me to dance. I wanted to dance from the time I could think. It's as simple as that. I was inconsolable when Eduardova slammed that door on us. But I waited out those two years and then began my formal studies with this great, great Russian teacher, who was very autocratic and quite severe. My schedule was hectic . . . you know German schooling. I'd go to my private school in Berlin, then I'd come home and do my homework, and then I'd get on a bus and go to ballet school. But I wouldn't have it any other way. I loved it. I adored it. I studied with Eduardova until the age of twelve. Then my mother took me to Paris, where I studied with Nicholas Legat. This lasted only a few months, because my mother became ill and we had to return to Berlin. There, I continued my studies with Victor Gsovsky. By that time, I was fifteen. Then, my mother decided we should move to London. Legat had also moved to London and I continued studying with him and also took classes with Marie Rambert. At Rambert's I met Anton Dolin. I became his partner at a very early age.

"Dolin took me back to Berlin to dance in a production of *Les Contes d'Hoffmann* for Max Reinhardt. We then returned to London. Then, when I was seventeen, my life changed radically. Léonide Massine saw me dance. Dolin and I were appearing in the play *Ballerina*. That was in 1933. Massine came to one of the performances. He came backstage and asked me to join Colonel de Basil's Ballet Russe de Monte Carlo of which he was the artistic director. Massine and Dolin had a fearful row about my leaving. Actually, I wanted very badly to leave. I wanted to enter a ballet company and so I did, and remained with the Ballets Russes for two years."

Zorina danced with the Ballet Russe de Monte Carlo from 1934 to 1936. She appeared in such Massine classics as *La Boutique Fantasque, Le Beau Danube*, and *Choreartium*. Indeed, the young dancer not only danced in these Massine works, but formed a strong emotional attachment to the handsome and by then world-famous choreographer. When I confronted her with the statement, "It is said that you fell madly in love with Massine and that Massine fell madly in love with you," Zorina smiled, and replied in a husky voice:

"Yes. . . . He was very beautiful, and I was seventeen years old. This, after all, was a giant in the ballet world. For a young girl, love gets mixed up with it all."

I mentioned that Massine was married to the character dancer Eugenia Delarova at the time. "Yes. He was married to Delarova, but I was not responsible for the split-up of their marriage. I don't deny that there was a love between us, but that is not what broke up their marriage. That's not the way it worked. I was the one who left the company, not Delarova. It was much later that they separated . . . much later that he left Delarova and married someone else."

I urged Zorina to speak about her two years with Colonel de Basil's Ballet Russe de Monte Carlo.

"Well, I'll tell you, it was a very peculiar episode. At that time, de Basil engaged me because Alexandra Danilova left the company to go to a far-off place called New York, to appear in the operetta *The Great Waltz*. I was engaged because I had made a bit of a name for myself through the play *Ballerina*, and I was promised certain roles. Obviously, I did not enter the company as prima ballerina. I entered as a soloist. But I was told that I would dance Danilova's roles in *Le Beau Danube* and *La Boutique Fantasque*—and I did. I made my debut in *La Boutique Fantasque*.

"I don't know what happened to Choura in New York, but suddenly she reappeared. Of course, she was a big star and in no uncertain terms, demanded her roles back. Anyway, I began to suffer a lot in the company. I didn't get the roles I should have gotten. I had a good career there and I learned a good deal, but it was a barbaric time. Don't forget, I was quite young, and a Nordic girl thrust in the midst of a lot of mad Russians, who spoke nothing except Russian and French. It was a peculiar atmosphere—full of tensions and jealousies. You have no idea!

"But I adored working with Massine. I felt he was a genius choreographer and a man of tremendously precise habits. His working habits were extremely interesting—and so unlike Balanchine's working habits. For example, he always carried with him a very large book, into which he would write out in advance every step that he planned to choreograph. In other words, he did an awful lot of homework. His symphonic ballets were all composed like this. He did them in a very simplistic way. For instance, in a work such as *Choreartium*, based on Brahms's Fourth Symphony, you could see the structure of the symphony physically interpreted, but so much less sophisticatedly than what Balanchine might do, because Balanchine is really a complete musician. Massine seemed to work with music on a more obvious level. He would take the motif of Brahms's Fourth and assign it to the prima, in this case, Toumanova. The horn section or woodwinds would be given to the male dancers. The violin section, to the female dancers—the *corps*. The piccolo or flute, or something airy like that, would invariably be danced by Tatiana Riabouchinska, who was very light and airy. In other words, you could visually see the structure of the symphony grow. Balanchine would never do anything like that. He would play a piano score at home over and over again. *That* was his preparatory work; whereas Massine would walk around with diagrams which he had recorded in his big book. Of course, that's a valid way of working. Balanchine, on the other hand, would come to rehearsals without a clue—or so he says. Actually, I think Massine worked on a very large scale, and I feel he was probably the only one who could do these large symphonic works. I don't think that it would have interested George.

"I considered *Le Tricorne* Massine's masterpiece. I mean, there wasn't a single performance of *Tricorne* that I didn't watch from the wings. And I learned a great deal from him watching him as a dancer. He had enormous authority. When he worked with us, he seldom flew off the handle. First of all, dancers are very obedient people. Dancers don't go around making a fuss. They are not like actors who will say, 'I don't feel this line.' We simply all stood around waiting for the choreographer to tell us what to do."

While Vera Zorina was dancing with the Ballet Russe in London, a smash musical opened in New York City—Rodgers' and Hart's *On Your Toes*, with choreography by George Balanchine. It catapulted Balanchine's first wife, Tamara Geva, to fame with her interpretation of the ballet sequence *Slaughter on Tenth Avenue*. English producers sought to open *On Your Toes* in London, and began their search for a dancer in Geva's role. Zorina was their choice.

"These people came to me and said, 'We've seen you dance. Can you act?' I said I hadn't a clue. I had never acted, never opened my mouth. Frankly I wasn't interested in any of it. Sometime earlier, someone from New York had approached me to appear in a Ziegfeld spectacle which I turned down flat. I said that a member of the Russian ballet doesn't do that sort of thing. But *On Your Toes* intrigued me. Also, I had seen it in New York and I had met George Balanchine socially. I thought that the ballets he had done for the musical were superb. I was most impressed and, of course, Balanchine already had a big name. And so, in 1937, I accepted to do the musical in London. I left the Russian ballet.

"When *On Your Toes* opened, Sam Goldwyn put me under contract. He wanted me to do a film—*The Goldwyn Follies*. I told Goldwyn I would sign nothing. Then I heard that Balanchine would do the choreography for the film. There would be two big ballets. I signed. And from then on, everything that I did in films and in Broadway musicals was in collaboration with George."

In 1938, Vera Zorina and George Balanchine were married. She was twenty-one; he was thirty-four. Zorina, now a Broadway star, was considered one of the most beautiful women in the world. Stories of her relationship with Balanchine abound. It is said that his passion for the dancer was all-consuming. At the time, Balanchine was creating dances for Hollywood and Broadway and for large sums of money. He led a glamorous, star-studded life. He rented an elegant apartment on Central Park South, built a fabulous house on Long Island, and assiduously courted his Nordic ballerina. It was reported that Brigitta, while thrilled to dance in Balanchine ballets, did not return his almost obsessive love. She seemed cool and aloof, it is said, despite the barrage of gifts Balanchine showered upon her. The culmination of this seemingly one-sided romance came with Rodgers' and Hart's *I Married an Angel*. Zorina was, again, a triumph. Balanchine had time and again proposed marriage. Finally, to his delight and amazement, she accepted. Following a performance on Christmas Eve 1938, they were married.

Balanchine had married his angel, but his "angel," it was said, did not consider the marriage heavenly. Balanchine fell into a depression and supposedly even went so far as to seek the advice of an analyst. In relating what I had read and heard of her relationship with George Balanchine, Zorina responded emphatically:

"I know nothing about an analyst. . . . Oh, I had heard that poor George would stand on the street someplace and look up at my window, being sort of moonstruck with me. . . . But, my God, what you're telling me is totally ridiculous. It's completely wrong. Of course, George has a way of telling stories himself. Look, he may have suffered somewhere during our marriage, but I never knew about it. Don't forget that I was a very different human being at that time—quite different than I am now. I was certainly more selfish—probably more self-involved, and always working very, very hard.

"All I know is that I loved George and thought he was a fantastically good and marvelous human being. Even then, he was certainly one of the greatest choreographers of all time. He was a great teacher. I would say that fifty per cent of what I knew or became was all due to George. I married him and I was very devoted to him. Don't forget, I was twenty-one years old, and George was considerably older. Also, our careers went in different directions. I was obliged to be in Hollywood making films I had no interest in making. . . . But I had a contract. I was obliged to appear in Broadway musicals. George, in the meantime, together with Lincoln Kirstein, was busy building a company. They would take off for South America. I would be in Chicago doing a show. It's really all very simple. Yes, we had problems, but we were together for five years before we were divorced. All this romantic nonsense about being desperate on a couch! . . . It doesn't even sound like George."

Zorina, long-legged, Garboesque, commanding, and enchanting on the Broadway musical stage, and an intriguing and beautiful presence on the screen, could boast of the best dance direction in both media. Balanchine directed her dance sequences in both the stage and film versions of *On Your Toes*. He guided her through *I Married an Angel, Louisiana Purchase, The Goldwyn Follies, Star Spangled Rhythm,* among others.

"George's interest was to present me in the best possible way. I remember when we were in New Haven trying out *I Married an Angel*, opening night was a terrible mess. George had created a surrealistic ballet, but the costumes were completely wrong. He went out and brought about twenty different kinds of toothbrushes: pink, yellow, green, red, and he strung them on a string and hung them around my neck. It was very amusing, and it worked. What I loved about working with him was that he was totally collected at all times. I loathe screaming and yelling. When somebody does that, he usually doesn't know what he's doing. George was always in command, always quiet, always very sure of himself. Working with him in the theater was a dream, because George is a total theater man, and I'm a theater person from A to Z. Making films was a problem, however. The agony was in repeating and repeating things endlessly. It was especially terrible for a dancer. The only one who really understood that and could talk about it was Sonja Henie, who was making her skating films at the time. You see, a ballet that would take three or four minutes on the screen would take a week to shoot. The pitch for a dancer is just agonizing. Anyway, I really didn't have a major Hollywood career. I was a dancer, and I needed the stage."

Fame had come to Vera Zorina through the stage musicals and the screen. In 1943, S. Hurok engaged Zorina to appear as guest artist with Ballet Theatre. She was returning to the ballet, but the ballet world, considering itself pure and untainted, did not receive her with open arms.

"I came back to Ballet Theatre with Balanchine, and I was as happy as a lark. It was like being home again. I was asked to dance in an ill-fated ballet called *Helen of Troy*. It was choreographed by David Lichine—and not very well. George came in and patched it up for me. Still, it didn't quite succeed. I also danced in *Apollo*, and the Ballerina in *Petrouchka*. Stravinsky conducted his own music. I thought that I danced better than I had ever danced before or after. But I remember with pain that people were quite bitchy about me. I was a 'Star.' Hurok brought me in. I was getting top billing. I was making twice as much money as anybody else. I didn't ask for *any* of that. Hurok was busy making a business out of it. So, 'Zorina came back,' and then a critic came—I forget his name—and said, 'Anyone who calls herself Zorina can't be a dancer.' It was cruel and unintelligent. You see, the ballet world didn't want you to go into any other medium. They get nasty. You're supposed to stay poor and in the background. Still, I loved that time. I remember dancing with Eglevsky and with Hugh Laing. I remember Jerry Robbins danced Hermes in *Helen of Troy*.

"Dancing meant a great deal to me. I suppose I was what you could call a legato dancer. I was never very good at little, fast, birdlike steps. I do regret never having danced all the great roles that one should have danced. I never had the great title of prima ballerina. I didn't stay with one company long enough. I always wanted to dance in *Les Sylphides*. I would have developed in George's ballets. . . . You know that long-legged thing. Dancing in *Apollo* was like a dream. In fact, anything George did would have been right for me. But, to tell you the truth, I've never been interested in standing still in one medium."

Zorina did not stand still. She was still dancing in 1968 when she both danced and recited Stravinsky's *Persephone* in Santa Fe, New Mexico. Since 1948, she has concentrated on the very specialized career of narrator-performer in such works as Honegger's *Saint Joan*, Milhaud's *Les Choëphores*, and Debussy's *The Martyrdom of Saint Sebastian*, among others.

"It just happened. . . . Artur Rodzinski was then the conductor of the New York Philharmonic and he had programed Honegger's *Joan of Arc at the Stake*. He asked me if I would like to do it. Out of that came one engagement after another with major symphony orchestras. I now find myself with a repertoire of twelve works that I do to this day. I find it enormously satisfying."

In addition to Zorina's career as narrator, directing operas has filled her recent years. Working with the Santa Fe Opera Company, she has directed productions of Strauss's *Capriccio*, Poulenc's *The Dialogues of the Carmelites*, and Puccini's *La Bohème* and *Madame Butterfly*. For the New York City Opera, she has directed *Cavalleria Rusticana* and *I Pagliacci*. She lives with her husband, Goddard Lieberson, president of CBS Records Group, and their two sons, and shuttles between homes in New York City and in Santa Fe.

"I'm now doing the long-delayed job of living. I never fret over something that's done with. I think my life is marvelous. I'm so happy. I'm plain old happy. I have two beautiful houses. I have a good marriage. I do things that most women do in their twenties. I do gardening. I'm interested in cooking. I lead a sort of leisurely life. When you're in the theater, you work incredibly hard. You can't do anything. Your life is regimented and you must store up your energy for that one burst of light. I've worked very hard. I sweated. When you're young, you don't know how to be afraid. That only happens when you get older . . . you know more. Now, my work is being alive. It's lovely just to live."

Louis Peres

SONO OSATO

Diaghilev's Ballets Russes considered its home to be the opera house in the Hôtel de Paris in Monte Carlo. Only a few miles west, in the town of Menton, there lived an Irish-American woman, the wife of a Japanese photographer, and her two young daughters. She often traveled to Monte Carlo to see ballet performances. On one such occasion, in 1928, she brought along her eldest daughter, aged eight, to see the Ballets Russes. The girl entered the theater and she considered it very elegant and mysterious. The program included *Cléopâtre*, the Michel Fokine ballet with music by Anton Arensky and décor by Léon Bakst. While other ballets were performed at this performance, the child could only remember *Cléopâtre*. She was spellbound by the shimmering costumes and particularly by the dancer who danced Cleopatra's slave. She looked at her program to search out his name, and saw that the Slave was Léonide Massine. Looking back to the stage, she became mesmerized by the moment when Cleopatra, portrayed by Lubov Tchernicheva, handed her slave a goblet containing poison, demanding him to drink it. The two figures on the stage stared at each other for what seemed an eternity. The little girl became terrified as she watched the Slave's feet. They were quivering. The muscles and tendons of his toes cringed. He drank the poison and fell back rigid. The child became even more worried when the dead slave was covered by a cloth. She hoped the cloth contained some holes through which the dancer could breathe. In a moment, the ballet was over. The curtain fell.

This dramatic, unforgettable experience was Sono Osato's first encounter with the dance. By the time she arrived home from this matinee performance, she had made up her mind to re-enact the scene she had witnessed. She and her younger sister brought a little chaise longue into their garden, as well as a gramophone. Sono found a record of Chopin music, put it on the gramophone, and assumed the Egyptian pose of Cleopatra. She had handed her sister a palm frond, and the smaller child stood fanning the reclining figure. The sun was hot, melting the Chopin record. It brought the small performance to an end, but did nothing to diminish the fires that had begun to ignite Sono's imagination.

The child was soon to witness another memorable performance. Mrs. Osato brought her daughters to Paris, where they were taken to a benefit gala. Suddenly, a young girl, not much older than Sono, appeared on the stage, dancing a brilliant solo. This was Tamara Toumanova, whose extraordinarily accomplished and poetic dancing made Sono's fantasies soar once more.

Today, Miss Osato lives in a duplex apartment on New York's United Nations Plaza. She lives there with her husband, Victor Elmaleh. Their two sons, Tony and Niko, now in their early twenties, lead their separate lives. On an October afternoon in 1972, I visited Sono Osato. She continued to radiate the performer's glow. Her delicate Oriental features bear the dual qualities of dazzle and repose. As with most former dancers, her movements and gestures have a natural flow. She wore a silk shirt and slacks, and small gold earrings. Everything about Miss Osato reflected innate taste. The room in which we sat, with its spectacular view of the East River and the United Nations Building, was a study in understated opulence. Far removed from the bustle and struggle of the ballet and Broadway worlds, Sono Osato leads a quiet life. But this singularly beautiful Japanese-American woman, who has remained in the memory of so many, was most willing to recollect her years as a dancer.

"I was born in Omaha, Nebraska," Miss Osato began. "I presume you want the year . . . it was August 29, 1919. I was born there because my father had come from the West Coast after the San Francisco earthquake. At the time he met my mother, my father was the society photographer for the *Omaha Bee*. One day they said, 'Osato. Go up and take the picture of Fitzpatrick's daughter.' Fitzpatrick's daughter was my mother, Frances, who had come from Washington, D.C., where her father had been an architect during Theodore Roosevelt's term of office. Apparently, my grandfather had some plans for earthquake-proof buildings which were stolen. Anyway, they came to Omaha because I think my grandfather had a job of some kind to do. . . . So my father went up and saw this beautiful eighteen-year-old girl and photographed her. They fell in love and got married, and I was born there."

Sono began her formal studies in Chicago with Adolph Bolm, who had been one of the leading character dancers in the Diaghilev company. She trained with him once a week for several years. When Bolm left to go to San Francisco to become ballet master of the San Francisco Opera, she continued her studies with Berenice Holmes. "She was a most wonderful dancer and teacher and I learned more from her than from anyone else," Miss Osato remembered. "I studied with her until 1934. That year, the Ballet Russe de Monte Carlo came to Chicago. I went to several performances. One night when we were all eating supper at home, the phone rang. It was Ludmilla, a friend of Miss Holmes's. She told my mother that she had arranged an audition for me with the de Basil company, and that I was to come to the theater that night, because the company was leaving the next day. I put on my practice clothes, and we dashed to the theater. They were just concluding *Les Sylphides*. We got seats way up in the gallery to watch the performance. Of course, everyone looked about an inch tall . . . but it was beautiful with everything bathed in blue moonlight. And I saw Riabouchinska dance in it. Anyway, the performance over, I rushed backstage, and found the place in an uproar because the workers were packing up the scenery and everybody was rushing around. In the midst of all this excitement, I saw a very beautiful, pale woman in street clothes, with the most marvelous legs. It was Alexandra Danilova, whom I had not yet seen dance. At any rate, with all this great confusion going on, de Basil came up to me and said, 'All right, little girl, let's see what you can do.' I was in a trance. I did a few steps. There was no accompaniment—no music. I just started to dance with all this bedlam around me. Then I stopped. De Basil didn't seem to change his expression. He went over to my mother and said, 'We'll take her for three years. Go home and reflect.' Well, when he said that, I could hardly breathe, I was so beside myself. De Basil told my mother that I was to join the company in Philadelphia in a few months time."

When the time came for Sono Osato to join de Basil's Ballet Russe de

Monte Carlo, the young girl and her mother traveled to Philadelphia on a Greyhound bus. Sono appeared at the Academy of Music, where the company was just then rehearsing *Swan Lake*. The fifteen-year-old girl felt out of place. She was the youngest member of the company, and the only American.

"I think that most of the time, I was in a daze. I got thrown in and I had to catch up somehow. The only thing I was conscious of was how people looked, how they behaved, how they talked to each other. Danilova became a standard of excellence. What I so admired about Choura—aside from her tremendous style and elegance—was that she never gave less. In other words, she would give exactly the same performance whether she were dancing opening night at the Metropolitan Opera or a one-night stand in Joplin, Missouri, or Butte, Montana. She never played down. Her performances were always 'full out.' I grew to admire her tremendously. In those days, Danilova wore a certain perfume . . . I think it was Coty's L'Aimant. So, wherever Choura went, there was always this marvelous perfume."

The artistic director and chief choreographer of the de Basil company was Léonide Massine. Miss Osato recalled his personality and his working methods:

"He was a very silent man, and it was very difficult to make any kind of contact with him. You never knew what he was thinking or feeling. The only ballet that I learned from the very beginning under his direction was Berlioz's *Symphonie Fantastique*. His way of choreographing was, I suppose, the traditional one. He would do a movement or a series of movements, which you then copied. But there was never any verbal or intellectual reason or explanation of what the movements meant or what he wanted them to mean. There was no verbal contact.

"If what you did seemed right, Massine would stop correcting. That was it, and then you'd go on. That's how you'd perform it. I suppose his choreography was very much like constructing a building. There's the groundwork, then the steel girders, then the walls, then the heating, then the plumbing. Afterward, came the embellishments. He would want a certain expression—he'd want your head raised a little more here, the chin down a little more there. So you had to retain. But you never knew what he *really* wanted, or what you were doing. For example, in the fifth movement of *Symphonie Fantastique*, there was a group of priests in long, brown robes and bare feet. They would enter and around them dozens of men and women were doing very grotesque, jerky movements. I was among these dancers. But all the time that I did the ballet, I never knew who we were. I never knew why we were groveling, why we were rolling on the floor. He never explained anything. Because of that, you could never try to bring some of your *own* feelings to his movements. You either did it, and did it the way he wanted it, or it wasn't right, and he corrected it."

Sono Osato danced with the Original Ballet Russe for six years. The life was one of constant travel and interminable work. Her advance from the *corps* to the rank of soloist was slow. The company was not only large but also had half a dozen soloists and four prima ballerinas. It was the dancer-choreographer David Lichine who gave Sono her first great opportunity when he chose her to dance the Siren in *The Prodigal Son*. It was the role danced by Felia Doubrovska when the work was created by George Balanchine for Diaghilev. Part of her thrill in dancing this role was wearing the same Rouault costume and head dress that Doubrovska had worn in the original production. Still, this opportunity did not exclude her from returning to the *corps*, where she dejectedly felt she was fated to remain. "There was no real advancement other than a very occasional performance of *Prodigal Son*."

During the rehearsal period for Balanchine's *Balustrade*, in which Sono Osato was again given a minor role, she felt it was time for a change. Over six years had passed and she thought that, having mastered the repertoire, it was time for better roles, better salary, and a better contract.

"I was tired of replacing people who fell ill, of never having sufficient rehearsal time, and of the very hard working conditions. I gave the management two weeks to come through with a new contract. The two weeks passed and I had received no communication. I came to realize that this was the end for me. I couldn't go on. I remember going to the theater that night, of taking my make-up, all my Woolworth jewelry, all my false hair and tights, and packing them in a suitcase. I quietly slipped out the stage door."

Sono Osato remained in New York while the company went on tour to South America. She took classes at the School of American Ballet. She worked with Balanchine and Oboukhov. These were difficult times. The dancer was unemployed. Finally, she requested a job at Ballet Theatre, and was promptly hired. It was the early Forties. While with Ballet Theatre, Sono Osato created the roles of Rosaline in Antony Tudor's *Romeo and Juliet* and Lover-in-Experience in Tudor's *Pillar of Fire*. She recalled her two years with the Ballet Theatre:

"The interesting thing for me at Ballet Theatre was working with Tudor. After six years of working with Fokine, Massine, and Lichine, the approach of Tudor was altogether eye-opening. Tudor impressed me enormously. First of all, he was very, very quiet. But when he spoke, he spoke extremely well. Unlike Massine, he had the ability to convey his ideas by verbalizing them. When he was choreographing *Pillar of Fire*, Tudor asked the dancers to move. Then, as they were moving, he would say, 'It is late in the afternoon. Dusk is falling, and you are walking together to get a soda.' Well, I had never heard a choreographer set an atmosphere verbally. He would set the weather, the time of day. He would talk about the small town in which these things were happening. He gave you a sense of place, a sense of color. When he said 'dusk' it brought on a certain kind of fatigue and lethargy. What he was doing was evoking an atmosphere in which the dancer could use his own fantasies, his own emotion. It was never a rigid 'Do this.' Dancing under Tudor gave you a completely different feel and quality to your sense of motion.

"Tudor would always work with a recording of the orchestral work—in this case, Schönberg's *Verklärte Nacht*. He would use the recording, then he would block with piano, phrase by phrase. Very often, he would hum. I remember thinking how difficult this was, because that particular piece of music is not at all rhythmic. There is really nothing to guide you. It was a very long piece, and very difficult to count. I never counted. Some dancers count and some don't. Working in that ballet with Tudor, I simply felt that the music would enter my body and that eventually, with repetition, my body would understand the phrase of music and respond to it correctly. Of course this ballet made a star of Nora Kaye. I remember it all so very well. You don't work together on a ballet from beginning to end, and not remember.

"The first time I became aware of Nora was coming to a rehearsal and not knowing very much about the character she would portray. Nora always used to wear a navy blue woolen skirt that came to her calves. Underneath, she wore her black woolen tights, and sometimes leg warmers. That day, at rehearsal, she was seated in a chair. She was extremely concentrated, very still, very quiet. Tudor walked over to the record player and put on the record. When the music began, Nora did one single gesture with her hand. She pulled her hair back. Watching it, I got goosebumps. That was a gesture that conveyed so much of this woman's frustration. Her character was established in that one, single gesture. I have never seen anything that potent.

"*Pillar of Fire* was one of the most important works of my dancing life. I was absolutely fascinated by Tudor's understanding of the power of the simplest gesture, by the differences in the characters, and how in dancing he could establish a kind of sexuality, frustration, repression, envy, fear. I never got to know Tudor personally, but I really didn't care because the way his mind and talent worked was so interesting and fascinating. In any case, a dancer rarely gets very close to a choreographer. I was an instrument like the other dancers. My motivation was to be as pliable and as receptive as possible. I can honestly say that to this day, I consider Tudor the greatest choreographer I have ever worked with. I always wished that I could truly dance the way he visualized his movements. But, I don't think the human body can do the movements he wanted because of the body's limitations. I mean, it would not be possible to stay up on toe long enough truly to achieve what was on his mind. It seems to me that most movements in choreography are possible, but that Tudor's, if they are to be realized to their fullest, are almost impossible for a human to do. You see, Tudor's movements don't resemble anyone else's movements. Actually, they are impossible to talk about. The people who came closest to achieving Tudor's vision, at least in my time, were Nora Kaye and Hugh Laing."

Osato's career at Ballet Theatre spanned from 1940 to 1942. She loved the company. She loved the fact that it was basically an American company. She was not conscious of the hierarchy so prevalent in the Ballet Russe. She danced with a new generation of dancers who were just as serious about upholding the dancing tradition, but had their own way of achieving it. While Sono Osato was given a wider range of roles, she did not finally find a true flowering of her gifts.

In 1943, one year after Osato left Ballet Theatre, she met and married an outrageously handsome Turk, Victor Elmaleh. He had just been discharged from the U.S. Army, ready to embark on a career as an architect. There was very little money. Happy but poor, she took her situation to Nora Kaye. Miss Kaye suggested that Osato try getting into a Broadway show. What is more, Agnes de Mille was just in the process of choreographing dances for the Mary Martin vehicle *One Touch of Venus*. Osato decided to write to Agnes de Mille.

"I asked her if she could use me—but *not in the chorus*! And I underlined that," Sono Osato recalled. "She wrote back a very nice letter saying that, yes, she could use me. In fact, during the show's run in Boston,

Agnes choreographed a solo for me, which was charming. She was the first choreographer who saw that I could be comical. We opened in New York and the show was a success—and I had a personal success. This was so strange, because in ballet, reviews come and it doesn't quite mean the same thing. The Broadway reviews meant something else. Anyway, when *One Touch of Venus* closed, I did not work for almost a year. Then, in 1944, came *On the Town*."

Young, sexy, and dazzling to look at, Sono Osato brought enormous charm and piquancy to the popular stage. In *On the Town*, she not only danced but spoke lines, proving herself a talented actress. As Miss Ivy Smith, a leading role, she added immensely to this innovative musical. She danced in the ballets created by Jerome Robbins to music by Leonard Bernstein. Miss Osato stayed with *On the Town* for ten months. She was twenty-six years old, she was married, and she wanted a child. She left the hit musical, and she settled down to domestic life. Her son Niko was born. Soon, her second son, Tony, was born. In 1949, she was persuaded to dance in *Ballet Ballads* for Experimental Theatre, and in 1955 appeared in a Broadway review. This marked her farewell to the stage.

Thinking back on her career, she smiled. "I never achieved great fame —no heights of incredible glory. But I think that any strong endeavor that gives you a sense of joy is the greatest thing in life. It would be nice if anyone who worked this hard and had this feeling could achieve great fame. What's important is the act of doing it. If I could point to the most powerful experience of my ballet career, it would be the rehearsals of Antony Tudor's *Pillar of Fire*. That was the greatest artistic and emotional experience I've ever had. What I got out of it was immense."

ROSELLA HIGHTOWER

The Parc Gallia in Cannes once housed a spectacular hotel-casino erected by the Russian nobility at the turn of the century. The Tsar and his entourage summered in the spacious apartments. They gambled the nights away in the Casino, and were entertained by spectacles held in their private theater. The Parc Gallia flourished as a tourist hotel up to 1961, when the structure was razed and replaced by a modern, sterile condominium. The American ballerina Rosella Hightower saw the old structure being demolished. Her heart sank to see the glamorous old building go. It had been her dream to purchase the theater and a wing of the hotel in order to convert it into a ballet school. Circumstances and bad timing made the purchase impossible. But with characteristic drive and determination, Miss Hightower did convince the authorities to save what were the hotel's old kitchens—a two-story structure, now hidden behind the white, terraced apartment complex. This small, simple building is now the Centre de Danse Internationale. One of the best ballet schools in Europe, it is run the year round by Miss Hightower and her husband, Jean Robier. There isn't a dancer who has not at one time or another stopped at the Centre. It has become a meeting place of the international dance world, with Miss Hightower as its inspiring friend and representative.

In August 1972, I rented a small apartment in the very condominium that replaced the old tsarist hotel. Miss Hightower very kindly paid me a visit so that we might talk about her extraordinary past and her exciting present. A diminutive woman with blond hair, she does not, at first sight, display the dazzle of her past. But this was the dancer over whom Serge Lifar and the Marquis de Cuevas fought a duel. This, indeed, was the toast of Paris for some twenty years. One of the most spectacular ballerinas of her day, Rosella Hightower brought her art to every corner of the world, dancing indefatigably with several major ballet companies. She has danced with every *premier danseur* from Anton Dolin to Erik Bruhn to Rudolf Nureyev.

For a girl born on a farm in Ardmore, Oklahoma, Rosella Hightower's story is nothing if not fabulous. Over a drink we discussed her life in the dance.

"I was born on a pecan and cotton farm," she began, "but my parents soon decided that a farm wasn't a place for them. They were young and they wanted to go to a big city. Their idea of a 'big city' was Kansas City, Missouri. My father found himself a job on the railroad. My mother also worked. As I was an only child, someone had to be at home to take care of me, so my father asked two of his younger sisters to come keep house for me. They came, and my young aunts proved absolutely charming. They loved to sing and dance. They loved to go out, and wherever they went I was brought along. We went to all the vaudeville shows, all the dances, all the musical events. That's how I came to develop a taste for the theater.

"I was about eight years old when I asked my mother for dancing lessons. She consulted with my father, who said that it was out of the question. There just wasn't enough money. But my mother, like most mothers, gave in to me, and, in secret, found me a dancing class. What's more, she was very thorough about it. She went to see all the dancing teachers in Kansas City. Finally, she found one she thought would be good. In fact, she had found the best teacher in the whole Central United States. Her name was Dorothy Perkins—an amazing woman."

The little girl was enrolled in Miss Perkins' class, which she attended once a week. Rosella soon learned that the teacher had studied in New York and in London. She had, in fact, followed the Diaghilev company on tour for several years. After an accident that paralyzed her right leg, Miss Perkins returned to America and began to teach. From the very beginning, Rosella Hightower received excellent training and showed extraordinary promise. She remained with Miss Perkins for nine years. At this time, the teacher decided that Rosella must go to New York. Actually, and better still, she wanted her gifted pupil to go to Europe. When Rosella agreed that it would be wonderful to do just that, both teacher and pupil realized that it takes money to go to Europe.

"Well, Perky, as I called her, went into high gear on raising money for my trip. She went to the bankers of Kansas City, she went to the Kansas City Country Club, and she passed the hat. Everybody contributed." The idea for the young dancer to go to Europe was not just a whim. "I had auditioned for Léonide Massine, who was on tour with Colonel de Basil's company in St. Louis. I danced for Massine and he said, 'All right, if you can make it to Europe, I think I can take you into the company that I'm forming in Monte Carlo.' So I left Kansas City and went straight to Monte Carlo. When I got there, I discovered that Massine had said the same thing to about two hundred dancers in every country of the world. His idea was to form a company of about sixty, but he found about two hundred and sixty people on his hands. Two hundred of them would have to be sent away. The elimination period lasted about two or three months. I stuck it out to the end and when everyone was eliminated, I was still there. I was not, however, in the company.

"The next thing that happened was that the company had to go to London for its first big season in Drury Lane, in 1938. By this time, I had run out of money and had to wire urgently to my family for some cash so that I could go to London. I was sure that once there I could get into the company. My mother managed a miracle. Money arrived and I followed the company to London. No sooner did I get there, than a girl broke her foot. I immediately replaced her, and became a member of the Ballet Russe de Monte Carlo. Of course, I entered in the back line of the *corps*. . . . One of the reasons for my being in the back line was that the company's cofounder, René Blum, considered me physically unattractive. He liked the lovely little French girls—you know the type. In fact, time and again, Blum wanted to get rid of me. He just thought I was the ugliest duckling he had ever seen. But Massine kept saying, 'Wait. You'll see. Leave her in the back line, and let's wait.' I was kept hidden from view for about a year. Then, the war broke out."

When war was declared, the company was on a vacation period. Rosella visited Cannes for the first time and fell in love with the place even then. With the outbreak of war, France was in a state of chaos. Rosella managed to get on a train to Paris, where the company had reassembled.

Colonel de Basil and René Blum told the company that they would continue, and proceed with rehearsals. Again and again the company was told not to worry. During a dress rehearsal of the Dali-Massine ballet, *Bacchanale*, the company was informed that Massine had left for America. Nobody had warned them of his sudden departure. With this astonishing news, the company disbanded. Rosella Hightower was one of the last Americans to leave Paris. She took the last boat out of France bound for New York.

"When I got off the boat," she recalled, "standing on the pier was none other than Léonide Massine. He stood there as if nothing had happened and said, 'We have a rehearsal in three hours. I've gathered a whole new company together. We have to redo our whole repertoire and you, Rosella, are the only one who knows it.' I couldn't have been more shocked. At the time, the Ballet Russe was doing *Gaîté Parisienne, La Boutique Fantasque*, and Beethoven's *Seventh Symphony*. Anyway, Massine had formed a whole new company, also called the Ballet Russe de Monte Carlo."

I asked Rosella Hightower to describe Léonide Massine during that period with the Ballet Russe.

"In those years he was the most amazing person. He was certainly the most energetic, the most dynamic individual I had ever come across. I just didn't realize that anyone could work that hard and that long without stopping. He was a beautiful, handsome man—extraordinary face. But he was not communicative. He always worked in complete silence. Massine never said two words, but he was incredibly active. He worked in class, he worked at rehearsals, and so, everybody else worked. He danced 'full out,' so everyone else danced 'full out.' During every performance, he would sit in the front wing observing what was going on onstage. But he never talked. And if he did talk, he was extremely shy. Whatever he said often had nothing to do with the situation. He was like that with everybody, and we had the most fantastic ballerinas in the world at the time. There was Danilova, Baronova, Toumanova, Markova, Slavenska. We had a tremendous list. At the time, Massine was married to Eugenia Delarova, who also danced with the company. I loved Genia. She helped me so much. She was the first person who taught me to use make-up for the stage, how to fix my face so that it was 'right.' Genia is still one of my closest friends."

In America, Miss Hightower was prepared for some of the hardest work of her career. Having often been thrown into roles to replace disabled dancers, she knew most of the repertoire. She was often given solo roles and was quick to learn new roles at a moment's notice. She entered the new Ballet Russe as principal dancer, and for the next six years toured with the company under the auspices of Sol Hurok.

"We performed at every Army camp. I knew every city in the States. I knew every theater in the States. Finally, by the end of the war, I had had enough. I thought that if I continued like that, and at that pace, I'd either have a nervous breakdown or else I'd give up dancing. Somehow I knew that I had to get back to Europe. I felt that it was the only place that could save me. At any rate, we gave our last season in New York. The company was to open at the Metropolitan Opera with *Giselle*. Markova was scheduled to dance the opening night. Suddenly, she became ill and had to be taken to the hospital. I danced in her place. In the audience that night was the Marquis de Cuevas. He came backstage and said that he had formed a ballet company called Grand Ballet de Monte Carlo. He asked if I would sign as prima ballerina. I did, and that's how I got back to Europe."

Marquis George de Cuevas, a Chilean-born patron of the arts, splashed onto the New York scene in 1939, when he sponsored a large exhibition of old masters at the New York World's Fair. Through his marriage to Margaret Strong, granddaughter of John D. Rockefeller, de Cuevas became privy to the Rockefeller fortune. In 1943, he founded the Ballet International and it made its debut in New York in 1944. It proved a fatal financial venture. But the Marquis was undaunted. If New York would not accept his ballet enterprise, Europe, he felt, would be far more receptive. He formed the Nouveau Ballet de Monte Carlo in 1947 and then changed its name to the Grand Ballet de Monte Carlo. It was at this point that Rosella Hightower joined the company, along with dancers such as Marjorie Tallchief and William Dollar. Its ballet mistress was Bronislava Nijinska.

The volatile and eccentric Marquis changed his company's name again in 1950, this time calling it Le Grand Ballet du Marquis de Cuevas—and changed it yet again during its last years to International Ballet of the Marquis de Cuevas. Most major dancers of the day appeared with his company, from Markova to Toumanova to Massine to Lichine to Erik Bruhn. But it was Rosella Hightower who remained its most steadfast dancer.

"The Marquis represented the contrary of everything I had ever seen, heard, or had in my life up until then. He was a uniquely fabulous person. He represented the European aristocracy. Although he was South American and came from a famous Chilean family, he was a true European—living among them, speaking their languages, thinking in their way. He had a passion for all the arts. I think that it never occurred to the Marquis that ballet would be his future. In his early years, he led a very social life, surrounding himself with every conceivable form of art. Finally, I think he became bored. It was then that he met and married Margaret Strong.

"The two were such eccentric personalities. Each was a complete egoist, and a kind of competition rose up between them. They became competitive and yet understood each other very well. Still, I don't think the Rockefeller family ever approved of the Marquis. He was so extravagant. He tried to impose his personality on New York with that World's Fair exhibition—he spent a fortune on it. When that was over, there was an emptiness in his life. That is when dance began to intrigue him. He formed his company in New York which was a flop. He said afterward that America has no sensitivity. And so he went to Europe and for the next ten years spent his wife's fortune on proving that his company was one of the best in the world. And, you know, it really was a good company. We had Nijinska whose ballets we danced and who was particularly good to me. I became her protégée. She understood my way of dancing."

Rosella Hightower's way of dancing was described as "supremely virtuosic." A natural physical force and an exceptional stamina produced a dancer who not only performed reliably but with enormous élan, bravura, and lyricism. She performed almost every day for years on end. The Marquis could not have wished for a more loyal or dedicated dancer.

"My time with de Cuevas was the highlight of my career. The Marquis permitted many, many experiments. Nothing too modern, of course, because he was a traditionalist. He loved the past. He loved the period of Louis XIV, and above all, he loved France. All of our triumphs occurred in Paris—all of mine had to do with Paris. Of course, the Marquis was the kind of person who abhorred calm and quiet. He liked things to be bubbling and exploding all the time. If they weren't, he would contrive to make them so. We were all constantly living in a volcano. He would provoke storms. This unsettled everyone all of the time, but we got used to it finally. We never knew from one day to the other what mad things were going to happen, and it kept us all working and living at high pitch. And yet, despite it all, the de Cuevas company was one of the most famous in Europe for twenty years, and it provided me with a wonderful showcase. Also, the Marquis really loved me. Whenever he introduced me to anyone he would say, 'This is my eldest daughter.' He said this because I was the one he could count on. He knew that I would always be there."

While with de Cuevas, Rosella met and fell in love with one of the company's costume designers, Jean Robier. They were married in 1952. When she became pregnant three years later, Rosella returned with Robier to the United States. She wanted her child to be born in America. Their daughter Dominique was born in 1955. For two years she was a guest ballerina with Ballet Theatre. Because Robier had difficulty in adapting himself to life in the United States, he and Rosella decided to return to Europe with their daughter. They returned to the Marquis de Cuevas, who reluctantly accepted them back.

"The Marquis was very hurt that I had left him. He was jealous of my husband. Then, when I danced again in Paris, he forgave us. I danced a wonderful ballet that John Taras created for me, *Piège de Lumière*. It was a marvelous, wonderful work. The Marquis was thrilled and all was well again, until the famous duel. Yes, it was another one of the Marquis's provocations. The Marquis challenged Serge Lifar to a duel because of me. You see, at the time, Lifar ran the Paris Opera and the Marquis was in direct competition with him. These were two major ballet forces in Paris.

This went on for quite a while, until, one day, Lifar and the Marquis decided to become friends. De Cuevas announced that Lifar would come and restage some of his ballets for our repertoire. Everyone was very happy about this because they had really been bitter enemies. And so, Lifar came, and we did his *Noir et Blanc* [retitled *Suite en Blanc* in 1946] and some other things.

"The big opening night of *Suite en Blanc* came. I danced the premier role. Everything went smoothly until the Coda. I don't know what happened to me, but I forgot my entrance. This was a big climactic moment with *fouettés* and other complicated things. But I simply forgot to come on. I missed my entrance. Nobody was on the stage and the music was going and going. Well, as I heard later on, Lifar was furious. He said something detrimental about me and the Marquis immediately picked it up, and words became heated. The Marquis slapped Lifar. Lifar threw his glove to the ground and the Marquis picked it up. That's how this thing with the duel started. I don't think it was very serious at first, but the fact that it all happened in public turned it into a *cause célèbre*. Of course, both men were great performers. They couldn't resist the fact that suddenly everyone in the theater turned toward their box and saw what was going on. I think they went much further than either of them would have gone otherwise, because it was an incident that could have been forgotten about. The press picked it up, and they both loved publicity. With the Marquis, anything that was publicity for the company was fine with him. Lifar was equally publicity-crazy. They were both terrified of looking ridiculous. So, they both realized that they had to go through with it. They took fencing lessons. Each one had a different fencing teacher. It became a big thing in France.

"In the meantime, the Marquis wasn't at all well. His fencing teacher would have to come and drag him out of bed for his lessons. Lifar was much younger and more physically fit. Anyway, the tension began to mount and the publicity grew. Big magazines now took it up. It got to a point where the Marquis and Lifar could not leave their apartments without being followed by the press. Finally, a date for the duel was set. The whole thing was carried through to the end. The duel took place in Paris. Serge was nicked in the arm. The thing was over. Everyone was greatly relieved. The two then became the dearest of friends. But I was right in the middle of it. I had started it all."

Rosella Hightower recounted that, after the duel, the Marquis became very ill with cancer. His health deteriorated but he held on and expressed one last desire. He wished to take his company to Russia. He wanted to present his company in *The Sleeping Beauty*, a ballet that had had enormous success in Paris with Hightower dancing Aurora.

"The Marquis really thought he could manage this Russian trip. He was a most determined man. It was like one last whim before the end. Well, we never got to Russia. It was 1961 and we were quietly rehearsing a new ballet choreographed by Edward Caton. The theme was inspired by paintings of Botticelli. There were three tableaux. One was based on *Primavera*, the second on *The Birth of Venus*, and the third on *The Annunciation*. The Marquis had his heart set on doing this ballet. He wanted me to do the third tableau—*The Annunciation*. I told the Marquis that I just couldn't dance the Virgin Mary. It just couldn't be done. He said, 'It is my will. I want it done and it will be done.' I said, 'But the Virgin Mary can't do a *pas de deux*.' The Marquis insisted. Anyway, Eddie Caton said that the Virgin must be a solo and we must show what she is thinking—what her premonitions were. Actually, I liked doing it very much. The Marquis was brought to see this ballet. He saw the premiere and then he went home . . . and he died."

With the Marquis's death in Cannes in 1961, Rosella Hightower quit the company. She felt she could not continue under a new management. She did, however, decide to remain in Cannes. It was then that the idea for a ballet school took root in her mind. She wanted the school to prepare professional dancers. She wanted to take students who would live at her school the year round. Rosella sold all her possessions, including those in the United States, in order to purchase the house which is now located in the Parc Gallia. To raise further funds, she embarked on a series of guest appearances throughout Europe.

Today, Rosella Hightower is firmly established as the director of Le Centre de Danse Internationale. She holds classes along with a staff that includes such former dancers as José Ferran, Arlette Castanier, Sonia Sundberg, and other professional teachers. Guest teachers have included Maurice Béjart, Anton Dolin, Serge Golovine, and Raymond Franchetti.

"In teaching I have found something that can only come through the synthesis of thirty years of dancing. Finally, what I discovered was that in dance the body is the beginning and the end. A school is not an end in itself. We teach dance, but we teach about the body first—how it works, what its anatomy is. Dancing is a science that transforms into an art. As for my own career, I am not the sort of person that has to be a 'star' right up to the end. That's not my mentality. It never was. Even when I was a ballerina, people used to criticize the fact that I did not take advantage of my 'stardom.' But that is not my character. I'd much rather spend my energy now in building new dancers. It gives me tremendous satisfaction. It's like having a second career. I'm carrying on. I love the young people around me, and I get a good response from them. Everything I have done I now give to the new ones . . . the ones who will be dancing next."

LEON DANIELIAN

▌n June 1973 a film opened in New York City called *First Position*. Its subject dealt with the ballet world and centered on the lives of young ballet students at work in a major ballet school in New York. Directed by William Richards, it attempted to capture the struggles, disciplines, frustrations, rewards, etc., of the very young dancer, showing him in the classroom, the rehearsal studio, and in private life. While some of the flavor of this highly specialized profession came through, the film proved something less than inspired. However, *First Position* offered a most poignant glimpse of the director of the American Ballet Theatre School—Leon Danielian. We see him teaching class in a wheel chair. Crippling arthritis had cut short the career of one of America's most virtuosic dancers. During the course of the film, Danielian discusses a forthcoming operation that would hopefully enable him to walk again. Several of his pupils take him to the hospital, and some weeks later he returns to the classroom, walking with the aid of a cane.

It is the irony of the dance world that arthritis has abruptly shortened the careers of several major dancers. Leon Danielian, Doris Humphrey, William Dollar, and Ruthanna Boris, to name but four, have suffered a disease that has tragically removed them from the public eye. But through their own tenaciousness and courage, they turned their talents to teaching and choreography. In the case of Danielian, the disease felled a dancer whose brilliant career spanned twenty years. Of Armenian descent, the handsome dancer joined the Ballet Theatre at its inception in 1939, at the age of nineteen. In 1942, he became *premier danseur* in Colonel de Basil's Original Ballet Russe, remaining with the company until it disbanded. Also at this time and until 1961, Danielian danced principal roles with the Ballet Russe de Monte Carlo. Further guest appearances took him to every corner of the world, partnering major ballerinas of the day. He spent a season with Ronald Petit's Ballets des Champs-Elysées in Paris and was a principal guest artist with the San Francisco Ballet. His virtuoso style encompassed classic and *demi-caractère* roles, each noted for exceptional speed, cleanliness of line, theatricality, and lyricism.

Danielian continues to be the director of the American Ballet Theatre School. He has a very slight limp, but holds himself with a spunky, martinet-like posture. Visiting his class, one finds Danielian in full command, moving from student to student correcting placement, *port de bras*, and technical execution. His instructions are voiced in a clipped, direct manner. A highly-intelligent man, he brings to the classroom enormous knowledge, flavored by an irrepressible wit. He is clearly an American teacher training American dancers, but this forthright quality is suffused with a theatricality garnered from his years with European companies.

I visited with Leon Danielian in the winter of 1972. He lives in a small West Sixties apartment—a place notable for its economy of décor and simple comfort. Articulate and charming, he talked about his life over drinks:

"I was born in New York City on Thirty-third Street and Third Avenue," he began. "I've kept my family name—I haven't changed it. Like many Armenians, my father was in Oriental rugs. My mother was simply a housewife. But she studied drama in Tiflis, the capital of Georgia, the same city that George Balanchine is from. I have a sister who works at Bonwit Teller as a saleslady. I had no idea what wealth was, so I didn't miss it. It was only when I grew older that I realized how very very poor we were.

"I was not a musical child. In fact, I had a great deal of trouble about that. I had to sort of educate myself in music. We did not have a radio until I was thirteen. But we had a record player, and we would have Armenian music. We did a lot of folk dancing. We were brought up in the Armenian colony in New York. Mother had a friend called Seda, the daughter of an Armenian composer. She had a little dancing school in Washington Heights. She was known as Madame Seda and was once a student of Mikhail Mordkin. Mordkin, as you know, was Pavlova's partner for many years. Anyway, I studied with Madame Seda, and when she thought that she couldn't teach me anything more, she sent me to study with Mordkin, who had a school here in New York. I was given a scholarship. I was about twelve. By 1935 or so, when I was fifteen, Mordkin was creating the Mordkin Ballet Company which materialized two years later in 1937. This was then realized into the Ballet Theatre."

Danielian's life with Mordkin was not particularly encouraging. The Russian was of the old "fire and brimstone" school of teaching. It seems to have been more about Mordkin than about the disciplines of ballet. Mordkin would walk into the classroom and all the students would have to stand at attention. Danielian claimed that the Russian was not particularly interested in teaching, that it was just a way of making a living, that he really wanted to perform. Still, Mordkin created a certain kind of excitement. If students danced well, he would scream out, "Maryinsky! Bolshoi!" He would scream out the name of immortals like Taglioni, Elssler, as well as the names of all the ballerinas he had danced with. Finally, he would shout "Pavlova!" This was all most exciting for young Leon, who began to sense what theater was all about.

"Of course, Mordkin seemed terribly old to me. He was probably about fifty-five. He would never really communicate with us, mainly because he spoke very little English. Everybody came to school and it was put to them that if they wanted to be dancers, they should learn to speak Russian. We trained through imitation. Mordkin would demonstrate, and we would imitate. As much as I worshiped Mr. Mordkin, I can't say that I learned very much from him. But I stayed with him from 1933 until the formation of Ballet Theatre. I still believe that a student should stay with one teacher until he's able to grasp what another teacher can give him.

"I joined Ballet Theatre at the age of nineteen. About eight dancers from the Mordkin Ballet automatically transferred. Unfortunately, I never did any *corps de ballet*. Michel Fokine, who was ballet master, gave me a solo role in *Le Carnaval*. I was Harlequin, which was a wonderful part for me. Then, Dolin came from London and he put me in the *pas de trois* from *Swan Lake* with Alicia Alonso and Nora Kaye. Now, you must understand that we were all children at that time. Alonso and Kaye were two girls out of the *corps*, but Dolin had a very keen eye. He saw Alonso and Nora Kaye immediately. He knew their value. Then, Andrée Howard came to join the company and we did her ballet, *Lady into Fox*. She gave me a very nice part in that. I began receiving very good press. In those days, Ballet Theatre had three wings. There was the British wing, headed by Dolin, and it also included Antony Tudor, who brought Hugh Laing and then Andrée Howard. There was the American wing that Eugene Loring headed. Then there was the classic wing that Fokine headed— which irritated Mordkin, who was also with the company at that time, and who soon after left the organization."

Leon Danielian remained with Ballet Theatre through the end of 1941. He left because of a shift in company policy.

"The reason I left Ballet Theatre was funny. I had gotten very, very good notices, certainly well above average for a nineteen-year-old boy. Then Lucia Chase decided to go Russian. She brought in German Sevastianov and made him managing director of Ballet Theatre. He was married to Irina Baronova, at the time. Lucia brought in Alicia Markova and Yura Skibine and a whole group from the Ballet Russe. I thought, If the Ballet Theatre is going to Russianize, I'm going to the real thing. What is more, I was earning seventy-five dollars a week, and Sevastianov didn't know who I was and had never seen me dance. When I went to negotiate a new contract, he offered me sixty-five dollars. In the meantime, during my first season, de Basil saw me and offered me a hundred and twenty-five dollars, which was an enormous salary in those days, but I turned it down because I wanted to be faithful to Ballet Theatre. Anyway, the upshot of it all was that I joined the de Basil Ballet Russe."

Colonel de Basil's Original Ballet Russe boasted two prima ballerinas, Alexandra Danilova and Mia Slavenska. Eventually, Slavenska formed her own company, leaving Danilova as prima ballerina, with additional ballerinas coming in as guests. Igor Youskevitch, Frederic Franklin, and now, Leon Danielian were the principal male dancers. Franklin was ballet master. Danielian danced the same repertoire he had been dancing with Ballet Theatre—*Les Sylphides, Swan Lake*, and others. When Youskevitch was drafted into the U.S. Navy, it fell to Danielian to partner Danilova. He recalled his relationship with the great Russian ballerina:

"She was difficult as all hell, I adored her. I worshiped her, but she was *so* difficult! She was a star, and I've seen very few like her. But when we danced together, there was no end to her complaints. Always the put-down. I was too small. I was not capable enough of supporting her. Anything that went wrong was my fault. We never came onto the stage with the confidence that one should have. There is no question but that Danilova was the dominant person in that company. When Slavenska was there with her, Danilova insisted on topping her. There would be no such thing as a gala opening night for Slavenska. It *had* to be Danilova. Freddy Franklin was also a very dominant personality. Like Danilova, he went to battle. Eventually, the two of them tried to control the company. Not that they weren't able to do so. They were superb . . . there was nothing that they thought they could not do. For example, Danilova insisted upon doing *Giselle*. I always thought she was totally wrong for it. And yet, I never knew what a prima ballerina was until I saw Danilova. When Danilova came out on stage, and did a fifth position on *pointe*, it was like an exclamation mark.

"You know, this nonsense that Choura was so old. She was never old. She was in her thirties when we danced together. Of course, we had jet-propelled Toumanova, honey-colored Riabouchinska, and Slavic Baronova, who were . . . what? . . . sixteen, seventeen, eleven, I don't know the idiotic ages they were. So of course Choura looked like an older woman by comparison. Choura was never old. She retired in her mid-fifties. In fairness, I must confess, I wasn't a very good partner at first. I was thrown into it and poor Danilova did have to go through hell. But later, there came a point when I didn't even want to dance with her. I felt I didn't need that problem. I worshiped her . . . but to get the salt in the sores all the time. I mean, the minute the curtain went down, she let me have it in front of the whole company. At one point, I got so disgusted that I wanted to give up my whole career."

But Danielian did not give up his career. He continued to dance major roles becoming particularly adept in *demi-caractère* roles in ballets by Massine.

"I never had the inclination to be in Massine ballets. I never wanted to do *Gaîté Parisienne*, for example. But Fred Franklin thought I'd be rather good in it. Then I saw *Gaîté* from out front and thought it would be fun to do. When I danced the Peruvian in that ballet, I decided not to think of the way Massine had danced it but thought instead of Chaplin. I worked from Chaplin. It was a great success. Some years later, Massine came to see me dance in some of his roles, and he was really quite sweet, because my interpretations were very different from his own. Also, many of the steps had been changed. I think the vitality behind the performances is what he wanted. It was the same vitality as his and so he didn't mind the changes. I did work with him personally when he restaged his *Harold in Italy*. Actually, he allowed you a great deal of flexibility."

During the war years, the Ballet Russe de Monte Carlo, under the direction of Sergei Denham, traveled extensively throughout the United States, Canada, and Mexico. Europe was obviously closed to travel. The company played tank towns and Danielian profited enormously because he felt that he learned about the theater as one could never learn otherwise. A different stage in every town and a different audience. The curtain went up and the vibrations of the audience came across to all the dancers. The

Ballet Russe was the only company that toured in those days. Ballet Theatre tried to, but with less success.

"Somehow the glitter and the life was so glamorous. Wherever we went huge parties would be thrown for us—and we were penniless. I remember I had one corduroy suit and one dark suit. That didn't matter, because I had friends all over the country. I'll be very immodest and say that there isn't a stage that I set foot on where I wasn't received with real love. And I don't mean just the big cities like New York, Chicago, or San Francisco, but all the ridiculous little dinky places."

Despite the glamour and the invaluable experience of being a member of Denham's Ballet Russe de Monte Carlo, working conditions were far from ideal. Danielian as well as other dancers in the company could not abide Mr. Denham.

"Well, he's dead now. I really didn't like him. He used many of us. He was cruel; he was thoughtless; he overworked us. He did many things financially which he shouldn't have done. He would not pay for our unemployment insurance, and our salaries were very low. I got shrewder, however, when I made guest appearances or when I taught. I did very well financially. So whenever I came back to dance with Ballet Russe, I made my demands. But if he could, Denham would squelch you. And the work! Four ballets a night. I danced three ballets in a matinee and four in an evening. I mean, it was insane. He wouldn't even say thank you. If somebody were ill, he'd just shove you into a role. Finally it became depressing. Also, the company became a road company. It was awful to see. You know, the wings were taken away—the extra bits of décor that *made* a ballet. It really became like a road show. And that's why I left.

"I danced from 1943 until 1951 without a break. In the summers, I did summer stock. I did operettas, and one summer I acted in a play. Then, in 1951, I went to Paris and danced with Roland Petit's company, Les Ballets de Paris. That's where I met Yvette Chauviré and she and I did a little tour of the casinos in the south of France. Then we went down to North Africa. It was a fascinating experience. Actually, I never officially left the Ballet Russe. It was my home base. It's just that I became a little more difficult with Mr. Denham. They wouldn't do a ballet for me. With Franklin and Danilova you couldn't get anything. Anyway, I kept going back to Ballet Russe. Then I would leave. At one point, I went to the San Francisco Ballet as a guest artist. But the point that I'm trying to make here is that no matter where I went, I always returned to the Ballet Russe. You see, there is no point in being an independent dancer, unless you have a 'home.' This is what I tell the boys and girls today. I tell them, 'Be a member of a company, and then be what you want. Don't leave your home base. It doesn't work unless you really belong to a major organization.'"

It was at the conclusion of travels to the Orient, Central and South

America with the San Francisco Ballet that Leon Danielian became seriously disabled by crippling arthritis.

"My career stopped a little sooner than it might have. . . . A long time ago, in a certain teacher's class, whose name I'd rather not give, I had already felt it. The teacher was pulling my leg and I felt a strange pain. Then it went away. We are so physical, you know, and when you work your body, you can work pain out of it. I didn't feel the pain for a long time, but I remember, people would tell me that I was limping a little bit. I was totally unaware of it. It got so, that I was never sure when I was limping and when I wasn't limping. Anyway, it was a good ten years of working in pain. Then, I went into *Man of La Mancha*. No one ever knew about the arthritis. I was dancing in the play, and suddenly, I couldn't get down on my knees and pick myself up. I would forget my lines. I was in agony. I just had to ask to be out. It was time to stop. . . . The thing that was so bad was that I had to give up the television shows and everything else that I was starting to do. I lost a gold mine. But it was all fortunate in a way, because the decision to be a teacher was such a happy one."

What does Danielian impart to his students in the classroom?

"I think a ballet teacher must be a very objective person. In the classroom, the pupil must not imitate. I think I was a highly stylized dancer—one that someone could imitate. I know of one young man who used to imitate me in everything. That must not be done in the classroom. I don't teach as I used to dance. I was small, and I had a certain *port de bras* on stage that I would not teach. I teach the simplest *port de bras*. I think that each dancer is like a sculpture. You teach the dancer to sculpt his own body. You suggest it; they must do it. They must mold their bodies into a perfect little machine that can do classical dancing. Then, if you want to 'break the wrist,' or have an angular elbow, or tilt the head, it can be done. But, you must teach very, very basic classic style first.

"To me, the dance is theater. Some dancers don't regard it as theater. They think it's an art, or a form of athletics. I don't see dance as, say, George Balanchine sees it. I don't see dance as being necessarily 'youth' or necessarily feminine. I think some of the joys of theater that I have experienced are when a man and a woman dance together. I saw Youskevitch at forty put out his hand, and a forty-five-year-old woman, Danilova, took it, and they danced. They knew what they were doing. It's like Fonteyn. It's a woman dancing. I love some of the young kids. I adore little Gelsey Kirkland. Naturally, I favor her, she studied with me a long time, but she's not yet a woman.

"I don't want a machine in a dancer. The flaws of an individual are sometimes so marvelous. Visually, the effects of their imperfections become beautiful. What they can't quite do, they cover with so many other wonderful things. Today, so many of the dancers disregard the fact that ballet is theater. Mr. Balanchine forgets it. Mr. Balanchine's dancers are so stylized, they can't do anything else. Of course, the whole conception of the New York City Ballet is superb, but it's also idiotic. It's fortunate that we have the American Ballet Theatre and visiting companies. . . . It would be like burning down the Metropolitan Museum of Art and having only the Museum of Modern Art. . . . It's simply looking at Matisse and Picasso, and never looking at Rembrandt and Raphael. There's nothing wrong with *Giselle*, and I adore *Agon*."

Danielian's personal life seems as happy as his professional life.

"No, I'm not married, but I play a great deal. I thought the arthritis would hinder it. It hasn't done anything of the sort. I have a tremendous personal life, but it's not involved with dancers. Sometimes I worry about the boys and girls. They had a day off the other day, and they were all together. I could never do that. I have to go elsewhere. I received my education from my friends. Don't forget, I left school when I was in the eighth grade. I don't go to church, but I'm very close to our Archbishop on an arts committee. So, I have a little Armenian life. I spend time with my Armenian friend Rouben Ter-Arutunian. I have many friends, although friendships are difficult because they are like love affairs. They have to be treated the same way."

PATRICIA WILDE

peaking about Patricia Wilde, Leon Danielian said, "Pat could do anything we boys could do—and then some. She could leap, she could jump, she could turn, she could do thousands of beats. There wasn't *anything* that girl couldn't do—a fabulous dancer!"

And indeed, Canadian-born Patricia Wilde could set the stage on fire whether in George Balanchine's *Firebird* or his *Western Symphony*. It is a fact that in the case of *Western Symphony*, her ability was so unique that Balanchine deleted the third movement from the ballet because few dancers could match it. Wilde's amazing strength, the steely poetry of her technique, her musicality, and her exuberant speed transformed whatever role she assumed into a tour de force. As with all great dancers, these personal qualities needed to be ignited and given full rein by the vision of a master choreographer. Miss Wilde found her Prometheus in George Balanchine, who created many ballets for her.

Today, oddly enough, Patricia Wilde is ballet mistress of the American Ballet Theatre, a rival company of Balanchine's New York City Ballet. She is a principal teacher at the American Ballet Theatre School, as well as professor of dance at the College of Arts and Sciences, Purchase, New York. Her administrative talents were put into use when she was invited to direct the dance department at the Harkness House for Ballet Arts in 1965, and when she formed the school attached to the Ballet of the Grand Théâtre de Genève in 1968.

In February 1973, I observed Patricia Wilde teaching a class at the American Ballet Theatre School. She walked into the classroom, a striking figure in white leotard and overskirt. Her hair severely pulled back, her large blue eyes set in a friendly face, she offered an image of alertness and vigor. Already sensing their instructor's extraordinary energy, the students aligned themselves with tensile expectation at the *barre*. Miss Wilde is one of that select group of teachers who is still able to demonstrate positions and combinations "full out." From the first *pliés* to center and traveling combinations, everything was demonstrated with enormous clarity and assurance. Miss Wilde's corrections always center on logic and muscular possibility. Nothing is forced and there is no room for the slightest sloppiness. She brings to her students a certain terse decisiveness. A stickler for precise placement, she scans the room for deviations from the correct alignment. She is quick to think up a variety of interesting combinations and will show these with an élan that clearly inspires the class. Miss Wilde's classes seem shorter than they are because both her mind and her body are fast and agile. The speed is reminiscent of her Balanchine experience.

For fifteen years, Patricia Wilde was a principal dancer with the New York City Ballet. She joined the company in 1950 and left in 1965. These were the years of her full flowering as a performing artist under the guidance of George Balanchine. Her career, however, began with the Marquis de Cuevas's Ballet International at its inception in New York in 1944. Miss Wilde consented to interrupt her hectic schedule to talk to me about her life as a dancer and teacher. Because she lives outside of New York City, she visited me at my apartment a few days after I viewed her class.

"I was born in Ottawa, Canada, in 1930," Patricia Wilde began. "My mother and father were separated and I was the last of five children. Of these, only my sister Nora and I were sent to dancing class. Everyone else was scientifically inclined. When my sister went to her ballet classes, I used to go along. I was about three years old and would embarrass my sister to death by kind of sleeping against the *barre*, or rushing to the middle and jumping around. Little by little, I became interested.

"The teacher was Gwendolyn Osborne, who was a beautiful dancer but a nervous wreck. Luckily, this did not affect her teaching, although it did affect her own career. She was a very good teacher and pushed both my sister and I on our way. We considered our dancing lessons the most important things in our lives. I remember that our mother would use the lessons as a form of threat. I mean, whenever there was punishment, she would never hit us, but simply say we couldn't go to our dancing class. That's when the tears would come. Anyway, there came a point where I couldn't imagine doing anything else. Going to those classes was the most important thing in my life. At one point, Miss Osborne took us to New York to audition for entrance at the School of American Ballet. Both Nora and I auditioned for Mr. Oboukhov. It was a terribly hard audition, but we made it. I was eleven years old and Oboukhov put me in 'C' class."

But eleven-year-old Pat was too young for "C" class. The administration told her that she must wait a year and then come back. Nora, who was older, was kept, began her studies, and ultimately entered the Ballet Russe. When the year was up (Pat considered it the most frustrating year of her life), she returned to New York anxious to take up her studies at the School of American Ballet. She applied for a scholarship. For reasons that had nothing to do with her abilities, Pat did not obtain one. Disappointed but undaunted, she enrolled in the Professional Children's School, moved in with her sister, and looked around for a teacher. She found the ideal one in Dorothie Littlefield. Miss Littlefield, a major ballet teacher in Philadelphia, was then giving classes in New York's Steinway Hall. Pat studied with Miss Littlefield for one year, making extraordinary progress.

"After a marvelous year with Dottie, I learned that the Marquis de Cuevas was starting a company in New York. It was called the Ballet International. I was invited to come and take company classes. After awhile, I was taken into the company. I was thirteen years old. I don't know how it worked, but they allowed me to sign a contract. I mean I was way underage, but many of the older dancers in the company knew me and knew that I was responsible: Being with the Marquis was quite an experience. He had hired everybody. He set up his theater on Columbus Circle, he brought in Massine, Dolin, Nemtchinova, Oboukhov, Vilzak, Eglevsky, Marie Jeanne, Viola Essen. I was in the *corps*. I don't know how many different versions of *Swan Lake* and *Giselle* we had. Everybody that came in did a different version. . . . I was given a few small roles—some solo parts, little things here and there. There were lots of intrigues in that company, but I was so young, that I really didn't know what was going on. I was too busy learning what I had to know. And it was wonderful working with all of those people. I stayed one full year with Ballet International, from 1944 to 1945.

"Then, the company disbanded. I was very lucky, because just then, George Balanchine took a group of ten kids from his school to Mexico City for the summer. He also took along Nicky Magallanes, Marie Jeanne, and Bill Dollar. I was among the students. We performed at the Teatro de Bellas Artes and did a few evenings of ballet and some operas. It was marvelous. I did the lead in *Les Sylphides* with Bill Dollar, and I did the second part in *Constantia*. Mr. B. also rehearsed us in *Concerto Barocco*. When we came back from Mexico, I joined the Ballet Russe."

Patricia Wilde's Ballet Russe period spanned from 1945 to 1949. The leading choreographers for the company were Massine and Balanchine. It was for the Ballet Russe de Monte Carlo that Balanchine staged *Night Shadow, Danses Concertantes*, and a new production of *Concerto Barocco*. Pat Wilde, already possessed of a strong and secure technique, began to be used more and more by both Balanchine and Massine. Her dependability and excellent memory were quickly taken advantage of, and she was thrown into any number of roles on very short notice. Not only was she depended on as a dancer, but choreographers discovered that Pat could assist in the staging of their ballets. Massine, for example, placed her in charge of restaging his work *Rouge et Noir*. More and more roles came her way. She danced in Massine's *Seventh Symphony*, the lead Can-Can Girl in *Gaîté Parisienne*, and the lead in de Mille's *Rodeo*. Miss Wilde recalled some of the atmosphere of the Ballet Russe:

"Of course, Danilova was the prima ballerina. You were never allowed to forget it. Actually, she was quite pleasant toward me. I can't say that she took me and hugged me particularly, but she wasn't nasty to me. She was a real trouper. We were on those terrible train trips. She went through it all, sitting up in coaches, suffering all sorts of discomforts, but she did all her performances without a gripe. She never made exceptions for herself. She went right along with everyone else. I'll never forget those terribly exhausting Ballet Russe tours . . . I felt that the company was starting to go down. Also, Balanchine wasn't around any more, and the intrigues were beginning to get unbearable. It was hideous, and I felt that it wasn't going to get any better. That's one of the reasons I decided to leave the company."

When Patricia Wilde danced with the Ballet Russe, the company was headed by Sergei Denham. It seemed that every dancer with the company felt some sort of animosity toward their director. Pat remembered him with equal dismay:

"It was the whole business of Nina Novak. She was a dancer in the company and Denham's special friend. He would let her dance anything she wanted to. She would refuse to come to certain towns, and one of us would have to fill in for her. Then she'd appear and do roles that she was never supposed to do. This was affecting everyone's morale. Denham was awful. We'd all be in the coaches, and he'd be in his special compartment. We'd see the champagne and the dinners going by. He'd say that he couldn't get us a sleeping car, and of course, we'd find out that it was because he didn't try—he didn't want to pay the extra money. There were situations where we'd have to stand up in the coaches and arrive to perform. We practically struck at one point. It just got to be too much. Anyway, in 1949 I quit.

"I decided that I wanted to study for a year. I wanted to go to Europe. I went to Paris and worked with Olga Preobrajenska. At the time, Roland Petit was having a season, and he asked me to guest in *Le Beau Danube*, which I did. Petit asked me to join his company for their first American tour. I refused. I thought it would be a huge flop. As it turned out, they were a smash hit. Actually, I don't think Roland's company was the right one for me. So I stayed in Paris and studied."

George Balanchine, who had worked with Patricia Wilde when she was with Ballet International and the Ballet Russe, wanted to enlist her services when he and Lincoln Kirstein formed his New York-based Ballet Society, the precursor of the New York City Ballet. He contacted the dancer and persuaded her to return to the States prior to Ballet Society's tour to London. Wilde agreed, and returned to New York. Once again, she was the last-minute "savior" when replacements were needed in an emergency.

"On opening night in London, Maria Tallchief hurt herself. I went in for her. From then on, I don't know how many things I had to do. I had a whole repertory to learn because Maria was out. I had to understudy ballets. Other people injured themselves, and again I was the one to fill in. I don't know how I did it all. I guess it was a question of my making a career. You just do what you have to do and hope for the best. Anyway, that was the beginning of my fifteen years with George Balanchine. Those first years were marvelous. It was entirely different from the way the City Ballet is today. In those days, each one of us was very important to the company. There weren't enough people to rehearse you, so you had to keep yourself in training and prepare yourself for the roles. It was very difficult. There were fewer of us. There was Maria, Tanny, Diana, Melissa. . . . Everyone had a unique talent, especially Tanny. She was divine. I remember that she used to get scared to death when she had to do *Swan Lake*. But she was *so* great. The way she danced *La Valse* and *Bourrée Fantasque* was fantastic. And then came her illness."

Patricia Wilde became visibly moved as she recounted the tragic end of Tanaquil LeClercq's brilliant dancing career: "We were on tour and landed in Copenhagen. We were all having a good time. One day, Tanny said she was feeling very tired. She had to do *Swan Lake* at a matinee. She felt sort of sick. She did it, and then that night she had to dance *Bourrée*.

We used to do *Bourrée* interchangeably. On that same night I was doing *Pas de Dix*. When I finished, I went into the dressing room and asked her how she was feeling. She said that her back felt strange and she asked me to look at it. So, I thought maybe she had a cold or something. I asked her if she wanted me to do *Bourrée* for her, and she said no, because she was already there and was made-up. So she went out and danced it, and after that night, she never walked again.

"We didn't know what it was. They said it was a virus. Anyway, that night she woke up and was in agony. She couldn't walk. Mr. B. was married to her then. He had to carry her. He called the doctor. The doctor said there was a virus in the south of Denmark—that it's effect was paralysis, but that it would last for only a few days. They took Tanny to the hospital and they didn't start treating her for polio right away. The thing is that it was the year when the Salk vaccine came out and they were giving it only to teen-agers and to pregnant women. So that's how it was. Tanny's fever was raging all of the time and more and more damage was done. The company had to leave Copenhagen to continue the tour. We left and we still didn't know what was the matter with her.

"Mr. B. stayed with her, as did her mother who had been along on the tour. We took the train and all of us were terribly upset. When we got to the station, an attaché met us and handed us forms requesting medical information. We all had to be vaccinated because it turned out that Tanny had contracted polio. Mr. B. was away from the company for nearly a year. Finally, he brought Tanny back to America. In the beginning, she didn't want to see any of us. But, you know, if it had happened to anybody else, it would have been much, much worse. Tanny has such a wonderful mind—she's so bright—and she's been able to find things to do in so many areas. I think it's so wonderful that she is connected with the ballet again, teaching classes at Arthur Mitchell's school in Harlem."

While Patricia Wilde was dancing with the New York City Ballet, she met and married George Bardyguine, then a stage manager for the company. They have two children, Anya, age five, and Yuri, three. Balanchine, never happy when his ballerinas marry, was characteristically "put off" by the news that one of his leading dancers would take a husband. Miss Wilde remembered the circumstances of her wedding day:

"It was very funny. The day we got married happened to coincide with Mr. B.'s staging of *Nutcracker*. . . . We were all gathered and he told us what parts we would be dancing in it. I was to do Merleton. At one point, I went over to Vida Brown and told her that I had gotten married that day. She asked me if Mr. B. knew. I said that I hadn't told him. After rehearsal, I *did* tell him. He was fine about it. Then he said that he would need me for rehearsals that evening between seven and nine. I was taken aback but came to rehearsal anyway. In the meantime, my husband and my in-laws were having dinner and waiting for me. This, after all, was my wedding night. Anyway, I was rehearsing and nine o'clock came around. Mr. B. wasn't looking at the clock. He asked me to do incredible things, like *entrechat-six* from *pointe* to *pointe*, *tours en l'air*, and one incredibly difficult variation which had no end. We finished at ten o'clock. I rushed to join my wedding party. But you know, Mr. B. didn't call me again for two weeks. That rehearsal period was his wedding present to me! What's so ironic is that on the opening night of *Nutcracker*, I had mononucleosis, and I couldn't do it at all!"

Dancing for fifteen years for George Balanchine ultimately took its toll.

"The company was changing, and I really wasn't happy with what I was doing. I didn't seem to be extending myself in the ballets that I was doing. I was dancing the same things over and over again. Even if Balanchine did a new ballet, it felt to me as if he were choreographing exactly the sort of thing I had always been doing. It wasn't true, of course. He composed beautiful ballets. But I didn't appreciate them enough because I had been in the company for too long.

"When the Harkness Ballet called me and said that they wanted me to become the director of its school, I thought it would be the beginning of something new and exciting. I accepted the job. I started the school, then went up to Mrs. Harkness's country place 'Watch Hill' and started a summer school. I also taught the company. I never worked so hard in my life. Then an awful lot of intrigue started going on. Finally, I couldn't take that. I couldn't agree with what was being done, and so I resigned. I stayed at Harkness for about a year and a half, and left in 1967."

From that year on, Patricia Wilde has made teaching her life. After her time with Harkness, she taught both at American Ballet Theatre and New York City Ballet. She also directed the school of the Grand Théâtre de Genève. By 1970, she was permanently installed as ballet mistress of the American Ballet Theatre. She spoke of her teaching methods:

"I teach a mixture of everything that I have learned. I had many different teachers in Europe and all of the teachers at the School of American Ballet. I do certainly teach everything Balanchine has taught me. But, I must say, looking at his company these days, I find things have changed to a very great extent. I think the change came with the company's move to Lincoln Center. I don't think it's quite as careful as it was. The movements are much bigger, probably so that you can show them to the back of the house. That's too bad, because they have lost that tiny movement that might have been more elegant—a little more refined. There aren't *real* fifth positions now. The dancer's turn out, their placement, is quite different, just because they want to make the movements very big.

"Anyway, when I teach, I like the fact that I can really show how things are done. I remember working like a dog on my feet, because I looked at my teacher Dorothie Littlefield, and she had beautiful feet, and I worked and worked to be able to have beautiful feet. I think that if you've once seen someone do a step, then you feel it's possible, and you have that vision in your mind. If a student can see a teacher balance and turn, then he knows that it can be done and that it's worth working on. I feel I'm able to get something across, and that gives me enormous satisfaction. I've had a fantastic number of kids in my time, and many have turned out well. Lar Lubovitch was a boy I brought to Harkness. He was not a developed dancer, but I felt he could do something. I gave him a workshop, because he had the drive and the possibility. He has his own company now, and his principal girl, Jeannie Solan, was just a little kid when I had her. Warren Conover, who is a soloist with Ballet Theatre, and coming along very well, was also a young kid when I had him at Harkness. Now I have kids dancing all over the world."

Because American Ballet Theatre imports from Europe several of its star dancers, I asked Miss Wilde how she is able to meld their talents into the style of the company.

"They are very good about anything you tell them. Of course, all of those stars find it very difficult at first. After all, they come to us as a success, and we can't expect them to change what has made them a success. With Natalia Makarova, for example, it was very easy to work on ballets that she had not done before. When it came to *Giselle* and *Swan Lake*, things were very difficult. She had danced these works in Russia, and she had a reason for every movement she made. So it took a tremendous amount of time to tell her that something didn't look right within the context of our way of doing these ballets. She listened, and I think she's much warmer now than she was when she first came to us. We've changed Paolo Bortoluzzi, I think. He's not as mannered as he was when he danced with Béjart."

Pat Wilde—forthright, intelligent, and leading a full life as teacher, wife, and mother—looks back on a career that has enriched the world of American dance:

"I wouldn't have wanted it any other way. I really did what I wanted to do. I had a goal, and I think I fulfilled it. The point is, if you're going to be a dancer, you can't possibly want to do anything else. You really wouldn't be living if you did something else. Dancing has to be the most important thing."

The Current Scene

DANCERS OF THE ROYAL BALLET

MARGOT FONTEYN
— guest artist

On May 18, 1972, Dame Margot Fonteyn, hailed the greatest ballerina in the world, turned fifty-three. At best, this is a precarious age for any woman. For a ballerina, no matter how gifted, it is usually a time for looking back—a time for recollection, retirement, rest, teaching, or the possible writing of a book of memoirs. For Dame Margot, May 18 was just another Thursday.

It has been tradition with her never to dance on the actual day of her birthday. But she had done so on the previous evening, dancing with

Rudolf Nureyev, during her guest engagement with the Royal Ballet, at the Metropolitan Opera. On such pre- or postbirthday occasions, no matter in what part of the world they may occur, Miss Fonteyn's fans invariably rise to their feet and sing "Happy Birthday, Dear Margot!" A deluge of flowers is tossed upon the stage, and the curtain calls are endless. Dame Margot, who has been acknowledging deafening applause, roars, and accolades throughout her thirty-seven dancing years, always responds with her usual cool and radiant grace. In recent years her curtain calls alone have become major events, because the public is never quite certain whether or not it is witnessing her presence for the last time.

Indeed, speculations regarding Margot Fonteyn's retirement have been rife for nearly fifteen years, and for nearly fifteen years, she has brilliantly eluded any such possibility. British ballerinas of unquestioned talent have long been waiting in the wings to assume her crown, while her male partners, from Robert Helpmann to Michael Somes to David Blair, now well past their primes, seem content to have at least been momentary meteors in a legendary partnership. Dame Margot, untroubled, clear-eyed, and obviously indestructible, continues to dance with immaculate precision and breathtaking élan.

With the years, something has, of course, been lost. For example, she no longer dances *Giselle* ("I don't think I'd dance it well any more"), and she no longer attempts the thirty-two required *fouettés* in *Swan Lake* ("Twenty-four are quite enough, thank you"). But something has been gained as well, most notably, an uncanny and incandescent sense of characterization—a true musical and lyrical maturity that lends her every movement and gesture an incomparable sense of inevitability. Her achievement is one of great artistic depth. She makes of dance a metaphor and symbol of what ballet is finally all about. It is an attribute that only consummate artistry, experience, and durability engenders.

Margot Fonteyn dislikes interviews. In point of fact, she had resisted seeing anyone during that New York engagement, claiming fatigue and, one suspects, a certain boredom with having to repeat herself. "I'm really not very good with words," she told me during my first attempts at seeing her. "But I'll call you when I have the time"—a heart-sinking kind of promise. Nonetheless, on an early Sunday morning my telephone rang, and Dame Margot herself was on the wire. "I'll have an hour or so today, if you'd like to come over to the Metropolitan Opera. It's Sunday, so there isn't a soul around, and we can have some peace. I'll be practicing for a few hours, so come around noon."

Dame Margot received me in her dressing room. She had just changed into her street clothes—a navy blue-and-white striped Yves St. Laurent dress. She wore a gold bracelet-watch and large pearl earrings studded with tiny diamonds. Her black hair was swept up, accentuating her heart-shaped face and her large, luminous deep-brown eyes. I commented on her elegant appearance. "I love clothes—and I buy clothes. I was young at a time when clothes were very elegant. Now, they're rather confused. I was brought up in the elegant era. Halters are now the rage, but they don't suit me." Presently, she applied a touch of powder from a black-and-silver étui she held in her hands. She sat in front of her dressing-room mirror with what can only be called regal poise. Snapping her compact shut, and placing it in her purse, she turned to me with a dazzling smile. "Now, then, what can I tell you?"

"You have been called the greatest ballerina in the world. Don't you find that a grave and great responsibility, if not something of a burden?"

"I don't listen to people who say that sort of thing. I don't think there is a greatest, first, best, in anything. I simply don't think about it. And, another thing I don't think about is my age, which you are undoubtedly about to ask me. Yes, I'm fifty-three years old, but, again, I don't think about it. I only think of what I must do tomorrow—that I must dance *Swan Lake*, that I must dance *Sleeping Beauty*. I go from day to day. I don't clutter up my mind with a lot of externals and things I have no control over. Perhaps I *survive* by not thinking about all these things. All I'm concerned about is concentrating more and more on what has to be done—and I feel I must work continually harder. Another thing I'm certain you will want to ask is: 'When are you going to retire?' Well, once again, my answer is, I don't think about it.

"I remember dancing at the old Met and saying to someone, 'Well, when they build the new Met at Lincoln Center, I certainly shan't be dancing there.' Well, that was—how many years ago? And here I am, dancing at the new Met. So, you see, one *thinks* about retirement, but I've been lucky enough to have been able to go on dancing, and I suspect I'll go on dancing until I can't any more. But, I assure you, I don't think about it. I only think about doing things well."

During the last few years, Dame Margot has appeared very little in New York. But she has been traveling and dancing ceaselessly in all corners of the globe. Just prior to her New York visit, she danced in Cape Town, South Africa. Her appearance there caused a political furor. The controversy centered around the ballerina's appearance at the newly built "whites only" Nico Malan Opera Center. Dame Margot became the target of the Coloured (mixed-race) Labor Party movement, which opposes segregation. There were demonstrations upon her arrival at the Cape Town airport, and demonstrations during her performances at the Opera Center. When she danced at a theater for "coloureds only"—a theater that seats two thousand, only two hundred coloureds purchased tickets. Interestingly enough, despite the rigid segregation laws, two hundred whites managed to get in by "passing" as coloureds—the women wearing saris and dark makeup, and the men wearing dark glasses.

Dame Margot recalled the experience with a certain anger:

"You see, everybody who goes to perform in South Africa performs for segregated audiences. You dance for white audiences and for colored audiences. Anyway, they built this new Opera Center and it was built from public funds—taxes from the city of Cape Town—and everybody in the city subscribed and gave money, including coloureds. Then the city decided that the Nico Malan Opera Center would be for white audiences only. The coloureds then raised a petition demanding that no artists from abroad appear there, hoping thereby to change the policy of 'whites only.' What happened was that a great deal of pressure was put on me to refuse to go and dance at that new theater. But I had been asked to go by David Poole, whom I know, and who directs the ballet company there. David Poole is a white South African, who had been ten years in England with the Royal Ballet, and I was happy and proud that he went back to his own country to run a ballet company.

"And so he asked me to come, and I accepted. Then the furor started. I was asked to cancel; but I went for artistic reasons, and I felt I should not be pressured into canceling for political reasons. In my eyes, this is a domestic matter to be dealt with in Cape Town. I don't believe for one moment that had I canceled it would have made the slightest dent in the government's policies. It would have done no good at all. It would have been a tiny scratch on the back of a dinosaur. Finally, I became quite angry with people who wrote letters—especially letters from South Africans living in England telling me what to do and what not to do. In my opinion, white South Africans who don't live in South Africa would do better to go back there and do something about their own country, rather than telling me what I should do about their country. Naturally, nobody could possibly agree with apartheid—not from the outside, anyway. Obviously, my going there didn't mean I was supporting apartheid. I couldn't possibly support it. But I still think that if you're a dancer, and if you have a chance to appear in a country like South Africa, you should go.

"What pleased me most, and made me feel justified in going, was that Eartha Kitt was in Cape Town at the time I was there, and she was totally sympathetic and understanding, and thought that I had done the right thing. That made me very happy."

Because she has been so mobile, although dancing very little in England ("I'm seldom in London, because I don't wish to be in other dancers' way"), I asked Miss Fonteyn where, exactly, she made her home these days. Married to Dr. Roberto Arias since 1955, she has in recent years been very much on her own, and very much alone. Dr. Arias, a former Panamanian Ambassador to Britain, and a highly controversial figure in Panamanian politics, was shot in 1964 by a political colleague in Panama. Since that time, he has been paralyzed from the neck down and is confined to a wheel chair.

Dame Margot did not answer immediately. She paused, bowed her head, and reflected for a moment or two. Then, lifting her head, she answered: "My home is where my husband is. My husband is mostly in Panama—he's there now. Of course, at the moment I'm traveling a great deal, but I'm with him as often as possible."

There was another pause. Suddenly she said, "I am now completely accustomed to the way he is now. I don't any more think of my husband the way he used to be . . . you know, walking and moving about. I just think of him as he is now. *That's* the person he is. I move. He doesn't. Some people think he can't communicate. But he does. He had a great deal of difficulty with his speech at first, but it gets better all the time. He doesn't have much volume when speaking, and so he whispers mostly. Some people can't make out what he's saying—but I can. Anyway, he's got a marvelous brain. I feel it's rather a fair division: he thinks; I move. Of course, it's dreadful what has happened to him, but he doesn't let it be a tragedy. Not at all. Something like that is a terrible shock at first. It has taken me a very long time to get past it. But it's no longer a tragedy. Obviously, it must, at times, be very, very difficult for him—incredibly frustrating. But he manages. He is such an exceptional person. I can't imagine many persons taking it as well as he does. He says, 'Our separations are purely geographical,' which is one way of expressing how two people are, in fact, one person. There's not much I could add to that. He can think and express himself in words, and I can't very well. It is better for me to dance, and let him think and speak."

I told Miss Fonteyn that it had been suggested that one of the main reasons she danced so frequently was because she must earn sufficient money to pay for her husband's medical care—said to be astronomical. The dancer looked totally startled:

"That's not true at all! What an absurd idea! It costs very little money to take care of my husband. He takes almost no medicaments—practically none. He has a manservant in Panama who looks after him, getting him in and out of cars and airplanes, and things like that. We have a nurse sometimes, but he doesn't have a nurse permanently. Of course, he had the good fortune of being in a hospital in England, which is very much cheaper than had he been in one in the United States. It really costs incredibly little. People *will* say anything, won't they?"

The annals of ballet are filled with legendary partnerships. One reads with awe and nostalgia of the brilliance and magic created by such dancers as Karsavina and Nijinsky, by Pavlova and Mordkin, Markova and Dolin, Alonso and Youskevitch, Danilova and Franklin. Today, the undisputed ecstasy-provoking pair is Margot Fonteyn and Rudolf Nureyev. While each dances with many other partners, their appearances together are charged with almost overwhelming passion, nobility, and symmetry.

Miss Fonteyn spoke enthusiastically of her partnership with Nureyev:

"Clearly, Nureyev is a very sensational dancer—an extraordinary virtuoso dancer. He's the kind of dancer one simply doesn't come across every day. When I first saw him dance, I had the choice of *not* dancing with him. That is to say, I knew that if I danced with other partners who were less sensational I would perhaps have to make less of an effort myself. To dance with Nureyev would have meant that I would have to make a superhuman effort.

"As it turned out, it was often easier to dance with him than with other people. For instance, we would be dancing *Le Corsaire*, and Rudy would go out and do his variations, and the whole theater would be set on fire. Well, after that, I would come on and do my own variations—not with any enormous amount of technique—but the whole theater was already in such a state of excitement that I was now included in it, and it too became something. I was more relaxed, more at ease, because somebody had already supplied the theatrical fireworks. This is what brought the public into romanticizing us. People like to romanticize, and that's quite normal.

"Anyway, I chose to dance wtih Nureyev because it was a challenge. I knew I was dancing with a boy half my age—a boy who could leap ten feet in the air. I knew it and everyone else knew it. But I took up the challenge —it was the more risky and dangerous thing to do. Like my husband, I tend to do the rather dangerous things. Also, the fact that Rudy has this very strong theatrical personality is an enormous help, especially to someone like me who does not depend entirely on her technical accomplishments. I have always depended more on my presence, on my way of doing things, on expression. Well, to have somebody who helps to create theatrical excitement . . . what could be better? As a person, I find Rudy extremely intelligent. He has a very quick mind. People think he's temperamental, or, as the English say, naughty. But they misunderstand his temperament and his naughtiness. The point is, he's never boring, and one can have a great deal of fun with him."

I reminded Dame Margot of the headline-making hippie party she and Nureyev attended in San Francisco in 1967—a supposed pot party that was raided by the police and which culminated in Fonteyn and Nureyev, among others, being placed under arrest at a police station.

"Oh, that!" says Dame Margot with a laugh. "But don't you see, that was the year when, if you were in San Francisco, everyone said, 'You must go to the Haight-Ashbury section and look at the hippies!' What actually happened was that after a performance we all went to supper. At the stage door, a man came up to us and said 'Come to a party,' and he handed me an address. I remember the man distinctly. He was an Irishman—a very impressive, Biblical kind of character with dark eyes and long hair. Well, we went on to supper, and afterward I said, 'Why not go to that party?' And so we went. There were a lot of us—about ten people. Now, the police didn't appear because of any pot, but because a neighbor had complained about the noise. When the police arrived, our hosts took fright, and told us all to run up to the roof. Of course, when the police saw that everybody was rushing off, they started looking for other things—like marijuana. It's the sort of thing that *can* happen when you merely go sightseeing! Anyway, we were all arrested and brought to the police station. It was really too funny. I've never smoked pot in my life. I've never even touched a cigarette. At any rate, all charges against us were finally dropped."

Dame Margot is not given to talking of her private feelings. When asked of the state of her inner life, for example, she became exceedingly tentative, and visibly put out:

"My inner life? Oh dear! I don't think I have any idea what my inner life is like. I've certainly never been psychoanalyzed. I wouldn't like that at all. Not one bit. I suppose I'm secretive by nature, and I wouldn't want to tell a perfect stranger all about myself or all about my thoughts and feelings. I'd rather keep my troubles to myself and live with them. I would say it would be very hard to get to know me. Even if I knew what my inner life was like—which I don't—I doubt whether I would be willing to talk about it.

"And I can't begin to tell you what goes through my mind when I dance. All I can say is that hundreds of little bits and pieces all put together pass through my mind—hundreds of different thoughts, feelings, worries, emotions, images—hundreds of things. Of course, that's only what I *think* happens; because, really, one has no idea. I have no systems for propelling myself onto the stage. I simply go on. If I began thinking and analyzing about the way I dance, then, perhaps, I wouldn't be able to do it. I simply use my resources. I try to make a contribution. That's really all there is.

"Remember, in the dance, everyone is different. Everyone must find a way of being themselves on the stage, which, I suppose, is a very difficult thing to do. It took me a very long time to come to know myself as a dancer. I suppose it came from being on the stage a lot of years—of dancing many, many roles, of observing others, of receiving help. I learned a great deal right from the start by working with Robert Helpmann, from dancing the ballets of Frederick Ashton, from being under the direction of Ninette de Valois. One learns a little bit from everything and everyone.

"I know what I *can't* do. For example, while I admire the choreography of George Balanchine, I'm not physically equipped to be a good Balanchine dancer. I danced only one of his ballets—*Ballet Imperial*, and I danced it very badly. Still, I think he's an extraordinarily inventive choreographer."

What sustains Dame Margot? There have been rumors of lovers. At this, Miss Fonteyn burst into peals of laughter.

"But, of course! I have hundreds of lovers! The only trouble is finding the time to accommodate them all. I mean, one *does* have to rehearse, eat, sleep, give performances. Oh, how people will gossip! Whatever you do, they're going to say something. Ninety-five per cent of what they say is inaccurate. Occasionally, of course, they might be right. But I fear people judge others by themselves. People say, 'What would I need to sustain *me*?' And then, they put that on me. Having lovers doesn't happen to be what I need to sustain me. Can you imagine how complicated life would be if I got embroiled with a lot of men? One simply couldn't cope with it. It would be impractical. Heavens! What an idea! Well, one thing I've learned is to take no notice whatever of what people say. What I do is dance."

Louis Peres

RUDOLF NUREYEV
— guest artist

With an insistence bordering on the obsessive, his eyes keep darting to the mirror. He scans the fluid line of his body, seeking always a greater perfection of shape, contour, and movement. He moves before the mirror like one possessed. The mirror, every dancer's aid and guide, becomes an incantatory object to Rudolf Nureyev. Here in this rehearsal room beneath the mammoth stage of the Metropolitan Opera, Nureyev appraises himself, and there is that in his eyes that suggests Narcissus lost in his own exquisite dream.

Actually, there are two reflections in the mirror. A *pas de deux* is in progress. Monica Mason, one of the Royal Ballet's principal dancers, is rehearsing her first New York *Swan Lake*, which she will dance the following evening, partnered by Nureyev. Miss Mason is somewhat tense, despite the elegance and beauty of her movements. Not so Nureyev. Dressed in blood-red leg warmers and a close-fitting orange shirt, he is the ardent, self-possessed partner, now eloquently supporting his Odile–Odette, now rushing from her with an ecstatic leap, now returning with an intake of breath and a sweeping, sinuous thrust of the body. And yet again, with every turn, the mirror is Nureyev's eternal magnet.

Suddenly, Nureyev stops the rehearsal. Something has just crossed his mind. He begins to laugh. Miss Mason looks puzzled.

"Oh, I must tell you my dream, Monica. I had an incredible dream last night. I dreamed I stood in the wings at La Scala. I was ready to go on. But to my horror, I saw that they were doing *La Traviata*! Can you imagine it? I became paralyzed. I turned to someone and said, 'But this is an opera, not a ballet. I *can't* go out there.' And the person answered, 'Yes, yes, you *must* go on. You are singing the role of the father—of Germont.' And I said, 'But I can't *sing*!' 'Of course you can sing, and you know the role very well.' And then it occurred to me that perhaps I *could* sing Germont, except that I could sing it only in the mezzo-soprano range. So, I took a deep breath and stepped onstage and sang the entire role—but as a mezzo-soprano! What do you say to that?"

Much laughter from them both. "I'm sure you gave a *lovely* performance, Rudy," says Monica Mason. The rehearsal continues, and the two dance with tremendous concentration. There is some halting, some slight faltering on Miss Mason's part, but eventually an altogether magical rapport ensues. The rehearsal lasts for another twenty minutes before Nureyev calls it quits.

Now, Nureyev and I sit in a small lounge outside the rehearsal room. His face is flushed. His hair falls loosely around his head. He seems spent. There are some awkward moments of silence between us. Nureyev dislikes being interviewed. I begin by commenting on his energy and his incredible capacity for concentration. He is startled by what I say.

"Is energy and capacity all you credit me for?" He draws himself up rather haughtily. I have offended Rudy. I quickly volunteer some rhapsodic words about his dancing. He begins to smile. I continue in my praise. "No, no—don't go on. It's all right. It's all right." Nureyev is beginning to relax.

At thirty-two, Rudolf Nureyev intuits the measure of his genius, and he does not take it lightly. He is aware of the spell he has cast on his public—aware of the fact that when Nureyev dances—with or without Margot Fonteyn—temperatures rise and audiences become transported by the elusive qualities that produce total, if not blinding stardom. A roar goes up the moment he flies onstage. His physical presence is enough to set thousands of spines tingling. There is about him an animal vitality and magnetism that generates a whole gamut of kinetic responses—as though he were possessed of motor forces that he, himself, can barely hold in check.

It is said that Nureyev has given a rejuvenating life to Dame Margot Fonteyn, who, in her fifties, continues to dance with unsurpassed beauty of style and technique. It is also said that he easily eclipses every male dancer around him, a fact that does not endear him to the few high-voltage names he has occasion to dance with. In short, since his defection from the Soviet Union to the West in 1961, when he was a member of Leningrad's Kirov Ballet Company, his international fame has been absolute. When, in 1962 he was invited to be a guest artist of the Royal Ballet, he accepted with alacrity. From that moment on, and through his legendary partnership with Fonteyn, Nureyev has become the company's greatest drawing card.

Still and all, dancing with the Royal Ballet has had its limitations. I asked Nureyev whether being a permanent member of the company might not solve his problems.

"I have tried to be a permanent member of the Royal Ballet," he answers, "but it seems not to work—or, shall I say, it seems not in the interest of the Royal Ballet. I don't know the mechanics involved, but they do what is to their best advantage without hurting me too much. You mustn't forget that the company is very, very good, and there are many very good English dancers in it. If I stay around too much, I might suppress them, or take their parts away. They have probably made the best arrangements.

"The point is, I really have to dance more often, and so, I travel around. If I don't, I will crumble. Yes, I can see myself as part of the permanent company, but only if they give me three to four performances a week. But you see, they cannot. There is Anthony Dowell, there is Michael Coleman, there are other male dancers. And the females also, they must have their chance to be on stage. The trouble is that with two or three *Swan Lake*s a year, I will never be in shape. Three *Giselle*s at Covent Garden are not enough for me, and so, I must dance the classical repertory in other places.

"Don't forget that a dancer's life has a span of perhaps twenty or twenty-five years. In that time you have a good period at the beginning, or in the middle, or even at the end. This good period lasts, at best, five to seven years.

"It is difficult to spread this very good period evenly, and when you are at your peak, you live off it later on. You live off your fat, so to speak. I feel I am in a very good period now, and I really have to dance nonstop."

As Nureyev speaks, his filmstar face is illuminated by some inner excitement. For a moment it seems as though he might spring into instant motion to give an added sense of reality to his words. Caught by that moment of impending movement, I urge him to describe the feelings he experiences while actually dancing.

"First, I must tell you that for me being onstage is really very abnormal, there is something very artificial about it. I must give more, and so, my emotions run very high. *Because* I feel so alien to the stage, I have a need to be on it more, and more, and more. I find it difficult to get used to, each time. For some dancers, being onstage doesn't matter so much. Their heartbeat doesn't change—nothing really changes. But for me, just standing in the wings, before going on, I am already exhausted, dead. Already my knees are shaking. It's extraordinary how terrified I am. When I have to dance in *La Bayadère*, for example, a terrible fear goes through me. But when one goes onstage, it *should* be something extraordinary, it should be like a sacrifice. You cannot go onstage as if you were going to the office. Still, many dancers do this. Yes, they can do wonderful turns, but still, it seems as if they go onstage to do office work.

"For myself, the moment I am on the stage things become multiplied and magnified. It's like having an atom reactor inside of me. There is a chain reaction, and, suddenly, my whole body bursts into flames. I suppose if someone were to photograph everything technically, it would probably look all wrong—the line would probably be wrong, etc. But the excitement overflows and spills into the audience, and enflames *them*. I don't know if I enflame the other dancers, however."

On a certain Friday night during an engagement of the Royal Ballet in New York, Nureyev danced the role of the Prince in his own choreographed version of Tchaikovsky's *The Nutcracker*. The Princess on that occasion was danced by Merle Park. Toward the end of the ballet, and in the middle of a long and complicated *pas de deux*, Nureyev abruptly left Miss Park, and, in an apparent fury, walked offstage. It was a shocking moment. A murmur of disbelief ran through the audience. Merle Park was left to her own devising for what seemed an eternity. Then, just as abruptly, Nureyev walked back onstage and finished the *pas de deux*.

On the following day, the newspapers reported that Nureyev had apparently kicked Miss Park in the leg, and for this clumsiness became enraged and walked off. Nureyev, it seemed, was also dissatisfied with the tempi set by the conductor throughout the entire evening. His own version of the incident differs somewhat:

"When there is no understanding and no trust between you and your partner, it doesn't matter how well you dance. It becomes like a two-headed eagle; you're doing one thing and your partner is doing another thing. That is what happened on that Friday night. It just didn't work, and I simply couldn't go on in that way, and so I had to walk off.

"When I dance with Margot, it is one aim, there is one vision. It is painful arriving at that vision, but when we have found it, we go there together. There is no tearing us apart."

Nureyev dances all over the world, except, of course, in Russia. I wonder whether he now regrets not dancing there. Are there any pangs?

"No. No pangs. No regrets. Besides, I think that at the moment the Russian ballet companies are in a kind of mess—they are sort of disoriented. They are neither here nor there. They are not in the past, not in the future, not even in the present. And I don't think their performances are all that good. I don't know whether people think I have progressed or regressed since leaving Russia. All I know is that I have done well, and didn't waste my time."

When Nureyev is not dancing, he is a night person. During his New York visit he attended quantities of parties at which he appeared dressed in the most up-to-the-minute fashions. Wearing boots with spurs, and jumpsuits designed especially for him, he will often dance the night away, or be seen at any number of Off and Off-Off Broadway shows. He went to see *Oh! Calcutta!* and enjoyed himself enormously:

"The new permissiveness is all for the good," he said. "Of course, it must be done well—and I must say, I thought the *pas de deux* done in the nude in *Oh! Calcutta!* was really very beautiful. Of course, if the dancers didn't have beautiful bodies, it would not be the same."

Would Nureyev ever dance in the nude?

"Well, it's not exactly my aim, but if a choreographer I respected would do a ballet in which dancing in the nude was integral and necessary to the work, then I would dance in the nude. Why not?"

Would Nureyev ever get married?

"Oh, come on," he said, grinning broadly, "it would never be an honest or sincere relationship. I would *only* think of myself. I would *only* think of my dancing. I would *only* think of my being up there, on the stage. Who has the guts to really share that? I don't think anybody does. And believe me, I don't want surfriders. I don't want anybody riding the surf from the waves I make."

Nureyev pauses. Then he adds, "Of course, I have a personal life. Something goes on, I'm sure. But I don't think the public should know about that. Do you?"

The above interview, which appeared in the Sunday *New York Times* on June 21, 1970, found Nureyev in a very loquacious mood. This was not the case two years later when I interviewed him in London for this book. I had gone to observe rehearsals of *Labyrintus*, the ballet by Glen Tetley which the Royal Ballet was presenting that 1972 season. The rehearsal was not going particularly well. Nureyev seemed exhausted, and out of sorts. Tetley was having some difficulties showing Nureyev a certain fall.

The dancer tried it again and again until he finally achieved it. The effort brought on a dark mood. He did, however, agree to go to a nearby restaurant for our talk.

Nureyev, nearing thirty-five, had been dancing all over the world in nonstop succession. There seemed something anxious about him that afternoon, as though he were terrified of the prospects of having to stop dancing, even for a moment. His guest appearances with major ballet companies around the globe have become a fifty-two-week-a-year matter. The strain shows in his eyes, and in the taut, drawn lines around the mouth. He is still handsome, and continues to exude his famed animal vitality.

In the restaurant he ordered large quantities of tea. At that hour—it was three o'clock in the afternoon—the restaurant's kitchen was closed. There were no steaks, no hot dishes. Nureyev resigned himself to cold salmon and avocado salad. During that week his film, I Am a Dancer, had opened in London. Nureyev was not pleased with the results. ("It wasn't conceived as a film. It was meant to be a television special. I wish it had been done more properly. I wish people were less greedy. . . .")

The film was indeed an idea that misfired. While it showed Nureyev dancing in various ballets with various partners, it almost judiciously avoided any real comment on Nureyev the man. A few excellent scenes showing Nureyev taking class were not sufficient to acquaint the public with the inner workings of the artist. Nevertheless, I Am a Dancer once again showed Nureyev's unbridled magnetism as a performer. It would be safe to say that he has singlehandedly brought world-wide attention to the male ballet dancer.

That afternoon, he seemed intent on being uncommunicative. Nureyev kept hesitating with his answers, and at one point I asked him whether he would rather not do the interview. "Well," he said, "there are some interviews that go as pleasant conversation. One doesn't feel burdened." His diffidence grew by the minute. Did he feel that there were things that misinformed the public about him? "I don't know. If there were, it obviously didn't hurt me." I suggested that he was being moody and quixotic with me. "I think one should be quixotic. I think it's very nice to be moody." Perhaps he is simply shy. "Probably. I really don't know anything about myself. Do you know about yourself?" Had he been psychoanalyzed? "No. No. There are things not to be known, and they should stay untouched. One should leave one's impulses to chance. It is better to do that rather than to calculate, prefabricate, analyze, and kill that something in us that we do not altogether understand."

I continued to probe him with various questions and found him to be ever more recalcitrant. Finally, I brought up his enormous dancing schedule and the possibility that he might by now have become an extremely wealthy man. At that, Nureyev exploded. He began to push all the buttons on my tape recorder in order to turn it off. "You don't need this information. It is none of your business." I quickly turned to his dancing. What was it like dancing with the Kirov Ballet? "Well, when I finished school at the Kirov and was later in the company and dancing *Giselle* I overheard the usherettes say, 'When this boy dances, he doesn't know where the earth or the sky is.' It struck me then that it was true at that moment. What I feel now I would definitely not like to analyze."

Nureyev would not pursue the question. What does he do when he is not dancing?

"I just lie down and then I get up. I go to swim. I go to the cinema. I go to my house in Monte Carlo. It has big rooms and it is constructed in such a way that when I walk, I don't meet anybody. I keep to myself. When you are in the public eye, you see so many people. There should be a contrast, a break. Sometimes I read. I listen to music. But there are so many things always on my mind. New productions, films."

Prior to his engagement at Covent Garden, Nureyev had gone to Mexico to dance with the Paul Taylor Company. He considers Taylor one of the most gifted choreographers working today, and has found Paul Taylor to be a man with whom he can be totally at ease. Whenever Nureyev is asked to a party or gathering, he never fails to insist that Paul Taylor be invited also. He commented briefly on Taylor's work. "He is the best choreographer. What I like about his work is the musicality. It is always so incredibly musical. And all of his ballets are always well balanced, well proportioned—always very inventive. The language of his movement goes as a story goes."

Has Nureyev thought of choreographing a modern ballet? Heretofore, his choreographic work had been limited to reworking classical ballets such as *Raymonda, Le Corsaire, Don Quixote, The Nutcracker,* and *The Sleeping Beauty.* "No, not yet. I won't rush into it. At the moment, I must do what I think nobody else can do, or nobody else wants to do."

I asked Nureyev what he looks for in a partnership. Of the many ballerinas he has danced with, who are his favorites?

"Of course, Margot. I liked Rosella Hightower; in certain ballets, Carla Fracci. I look for understanding. Sharing, finding similar ground. Finding a similar approach to a particular piece. We discuss it. Quite often, a partnership has not worked out. When that happens, I try not to repeat the performance."

What is dancing to Nureyev? "It is fulfilling one's wish from childhood. For me, the wish is as strong today as it was then. It never bores me. It gives me satisfaction."

I tell Nureyev that Balanchine considers ballet an art in which only woman reigns supreme, but he, Nureyev, had once claimed that ballet does, and should, celebrate the male. "I have never claimed this. It is Béjart who claims that ballet is male. I claim that it is just in between."

Is there anything Nureyev would like to tell young people who wish to become dancers?

"Give up before it's too late. It's a very hard life. It's very strenuous and becomes unrewarding very soon."

Would Nureyev comment more fully on his great partnership with Margot Fonteyn?

"One tries not to speak too much about certain things that are very close to you. One must not devalue. It was fortunate just to have met her. I must now go."

When Nureyev came to New York City in the spring of 1973 to dance with the National Ballet of Canada at the Metropolitan Opera, we met again. This time he was extraordinarily cordial. With the Canadians he danced in his new staging of *The Sleeping Beauty*, in *Swan Lake*, and *La Sylphide*. During the three-week engagement, he danced every single night. On the very last evening, Nureyev injured his foot. Later, it was ascertained that the injury was slight. He had been doing his *jetés en tournant* in the last act of *Sleeping Beauty*, and he landed incorrectly, twisting his ankle. He limped offstage, but returned for the Coda, walking through it, mostly. There was a party for Nureyev to celebrate the end of his New York engagement thrown at an East Side restaurant by his close friend Monique Van Vooren. He arrived limping, with his young friend Wallace Potts. Miss Van Vooren had invited Sol Hurok, Patricia McBride, Jean-Pierre Bonnefous, Paul Taylor, and Patricia and Clive Barnes among others. As it happened, it was Mr. Barnes's forty-sixth birthday, so the event turned into a double celebration. Nureyev was extremely cheerful and talkative. Everyone, of course, commiserated with him on his injury. He replied, "I was punished for having gone to see a matinee at the New York City Ballet. I should have stayed home and rested for my evening performance." Sol Hurok lifted his glass, saying, "Long life, good health and many more performances with Sol Hurok." Nureyev, in a brown satin jacket, brown pants, boots, and a leopard-skin cap, proceeded to enjoy himself throughout the evening, chatting amiably with everyone, including two young women, also guests, who are Nureyev's most ardent fans. They fly everywhere to catch his performances. No doubt they were talking of Nureyev's upcoming itinerary. He would be flying off to Europe on the following morning, and would be dancing nonstop wherever he chose. The most famous male dancer in the world follows his destiny at breakneck speed.

ANTOINETTE SIBLEY
and ANTHONY DOWELL

Their partnership is on the verge of becoming legendary. Their appearances together at the Royal Ballet, of which they are principal dancers, or as guest artists, are becoming events. Their looks are extraordinary. Dowell is the image of the poetic, Byronic, youthful partner. Sibley, dark, intense, with Ingres-like features, is the essence of the romantic ballerina. On stage together, they suggest something of the nineteenth century—a kind of young, ardent impetuosity tempered by a regal calm. In Frederick Ashton's *The Dream*, a work composed on them, they transform into magical figures, drawing on their technical brilliance to transmute gesture and movement into art. In *The Sleeping Beauty* or *Swan Lake*, they lend to their principal roles an ecstatic radiance. In short, Sibley and Dowell have found that mysterious meeting ground that makes of two dancers a single magnetic force.

The two are very close friends. Offstage, they give the impression of being somewhat removed, occupying their own private sphere. When, for example, Sibley and Dowell came to dance in Spoleto at the Festival of Two Worlds during the summer of 1973, they performed with equally celebrated dancing couples in Jerome Robbins' ballet *Celebration: The Art of the Pas de Deux*. It was clear from the outset that Tony and Antoinette would not be mingling with their fellow dancers. In restaurants, they would occupy a table for two, while dancers such as Carla Fracci and Paolo Bortoluzzi or Violette Verdy and Jean-Pierre Boonefous, Patricia McBride and Helgi Tomasson would be crowded together with any number of friends, sharing each other's company with much conviviality. Dowell and Sibley dined together, visited the night spots together, and it was clear that they found continual pleasure in maintaining a sort of special, conspiratorial privacy.

It was in London that I met with the two English dancers. Miss Sibley was quick to suggest that she and Dowell be interviewed together, and invited me to visit with them in her London house. When I appeared at the appointed hour, neither dancer had yet arrived. A relative of Miss Sibley's greeted me at the door, and informed me that the two were delayed at a rehearsal. I was ushered into a pleasantly cluttered living room with old-fashioned, comfortable furnishings. There were couches, settees, easy chairs, small tables holding charming bibelots, and the place reflected a sense of familial, homy unpretentiousness. A beautiful black cat, whose name I learned was Deushka, wove itself cautiously around my feet, then, with a dart, leaped upon my lap. In a little while, Sibley and Dowell arrived. They were in high good spirits, a bit out of breath, and full of apologies for their delay. Instantly, preparations were made for tea and sweets and the three of us settled down for our talk. Miss Sibley looked beautiful in a pale-brown silk-print dress. Dowell looked dashing in beige trousers and a white shirt and foulard. The cat, Deushka, was the first topic of conversation.

"She walked into this house a few days after Michael Somes and I were married," said Miss Sibley. "She just walked in and took over. Michael made me take her around to all the houses so that I might give her back to her proper owner. No one claimed her, and so I brought her back. But Michael didn't believe me. So *he* took me around with him. We had to do the whole thing over again. I was never so embarrassed in my whole life. All the people said, 'But we've seen you already!' Then, of course, the cat made a beeline for Michael because she's mad about men, and that was it.

I used to call her Darling, but Madame Nijinska came one night and told me that the Russian word for Darling was *Deushka*, and that's how Deushka got her name."

When tea was served, talk turned to Sibley and Dowell. I learned that Miss Sibley was born in Bromley in 1939. She entered the Royal Ballet School, then joined the Royal Ballet in 1956. She has been a principal with the company since 1960. Mr. Dowell was born in London in 1943, and also studied at the Royal Ballet School. Toward the end of his training, he joined the Covent Garden Opera Ballet; then, in 1962, transferred to the Royal Ballet.

"Anthony and I never met in school. I'm older."

"I know exactly where we met," Mr. Dowell adds. "We were both put to understudy *Symphony*, a ballet that Kenneth MacMillan was doing. I was in the *corps*, but Antoinette was covering Lynn Seymour. I was understudying the lead boy."

"I hadn't got a partner to work with in the ballet," Miss Sibley continued. "Then, eventually, I realized that Anthony could help me as a partner. That was the first time we ever met. I think it was in 1963. But the first time we danced properly in a performance was when Sir Frederick Ashton did a ballet called *The Dream*, especially for us both."

I asked Sibley and Dowell how it all began for them.

"Well, it was really my parents who wanted me to dance," Miss Sibley said. "I was sent off to boarding school because of the war. At boarding school, we did all kinds of dancing, not just ballet. So, I wasn't trained specifically for ballet. But then I got quite good at it, and they sent me off to the Royal Ballet School. The school was at Barons Court, where we still all go to take class and to rehearse. I have been going there since I was nine years old. I was reckoning it up the other day, and I was shocked to realize that I've been walking along those same pavements since the age of nine. Incredible! Actually, I never had an urge to dance. Whenever I saw a ballet, it never occurred to me that I would ever be doing principal roles. I think dancing was really something that just happened to me. It was never anything I, myself, was looking toward. It just happened."

"We're sort of similar," said Anthony Dowell. "My mother wanted my sister to dance, and I was taken along to her dancing classes, and I loved it. It was all forms of dancing—not just ballet. Gradually, one finds what one's natural talent is. So it was easy for me to fall into classical dancing. Of course, the rot doesn't set in until you're sixteen. At least, it did with me. I started when I was four or five, and my first teacher was June Hampshire. Then, I went to the Royal Ballet School where I had a great mixture of teachers. I also went to White Lodge, where we had to take regular schooling, together with ballet. I loathed all that shit we dived into at White Lodge. I was hopeless at everything. I was just plain dumb. I mean, they gave you the feeling that if you couldn't do mathematics, you

THE PRIVATE WORLD OF BALLET   120

would never make it as a dancer. Well, it doesn't necessarily follow that if you're gifted artistically, you're also going to be gifted mathematically. At any rate, I finally made it into the Senior School, and I did a year in the Opera Ballet at Covent Garden, which was considered a sort of apprenticeship. After that, I joined the first company—the Royal Ballet—in 1961."

Antoinette Sibley began to tell me some of the drawbacks of being a ballerina:

"If you knew what it was like! There is time for absolutely nothing. I mean, I went to a hairdresser the other morning. I hadn't been to a regular hairdresser in one entire year. It was terrific. They put your feet up. They give you coffee. And as I sat there, I looked at all the people around me. I realized that these women could do this twice a week. And when they're not at the hairdressers, they go shopping for clothes. Or they fetch their children back from school. They read books. What it all boils down to is that you'd like to be doing an awful lot of things—except, you can't. You can't cancel morning class. That means you cancel going out at night. First comes the work. It really does. You feel you're living in a convent. Of course, I rebel all the time.

"I have a tremendous amount of outside interests. When I have a minute, I get very impulsive. I have these sudden urges to go to the theater, to read books—to do a hundred thousand things. But I get so very tired because the dancing and rehearsal schedule is so time-consuming. There just isn't time."

"I don't really miss the world out there so very much," adds Dowell. "It's because I'm sort of a hermit. I don't enjoy parties at all. I do enjoy the theater, but I'm not really desperate to escape the world I'm in. What does bother me an awful lot about being a dancer is the constant tension of performing. I get frightfully nervous. It's at those lonely moments when you're on your own—waiting to go on. The feeling that you can't relieve your nerves. I always slightly resent the people out in the audience because they're not at all as nervous as I am. Their stomachs are not doing dreadful things. They may have other problems, I know; but they don't have the terrible nerves I've got to deal with. You see, dancers can't take calming pills or drink, or what have you, to quiet down. With us, it's a continual battle, coping with nerves."

"Yes, it's a continual battle," says Miss Sibley. "Also, you're always worried about injuries. Well, it just never gets any easier. That's the frightening thing."

We turn to the subject of the Dowell-Sibley partnership. What, in their opinion, makes them so perfect for one another? Mr. Dowell has some clues:

"Well, it's how one looks together. The proportions have to be right. The way each of us is built enhances the other. Also, it's the way we hear music. After a time, one sort of knows exactly what each of us needs from the other. I *know* what Antoinette will do at any given moment. I know how she moves. Of course, I have not had many other partners. I started with Antoinette straightaway. She, of course, has danced with many others, and so, would be in a better position to tell you why our partnership seems to work so well."

"Yes. I worked with literally every dancer there was. Of course, I started very young doing very big ballets, and the men I danced with were all very wonderful. But with Anthony it was something quite different. It seemed so logical that we should dance together. As he said, a lot has to do with our proportions, and with the way we hear the music. But it is also an emotional thing. It has to do with our temperaments, even with a sort of cut-offness that both of us have in us. It's hard to explain. Actually, it's all very mysterious. I'm constantly surprised at the fact that it works so well for us. It's quite extraordinary—quite incredible."

Miss Sibley was willing to talk about her marriage to Michael Somes— something Mr. Somes declined to discuss.

"We separated in 1969," she said. "We partnered together and while it's sometimes easy to be married to one's partner, it didn't quite work out that way for us. I mean, he was constantly rehearsing me. There comes a point where you can't take that home with you. It was a hopeless situation. Michael was such a disciplinarian. If someone tells you off, you take it as an insult. You can't help it. So you fight it all the time. It's no good, your telling yourself that that's part of your job. Anyway, a lot of other things came into it. Also, our hours were very different. He was at the theater all the time. I was not. I had my schedule of performances. It was not an easy relationship. If we were easy people . . . but we're not.

"Of course, it all started off as a very passionate thing. It was a fairy tale—an absolute fairy tale. He was rehearsing me for my first performance of *Swan Lake*, which I had to learn in ten days. I was only twenty. It was a huge strain, and I was on every night doing other ballets. In the end, Ninette de Valois asked Michael if he wouldn't mind dancing *Swan Lake* with me. Well, you can imagine! At the time, I was twenty and in the *corps de ballet*. He was Michael Somes, Margot Fonteyn's partner. And he agreed to dance with me—this goose. He was really quite something. So it all started to happen between us through rehearsals. I suppose the fairy-tale aspect of it all got to me. It became a passionate thing—and he was a very good-looking man." Her divorce from Michael Somes left Miss Sibley single once again, but that status was changed on July 13, 1974, when she married Panton Corbett, a banker.

Anthony Dowell admits to leading a very sheltered personal life. The various stigmas attached to being a male dancer have eluded the handsome young ballet star:

"I was very protected, really. It always sort of amazes me now, when I think back, of how marvelous my parents were. There was never a time when they objected to my taking up the dance. They never thought that it might be wrong for a boy to dance. I mean, there were slight influences from other sides of my family, who thought that it might not be right for me to enter this profession. Of course, no one, not even my parents, knew that I was going to make it as a dancer. Now that I have made it, everyone's very happy.

"What does annoy me is when people continually send up the male ballet dancers. And even in variety shows, a comedian can't wait to get into tights and do a send-up of a male ballet dancer. It's a great laugh, except that no one realizes that to be a ballet dancer takes probably twice the stamina it takes to be an athlete. Because, you see, we not only have to learn to build terrific strength but we're also not allowed to show it. We go through everything an athlete goes through, but we've got to make everything look so easy. And people have the mistaken impression that we never do anything during the day, except have lunch or tea. They think we just go to the theater at night and start performing. It would be so nice if people really knew what dancers go through to become dancers."

Anthony Dowell lives at home with his family:

"I've always lived at home. I think people tend to think of me as a slightly odd case. The fact is, I was very lucky, as a child, to have had a tremendously happy home life. I naturally thought everyone did. It's only now that I realize that my situation is one in a million."

"Oh, yes. It's an unbelievably happy family. I mean," Miss Sibley said. "To go there is a tonic. It's better than any whisky. It's really fantastic. Of course, my parents are also quite proud of me. My father, particularly, even though he keeps telling me that some of our other dancers are much prettier. Well, I'm getting old, aren't I, Anthony?"

Both Sibley and Dowell now attempt to explain something of what goes through them while in the act of performing:

"It's pain," says Dowell.

"Yes, pain, pain, pain," says Sibley. "You see, it's such a composite art—you can't just think of one thing. First of all, you must concentrate on the character you are. For me, that's the very first thing. I *become* the person I'm portraying. I don't *act* that person, I *am* that person. Then, of course, there's the music. The music is a guideline to everything. Then there's the story. The story indicates the way in which your character moves. For instance, you can do an arabesque twenty different ways. But it all depends on the role you're doing. So all of that comes together during the performance."

"Actually," Dowell says, "it's awful when the mind starts working overtime. You see, things can go one way or they can go another way, and that can become an obstacle. I mean, you start to think about the steps that are coming up, and that sort of thing can get you in trouble because it impedes the flow of what you're doing."

"Anthony is right. You can start off, and you might do one step that doesn't go well, so you begin thinking that you've failed. Well, you then start trying to adjust and carry on, and you usually do. Of course, when you dance something like the *Black Swan pas de deux* and the variations, there is only *one* way of doing it. And you can't let anyone know that it hasn't worked that day. The point is, no matter how great you may be, you've got to live with the constant possibility of failure. I think that the greater an artist you become, the more you can live with that possibility. Conversely, you can find something really valuable because you are acquainted with failure."

I ask Anthony Dowell whether the advent of Rudolf Nureyev has in any way impeded or threatened his position with the Royal Ballet.

"Well, I was very lucky. When Rudolf first came to our company, I was just starting. I hadn't really gotten my first big chance yet. I wasn't going to lose performances, as some of our more established artists did. I must say, some of our male principals had a tough time of it. Suddenly, they lost performances because the great dancer was arriving. As if no great dancing had ever happened before. For me, it was marvelous, because I watched a lot. No matter what anyone says, Rudolf has the most fantastic training. I mean, you'll talk to him about it, and he'll tell you about his hangups—about the way he's built or the way his legs are, and the way he's had to overcome his physical drawbacks. Just talking to him is absolutely fantastic."

"Rudy is the most helpful artist," adds Miss Sibley. I have danced *La Bayadère* with him. He decidedly knows what he's about, and one does respect him for what he says. And he's tremendously helpful. The only way we have lately become threatened by him is in losing performances. It does happen sometimes."

The couple's greatest complaint is a lack of new ballets choreographed especially for them:

"All dancers are desperate for new ballets," says Dowell, "because it's one's food. It's what extends you—it's what nourishes you. We've only had two ballets made on us in eight years."

I asked Miss Sibley whether she might not have wanted to dance in Glen Tetley's *Labyrintus*, which would involve her in more avant-garde choreography.

"Well, I was going to do a very modern work, but finally I had great difficulties with the music. I was asked to be in Tetley's *Field Figures*, but I was too busy at the time. Actually, it's the music that I can't relate to. I can't relax with electronic music or very abstract music. You see, my whole thing is that when I dance I've got to put myself inside the music.

It's the music that gets me through. Well, there is some music I just can't deal with."

What, I ask Sibley and Dowell, are the most elating and the most terrifying aspects of their work? Dowell laughs: "The most elating part is when it's over!" Miss Sibley chides Dowell, then says, "No. The elation is something very rare. Of course, you're elated when you're dancing well, and you're elated when you get through dancing without an injury. But then, there's also the terror—the terror that you will injure yourself. Because, then, you're off—you're out, and that's the thing a dancer loathes more than anything else in the world. I mean, what are you going through all this agony for unless you can be on?"

Anthony Dowell sums it all up:

"The fact of the matter is that ballet dancing is the most unnatural thing in the world. You're constantly in agony, but you've got to come out onstage and make it seem as though it were the most natural way of moving. It's not. It's against all human possibility."

Dominic

MERLE PARK

When, in June 1970, I interviewed Rudolf Nureyev for *The New York Times*, the dancer commented on a mishap between himself and Merle Park during a performance of Nureyev's version of *The Nutcracker* that they had danced at the Metropolitan Opera in New York City. He claimed that he and Miss Park erred during a *pas de deux*, causing Nureyev to abruptly leave the stage. (This, of course, may conflict with some of the other stories, but they all conflict with each other!) Miss Park was left to her own devices for several minutes, until her partner returned to the stage to finish the figure. During our interview, Nureyev made a disparaging remark about Miss Park which had caused the ballerina a certain amount of anguish.

Unbeknownst to this writer, the article, or a portion thereof, was reprinted in the London *Evening Standard*. Friends of Miss Park telephoned her to tell her that Nureyev had, in so many words, blamed her for ruining the *pas de deux*. This was the first Miss Park heard of the incident, not having been aware of the interview which had originally appeared in the *Times*. She was angered and considered bringing suit against the dancer and the *Evening Standard*.

When I came to London in the summer of 1972 to interview dancers of the Royal Ballet, I had no inkling that any of this had transpired. When I attempted to contact Merle Park so that I might interview her, the Royal Ballet's press officer told me that she did not wish to meet the man who had printed damaging remarks about her. It took considerable prodding on my part to convince the press officer that I had not, in fact, made those remarks, and that it would be an excellent idea for Miss Park to give her side of the story. Finally, the ballerina consented to see me.

One of the Royal Ballet's most enduring and exquisite dancers, Merle Park leads an affluent life. Unlike some of her fellow dancers, she lives in an elegant house facing the Thames. Expensive paintings hang on her walls. The furniture is antique. The living room into which I was ushered was a model of understated luxury. Miss Park greeted me cordially, offered a drink, and introduced me to her husband, Sidney Bloch, who soon left us together. The dancer wore a superbly tailored silk dress. She looked radiantly self-possessed. Her large blue eyes suggested intelligence, vitality, and, vis-à-vis myself, a certain suspicion.

We immediately touched on the *affaire* Nureyev.

"Well, I was rung up," Miss Park began. "I hadn't seen the paper. Someone said, 'What a lousy thing to have happened.' Well, I couldn't believe it. When I saw the article I rang up Rudolf, and I said, 'Is it true that you said I kicked you in *Nutcracker*? And he said, 'Oh, no . . . no, no.' Then I told him how annoyed I was, and asked him again if he had said those things. He said, 'Oh, maybe I did say it, yes. But don't worry about the papers.' I was very cross with Rudolf. After all, you just don't *do* that sort of thing. All right, a mistake may have been made, but you don't come out with it in print. And so I went to Queen's Council and said that surely this is libelous. It made out that I was a bad dancer. I am, after all, earning one of the top salaries at the Royal Ballet, and what would the taxpayers think, reading that Rudolf Nureyev says that Merle Park is a bad dancer. And yet, I dance with him every second night at Covent Garden. This had to be put right. Council said that this *was* libelous, and a letter was sent off to Rudolf. The same letter was sent to the Board of the

Royal Ballet, to Sir Frederick Ashton, and to Rudolf's agent. Because, if it had only gone to Rudy, he probably wouldn't have even opened the letter. Anyway, I demanded an apology. And I got it. He also wrote this long thing in the *Evening Standard*, with a picture of us both, saying I was one of the best partners that he had ever danced with. He's been a lamb ever since. Anyway, that night at the Metropolitan Opera, we actually kicked each other. It was inevitable. We were doing a step—a strange piece of his choreography. We had to run around each other, and because I happened to be in time with the music, which was double speed, and he was at the slower pace, we kicked each other. We did. We were in each other's way. That's what it was.

"I'm tremendously fond of Rudy. I think we are of each other. Thank God, we don't have to live together. I think we respect each other; that's what it is. Of course, I have walked out of rehearsals when he misbehaved. Then he comes after me and says, 'Let's do it again.' So I come back. Usually, I am absolutely calm when he has a tantrum. I think this is the only way to treat him. He's a child, and he needs a mother."

Having said all of this, Miss Park was now willing to discuss her own life:

"I was born in Salisbury, Rhodesia. All my family are there, except my mom and dad, who are here looking after my little boy. So I have built-in babysitters. I was not a beautiful little girl in Rhodesia. I was skinny—a weedy little thing that wouldn't eat her food. So my mother took me to the doctor, and he suggested ballet or horse-riding. My mom sent me to ballet classes. I took tap classes, Greek classes, and acrobatic classes—the whole jolly lot. I wasn't so keen on the tap, but I loved the ballet. I also loved the Greek dancing, which is like Dalcroze. I wouldn't be as good a classical ballet dancer, had I not taken Greek classes. It gives you a marvelous sense of line. At thirteen I came to England to go to a ballet school and went to a boarding school as well. The ballet school was a sort of feeding-place to the Sadler's Wells. Two and a half years later, I auditioned for the Sadler's Wells, and they accepted me into the school. I had a year's grant. But within three months I was in the company. There were five of us taken in, and I was one of the lucky ones. I wasn't trained at all at the Royal Ballet School. Some say this is a good thing; I say it's not. I say there's a marvelous basic strength in their feet and legs. All my work is done through my head rather than through physical strength. It's a *will* to do it. I've been with the company twenty years."

Miss Park recalls her early years at the Royal Ballet. She speaks warmly of Dame Ninette de Valois, saying that she was fair, and a bit eccentric. One day, because of the illness of Rowena Jackson, Merle Park took her place, and the press discovered a new and brilliant dancer.

"I was thrown on in six hours, and overnight I was made. Of course, that's all nonsense. It takes fifty years to make a dancer. You can't become anything overnight. Anyway, when the press made all that fuss, Dame Ninette said that I would have to change my name, that no one was called 'Park.' So I went home feeling my career was finished. I had to find a new name. And I thought up two of them—Merle Andrée or Merle Denver. When I told these names to Madame, she said, 'Keep Park!' "

I asked Miss Park if she would describe the kind of dancer she is.

"I'm a rebel dancer, I guess. Basically, I try to lose myself in the music. To me, dancing is movement to music. I'm not so sure of musical beats or rhythms, but I am very sure of phrasing. I can hear the phrase. I stop at the end of a sentence, and I finish there. What I put in between is how I do it. It's my signature. Some people say my dancing is not rhythmical. It may be so, but I would say that my dancing is phrasical. Of course, the nerves are there, all day and all night. Of course, we are all masochists. We constantly ask ourselves, Why do we do it? Well, there's a drive. We were born to do it. You can't do anything else. You can give up, of course, but you won't be happy."

Miss Park was married for three years to the ballet critic James Kennedy. "He had a terrific personality, and perhaps that is why we clashed. We have a little boy. His name is Antony. Unfortunately, I am a great one for making mistakes in feeling. Luckily, I've always come out on top afterward. I couldn't be happier now. I've remarried a wonderful man. He gives me everything that's nice. They say that ballet dancers must sacrifice a great deal for their careers. I do not sacrifice. I cannot sacrifice a personal life—now that I've experienced it. It might be right for others, but it doesn't work for me. I have to be able to work the two together, and I must work my child into it as well. If my home isn't right, then I do not dance well. I cannot divorce the two. You see, I'm so basic. I'm so peasant. And I'm always a dancer. I'm a dancer climbing the stairs, I'm a dancer cleaning my teeth. That's me."

Merle Park on the stage is the essence of lightness and fragility. Whether performing *Coppélia, The Sleeping Beauty,* or *Romeo and Juliet,* she projects a kind of gossamer poetry. Her movements are never less than pure and her strength is obvious at every turn, but she has developed a unique style in which a sense of suspension and melodic line cause her dancing to have a special lyrical freedom. While she has danced all the major classic roles, she had, for years, avoided dancing in *Swan Lake.*

"I said 'no' to *Swan Lake* because I didn't think I was suited to it. I think that I never much cared for it at first. The only thing I was impressed by was the Neopolitan Dance. That's what I wanted to do. And that's what I did do, for years. Anyway, I finally agreed to appear as Odette–Odile. It's taken me a very long time."

Miss Park danced her first *Swan Lake* at Covent Garden in 1973 to high critical acclaim.

Like most dancers at the Royal Ballet, Merle Park spoke, in 1972, with unbounded admiration of Dame Margot Fonteyn:

"Margot is a great, great person. For me, this matters more than anything. I have always believed that unless you are a great person, you cannot be a great artist. Her career was built up for her by Ashton and by Madame. I adore her. She always says I'm her mom's favorite dancer—which I consider a great compliment."

I wonder whether throughout the years Margot Fonteyn had not overshadowed Miss Park's career.

"Of course not," Miss Park said. "Nobody has ever overshadowed my career, and no one ever will. What I am, I am. I am what I am meant to be. Of course, I would be sad to see Margot go, because I feed on her all the time. I would like her to be here all the time. I would actually like to see her directing the Royal Ballet. In fact, when Ashton left, she was asked to come and direct the company. She said no. But she *could* direct it. With her finger on the telephone, she could run the whole company. She's a wonderful organizer; everyone respects her.

"I feel the company at the moment has no direction at all. For us older dancers, the company is not what it used to be. Frankly, I feel that the Board must do something about it. We want direction. We have a lot of dancers and not enough works to dance. If I had my way, I would love to do all the Tudor ballets. If they would produce all the Tudor ballets with our second group, I would do them. But I don't think MacMillan likes Tudor. However, you can't be a dancer and also go into politics.

"What should really happen is that *I* should be running the company. This is my ambition. I'd give up dancing tomorrow if they'd give me the job. I would love to run the Royal Ballet. I know I could do it, and I would be awfully fair to my dancers. Without the dancers' respect, how can you have a company? That's what matters most. You know, enough work, enough enthusiasm, enough productions—those are the things that keep dancers constantly thriving."

There is no question but that Merle Park is a woman of high conviction and strong personality. She seems secure in her aims, and does not mind speaking out. Clearly a woman of the world, she combines a glamorous personal life with an intense artistic life.

"My rewards are that I love people. I mix so much. And I go around the world. And I earn quite a lot of money. I've never had money, and to earn a lot of money is marvelous. I like living well. I can live well on very little. If I'm in France, and I have some Brie cheese and a bottle of wine on a bench, I'm happy. And I'm happy just walking through a corn field. I love the sun. I love getting away. I'm a Libra—that's October. And I say, I'm balanced. Oh, I get terribly depressed. Terribly down. But I always remember that I can only go up. So, I somehow keep myself going. I really think I'm terribly easy. I hate scenes. And there's nobody that I hate. Of course, I get terribly distressed. I cry easily. If I see hungry children, or I hear that parents have mistreated children, I get very upset. I hate wars. I loathe them. And I hate people who are horrible to old people and to animals. The most important thing is to be oneself, knowing oneself, and believing in oneself. That is what I am all about."

Roy Round

LYNN SEYMOUR

She was born in Wainwright, Canada in 1939. When Lynn Seymour danced at the Canadian Ballet Festival in 1953, the intensity of her performance was duly noted. The following year found her studying at Sadler's Wells. In 1956 she danced with the Covent Garden Opera Ballet. In 1957, she joined the Royal Ballet, where she is currently principal dancer.

The choreographer Kenneth MacMillan created a number of ballets for her, including the role of Juliet in his highly tauted *Romeo and Juliet*. But she has danced in all the major classical ballets, and is considered one of the great actress-dancers of her day. Unlike some of her fellow dancers, she is possessed of an unusually complex character. Lynn Seymour is enormously interesting, both on the stage and off. There is about her a strange, driven quality. The dynamics of her personality spill into the dynamics of her artistry. One might suggest that there is something fascinatingly neurotic about her.

Circumstances caused me to arrive late for my interview with Lynn Seymour. As I approached her London house, which was in the process of being remodeled, I glimpsed a somewhat nervous figure in a long summer dress, pacing the floor, smoking a cigarette. The pacing and the manner in which the figure carried itself had something of the same dramatic thrust that it exudes on the stage. A certain tension, and a curiously obsessive concentration, yielded the sight of a woman filled with a teeming inner life.

She seemed rattled by my lengthy delay, but greeted me with cordiality. It was late afternoon and the weather was mild. Miss Seymour poured us a drink and suggested we have our talk in her garden. We sat on the grass. An apple tree, a pear tree, a bank of flowers surrounded us. Though quite small, the garden gave the impression of being spacious. I commented on how pretty everything looked. "I know nothing about flowers," Miss Seymour said. "I didn't put them in myself. I don't have time to tend to nature, although I'd love to." Noting some children's toys, I learned that they belonged to Miss Seymour's twin boys, presently taking a nap in an upstairs room.

We quickly launched into her beginnings.

"I started my training in Vancouver," Miss Seymour said, "although I wasn't very serious at all. My mom made me a pair of bloomers and a halter top in which I used to love doing backbends and splits. I had an awfully nice teacher, with a lot of qualities. She was madly musical, and in love with the theater. I think she had done something in New York. I believe she was sort of a showgirl at the Latin Quarter. Naturally, hearing that, I thought she was the bee's knees. She was fabulous with children. She had long, long legs that were always covered in those mesh-y tights. She was wonderful. Actually, she was intensely serious, and imbued us with a love for dance. I mean, it wasn't your 'holy' bit. More workmanlike, really. Her classes weren't airy-fairy at all. She taught one about the gypsy side of it all, which was rather romantic. She taught us to work hard—it wasn't about being an ethereal creature. I learned all of this before I was twelve.

"Then a marvelous man called Nicolai Svetlanov appeared on the scene. He had fled Moscow. You know, one of those White Russians who walked from Moscow to Manchuria. Then he went to Shanghai. Anyway, he was a fabulous teacher. His big thing was adagio. He was a real partner-type—one of those ageless, Mongolian-looking people. He had incredible eyes.

You couldn't look into them. It was too much. He and a female Russian dancer used to do a night-club act in Shanghai. He was incredible, and it was with him that I started to work very seriously. I was thirteen at the time."

By fourteen, Lynn Seymour had arrived in London and began studying at Barons Court. She had come to England by herself.

"Actually, I had everything to learn, and I sort of wore it on my sleeve. I was an outspoken girl, and a bit of a dumb bore. Everyone felt I was horrible. But you know the English, and their reticence. The last thing that you're supposed to show is that you want to do something. Luckily, I had some marvelous teachers, which helped a lot.

"In my third year, everyone in my class went on to great things, but they didn't think I was ready, so they sent me over to the Sadler's Wells Opera Ballet, which was about the last thing they could do with you. So there I was, dancing in *Rigoletto, The Bartered Bride, The Pearl Fishers.* I sort of flashed about in all those. Actually, it was very good experience, because we learned about theater and all those operatic trappings. It all lasted one year. Then, I joined the Royal Ballet touring company. I consider it the best time of my dancing career. Because when I finally came to Covent Garden, a lot of lousy things began happening to me. I got injuries, I got sick—things started falling apart. Also, adulthood set in, and all the problems that go with it. Nevertheless, there were good times as well. I danced big roles very early on."

In performance Lynn Seymour offers singular pleasure. Physically, she does not appear to have the perfect dancer's body: she has a tendency to gain weight, although never to a point where it seems to interfere with her flawless technique. The coolness of the English dancer is not one of Miss Seymour's characteristics. She is an emotional dancer. Whether she performs Aurora, or Giselle, or in MacMillan's *Anastasia*, or in an ultra-modern Glen Tetley ballet, she seems consumed by whatever role she is portraying. Her beautiful round face, with its enormous brown-black eyes, is incredibly expressive. Her body transforms into an instrument of subdued lyricism. Her dancing has about it something strangely brooding.

When she made a guest appearance with the New York-based Alvin Ailey Company, dancing in Ailey's *Flowers*—a ballet based on the life of the late rock star Janis Joplin—she produced an uncommon characterization that perfectly embodied the tortured, drug-ridden singer. Alternating between frenzy and ecstasy, she gave to the role a dimension not usually associated with the pure classical dancer. In short, Lynn Seymour can veer from emotion to emotion with unique realism while retaining a perfectly modulated and disciplined technique.

As we sat in the cool garden sipping our iced drinks, Miss Seymour continued to tell me about herself. I asked her about her twin boys:

"They're not identical twins, not a bit. They're quite different in character. It's helped an awful lot, having them. It puts everything into the right perspective. The boys are three years old. One is named Jerzy and the other Adrian. I don't have a husband any more. I've been through two. It was my second husband with whom I had the twins. Both my husbands were dancers, but in the end, they went on to other things. My first husband is now a successful photographer and my second husband is a talented industrial designer. I doubt that I'll marry again. I'm off that scene." (However, Miss Seymour re-entered the scene when she married yet another photographer, Philip Pace, on January 7, 1974.)

Is it difficult being a woman alone with a career and children?

"Quite often. I mean, as far as the law is concerned. For example, I had terrible trouble buying my house because I was a woman. Any man with even half my earnings could have had it immediately. Things like that. Of course, I have a nanny who takes care of the children."

Discussing her dancing, Miss Seymour claimed that it is the music that inspires her first:

"You try to be part of it. The rest has to do with your imagination—with what you're trying to translate or realize. For me, the real key is concentration. It's quite the opposite of what everyone says dancing should be. Everybody talks about 'pushing-out'—you know, giving out a lot. In fact, for me, it's quite the opposite. I make my dancing extremely concentrated. There are so many things to worry about onstage. There's the physical thing—the craft. There's your partner, there's the music, the lighting. There are so many aspects. And you have to use them all, and feel. I think in order to do that, you have to hang on like mad. You can't let go. You've got to put it all together."

I asked Miss Seymour about her partners.

"My first partner was Donald Macleary," she said. "We did our first Swan Lake together. I still think he's probably the best partner in the world today. He was so marvelous that some greater ballerinas sort of grabbed him, and I had to start again with another partner. I then danced with Desmond Doyle for a short time, and then, with Christopher Gable—which was fabulous. We created Romeo and Juliet together. I've danced with Rudolf Nureyev. I love working with him. He has such marvelous force. It's a great engine, you know, and it sustains the whole performance. It's amazing. Also, I love him dearly as a person. I think I'm one of his greatest friends."

I wondered whether Miss Seymour could talk about the psychological factors that give such drama to her roles.

"Well, when I dance, I don't divide it from my personal life. Actually, I don't think anybody can. But I think that more than half of it is really the technical and physical side of it. The rest is just sort of a sophisticated veneer. In ballet, everything is really technique. And what's so awful is that the technique is not always within grasp. When I danced in the film *I*

Am a Dancer with Rudy, I was too much of a coward to go and see it. Whenever I see myself dancing, I practically die. I don't really know how I dance, and I prefer to live in ignorance."

I had gone to see Lynn Seymour, Nureyev, and other Royal Ballet dancers in Glen Tetley's *Labyrintus*. The difficult Luciano Berio score seemed practically impossible to dance to. I asked Miss Seymour what it is like dancing to very abstract music.

"It's really quite simple," she said. "Actually, it's kind of four-square, or triangular, or round. Certain sections of the music give you the signposts, while the rest of it is muscular memory. So, you move from signpost to signpost and you hit things at just the right moment. Finally, you begin to really feel it. What I find so curious is that with music of strict tempi, you use it personally to get a dynamic force for technical things. You use it for a jump, or whatever. In this case, you go on your own impetus all the time, except for occasional things. It's more the atmosphere of the music that propels you. It's a very fluid thing.

"Of course, Tetley showed us the movements, but, finally, you're on your own, and work almost instinctively. When you're enmeshed or contorted with your partner, you feel each other's balance. It's sort of a give-and-take. You can tell where the movement is going. That's the whole thing of dancing with a partner. You can extend and do things that you can't do alone. It's a feeling . . . an antenna."

What goes on inside Miss Seymour as she dances?

"Fear. I think one of the greatest fears for me is to get too tired. Fatigue comes from sustained dancing on the stage. It is less fatiguing in class because the work is more concentrated and comes in smaller doses. You don't do a four-minute variation in class. You do things that will build you up to be *able* to do it."

And what of the sacrifice entailed in becoming a dancer?

"I don't really believe that a dancer sacrifices too much," Miss Seymour said. "Of course, it would appear that I had to sacrifice a personal life. I think you also sacrifice a lot of nerve ends. Then, there's the education. I'm not the kind of supercharged person like Nureyev who goes out and is constantly learning about things. He's rabid for knowledge, and he has enough energy to go after it. I'm sorry I've missed a lot of formal education, but when you're studying to be a dancer, it's like being punch-drunk in a funny way. You're just too tired to be able to study. It's only when I've been laid off or ill that I've actually consumed books and gone to see things. It's at times like that that I say to myself, Good Lord, this is stupid, I'm just like a vegetable. I should know more. But when you're working, you're in that scene, and it's about all you have time for. Despite it all, I have no regrets about being a dancer. No regrets at all."

Roy Round

MONICA MASON

There is nothing quite so disturbing as seeing a ballerina on crutches. But that was how Monica Mason greeted me at the door of her London apartment in Heatherfield Gardens. The dancer was injured while performing as the Queen of the Wilis in *Giselle* during the Royal Ballet summer season of 1972. Miss Mason, one of the company's most brilliant dancers, did not let the impediment of crutches interfere with her buoyant good spirits or indeed with her extraordinary appearance. She is among the tallest of the Royal's principal dancers, with splendid, open, patrician features. We sat in her sunny living room, Miss Mason's injured foot in a cast raised onto a small stool. She explained what had happened:

"I was preparing my first big jumping entrance as the Queen of the Wilis. When I landed on the stage, my foot caught on something and it got stuck. It turned sideways. It was very strange. Everything seemed to happen in slow motion. I heard something snap. It sounded like a pistol crack. Actually, I had broken the tiniest bone near my little toe. So, of course, I couldn't finish the performance. And I've been out for a month now."

Monica Mason was born in Johannesburg, South Africa, on September 6, 1941. As a very young child, she loved hopping and skipping to music. When she turned nine, she was exposed to ballet by way of visits of the Sadler's Wells. She recalled the joy on the dancers' faces as they performed, the happy expressions. It seemed to her that dancers must all be very happy people. When Monica was twelve, her father died and two years later her mother, wanting a change of scene, decided to move to London. Someone suggested that Monica try to get into the Royal Ballet School. She auditioned and entered the school at the age of fifteen. Her very rapid advance resulted in her joining the company within a year. For the next five years she danced in the *corps*, and when she turned twenty Kenneth MacMillan chose her as lead dancer for his ballet *The Rite of Spring*.

"You can imagine my shock. I was still in the *corps*, and suddenly Mr. MacMillan was going to create a ballet on me. I remember when we first started working on it, we used a little studio that no longer exists at Barons Court. We used to work, just he and I and the pianist, from eleven at night until one-thirty in the morning. We did that for about three weeks, to get that last solo done. What was so amazing to me was that MacMillan would not do anything on *pointe*. It was unlike any ballet I'd ever done. And so, I was given this lovely thing to do, and when opening night came it was really something. The Queen Mother was there . . . the Queen Mum."

Miss Mason in MacMillan's *The Rite of Spring* was a triumph, and the dancer was made a soloist in the company. She danced innumerable solo roles, then, four years later, in 1968, was made a principal.

"Just before I was made a principal, I had to do a complete *Swan Lake*. I learned it from Michael Somes, and he was absolutely marvelous. He taught it step by step. And he's a perfectionist. I remember his saying 'My girl, you're going to dance the lead in *Swan Lake*. Remember that this ballet is only as good as its ballerina. Of course, it sent me into shakes."

Miss Mason's first Swan Queen was a great success, and she dances the role to this day with particular finesse and *brio*. Because of her height, she lends special regality to the role. But this quality attends everything she dances. Her movements are clear and crisp yet sumptuously lyrical. Her bearing, the manner in which she holds her head, and her exquisite *port de bras* combine to produce in her dancing a great authority, immediacy, and precision. But Miss Mason can also deliver impetuosity and humor. This comes strikingly to the fore when she essays roles such as one of the Harlots in MacMillan's *Romeo and Juliet* or as the Hostess in *Les Biches*. An added sense of urgency contrives to give the impression that the dancer strives for a certain kind of attention. This last characteristic has at times been translated as fierce ambition within the ranks of the company.

"People always used to say to me that I gave the impression of being desperately ambitious from the moment I joined the company," Miss Mason said. "The truth is that it's not a question of ambition, but just an enormous desire to improve myself. I can honestly say that not for a moment did I think, Gosh, I'm going to be a soloist . . . I'm going to be a principal. It really never entered my head. When I joined the company I was utterly absorbed in doing what I was doing at the time. I was terribly keen on doing what I was doing as well as possible. My goal was simply to improve more and more. And I had such really tremendous dancers around me—people like Fonteyn, Nerina, Beriosova, who all danced gloriously. It just made you strive to be better. Then, when you've tasted a little bit of success, and when you know that the applause is really for you . . . then it starts. You start to think, Gosh, this is really nice. I mean, not from the point of view of the audience liking you, so much as desiring to do *more*—to do something bigger. You suddenly get the mad desire to say something of your own."

I ask Miss Mason whether she could describe the particular quality of her own dancing.

"I think that I don't really fall into the strictly classical format. I somehow don't fit into the role of a British classical dancer. I'm really too tall—five-foot-six. When I joined the Royal Ballet all the ballerinas, with the exception of Svetlana Beriosova, tended to be Margot's size. They were small, with probably better proportioned bodies than my own. I think that everything about my style of dancing is far more modern. Also, it's dramatically inclined. I seem not to be of the Old World. And yet, to dance *Swan Lake* continues to be a challenge. I mean, it's really a fairy tale that should have long ago become old hat and boring. But because the story is so very dramatic, it keeps readjusting itself to present-day implications. I don't think it can ever wear out. So, a dancer of today *can* make *Swan Lake* a story of today. I think this is the way I approach it."

There is no question but that Monica Mason exudes an enormous drive.

"When I was twelve and going to school in Johannesburg," she recalled, "I had a very unsympathetic headmistress. She certainly didn't like the ballet. Whenever I tried to get out of hockey or tennis, she never would let me off. But the moment someone tried to stop me from going to my lessons, the desire to do so became stronger and stronger. I used to think up the most outrageous excuses. In the end I'd become quite daring. You see, I felt that I was wasting my time running around the hockey field. I used to spend all my time keeping out of the way, trying not to get hurt. Anyway, nothing could keep me from my ballet lessons. Those very early years were actually quite wonderful. I never knew the meaning of spare time. I didn't know what it was like to sit and think, Oh, what shall I do with myself? That's why with this bad foot I'm sort of going batty. I mean, in a way it's wonderful to sit and do nothing. I am usually so tied into a routine."

Despite an all-consuming schedule, Miss Mason found time to marry a fellow dancer, Austin Bennett. The two have been married four years.

"I met Austin in the company, and he was at the same stage as I was. He was getting to do solos. But he got a knee injury—a very serious one—and he had to give up dancing. He's now with a music firm. Having been a dancer, he is totally understanding of what it's all about. We just get on marvelously."

We then touched upon dancing a major role such as Odette–Odile.

"Well, the most important thing is concentration," Miss Mason said. "You must shut out everything else. You don't want to be distracted or disturbed in any way. When you dance the Swan Queen, you want to feel that you've got wings instead of elbows and wrists. You become who you are supposed to be. Of course, you're continually listening for the music. The more you dance, the more you listen for the *quality* of the music—not just the rhythmic oompah-pahs. You must realize that it's not just a matter of stepping left-right, left-right. It's all about being expressive . . . of feeling something. Remember that dancers hear music very differently.

"When I was asked to create my role in *The Rite of Spring*, I played the Stravinsky music on the record player incessantly—so much so that my sister said that in the end even the dog could have danced it. It's a question of immersing yourself in the music until it becomes part of you."

We turned to the question of partnering.

"It took me a long while to find the people I most like to dance with. I can't think of anybody in the company that I've *disliked* dancing with because you're always two people struggling to achieve something together. Sometimes it doesn't work. But you can't really dislike somebody or hate them when this happens. You just find that you're not thinking along the same lines. When I did my first *Swan Lake* I was partnered by Desmond Doyle. He was just marvelous, and so sympathetic. Then I danced *Swan Lake* with Keith Rosson. He was, of course, much younger than Desmond, and that was fascinating because the two of us were trying to find a way together. Then I started doing quite a few performances with Donald Macleary. I'm going to be bold and say that he's probably the finest partner that one could possibly work with. He has an uncanny ability to anticipate trouble. He knows something is going to go wrong even before it's started to go wrong. He's just part of you. I've also danced with

Christopher Gable. He had such firm, firm ideas about what he wanted to do. He was extraordinarily sensitive.

"Then, I suppose, the next big break was to dance with Rudolf Nureyev. The first thing we did together was a *Swan Lake* in New York. It was the most amazing thing, because, next to being told I was going to do *The Rite of Spring*, it was a great shock to be told that Rudolf wanted to do a *Swan Lake* with me. I was so frightened the first rehearsal that I really couldn't speak. I didn't understand at all how to begin to work with him. I mean, when you are left alone with somebody in the rehearsal room together with a pianist and *that* somebody is Rudolf Nureyev, you really think, How do I begin? . . . What does he want of me? And, of course, he's so positive and so understanding. Yet, at the same time, he won't tolerate people who won't think. He's very impatient with people who don't know what they want. At the time, he must have realized that I was absolutely petrified. Still, by the time of the performance, I understood what he wanted and what I wanted. With Rudolf, it is the Now that is the important moment. What I've learned from Rudolf is to give the utmost. He's so passionate. He's so believable. He creates such a living thing for you when you're dancing with him. When he comes toward you, he's not just looking at you as a Prince, he's looking at you as Rudolf, and you know what Rudolf means. It means everything. It means you've got to *be* there. And it's got to be *right*. When I dance with him, he extends me so much. He makes me feel full, and stretched right to the last degree.

"He pours himself into every performance. That is why if ·something goes badly he gets very angry. He wouldn't dream of covering it up. He's furious because he hasn't been right—and he knows what he can do. That's what enrages him. He's so honest. Honesty is one of the most important things you learn when you work with Nureyev. He can't stand it if you say that something is all right if you don't really think it is. He always knows when you're pretending. You know, the English are always so reticent and polite. We tend to cover up, and that is what Rudolf finds so hard to take. Anyway, to dance with Rudolf is something quite fabulous."

Sitting there with her crutches at her side Miss Mason is visibly moved by the memory of her partnership with Rudolf Nureyev. It makes her doubly impatient to be indisposed. I comment on the relatively short life-span of a dancer.

"Yes, we actually have very few years. But then, I think that there are so very few people in the world who ever really get the chance to do what they want to do. For myself, if I stop dancing when I'm thirty-five, or if I'm lucky enough to go on until I'm forty, I would know that for fifteen or twenty years I've had the most fantastic life with the Royal Ballet. That's what's so worthwhile—to have had the chance to do and say what you've wanted to do and say.

"To be a dancer can be the most fulfilling thing. Of course, the life is all work. Anyone who wants to embark on it must be prepared for work, work, work. Also, it is important to watch and to listen. You learn so much by watching and listening. I think we've been very lucky in the Royal Ballet because so many great people have come to rehearse us and to teach us. For example, every time we used to put on *Petrouchka* or *Firebird* or *Les Sylphides*, the Grigorievs would come. Sergei Grigoriev was the *régisseur* with the Diaghilev company. Mrs. Grigoriev was the great ballerina Lubov Tchernicheva, who danced with Diaghilev. They would come and they would just sit and talk to us. Tchernicheva could say more in one sentence than you felt you could learn in a week of classes. She could express something so beautifully. And she could show us something so beautifully. When Nijinska came and mounted *Les Biches* and *Les Noces* for us, she could barely speak English. But she didn't need the language, because she could show it. And it was the same quality that this old woman projected that gave us such insight into these works.

"You know, people are always saying we've become so technically assured. But the thing we must never lose sight of is that in our striving for technical brilliance, we mustn't lose the quality of theater. When you're dancing a ballet like *Firebird*, you mustn't just think about the steps, but of the quality of the movements—the quality of the story—the quality of the music. Ultimately, if you're going to be a dancer you must never lose sight of the reason you're dancing. Of course, when one is young and a student, you are so busy watching and learning that you can't assimilate everything all at once. But, ultimately, the thing that you have to learn is that you are there to create something—that you are there to give life and meaning to something that is so very fugitive."

Roy Round

DEANNE BERGSMA

Another small and charming English garden. This one is rather jungle-like. Bushes, plants, flowers intermingle in freewheeling confusion. A great bushy cat slowly stalks amidst the greenery. The fawnlike beauty of Deanne Bergsma completes this lush tableau.

"The cat's name is Tamara. My husband found it, she's not named after anybody. It's because she's a Russian Blue. So she has a Russian name."

Miss Bergsma wears her hair in a pony tail just now. There is something tremulous in her smile, and when she speaks her voice has the delicate inflection of a child's. She is the tallest of the Royal Ballet's principal dancers. ("I've never measured myself. I would say I'm five-seven. I might be a little more or less.") This afternoon—there are some clouds—she wears a white shirt under a white sweater and black slacks. She was born in Harrismith, South Africa in 1941. She and her family moved to Pretoria when Deanne was four years old. There was a dancing school in the garden of the house where she lived, and that is how it all started. She went to school and took ballet classes in the afternoon. At twelve, she participated in the Royal Academy of Dancing exams. She was noticed and was invited to come to London to study at the Royal Ballet School. She and her mother booked passage and when they arrived in London, mother and daughter moved into a boarding house. Deanne began her studies.

"Frankly, we couldn't stand it. I spent three months at the Royal Ballet School and I loathed every second of it. And living in one room was simply impossible. My poor mother was just sitting there with nothing to do. We packed up and went straight back to South Africa. I finished my schooling and I spent a normal, healthy life, which I think was the making of me. If I had been shoved into a boarding school, I would've turned out quite differently. Before I left London, I was told that if I didn't put on a lot of weight I could rejoin the school. So, at age fifteen I went back to London, only to come down with a case of diphtheria.

"I went straight home again. Actually, it was quite awful because the doctor listened to my heart and said, 'My dear, you must give up all idea of dancing.' Well, that was fine with me. I really *didn't* want to dance any more. I was feeling rotten. I just wanted to stay home and forget all about it. When I got well again and it was ascertained that my heart was back to normal, the desire to dance came back. Once more I flew back to London. I was sixteen. After a year at Barons Court I joined the company, in the *corps de ballet*. However, I started doing solos the minute I got in. I was lucky. In some ways, being tall helped; in others, it didn't, because there are certain roles I can't do. When I turned eighteen I danced the Lilac Fairy and Queen of the Wilis. I've been a principal dancer since 1965.

"Dancing is best for me when something else takes over—when you are absolutely lost, and your body is simply an instrument that lets you do what you want to do. I like being carried away—lifted off. I believe that in order to dance a major role like the Swan Queen it is helpful to be immersed in life. Ballerinas are generally shielded and protected because of their rigid schedules. I don't like being protected very much because, then, you cannot feel the roles you dance. I think the dancer should garner as much life experience as possible. I don't like being enclosed in the magic circle that is the Ballet.

"In *Swan Lake*, when you lose your Prince, you've got to *know* what that feels like. You've got to live through the pain."

Bergsma's *Swan Lake* is a study in poignancy and bravura. But then, these qualities are her particular hallmark. In a way, she consumes the stage with her statuesque and dramatic presence. Her long, long legs and arms sweep the stage. And yet she contrives to lend delicacy and refinement to her every movement. Too, her interpretative approach is at all times believable. Bergsma *feels*. Her Lilac Fairy is goodness personified. Her Queen of the Wilis is the essence of mystery. In the classics, Bergsma projects a dreamy, floating quality. But Bergsma is not all gossamer and filigree wings. She can move with iron strength and staccato brilliance whenever it's demanded. Thus, the rarity of her dancing. One of her special qualities is ambiguousness, charged with emotional and intellectual experience.

While her Swan Queen resides in life, she is equally adept at abstract characterization. In Glen Tetley's *Field Figures*, for example, Miss Bergsma assimilates the classic technique with a free-flowing, almost improvised bravado. We discuss the experience of dancing to Karlheinz Stockhausen's music, which serves as its score.

"You've just got to know the music very well," says Miss Bergsma. "Then, you get rather fond of those plinks and plunks. You try to get to a certain place in a certain time in the movement. The key is awareness. You've got to be aware all the time. You've got to be aware of what the other dancers are doing. You've got to be aware of what the orchestra is doing. Of course, learning *Field Figures* was absolute torture. We'd never done anything like it at the Royal Ballet. It took us three months to learn. There are so many contortions, so much intertwining with your partners.

"Nureyev was my partner in *Field Figures*. He was difficult in rehearsals. I mean, he might just drop you on the floor . . . splat! He's done it many times. He was probably just tired, but during performance, he's marvelous. Everything works. At any rate, when you dance in a ballet like *Field Figures*, you've got to learn to anticipate *everything*. It's difficult, but also immensely releasing. It is an extension of everything you've learned from the classics."

Miss Bergsma is married to Keith Grant, who is the opera manager at Covent Garden. They have been married four years.

"It's working out marvelously, because we have a chance to see each other—we work in the same place. You know, he can pop out of his office and see how things are doing on the stage. Also, when I'm dancing and I have nothing to do during one whole act, I can pop in to see him."

I ask Miss Bergsma to reveal the most important qualifications for the making of a dancer.

"You have to have talent to begin with. But more than that, you've got to have determination. Also, you must have a very good mind. You've got to have a mind that's going to make your body do what you want it to do. It's not a question of intellect but of a kind of mental strength. That's what

Margot Fonteyn has. She doesn't let herself go for a moment, mentally. That's what's so sensational about Margot. She's so brave. Because sometimes you can see that she is in pain, and that she's dead tired, and nothing is working. She just can't get up on her feet, and you wonder how she's ever going to do it. I'm now talking about rehearsals. In a performance, it's quite another matter. She's brilliant. But that's what I mean. It's simply mental. Margot *makes* herself do it."

How does Bergsma feel before a *Swan Lake*?

"It all begins a week before the performance. A week before, you start to get very silent and moody. Your husband knows you've got to do a *Swan Lake*. You've got the *Swan Lake* blues. It's like a mountain that you have to climb. It's just there. And you've got five thousand shoes to prepare, and one rehearsal might work and another won't work. Then there's always the danger, at the last moment, that your partner gets ill or injured and you've got to do something quickly with somebody else.

"The *day* is always the same. The day of performance. You're so alone it's just horrible. You've got to cook your own steak, and you've got to shove it down your throat at about three o'clock in the afternoon. Then you sleep, and when you wake up you've got this awful feeling. I have a cup of tea, maybe. I get to Covent Garden. I go to my dressing room. Then, gradually, as you're putting on your make-up, you're gearing yourself for the ordeal. You warm up. Then you start getting a little more courage when you start talking to the other dancers. They may be joking. It's a relief—that. You start trying a few pirouettes, and you always go and watch the Prince do his solo. He usually inspires you. You stand in the wings, and you are lost in a maze of Swans. There's such a fluster of Swans getting to the rosin box. And they go on. And you know you're going to be the next one. And you pray. It's at this moment that you have simply got to forget about the whole thing, and just go on and do it. You've got to take each step as it comes, and you must try desperately to enjoy it. It takes years to do a good Swan Queen. I don't know if I'll ever achieve the perfection I strive for."

Miss Bergsma pauses, lifts her head, and smiles. "Dancing is an ordeal. But then, isn't everything?" Because of Miss Bergsma's husband's position at Covent Garden, there is a certain amount of socializing that she must do.

"We do go out. But I don't enjoy parties. They make me very nervous. I find it hard to communicate. You see, in class we don't talk. During rehearsals, we don't talk. You just look at yourself. Then, suddenly, you've got to communicate with speech. You must speak to your dinner partner. It's so strange speaking with your language and not your body. It is strange. I can communicate best by dancing. My own hell can be lived in dance. One certainly did that in *Labyrintus*, which I'm dancing this season. It's in that kind of ballet that you can be at one with the fact that you can't really ever get away from yourself. You can never break away. Other people are always bringing you back. It is like life, you know. Sometimes it's like wanting to chuck your whole career—and then you're drawn back and you find you're doing class and rehearsal. And all those mirrors that keep pulling you back. You keep on seeing yourself—thousands of you."

MICHAEL COLEMAN
and JENNIFER PENNEY

wo of the most enchanting and popular Royal Ballet dancers are
Michael Coleman and Jennifer Penney. Miss Penney is a slight, ethereal
looking girl, with small, delicate features, deep-set eyes, and a flawless
skin. She suggests a Fra Angelico angel. Coleman is extremely boyish,
invariably good-humored, with a wide and mischievous grin that continually lights up his charming, uneven features.

The two share their lives together in a neat little house in Chiswick, a
London area not far from Barons Court. Both Penney and Coleman are

principal dancers with the company, dancing major roles, though not necessarily together. They are not a duo à la Sibley and Dowell. On a sunny afternoon, the two young dancers made time for an interview. Miss Penney, wearing a brown T shirt and slacks and tiny gold earrings, prepared the obligatory tea. Mr. Coleman, in a yellow T shirt and mauve-and-blue-striped slacks, gingerly helped with the preparations.

For lack of a coffee table in their modest living room—it had been ordered, but had not yet arrived—we drank our tea cross-legged on the floor. They each began to tell me something about themselves.

"I was born in Vancouver, B.C., on April 5, 1946," Miss Penney said. "I started dancing lessons when I turned eleven. It was my grandmother who sent me to dancing school, and I honestly don't remember why—probably to get me out of the house. I was extremely indifferent to the dance. Actually, I used to hide in the orchard, because I didn't want to go to classes. I had absolutely no ambition to become a ballerina. Then, I began enjoying it a bit more. I began going twice a week, and would go into competition and win a ribbon or something, which I suppose gave me some incentive. As time went on, the lessons increased—and that was sort of that. At sixteen, I came to London and I got into the company. I was just lucky, I guess. I danced in the *corps* for about three years, and was given a chance to do solo things. About two years ago I became a principal."

Pouring out some tea, Michael Coleman told me that he also had no great initial desire to become a dancer:

"I didn't ever want to dance. I did it because all my friends did it at school. They used to go to tap lessons, and so I did, too."

Coleman was born in East London on June 10, 1940. His father was killed in World War II, and Michael lived at home with his mother and sister. By fourteen, Michael took some ballet classes together with his tap dancing. At fifteen, he decided to leave school and work as a copyboy for a small London newspaper, a job which soon disenchanted him. Next, he worked for a photographer and enjoyed the experience. Photography remains one of his hobbies. When Michael turned seventeen, he auditioned at Barons Court and was accepted. After two years of study, he joined the touring section of the company, then came to the principal company at Covent Garden two years later.

"There I was at Covent Garden, dancing with the company for about a year and a half, when I was again sent out with the touring company. I think for youngsters of nineteen and twenty, it's a marvelous experience. We toured the provinces and did foreign tours. You progressed much faster because you did so much more work and under bad conditions—bad stages, etc. Anyway, after a while, they sent me back to Covent Garden, but, believe it or not, I was again sent on tour, and I was beginning to feel that what I really wanted was to dance in one place. I mean, by then, I was already twenty-five years old. Finally, they let me stay put at Covent Garden, and, about four years ago, I became principal dancer."

When Coleman was twenty-three, he married one of the young dancers in the touring section. Four years later they were divorced. He and Jennifer Penney met in 1967, fell in love, and sometime later began living together.

When watching Penney and Coleman perform onstage, their artistry comes stunningly to the fore. Jennifer Penney, while perhaps not yet mature enough to give total depth to the classic roles, is possessed of an oddly moving poignancy. Her Swan Queen has a lightness and agility that is altogether remarkable; a special sweetness attends her Aurora—and her approach to the several classic roles she dances is never less than dramatically sound and technically brilliant. She conveys a youthful innocence that lends particular credibility to these roles.

Michael Coleman, for his part, is a dancer of extraordinary lightness and grace. His Blue Bird in *Sleeping Beauty* would be rare to match for its sense of miraculous suspension and agile clarity of line. His Mercutio in *Romeo and Juliet* is a study in wit, and dramatic braggadocio.

The conversation between the three of us on the floor turned to pleasant banter. We sat there like three characters in a playlet about ballet dancing. The playlet went something like this:

GRUEN: We all know that you have to work like dogs, but what I'm trying to get at are some of the by-products that go with creating a role. Jennifer, what goes through you when you dance?

PENNEY: That really depends on what I'm dancing. The feelings are different with each different role.

GRUEN: Well, what about *Swan Lake*?

PENNEY: It's terror. If you think less about the nasty things that you have to do technically, and just get into the story, you'll be all right. I usually fall in with the things that are going on around me—the continuity of the story that's being told. It takes your mind off the technical things.

GRUEN: When you're standing in the wings waiting to go on, what propels you onto the stage?

PENNEY: Absolute nerves. Nervous tension.

GRUEN: How do you handle nerves?

PENNEY: I don't handle them terribly well. But, in fact, I think they're very necessary. I can't imagine being without them. That's how a dancer just gets on the stage and by dancing gets rid of all that nervous energy.

GRUEN: And what about you, Michael? What propels *you* onto the stage? What are your thoughts? What happens?

COLEMAN: Well, in the classics, you just do what you can do. Your body can either do it or it can't. I mean, you have to put your mind to it. For me, I think I'm only being myself in a different set of circumstances. I don't really try to be a different person when I take on a role. I try to be more myself. I also try very hard to keep my sense of humor about everything. I try to make myself enjoy things.

GRUEN: When you have to take over a role previously done by another dancer, does the choreographer come in and teach it to you, or does the previous dancer help you?

COLEMAN: Usually it's the previous dancer. We are all natural mimics, and so it's easier to learn the role from someone who's danced it before.

GRUEN: And what about your nerves problem?

COLEMAN: Well, I definitely have nerves.

PENNEY: When Michael dances, everybody thinks he is the calmest person—that he never gets nervous.

COLEMAN: The way I handle my nerves is that I'm always trying to make people laugh. Actually, I try to keep a very simple philosophy about it all. I try to make everyone enjoy what they're seeing. I mean, basically, this is entertainment. If people want to consider it an art, that's okay, too. But our job is to entertain people.

GRUEN: Has Rudolf Nureyev's presence made any difference to you, Michael, as a dancer?

COLEMAN: Yes. I have the greatest admiration for him. I suppose we all copy things from him. It's not a conscious thing, but something seeps in, anyway. We have a very good relationship.

PENNEY: He's dreamy.

GRUEN: Not everyone adores him.

PENNEY: Well, he can be as evil as the next person.

COLEMAN: Sometimes he's full of shit—but aren't we all?

PENNEY: Six days out of seven, Rudy is wonderful.

COLEMAN: One must always remember that if we feel that we're on razor blades sometimes, Rudy's even more so. He works so hard. It's unbelievable. I've never seen anyone work like that.

PENNEY: Actually, it makes you feel guilty.

GRUEN: Has he ever partnered you?

PENNEY: We did *Afternoon of a Faun*. He was very gentle. He even apologized a few times. He takes everything so seriously. I mean, the few times Michael and I have danced together, he might be laughing behind his eyes, but Rudolf doesn't fool around much onstage.

GRUEN: What are the tortures of being a ballet dancer?

COLEMAN: It's like going to the dentist every single day.

PENNEY: Then, there's the continual competition. I find *that* hard. It's especially hard on us girls because there are so many good ones. The young ones are so eager. They work terribly hard because they realize that after awhile some of us get a bit tired. Someone is always at your heels dying for the chance to take your place. You can't ever relax.

COLEMAN: Yes, there's always that undercurrent within our company. Actually, this competitiveness keeps you on a constant alert.

GRUEN: Nevertheless, you love being with the Royal Ballet.

COLEMAN: Yes, I have a great loyalty to it. I think the company will go on, no matter what happens. If an atom bomb dropped, it would just carry on and get on with the job. It's fantastic.

GRUEN: Jennifer, what's it like living with a dancer? Some dancers prefer sharing their lives with someone who's completely away from the dance.

PENNEY: Well, not ever having lived with someone who wasn't a dancer, I don't really know. Actually, there's so much you've got to understand about a dancer's life. The odd hours, the feeling tired, the going away on tour. Someone who is not a dancer would never understand this. I couldn't imagine coming home to someone who had been at the office all day.

COLEMAN: I think after having been a dancer, you could never do a nine-to-five job. We see people in the underground who all look like zombies.

PENNEY: Yes. We complain all the time, but deep down, we think we're really very lucky.

GRUEN: Now, Michael, talk about partnering. You've danced with most of the principals in the company. Isn't there one you'd like to partner on a more permanent basis—have a partnership like Sibley and Dowell?

COLEMAN: Not really, I think I'm fortunate in that I haven't been labeled. Actually, I think it's a very good thing *not* to be working with one person all of the time, because you create bad habits. It's much better for everyone to be able to do anything with any partner.

GRUEN: What about some of the technical aspects of partnering? How do you lift all these girls?

COLEMAN: It has to do with coordination—using the muscles in your arms at the same time that you use the muscles in your legs. It's coordinated with the girl's use of her legs. It all comes together. Then, of course, there is the question of balance. It's no good trying to lift a girl if she's miles away from you. You have to get right underneath. Balance comes first. If you're not on balance, you can't even . . . pick your nose. I dropped a lot of girls when I started out. I was so tiny—I was minute. I hated it all when I started out, and I really had to push to make myself stronger.

GRUEN: How *does* one get stronger?

COLEMAN: You just make yourself do it. You work and you work. I always felt so stupid when I saw all those huge, big, handsome fellows around me, who could do everything. I just pushed myself to a point where I could do everything with as much ease as possible. It takes a lot of will power.

GRUEN: How do you feel about ballet criticism?

PENNEY: We never read it. It's better not to because it can upset you too much.

COLEMAN: We listen to the public. It's the audience that tells you if you're good or not. From a technical point of view, you can't really listen to a critic. You listen to the boss—the choreographer, the teacher—because they've all been dancers, and they *know*. I don't think one should get hung up on what the critics say.

PENNEY: It's so destructive, criticism. Especially for young dancers. I mean, a girl who's been working for ten years, day after day, and who then gets a chance to perform would just go to pieces if she were given an awful write-up.

GRUEN: What would you like to do once you decide to stop dancing?

PENNEY: I'd definitely like to have a child. It's not to be missed. Dancing is part of your life, but it's not all of your life. Of course, I'd like to wait as long as possible. I'd like to dance a lot, because I know that when I stop I'll probably never go back to dancing.

COLEMAN: It worries me sick to think of what I'm going to do afterward. I suppose I could teach, but I don't know if I'd be passionately interested in it. I'd really have to do something that provides me with a real challenge, and, right now, I don't know what that would be once I stop dancing.

ANN JENNER

principal with the Royal Ballet, Ann Jenner is Miss Electricity. Young, pert, large of eyes and pointed of chin, her very slim figure darts and dashes across the Covent Garden stage with particular speed and energy. To see Ann Jenner do the Neapolitan Dance in *Swan Lake* is to know the meaning of unbridled exuberance and vivaciousness. She was born on March 8, 1944, in Surrey. She went to the Baron School of Dancing when she was six, then went to audition at the Royal Ballet School and passed, much to her own and her parents' amazement. Ann was nine years old. After two years of study at Barons Court, she attended the White Lodge School at Richmond Park, where she remained until the age of sixteen. By seventeen she entered the *corps* of the Royal Ballet. She has been a principal of that company since 1969.

Deeply committed to her career, Miss Jenner offered some views on the life of a ballerina when I talked to her in the flat she shares with her husband, Christopher Gridley:

"I thought that when I got into the *corps de ballet*, life was going to be very easy—that it would be plain sailing. Well, I must say, that when you move up, things get harder and harder. In the *corps*, you're one of many, you're in a line, you don't have the responsibility that you do when you move up. It's awful when you're beginning to be on your own, with the audience out there. When you get to be a principal, the strain is really terribly hard.

"I take a class a day each morning at ten fifteen, except Sunday. Then I usually rehearse until half past five—that is, if there isn't a performance that night. When I dance in *Sleeping Beauty* it just kills me for the next few days. Nevertheless, on the very next morning, you're back in class with everybody else. Your performance is gone, it's past, it's finished, it's forgotten. You're back exactly where you were."

Miss Jenner speaks rapidly, and flashes frequent smiles. She is indeed quite beautiful, and I tell her so.

"Oh, thank you, but I always think I look rather hideous. It's because in this profession one spends one's whole life looking at oneself in the mirror. Finally, all you begin to see is what's wrong with you. You never see what's right. I don't think dancers are very good judges of what they really look like. I think it's because we criticize ourselves to an absolutely fantastic degree. I've been dancing twenty-two years. To most people, that's an eternity. Most people don't realize that one can still be quite young and have danced for twenty-two years."

One of Ann Jenner's qualities on the stage is a certain eagerness. It is an eagerness to please, and an eagerness inherent in her style of dancing. One senses the tremendous wish to succeed. I mention this to her, and she readily agrees:

"Oh, yes. People are always complaining that I've got too much personality. Of course, I think the audience likes that. But I don't think the management likes it that much. They like more uniformity of behavior on the stage. I always seem to stick out like a sore thumb. But that's because I enjoy dancing so much. I feel that the main aim of a dancer is to give pleasure. I mean, that's what you're there for, isn't it?"

When I interviewed Ann Jenner she had just danced Aurora in *The Sleeping Beauty*. This experience of doing a major role prompted my asking the young dancer precisely what happens on the day of such a performance.

"Well, it starts out with my going to class in the morning, as usual. Then, there is rehearsal. Management tries to give you the afternoon off if you have a performance like *Beauty* that night. I'm not really the sort of person who can go home and go to sleep when I've got something like that to do. And so, I keep my mind occupied with other things. Then I get to the theater early and start putting on my make-up. Then, of course, there is the business of wearing your shoes in. You have to bang them on the floor; you have to sew on ribbons—and all that. You have to walk around in your shoes so that they bend into the shape of your foot. They have to have the right softness or hardness.

"After you've made up and have your toe shoes in order, you sort of prepare a little tray with hairpins, comb, mirror, and you bring it backstage with you. Then, holding onto a piece of scenery or something, you do a warm-up. Of course, you also bring along six pairs of toe shoes to choose from. You need three pairs of shoes for *Beauty*. You choose your shoes according to how you feel in each act. For example, there are those that are best for balancing on one foot. Anyway, it takes quite a while to sort all that out. After that, you have some drink—some juice or a cup of tea, because you've got a half-hour before you go on. *Beauty* has a rather long Prologue in which Aurora doesn't appear. Then, there's that awful moment, while the Garland Dance is going on, and you know that when it's over, you've got to come out and do the Rose Adagio. You're standing there at the top of the steps. I can't tell you what it's like. It's as though someone's got hold of your stomach and tied two knots. You feel as if you want to turn around, rush out the stage door, and never come back. That's how awful your nerves can be before the Rose Adagio.

"You can't imagine what it's like holding onto one person and having him lift you up, and having to balance on one leg, knowing that the whole opera house is looking at you, plus all the people around the stage, including your own teacher, Gerd Larsen, sitting there on the throne as Berthe, your Queen Mother. It's terror. Once you've got the Rose Adagio over with, you feel better. If you've done it well, you've got more confidence. You feel you've achieved something—because that section is probably the most terrifying thing in the whole of dancing."

Eyes lit up, and sitting practically at the edge of the couch, Miss Jenner relives the agony and the ecstasy of her *Sleeping Beauty* performance. In her pretty navy blue dress she seems like an alert bird ready for flight. Having told her story, she now leans back and relaxes.

"People think that being a ballet dancer is the easiest thing in the world. They forget that they only see the finished product. People have said to me, 'It's a lovely life you lead. But what do you do with yourself during the day?' You see, they all think that you spend your whole day sitting around. They don't think that you've got to rehearse, take class, or prepare for a performance. It makes me livid."

Many dancers prefer to be married to other dancers. Miss Jenner is not one of them, but she is clearly lucky in her marriage.

"Christopher adores the dance. But he's in a whole other business. He works for UNIVAC—the big computer center. Being married to a dancer is never easy, but if you've got a husband like mine, it's marvelous. He's patient. He's understanding. Actually, we lead a very odd life. I may be off to performances four nights a week, and Christopher comes home to an empty flat. When I can, I leave him something to eat in the fridge. He never complains. The only time he gets angry is when I come home looking like death-warmed-over with my face all sunken in. He can't cope with the possibility of my getting ill. Anyway, we don't have a social life like other people. We can't have friends to dinner because I haven't got the time to get the food in and get it ready. Also, there are so many things I'm not allowed to do. I'm not allowed to ski, to ice skate, to ride a horse, to water-ski. It sounds ridiculous, but once you've broken a foot, you're out for ages. Anyway, Christopher, who loves all of these things, is terribly understanding about it. All I can say is that, when I retire, I shall make it all up to him.

"Of course, I could never last as long as Margot. She's incredible. I haven't got the discipline. I haven't got the strength. I couldn't do it. I think my achievement is to have become a principal dancer. To think of all the many girls who started out with me at school and didn't achieve that! I think that if I did Giselle, then I could quite happily retire. In a funny sort of way, I'm quite looking forward to having my freedom. It would be such absolute bliss not to have to live on schedule. It would be like a whole ton of bricks taken off my head. In the meantime, I'll go on. I think that when one reaches the age of thirty-five, then that is the time when you should start thinking about retirement. When that time comes, I will have children, and perhaps do something in a hospital. I'm fascinated by hospitals. Anyway, I've still got a bit of time before all that comes about."

Roy Round

GERD LARSEN

One of the Royal Ballet's principal teachers and character dancers, Gerd Larsen was born in Oslo, Norway. Her family had no interest in the theater. But young Gerd was continually listening to music over the radio and going to concerts. Eventually, she learned to play the piano. When she was eight years old, she began taking dancing lessons at the lone dancing school in Oslo. After some years, the child told her parents that she wanted to go to England, half pretending that it was to learn the language. Actually, she wanted to continue her dancing lessons. She had heard that there were excellent schools in England. Her parents thought their daughter's interest in the dance was only a foolish notion, but soon realized she was quite serious. They allowed her to travel to England on the condition that she also finish her formal schooling there.

In London she studied with Antony Tudor and began performing with the London Ballet. Later, she danced with Ballet Rambert and with the International Ballet. Her ultimate goal was to join the Sadler's Wells. When she auditioned for Ninette de Valois, she was told to return in a year—which she did. She was accepted into the Sadler's Wells company and entered the *corps*, remaining with it for several more years. In 1954, she was promoted to soloist. By 1956 Gerd Larsen had danced several major roles, but the management soon discovered that her forte was in creating extraordinary mime parts, such as Berthe in *Giselle*, the Queen in *The Sleeping Beauty*, the Prince's Mother in *Swan Lake*, and the Nurse in *Romeo and Juliet*. It was also discovered that Miss Larsen had great potential as a teacher, and to this day she teaches advanced and company classes at the Royal Ballet.

An enormously witty and charming woman, Gerd Larsen made me feel extremely welcome when I paid her a visit in her London duplex in the summer of 1972. Blue-eyed and blonde, she exudes a Scandinavian vigor. Her manner, however, was decidedly English, and following the English tradition, I was offered tea and biscuits. We began discussing her life as teacher.

"I was always inquisitive," she told me, "and so, when the company began to travel, say, to La Scala, Milan, or to New York or to Russia, I would look in on other companies to observe their teaching methods. I visited the Bolshoi School and the Kirov. I remember in Leningrad walking down Theatre Street and entering the famous Kirov Theatre School. I had just finished reading Madame Karsavina's memoirs entitled *Theatre Street*, and I was thrilled. One time, at the Bolshoi School, I observed a class taken by Plisetskaya and Ulanova—just the two of them—and it was absolutely fascinating. So, with the years, it all added up to my being exposed to a great many schools of teaching. Of course, the English ballet tradition is still very young. We have taken an awful lot from the Italian school—Cecchetti. Then, since the last war, we have been taking from the Russians—the Kirov School. We have taken from the Danes—the Bournonville style. Naturally, one has to be very careful not to mix them all up in a pot. One takes the best from all. I would say that it was Dame Ninette de Valois who created her own English style. It's often been criticized as being shortsighted, but it certainly was the grounding for my own teaching. I was taught by her and by teachers under her. Madame was herself in the Diaghilev company, but she wasn't one-hundred-per-cent influenced by the Russians. She was also personally trained by Cecchetti. So, our tradition is a mixture."

I ask Miss Larsen if she could describe the qualities inherent in the typical English dancer.

"Well, the English body is, of course, the dead opposite of the Slav body. One gets very carried away with the beautiful Russian backs and legs—and they are lovely, but that is a Slav body. The English are a very German race. We have a slightly stiffer and more slender body. The English dancer must first of all have a slender, light body. She has to have very light technique from the knee downward. We are very famous for our footwork. I also think our placement is one of the best in the world—one of the most correct. That is how we can get twenty, thirty, fifty girls to work the same way. We try to make the body work quickly. Of course, sometimes we work quite slowly in order to strengthen the muscles. Later, we speed them up. In other classes, when I have the top ballerinas, I must slow them down because of the heavy roles they are asked to do. They work so hard, poor dears. We don't ever seem to have a holiday. We have a few weeks in the summer. But all the year round, year after year, we never stop. To make the dancer not get overtrained, overworked, one must think very carefully how to build a year of teaching.

"The way I do this is to study our repertoire very carefully. Then I work accordingly. Well, with all the many different ballets we do, from *Sleeping Beauty* to Tetley's *Field Figures*, where dancers must roll on the floor, the classes must be very carefully organized. We've got to keep up our standard, and that means that I nearly kill myself and all my girls with classwork. I have to train myself to be with them bodily and mentally all the time. It's dreadful. You must be married to the company. If you let go and only do half a day, or half a week, you lose your sense of order.

"Of course, I do not teach the children. I get them after all the awful, dirty work is done. I see the products. And I still get a lump in my throat when I see one of my girls doing her first Queen of the Wilis, or her first Swan Queen. Because she was my pupil. Don't misunderstand, I'm not the only teacher. But I'm one of the closest to the company. I have not trained girls like Merle Park or Antoinette Sibley or Monica Mason entirely on my own. Still, all come to class in the morning. Another thing about a teacher who has been attached to a company for a great many years is that she must not bore her pupils. I have to be very careful about that, because if I'm boring, they become bored. But it's wonderful to teach my girls. I know their strengths. I know their capacity. I know their musicality. I know their limitations. I know their great talent, if it's there, or if it's going to come. It's fascinating to see them grow. I also know when they're not going to make it. After a few years, if someone is not going to make it, she must go, because otherwise the standard goes down."

To observe Gerd Larsen performing on the stage in one of her mime roles is to know a superb technician and character actress. As a queen, she walks with a sort of regality that suggests years of observation and study.

In gesture, facial expression, movement, Miss Larsen continually offers insight into character. Miss Larsen told me that she studies artists such as Marcel Marceau and actresses such as Sybil Thorndike and Dame Edith Evans. She has also studied and observed the poise and manner of England's Queen Mother—Queen Elizabeth:

"When I speak to her I watch her all the time. She's so very gracious. I always observe the way she carries herself and how lovely she looks wearing her tiara and her crinolines. Of course, Frederick Ashton has taught me an awful lot about style on the stage. You get things from all quarters."

Miss Larsen was married to Harold Turner, an important virtuoso dancer with the Royal Ballet, who also became one of the company's principal teachers.

"Harold was older than I when we met here in the company. He was one of the founders of the Sadler's Wells. He danced with Margot Fonteyn when she was very young. Then, he left to go into the Army. Many of our men went into the war. Anyway, when he came back, he fairly soon became one of our teachers and also danced. I'm afraid he worked terribly, terribly hard. He took on too much responsibility on the male side of the school. Nine years ago, he died. He had been rehearsing as the Old Count in Massine's *Les Femmes de Bonne Humeur*, and he walked into his dressing room and fell down dead of a heart attack. We have a daughter, who is a beautiful blond girl, not at all interested in ballet. She is Margot Fonteyn's godchild."

I ask Miss Larsen whether Margot Fonteyn still takes class from her.

"Oh, yes, and we are very close. Of course, I think Dame Margot is obviously a genius. But what I admire more than anything is her simplicity. She's such a simple, down-to-earth, natural person. And she is unpretentious. In a way, she is a saint. I lived through the drama of her husband's great tragedy. How she coped with that, I'll never know. I have seen her down many times. But she comes out of it. I suppose her dancing has saved her from many distraught moments. She is always kindness itself when it comes to other people in distress. She was marvelous with me when Harold died. Margot is the first to be there to help people in upsetting times."

And what of Rudolf Nureyev?

"People are continually saying that he's awful and impossible. He's not. He works. He's a perfectionist. So, if he loses his temper, it's mostly because he hasn't got something right, or others don't give him time to let something be perfect. He's always been very sweet with me. Other people are sometimes jealous of him—other dancers. But if they had any common sense, they would learn from him. I've learned from him myself. I'm reminded of many things when I watch him. I also argue with him. At times I've convinced him that what *we* do is often right. And I've stuck to my arguments."

Gerd Larsen has been teaching at the Royal Ballet for seventeen years. Have the years been fulfilling?

"Sometimes I think that I ought to stop. But you can't suddenly take a leave of absence from a company like this. I go along with the theory of Margot Fonteyn—to keep on going until one isn't physically able to do so any longer. I think I'll carry on until that time comes. Actually, I haven't missed an awful lot. If I met some lovely millionaire—and he has to be lovely, as well as being a millionaire—I might go off and marry him. My friends say I'd be awfully bored, and I think they're probably right. I think *that* kind of life after *this* kind of life would only be half full. I mean, that kind of happiness . . . I mean, what is happiness today? I lost my happiness losing my husband. I'm so very lucky that something as valuable as teaching has been created for me here at the school. It doesn't mean that I'm devoted *all* of the time. There comes a moment when I get sick of them all. So I go down to my cottage by the sea and communicate with that for a while. Naturally, in the life I lead now, I am missing something. But I suppose you can't have everything."

Roy Round

MICHAEL SOMES

Ｔhe dashing figure wearing a monocle placed fiercely over his right eye, who stands glowering in the wings at Covent Garden, admonishing ballerinas as they leap offstage, curtly telling them they were "miserable," danced "dreadfully," is Michael Somes. As the company's chief *répétiteur* and one of its most important teachers, it is his job to watch how the company's dancers perform. Everyone fears and respects Michael Somes. He is also loved. There are good reasons. Somes, the image of aristocratic restraint, was one of the company's most durable and brilliant *danseurs nobles*. For ten years he was Margot Fonteyn's constant partner. For longer than that, he danced principal roles in innumerable ballets created for the company by Frederick Ashton. He is remembered for his extra-ordinary technical élan in such Ashton works as *Les Patineurs*, *A Wedding Bouquet*, *Horoscope*, *Symphonic Variations*, as well as leading roles in all the great classics—*The Sleeping Beauty*, *Swan Lake*, *Giselle*.

Michael Somes asked me to come to Covent Garden for our talk. We met in the Green Room, which, it turns out, is totally blue. Seated on a blue couch in a room made depressingly dark by blue wallpaper and dark blue lampshades, Somes looked lost in the gloomy shadows created by the ineffectual lights. He seemed somewhat nervous, but soon settled into easy conversation.

"I was born in the West of England—in 1917—in Horsley and lived my boyhood there with my parents. My mother was a schoolteacher. She also taught a children's dancing class, and as a very young boy I went along with her and joined in. I was encouraged in my dancing and soon showed a sort of aptitude for it. Later, I appeared in many amateur shows and in competitions. All this resulted in my schoolwork going by the wayside. The headmaster kept saying that the dancing must stop, or I would never make a good tractor salesman or something like that. Fortunately, my parents were keen on my continuing to dance, and they urged me to go to London. Of course, in those days there was hardly any ballet in London. The Russian Ballet would come in—and that was about it.

"I was very impoverished, and among other places I went to look for a scholarship, Sadler's Wells accepted me. I was the first boy ever to receive a scholarship from Sadler's Wells. And so, they trained me, but I had no money to live on. There were no grants in those days. I was very poor indeed. One day I met Lilian Baylis, who was a marvelous person with a driving force and an ability to get money out of a stone. She knew very little about ballet, but she had a knack to choose people and to help people in the arts. She helped all of us at Sadler's Wells. Anyway, she told me that she had a friend at Oxford who had told her years previously that if ever there was a young male dancer who had talent, and who needed some support, he would help. He was neither a rich man nor a poor man, Miss Baylis told me, and she didn't even know whether he was still alive. But she wrote him a letter and found out that he was alive and living in Malta. He answered her that I was to write to him and to tell him whether I was healthy, talented and whether I was a Roman Catholic. So I thought, What would he like me to be? I wrote him the truth. I told him I was healthy, that I thought I had talent, and that, no, I was not a Roman Catholic. Eventually, I received back a check for a hundred pounds, which, in those days, was really something. Now, this was all done through someone else—through a solicitor. I was fitted out with clothes and a good pair of shoes and all those things, and I was fixed up with an allowance which was modest, but which enabled me to survive in London.

"I had never met the gentleman who was my benefactor. One day he came to London. Through the solicitor, I asked to meet him to be able to thank him personally. I was told this would be very difficult. Finally, this man, whose name was Glyn, agreed to come and see me dance at Sadler's Wells, and I was told that in order to recognize him I would have to look for the ugliest man standing by the ticket office. So I went and looked by the ticket office, and there was an old gentleman wearing the heaviest glasses I'd ever seen. He was almost completely blind. It was so ironic for a nearly-blind man to sponsor a dancer. He wanted a ticket in the first row. He came and he sat and could barely see me. I saw him a few times after that, but he never wanted to be particularly close or friendly to me. At one point I asked him why he wanted to know whether I was a Roman Catholic. He said if I had been, he wouldn't have sent me a penny. He was a bit eccentric. I never learned very much about him, except that he was a very lonely man. He was in his seventies, and after the war, he died."

This Dickensian story was told in a subdued and retiring manner, with Somes pausing here and there to search out his words. He was talking about the prewar years of 1935, 1936, 1937. He then went on to recount that he was part of the pioneering days of the Sadler's Wells, which later became the Royal Ballet. There was little audience for ballet in those days—only the faithful came—and the company and its dancers lived from hand to mouth. The name of Lilian Baylis came up again as Somes continued to tell of his beginnings—how she would collect old clothes which were then turned into costumes, how she was forever being helpful. Very early on, Somes discovered that he had an uncanny knack for re-membering the steps by any given choreographer merely by watching the dancers perform. Even before he began his life at Sadler's Wells, he would sit in the highest balcony watching the Ballet Russe doing the symphonic ballets of Massine, and then be able to show his fellow dancers all the steps.

"It's the only virtue that I've been blessed with. It's just something you have or you don't have. It's like having red hair. I remember all the early ballets of Fred Ashton, all the long-forgotten ones, and I can still show all the parts, including all the girls' parts."

In 1938 Michael Somes danced the young man in *Horoscope*, the first ballet created for him by Frederick Ashton. It was also the year in which he began to dance with Margot Fonteyn, then a very young member of the company. Soon after, he began doing all the classics. He was in continual demand for Ashton ballets, and his prowess and versatility developed with the years. When World War II broke out, he served in the Army. He was absent from the company for four years. Then, just before war's end, he suffered a severe accident.

"I got thrown off a truck rather stupidly. I ruptured my spleen, and I nearly pinked out, but I stuck it through somehow and convalesced for several months. Doctors said that I could never go back to dancing, that the muscles were shot. Well, that was out of the question. I didn't know how to do anything else. I only knew how to dance. And so I went back, and very slowly started to work—I pushed and pushed and pushed. It wasn't easy. I was very lucky, and by the time our company visited America for the first time I was pretty well near back to the top again. Robert Helpmann was the leading dancer then, but around 1951 he retired, and I sort of took over as leading dancer for the next ten years. I danced with Margot all that time."

I told Somes that I had seen him dancing with Margot Fonteyn and the great impression his partnering made on me.

"It's nice that you've remembered. It's flattering, because some people don't know that I ever danced with her. Sometimes I don't think that anyone ever remembers it. I'm not saying that bitterly, because I'm terribly happy for Margot and for Nureyev, who now dances with her. Their great success is a marvelous thing. It doesn't mean anything to me any more; I mean, if you've had that kind of partnership, then you don't worry about other people also having it. Anyway, ours was a very special partnership. The difference between ours and what she has now is that we grew up together. That's the first thing. We grew up together under the same influences and the same hardships. We had the same teachers. And we had Fred Ashton, who created for us at the same time. We worked together, the three of us. What was special about our dancing was that we were both blessed with musicality, and we had a great rapport. We knew exactly what we were going to do. I knew when she was just the slightest bit off, and needed a touch. I knew when she needed me to support and when she didn't. Also, I was taught to keep myself always slightly in the background. You see, she was a showpiece. My job was to see that that showpiece was presented immaculately and perfectly. The audience often was not really aware of my presence. In that lies a cue to what I was saying earlier, about people not remembering that I danced with Margot. But I really believed that my function was very much to put myself in the background. I projected her, and the greater her success, the more credit, I felt, came to me."

Somes continued to speak glowingly of Margot Fonteyn—so glowingly that I asked him whether he was in love with her in those days.

"Well, I suspect we were in love at some time. One usually falls in love with one's partners at some point. I mean, one gets so close. . . . We were very fond of each other, always have been, and we still are. Now, of course, Margot has even greater success and world-wide fame with Rudy. I'm not the least bit . . . I mean, it was something she needed."

When in 1963 Frederick Ashton choreographed *Marguerite and Armand*, for Fonteyn and Nureyev, Michael Somes took the role of Armand's father—a role that did not require him to do much dancing. It was poignant seeing an older Somes on the same stage with his former partner dancing with his young successor. I asked Somes how he felt watching the impassioned young Nureyev dancing with Fonteyn as he had once danced with her.

"Well, I'll tell you. There were two reasons why I did that ballet. First, I wanted to show the ballet world that there was no rancor or jealousy on my part. That even though I was there with Margot earlier on, I did not feel jealous of the new partnership. Second, I wanted to show younger people—the young dancers—that this can be done—that a former partner could take on a sort of super-walk-around part without losing one's dignity. I hoped that by doing this I would show the audience that it can be done. Of course, I have never had notoriety. I don't wish to be notorious. I don't want to run around the streets of Toronto naked. I mean, it doesn't worry me that I don't hit the headlines. Look, just being able to dance is all that should matter."

Michael Somes has been teaching company classes for a great many years. He is also responsible for teaching roles to young dancers ready for new parts. We discussed this aspect of Somes's career.

"To begin with, you can't go on in this business unless you're prepared to always be in pain somewhere. You've just got to accept it. If it were up to me, I would put a large sign over the door of our school at Barons Court: 'All Ye That Enter Here, Be Prepared for Ninety-Nine-Per-Cent Failure Every Day.' Because you succeed once in every hundred times. It's all failure. And there's that awful grind of going back and finding that you *can't* do it. Still, you must keep your head and realize that someone will always come along and bawl you out and shout at you and make you feel miserable. That's the position I'm in now. We try to make it as pleasant as we can, but it's a grind, and it's a discipline. I always say that my job now is sort of between being nursemaid, office boy, and butcher. I believe in being strict. But after the rehearsals, I never bear a grudge. I don't even hold an artistic anger. We always start fresh every day. What I do mostly is have sessions with the principal dancers on all our ballets. I rehearse everybody. Sometimes I have to teach roles from scratch. I also teach classes and, particularly, the men's classes.

"A male dancer differs from a woman not as much as one would think. He has to be able to lift, and he has to do more jumps. The stress is certainly more on that than it is for a woman. Also, a male dancer must be masculine. At any rate, it is very hard to do a beautiful line. I think one of the great tests of a good male dancer is to look at him, suddenly close your eyes, and see, like a photographic image, a perfect shape—a perfect line. Then you know that a dancer is getting somewhere. Physically, a male dancer must have a very, very well-proportioned body, and it cannot be stiff. You must always be working for mobility as against brute strength— especially in matters of partnering. I mean, one has to be strong, but one must be strong in proportion."

"What is a British dancer?" I ask Somes.

"We are more restrained," he says. "We are not flamboyant. We are more reserved. I think we can light up sometimes, when we need to. But sometimes I think we need a bit of a bomb underneath us. Of course, I think nothing succeeds like success. In America we are very successful, and so we dance better in America."

I now ask Somes what it is like observing Sir Frederick Ashton create a ballet.

"Well, I don't wish to sound immodest, but I know more about Fred Ashton than anybody else. About his choreographing? Well, he'll come in, look at the dancers. He'll get up and sort of putter about, piddle about. He'll do some old-shoe stuff that looks like yesterday's old fish. You're saying to yourself, Oh, how dreary, how boring! It's awkward, it doesn't fit, it doesn't look like anything. And he'll dig around. Then he does something, and it's good. He'll go home, come back the next day, and make some changes—some alterations here and there. Suddenly, the results are absolutely marvelous. You see, he's a perfectionist, but somehow he saves things for the end. That's really how he works."

As Somes speaks, he fishes his monocle out of a pocket and affixes it to his eye. His handsome face is subtly altered. It becomes a nineteenth-century face—both romantic, and slightly sinister. I am suddenly transfixed by the gleaming glass piece. He notes my staring, and removes the monocle.

"You're looking at this odd piece of glass," he says. "Actually it's the most functional apparatus I've ever had. Also, it has the side product of putting a lot of fear in people's hearts. But I think I can do that even without the monocle. Really, I don't like to make people afraid, but I believe in the strictest of disciplines. I believe in a little bit of fear. . . . I mean, I use it very, very carefully, and I don't believe in thundering at people. Many people think I don't like anything. They say, 'Oh, he never likes anything.' They also say that I'm a monster and a devil and absolutely dreadful—which I can be. But I'm none of those things, really. I can be quiet and gentle—and encouraging."

Michael Somes has been married twice. His first wife, Deirdre Dixon, died in 1959. Five years later, he married Antoinette Sibley, a principal dancer with the Royal Ballet. The two are now divorced. Somes was most hesitant in talking about his marriage to Miss Sibley.

"She's come along very well, and I try to help her and give her all the encouragement and knowledge that I can. I look after her as much as I can in her work. As for our marriage, I think that's one's private affair. I don't think one really wants to talk about that. But I think that professionally speaking, which is all we're interested in, she's a great dancer. I do everything and anything I can to promote her in her work."

With that, Michael Somes rose, bade me farewell, and made his way out of the blue Green Room.

THE STUTTGART BALLET

JOHN CRANKO

In June 1973 Jerome Robbins was staging and choreographing a new ballet presentation entitled *Celebration: The Art of the Pas de Deux,* which was one of the highlights of that summer's Spoleto Festival of Two Worlds. The extraordinary aspect of *Celebration* was the bringing together of five internationally celebrated ballet couples who would perform two *pas de deux* each from the established repertory, all to be framed by an introduction and finale choreographed by Robbins to music from Tchaikovsky's *Swan Lake*.

The dancers had arrived in Spoleto. There was Patricia McBride and Helgi Tomasson from the United States, Violette Verdy and Jean-Pierre Bonnefous representing France, Carla Fracci and Paolo Bortoluzzi from Italy, Antoinette Sibley and Anthony Dowell from Britain, and Malika Sabirova and Muzdafar Bourkanov from the Soviet Union. On the morning of June 27, a radiantly beautiful day, Violette Verdy and Jean-Pierre Bonnefous were walking from their hotel to a rehearsal at the Teatro Nuovo. Meeting by chance on the street, we greeted effusively. After a short, bright chat, the ballerina went off with her partner, singing merrily. Not a half an hour had passed before that same cheerful ballerina was distractedly walking the halls of the backstage area sobbing uncontrollably. The news which plunged Miss Verdy, and indeed the whole dance world, into the greatest shock and depression was that forty-five-year-old John Cranko, renowned choreographer and director of the Stuttgart Ballet, had collapsed and died in an airplane that was returning him and his company to Stuttgart following a triumphant American tour. When the news reached Jerome Robbins, he sent off a wire to Stuttgart which was signed by him and all the dancers of *Celebration*. The work was then dedicated to John Cranko, and a note to that effect was printed in the program.

Ironically enough, I had first met Mr. Cranko in 1965, in Spoleto. He and his Stuttgart Ballet had come to the Festival of Two Worlds to perform his recently choreographed *Romeo and Juliet*, and I remember being deeply impressed by Cranko, his work, and his dancers. At the time that I met him, which was at a party given by Gian-Carlo Menotti, following the performance of *Romeo and Juliet*, he seemed extremely shy and curiously ill at ease. Still, we chatted briefly and he graciously accepted my compliments. The Stuttgart Ballet had, at that time, been in existence for some four years and Cranko was still in the process of building it into what eventually became one of the major ballet companies in the world.

There was a double irony in my receiving news of Cranko's death in Spoleto. I had brought along from New York the tape he and I made together for inclusion in this book. It was the last tape I had made prior to my departure, and I wanted to have it along to transcribe. It was, to say the least, both eerie and moving to hear John Cranko's crisp, bright voice on the very day that he had died.

I had seen John Cranko outside of a rehearsal hall in the depths of New York's Metropolitan Opera House on May 31, 1973. He had just been rehearsing the company in his newly mounted version of *Swan Lake*. That season, Stuttgart was performing *Eugene Onegin, Swan Lake*, and a program of shorter Cranko ballets. The tall, brilliantly blue-eyed choreographer came out of the rehersal wearing a suit which he told me was made of Russian antelope. When the spirit moved him, Mr. Cranko was given to wearing colorful, mod clothes. We began by talking about his parents. It seems they had met during a performance given by the Diaghilev company in London in 1921. One of Cranko's earliest memories was that of his parents discussing and telling the child about Diaghilev and the fabulous dancers and ballets that he inspired. "They talked about Diaghilev and showed me pictures and this became a kind of world for me, rather like for other people, fairy stories. I grew up hearing about this enchanted world."

John Cranko was born in Rustenburg, South Africa, on August 15, 1927. His mother, though not a professional musician, played the piano with great passion. His father was an attorney with a great penchant for the theater. It was Cranko's father who was largely instrumental in putting the repertory theater in Johannesburg on a solid basis. What is more, he used to perform in revues when John was a small boy. With this background, it was not surprising that John Cranko fell in love with things theatrical.

"I had a marionette theater of my own, and I used to make my own marionettes. My father gave me pocket money to buy a record a week. I bought practically the entire repertoire of Gilbert and Sullivan. Finally, my father hinted that it might be a good idea if I found something else. So I tried ballet music. I bought *Schéhérazade* and *Firebird*, rather because of their names . . . especially *Firebird*. I started to try and imagine what they could possibly be doing. I think it was these imaginings and wonderings to music—that sort of fantasizing to music—that started me off to wish to be a choreographer. I never actually wanted to be a dancer. Still, when I was thirteen or fourteen, I did begin to take dancing classes in Johannesburg. It got to the point where I was neglecting all my studies.

"My life was sort of shattered by the advent of the Cape Town University Ballet which came to Johannesburg. They needed extras to do little bits for them, and I did bits for them. Then, of course, my school just went. I think my father realized that it was absolutely no good forcing me, and he allowed me to go down to the Cape and study every day with the Cape Town Ballet. Then it all really started. I stayed with them for about three years."

Not only did John Cranko dance with the Cape Town Ballet, but also began his first essays in choreography. He devised ballets based on Stravinsky's "A Soldier's Tale," Debussy's "Sacred and Profane Dances," and Strauss's "Tritsch-Tratsch Polka," the last, a work that brought him some attention. In 1946, Cranko danced with the Sadler's Wells Theatre Ballet, where he also continued to choreograph. By 1951, he had choreographed some nine works, including the hugely successful *Pineapple Poll*. During the 1950s, Cranko became an established choreographer. His works were being taken into the repertoire of Sadler's Wells, later the Royal Ballet. In 1957, Cranko composed the first full-length, entirely English ballet—*The Prince of the Pagodas*. His versatility was such that he could also immerse himself in British musical revues. An original revue,

Cranks, staged in London in 1955, became a hit, and it led him to write its sequel, *More Cranks.*

While John Cranko was affiliated with the Royal Ballet, the resident choreographer was Frederick Ashton. The younger man, while successful and obviously highly gifted, was not given the choreographic opportunities he both sought and demanded. In 1960, he devised his last work for the Royal Ballet—*Antigone.* In 1961, he accepted an invitation to become the head of the Stuttgart Ballet.

"Nothing really drastic happened with the Royal Ballet. The trouble was that they kept restoring the three-act ballets which were part of their repertoire, and, of course, Ashton was their major choreographer. Also, they had guests like Massine or Balanchine. I was doing a ballet every eighteen months, and it wasn't enough. By the time I got around to it, I was so nervous, that nothing tended to come out as I had wished. Actually, I never thought of leaving. Quite by chance, Svetlana Beriosova's father was ballet master in Stuttgart. I went over and saw the German state theater system which is dazzling, to anybody who lives in America or England. Well, I met the director of the Stuttgart, and he was very interested in building a ballet company. He was quite serious. When I returned, I talked to Ninette de Valois, and, at first, she was rather angry at the idea of my leaving. Finally, she said, 'Well, I thought it over, and you'll have two companies. You'll always be welcome to come back here.' I can't be grateful enough to her, because she would put a dancer on an airplane when I was desperate for one. . . . Things like that. I did not know Germany at all. I suppose there was a certain amount of prejudice and fear about going to live in Germany. But the longer I lived there, the more my fears were dispelled."

Cranko told me how the art of choreography affected him: "The rehearsal people are always amazed at how quickly I do ballets. But it's not the rehearsal time that is so important as the gestation or pregnancy. I found that I just can't force this. Little glimmers of ideas, of feelings, come. So that by the time one gets to rehearsal, one knows emotionally or instinctively what might happen. With every ballet I do, I am convinced that it's going to be the worst ballet of my life. I have in my mind what should happen or what the weight of the sequence should be. But the actual invention happens in the ballet room, and often it's very surprising. I think that one should catch what Max Ernst calls 'the divine accident.' Very often, I suggest a step to a dancer and he does it. Often, he doesn't get it quite right, or does it wrong, and just as often, the mistake is better than the original idea. That is why I feel that while I work, I am like a microphone, picking up every sound that's in the air."

I asked John Cranko how he has developed a personal style.

"Well, you see, I always pick tall dancers, but in class, they must have no style. They must dance as purely as possible, without any frills or furbelows. I would hate the personal characteristics of one teacher to mark his class. In our school, we try to teach the purest of ballet movement in the most unstylish way possible—the style should come through the choreographer. For instance, now we are rehearsing a ballet of Jerome Robbins, *Opus Jazz*. We do Balanchine ballets and MacMillan's. I do think the most terrifying criticism would be to say, 'Stuttgart Ballet danced *Opus Jazz*, by Jerome Robbins in the Stuttgart style.' They should dance it in the Jerome Robbins style. I think the question of style comes in the work and not in the training."

When I asked Cranko whether there was a "Cranko style," he answered that it varied with the intention of each work. Cranko is one of the few choreographers who has a reputation for favoring story-ballets. He is quick to point out, however, that the programs the Stuttgart presents in America are misleading:

"Don't forget, that when we first came to America, no one had really heard of the Stuttgart. If we had been the Vienna Ballet, or the Berlin Ballet, it might have been different. Mr. Hurok has to pay enormous overheads to rent the Metropolitan and to do a number-one tour. So the ballets that we do are ballets that would tend to fill a house. The riskier ballets we do in Stuttgart. There, we use more avant-garde composers and use ideas which are a bit more difficult to understand. For example, Glen Tetley will come next season to do a new work for us. We also are developing young choreographers of our own, and their work is much more complex than what we show in New York."

How does Cranko tell the dancers what to do when choreographing one of his own ballets?

"Mostly, I give metaphors. I will say, 'I want this to be like a bow, the string is being pulled, and the bow is bent, so I want you to make this particular shape.' I give mostly images that I hope will be then conveyed to the audience. One makes images of falling, of rising, of despair, of ecstasy, of being constricted, of being liberated. I give emotional movements. I feel the emotion first and then I try to transmit it, no matter how abstract it is. Of course, one has one's ups and downs, one's depths and one's heights. I think everything is fair game in art.

"But about the story-ballets. You see, I follow the Balanchine principle which holds that first and foremost a ballet is a composition with bodies in space and time, whether it's got music, or it hasn't got music, whether it's got a story and costumes, or it doesn't. A ballet must be satisfying, firstly, in Balanchine terms. I feel that one should be able to take a dance out of *Onegin*, strip it of meaning, strip it of costumes, and look at it as a valid, abstract composition."

When the Stuttgart Ballet came to New York, in 1973, one of its major presentations was Cranko's sumptuous new version of *Swan Lake*. The basic story had been reidentified by Cranko.

"The major task with *Swan Lake* was to try to rediscover the myth of *Swan Lake* and to reilluminate the myth. I did not want to do just a new production of it. I wanted to find its mythical truth."

In point of fact, Cranko's version of *Swan Lake* finds Prince Siegfried a developed character. As Cranko pointed out in a program note: "There have been many happy endings, where the lovers are reunited after death in 'fairyland.' But I believe that Tchaikovsky intended to write a tragic ballet. Siegfried is a tragic hero and must be vanquished. The tone of the music, especially in the Fourth Act, is tragic. Odette and Siegfried are not the sort of lovers who can live 'happily ever after.'" The ending of his *Swan Lake* finds Odette being swept away by Von Rothbart, while Siegfried drowns dramatically in a magnificently staged rush of waves.

The principal dancers of the Stuttgart Ballet are not primarily German. The company's prima ballerina, Marcia Haydée, is a native of Brazil. Her frequent partner, Richard Cragun, was born in California. Joyce Cuoco, a technical marvel, hails from Boston. Egon Madsen is a product of the Royal Danish Ballet. Judith Rein came via the Royal Ballet. The first genuine Stuttgart ballerina is Birgit Keil. Also German are Heinz Clauss, Bernd Berg, and Susanne Hanke.

Clearly, the company's most celebrated ballerina is Marcia Haydée, whom Cranko extolled with unqualified praise:

"My finding her was an act of destiny. When I started, it was very hard to get dancers. I had a vague reputation as a choreographer, but no reputation as a dancer. I think everyone was waiting to see what would happen. One day, Alfonso Cata, who is now director in Geneva, said there was this marvelous girl from the de Cuevas company. He said I knew her. I couldn't remember her. Marcia just appeared in Stuttgart and did an audition which was professional. I could see that she was a good dancer, and I liked her very much as a person. Of course, I had no idea of what was really in her. I engaged her, and it just started like that. I would say that Marcia fulfills her function as a ballerina by her love and responsibility to the company. She's tremendously concerned for the well-being of the younger dancers. She almost has a sort of built-in radar. Personally, we both understand each other one hundred percent. That's about the best way that I can define it."

At the time of his death, John Cranko was in the process of executing a series of new ballets for his company.

"The next ballet is to be an idea of my own. I haven't got a title, but the music will be by Rachmaninoff. The basic idea is around about the time of the First World War. It takes place in a small town where the men are all gone and a very young female teacher is in charge of a class of adolescent boys. She is dutifully married, but not through real love. A love grows between her and a young student. We see her instructing him and we see how a love begins developing between this boy and a girl of his own age.

The teacher allows this love to develop because it would be folly to try to be possessive about the boy. She leaves, and she is pregnant by the student. The husband believes that it is his child. For consolation, she will have the baby of the boy she loved.

"Another ballet I have in mind, is based on *Othello*. I'm not certain of the composer as yet. Another one will have music by Heinz Werner Henze, and will be based on the myth of Tristan. The episode covered by Wagner, with the love potion, is really the most boring and unnecessary episode. The Tristan myth is very long. We won't do the Tristan and Isolde episode. We'll begin with the killing of Isolde's uncle by Tristan. If it's a success, we intend to do a trilogy of three evening-length ballets. Each will have as its basis, one of the elements—water, earth, and fire."

John Cranko was much loved by his company. Everyone addressed him by his first name, and everyone knew that he would be available to them, whether to discuss a personal problem or a professional matter. He will be deeply missed. In March 1974, the American choreographer Glen Tetley was appointed to head the Stuttgart Ballet.

As I left John Cranko that morning at the Metropolitan Opera in New York, we spoke of his fulfillment as both choreographer and person.

"Of course one always has depression and glooms," he said with a smile, "but life seems to be working out."

"What does it mean to create dances?" I asked. He answered, "I think it means total expression of the things that one cannot say with words—the things of one's whole life, what one is, one's being, without being able to define them. I suppose if one could define them, one would be a writer. To try and find that thing which movement says, is what no other art can find. Havelock Ellis said that dancing was the first art. He said that the first two arts were dancing and building. All the performing arts came from dancing and all the plastic arts, like painting and sculpture, come from building. And the stars, of course, dance around the sun."

Louis Peres

MARCIA HAYDÉE

Offstage, ballerina Marcia Haydée is not beautiful. Aside from her large, liquid brown eyes, the Brazilian-born dancer, the undisputed star of the late John Cranko's Stuttgart Ballet, does not present the image of the ethereal, perfectly shaped dancer. Haydée on stage, however, is quite another matter. Elusive, mysterious elements enter her persona, and the seemingly tentative, uncaptivating girl transforms into a riveting presence which, brilliance of technique aside, communicates an intensity and passion that are as dramatically valid as they are visually tantalizing. Haydée is that rare phenomenon: a bravura dancer who is also a remarkable dramatic actress.

It is perhaps her private, physical anonymity that allows her to assume the variety of taxing and complex roles that she and choreographer Cranko have so brilliantly evolved together. In this collaboration, Haydée has no difficulty conjuring a proud, emotionally torn Tatiana in *Eugene Onegin*, exposing an urgently poetic and ecstatic Juliet in *Romeo and Juliet*, creating an explosive and fury-drenched Carmen or giving life to a studiedly witty and stylized Kate in *The Taming of the Shrew*. Clearly, Marcia Haydée is a protean dancer—something of a sorceress invoking the spirit of any given character and taking total possession of it.

My first offstage glimpse of Miss Haydée was in New York at the St. Regis Roof on April 19, 1971, when S. Hurok (who first brought the Stuttgart Ballet to America in 1969) was staging an expensive opening-night party following the Stuttgart's performance of *Eugene Onegin*. The company members and their friends slowly filled the heavily chandeliered room, while an orchestra alternated between slow-tempoed geriatric tunes and frenzied rock 'n' roll.

Haydée had not yet arrived, but her table was already occupied by Mr. Hurok, John Cranko, Miss Haydée's mother (a strikingly beautiful Argentine in a backless evening gown), her half sister (a lovely, dark-skinned girl, said to be one of Brazil's top fashion models), and Richard Cragun, a principal dancer with the company and for the last eight years Marcia Haydée's companion.

At last, Haydée makes her entrance. People rise, clap, and rush up to her. There are kisses, embraces, breathless compliments. She wears an incredible dress. Floor-length and totally transparent, its material is a light gray silk net, embroidered with constellations of silver brilliants. A tight, flesh-colored body-stocking underneath the dress outlines her five-foot three-inch, ninety-pound frame ("I feel very naked!" I overheard her saying), while white silk ribbons rise from her evening slippers, lacing her legs in Roman fashion. Her black, black hair was coiled into an abrupt knot atop her head. All fragrance and white powder, she had once again transformed herself into an ethereal princess, aware of her magical presence and stardom.

On the following morning I went to the Metropolitan Opera House, where I had arranged to interview Marcia Haydée. I was ushered into a rehearsal room, where company class was being held by ballet master Alan Beale. It took me several minutes to spot Haydée. Finally, I saw her working inconspicuously among a row of girls, leaping, rising *en pointe*, doing the required exercises. She wore a pink leotard, white leg-warmers, and a dark gray head-scarf. Haydée looked tired. Not an ounce of make-up covered her face. During a short break, she stood to the side sewing a ribbon on one of her toe shoes. Class over, she came over to me and after a friendly greeting, led me to her dressing room. Lying back on a chaise longue, she opened a small container of yogurt and slowly began eating it, I asked the dancer to tell me precisely how her name should be pronounced.

"It should be pronounced like the initials I.D.," she said. "Marcia should not be pronounced like Marsha. The 'c' is very soft—like an 's.' Haydée is my mother's name. She was born in Argentina. My real father is Portuguese, and I have a brother. My mother and father divorced, and my mother then married a man named López. They had another daughter, my half sister, and a set of twins—a boy and a girl. We all lived in Rio.

"I was three years old when I started to dance. You see, in Brazil, all the schools have ballet classes for little girls—it's part of the schoolwork. My mother tells me that I always wanted to be a dancer. So I was three when I started, and I have never stopped. As time went on, dancing became harder and harder, but I have never had a change of heart about becoming a dancer. Never. Of course, I soon learned there were many things I would never be able to do, like going to many parties, drinking, smoking—all those things a normal person enjoys. But when you are in it—really *in* the dance—then nothing seems to be a sacrifice.

"I left Brazil when I was fifteen. I went to England to study at the Royal Ballet School in London, and two years later joined the *corps de ballet* of the Marquis de Cuevas in Paris. I was in the *corps* for two years. I remember that John Cranko once came to do a ballet for the company. He didn't know me or even notice me, but I enjoyed watching him—I admired the way he worked."

When, in 1961, the Marquis de Cuevas died, Marcia Haydée found herself in Barcelona. She had heard that John Cranko had taken over the Stuttgart Ballet.

"I simply picked up the telephone and called Cranko in Stuttgart. I asked if I could come for an audition. He said, 'Come as quickly as you can, because in one week all contracts must be signed.' So I flew to Stuttgart and for two days took classes with Cranko.

"Now, you understand, my idea was simply to join the *corps de ballet*— I never thought of auditioning for first-dancer roles. Anyway, after those two days of classes, John decided to have me all made up and he put me in a tutu and told me to come out on stage and do a *pas de deux* and a variation I had never done before. I couldn't understand it—especially since I noticed that out in front were the director of the theater, his assistant, his secretary, and, of course, John Cranko.

"So I danced before all those people, and afterward John told me that I was hired as a principal dancer. Well, I was stunned—flabbergasted—and very, very happy. And that's how it all began for me. I danced in the repertoire of the Stuttgart, which at the time included *Swan Lake*, *Giselle*,

Coppélia, and *The Sleeping Beauty*. We still do these ballets, because we need the classics to keep the company alive and in shape.

"Of course, Cranko's ballets are classics all on their own. I mean, his themes are the great classical themes, like *Romeo and Juliet*, *Eugene Onegin*, *Carmen*, *The Taming of the Shrew*. But John's special qualities as a choreographer are that you don't really need to know the story beforehand. Every single situation is immediately understood—he has a tremendous sense of drama—*that*, I think, is his greatest quality. He has a great, great sense of theater. And he can dream up steps that are absolutely dazzling. I mean, he will ask you to do things that you *know* are impossible to execute. But, miraculously, you *can* do them. And it always looks right.

"At any rate, I love doing those long, full-length ballets of his. I love the continuity, because you can build and build . . . and grow with the roles. I just throw myself completely into those long and difficult roles, because when I dance them I actually *believe* I am Juliet. I *believe* I am Carmen. A lot, of course, is John. I know his ideas—I know how his mind works. And we talk about the characters, and I read about the characters.

"But when I work on the roles myself, it becomes a very private, very personal thing. For me, it's never a question of getting things technically perfect *first*. Everything must happen together. Each step must somehow reflect something in the character. Otherwise, things like a *pas de deux* have no meaning. In other words, when the choreographer starts working on the steps, you must already *be* the person the role calls for—certainly in your head. In that way, you help the choreographer—you are already in the role.

"But I must tell you that many of these ideas and feelings came to me while I was studying at the Royal Ballet School. I kept watching Margot Fonteyn. For me, Margot is the essence of the word ballerina. I am not saying that Margot is the only ballerina—there are so many superb ones today—but as far as I am concerned, Fonteyn was, and still is, my inspiration. It's not just the matter of her dancing—which is, of course, unbelievable—but the kind of person she is, the way she behaves. I believe Margot could live to be a hundred and still continue dancing."

Still slowly eating her yogurt, Haydée shifts position on her chaise longue and speaks of her admiration for Rudolf Nureyev.

"I have danced with Rudy in Stuttgart. He came to do *Swan Lake* and *Giselle* with us, and he's taken me to Vienna and Zurich. I love dancing with him, and I've learned a great deal from him. People say he is temperamental, but with me he has always been wonderful. Actually, I'm the one who's temperamental. I have a terrible temper. If anything upsets my work, I go into a blind fury. I get terribly angry, and I immediately voice my anger. It could be with the company, with a partner . . . with anything that harms my work. I believe every artist should have a strong temper and a strong temperament. I have both. But I also know my good qualities. I know about my art, about my ability to transform myself into many different characters. From the point of view of pure dancing, I'm sure there are many ballerinas who dance much better than I. Technically, they might be stronger. Physically, they might be more beautiful—they might have better legs, better feet. My strength is that I have a mixture of all these things— and somehow, it all adds up.

"Marriage? I think it's very difficult for dancers to combine marriage with ballet. I have never been married, and I have no plans for marriage. But I am in love. I think everyone should be in love. An artist has to be involved with other people—it's vital. You cannot be concerned only with yourself. You must be part of life, otherwise, you can't grow as an artist. It's true that the life of a ballerina is nothing but work, work, work. It's not about pleasure and beauty and having a good time, although that is what we want to offer the public. The real satisfaction comes when you do something well, when you satisfy yourself, when you know you have done your very best.

"Like everybody else, I have my great depressions—the greatest being that I may be growing stale, that I'll not be able to top myself. What really makes me nervous is having to live up to the expectations of the public. You know, when people write or say that there are only five great ballerinas in the world today and your name is listed as being one of them . . . that's very scary. I'm scared of the idea of people expecting miracles. That's very hard to live with . . . that's what scares me to death."

LES BALLETS DU XXᴹᴱ SIÈCLE

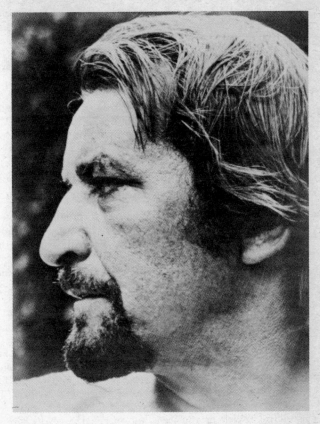

MAURICE BÉJART

When Béjart's Ballets du XXᵐᵉ Siècle returned to New York in the fall of 1972, its sole presentation was Béjart's ballet *Nijinsky: Clown of God*. It was performed at Madison Square Garden's Felt Forum, which seats five thousand. It was typical of Maurice Béjart to choose so vast a place for the viewing of his work. He does not believe in conventional theaters. Sports arenas, even the out-of-doors are his playgrounds, and his balletic vision is as grandiose as the space in which he chooses to give it life.

Nijinsky proved a highly theatrical spectacle. It charted the life of the famed dancer by way of careful reconstruction of Nijinsky's ballet poses (taken from photographs), and the bringing into focus of the dancer's greatest personal influences: Diaghilev; Nijinsky's wife, Romola; and the forces, real or imaginary, that ultimately led to his breakdown. Béjart employed recitations from Nijinsky's diary, electronic music, and music of Tchaikovsky. Jorge Donn, as Nijinsky, proved brilliant, and Suzanne Farrell, as Romola, danced ravishingly. Other dancers with the company, such as Ivan Marko, and Paul Mejia, assumed Nijinsky's various balletic guises to splendid effect. The company, numbering some fifty dancers, performed the work as though it were a masterpiece, which, of its type, it might well be. But the New York ballet critics were mainly down on *Nijinsky*. They found it pretentious, vulgar, unballetic, boring, and far too long.

A few days after the opening, I visited Béjart at the Hotel McAlpin, where he and most of his dancers stayed throughout the company's New York engagement. A man of extraordinary dynamism, Béjart, blue-eyed, black-haired, and sporting a mustache and goatee, seemed unperturbed by the reception allotted his ballet. Asked about the poor reviews, and their effect on him, Béjart smiled, and said, "Don't worry. I will proceed anyway. People have a strange idea about the press—especially in America. It is two things: it is a power and can influence the box office; second, it presumes to have something to do with the creators—the artists, which I think is all wrong. My managers, are, of course, sorry when houses are not sold out. But the ballets are my department, and I do exactly what I think is right.

"I am the severest critic of my own work. I can point out any number of my own works which I think are bad. I am exactly like a painter. You make a painting because you feel you have to do it. You want to make a red sky, so you make a red sky because you believe it's right. Then you look at it, and you see that it's either a mess, in which case you destroy it, or you like it. Well, then someone will come and say, 'Why have you done a red sky? It's vulgar and cheap! You should have done it green!' To that I say, 'To hell with you—my sky is red, and I'll leave it red!' Perhaps I won't sell the painting; perhaps no one will buy it. But it doesn't matter, because you know that one day people will understand you."

Maurice Béjart speaks very quickly. His English, heavily French-accented, is excellent. The rush of his words is marked by a certain nervous restlessness. Wearing black pants and a white turtle neck, he looked both alert and slightly menacing. There is, about Béjart, something violent —imminent anger, or joy, or passion, or defiance simmers just beneath the surface of his words. This withheld frenzy is often reflected in his ballets— works like his version of Stravinsky's *Le Sacre du Printemps*, or his production of Beethoven's Ninth Symphony—works that seethe with unrestrained propulsion and diabolical movement.

Born in Marseilles, in 1928, Maurice Béjart began as a dancer with the Marseilles Opera. He has also danced with Ballets de Roland Petit, the International Ballet, London, and the Royal Swedish Ballet. In 1954 he organized Les Ballets de l'Etoile in Paris. After his success with *Le Sacre du Printemps*, choreographed in 1959, Béjart was appointed ballet director of the Théâtre Royal de la Monnaie, Brussels, where his present company took the name Les Ballets du XXme Siècle.

I asked Béjart to tell me how he came to compose *Nijinsky: Clown of God*.

"It was a very long process," he told me. "When I was still very young, I read Nijinsky's diary, and I was very impressed. At that time, I had no idea it could be made into a ballet. Then, in 1962, my company was in Germany—in Bayreuth—where Wieland Wagner asked me to do the choreography for *Tannhäuser*. We lived in Bayreuth for two months. One day, a rather old lady came to see me backstage. She said, 'Please, Mr. Béjart, I'd like to talk to you. I am Madame Nijinska.' This, then, was Romola, the widow of Nijinsky. The next day we had lunch together, and we spent the whole day talking. She said she had seen in my ballet the qualities she had seen in Nijinsky's ballets. She told me that she was planning to make a film on the life of Nijinsky, and she asked me to do the choreography. I said yes. But the film was never made.

"Then, three years ago, I was reading Henry Miller, and I came across a phrase having to do with what books he would take along if he were to spend the rest of his life on a desert island. Well, one of the books he mentioned was the *Diary of Nijinsky*. I was very startled and amazed. So I read the *Diary* again, and said to myself that I must make a ballet of it. That's how it began. And I went deep into research. I studied Nijinsky's notes which he wrote into the score of *Le Sacre du Printemps*, I studied his photographs. I went very deep into his life. Then I began to choreograph.

"Some people are very disturbed by my ballet. They boo at the end. But don't forget, Nijinsky's own choreography was booed. I feel that if you take something from the soul of someone, you have to bear that soul's burden and his suffering. To this day I fight with certain critics over Nijinsky's choreography. They say, 'Oh, Nijinsky was a bad choreographer!' And I say, 'What makes you think so? You haven't seen any!' I believe that during the first ten years of this century, the most important people in ballet were Isadora Duncan and Vaslav Nijinsky. They were much more important than Fokine. Fokine came from Duncan—he learned everything from her. You see, Nijinsky was very avant-garde, and people didn't understand him."

What sets Béjart's company apart from other ballet companies is his use of space, his interest in reaching a wide variety of audiences, a predominance of male dancers, and very large-scale choreographic works. Béjart elaborated:

"I like large, complex ballets. I follow a vision. When I start to work, I have a total vision of the final work—this vision lasting but one second. Then, the vision vanishes. It is at this moment that I begin to build . . . slowly. There is a long process of construction. It's exactly as though I were constructing a building. First, I have a vision of the building as a whole, with everything there and finished. Then I have to start digging up the earth, put stone upon stone. And I build, with one necessity following the other.

"I found out a long time ago that dance is very important for our civilization. Ballet can be something very, very popular—something that can touch people very deeply. Here, for example, at the Felt Forum of Madison Square Garden, we try to bring ballet to a different public in a different place. Of course, some people are strictly against that sort of thing. But, you see, I compose ballets in order to communicate to people. I don't do abstract, beautiful forms unless it really speaks to people. I don't mean solely a *lot* of people. But a lot of *mixed* people—people from different social strata. That is very important to me. I have always been against playing for one category of people. By that, I don't mean that I will perform in a factory—for the workers. That is also limited. I want to play and perform for everybody—for rich people, poor people, workers, old people, young people. Then, you are in touch with life—with something real.

"As for my celebrating the male dancer rather than the female dancer, I do this because I have come to realize that our first dancing was folk dancing, where the real dancers were always the males—they were the more important element of the dance. In early folk dancing, the women were merely beautiful—they followed, they helped. I mean, look at Russian folk dancing. The men dance, and the women go around with handkerchiefs. In Japanese dancing, it's always men. The same in African dancing. In Africa women are often not allowed to dance or even appear. Look at the American Indian dances. They were and are always executed by the males. And so, I found out that the origin of dancing was built for the power of the man. Women come to add beauty and femininity."

Indeed, Béjart has created any number of fine male dancers—notably Paolo Bortoluzzi, who danced in Béjart's company for twelve years before joining the American Ballet Theatre as principal dancer. Béjart seemed unmoved by the loss of this particularly gifted young man.

"Many dancers leave the company," he said. "In a way, it's good that this should happen. The point is, we form dancers. My interest is to create dancers like Bortoluzzi. I mean, I really created Bortoluzzi. He started as a *corps de ballet* boy, and now he has become one of the best dancers of the day. My interest is not to keep people. There are other boys, and they must come forward—move ahead. It's like being a father. You've done everything for your son, and it's better that he goes off to other things. We are here like a tree that produces fruit."

When, under highly turbulent circumstances, Suzanne Farrell left the New York City Ballet, she accepted an invitation to join Béjart's company —a move that many people in the ballet world felt to be unwise. But Farrell and her husband, Paul Mejia (whom she married while both were dancing with the Balanchine company), seem happy with Béjart. Still, Miss Farrell appears somewhat out of place surrounded by the barrage of young, beautiful male dancers that Béjart clearly favors. I commented on this to Béjart.

"I don't feel that Suzanne is out of place in my company. Yes, she began as something of an oddity with us, but month by month she gets more in the spirit of the company. Every month she gets happier with us. For example, in my ballet *Romeo and Juliet*, which I had originally choreographed for a girl who has since left the company, she turned out the best Juliet I ever had—that I ever dreamed I could have. People say Farrell does not fit in with us—that she is a Balanchine product. But look, Bortoluzzi is a Béjart product, and now he dances with American Ballet Theatre. So it comes out the same."

When Maurice Béjart invited me to observe him compose a new ballet during his New York stay, I accepted with alacrity. He and his dancers met in the studios of the Robert Joffrey School, in Greenwich Village. The new work was a ballet based on Pierre Boulez's "Le Marteau sans Maître." I instantly noted that Béjart's choreographic methods are based on speed, and a rapid succession of steps and formations which seem to come to him almost on the spur of the moment. He shows the dancers what he wants, placing himself in the center of the floor, going through movements destined for this or that dancer.

Boulez's highly abstract score, with its strange, high-lying vocal line, its odd rhythmic musical clusters, elicited from Béjart kinetic and gestural responses that he quickly transmitted to his dancers. They moved in jagged counterpoint to the music, following their choreographer's patterns in space. Often, the steps and gestures were enormously exaggerated, and came in a tumultuous, rapid flow. Béjart took only a brief section of the music, then returned to it again and again, until his dancers had mastered the given movements. It was a process which took several hours. During a break, Béjart told me some of his feelings about the art of choreography:

"First of all, I think that you can use any music whatever for the creation of a ballet. If you love the music you have chosen, if you understand it, if you analyze it, work with it, then it can be used for ballet. Everything depends on the imagination of the choreographer. Next comes the matter of how a choreographer employs space. But, for me, space is something very difficult to be verbal about. The minute you try to verbalize about space, it is no longer space. I can only manipulate space. I am like a sculptor in that way.

"For me, ballet is an art form that is deeply connected to two things: cinema and sport. I love the cinema. I think it's a fantastic art, and I think that today's great thinkers are film directors—they have *everything* to work with. I believe that ballet has much to learn from the cinema—from the way it moves. And ballet has much to learn from sport, because sport, like ballet, is body performance. Dancers do daring things. They jump, have extensions, difficult movements, power. My own choreography comes from the connection and relationship to these two great arts. Also—I like my ballets to be sexy. Because it is part of nature, and I am a primitive. I am not a civilized man. Deep inside, I am a savage. That is why civilized people often hate me and my work so much."

Norma McLain Stoop

JORGE DONN

here are some dancers so under the spell of a single choreographer that they are willing to devote their entire career to him alone. Jorge Donn is one such dancer. Mr. Donn and Béjart's Les Ballets du XXme Siècle were in New York in the winter of 1972 performing *Nijinsky: Clown of God* at the Felt Forum. In this elaborate, full-length production created by Maurice Béjart, Donn danced the principal role of Nijinsky—a role requiring extraordinary strength and concentration. The young performer lent astonishing intensity to his portrayal of the mad Nijinsky, entering fully into the characterization and yielding a wide variety of psychological shadings.

The critics did not generally like *Nijinsky: Clown of God*, but as performed by the Béjart company, it proved a theatrical tour de force. Donn, Suzanne Farrell, Paul Mejia, Ivan Marko, and other principal dancers poured their various talents into an evening of spectacular dancing and *mise en scène*. I visited Jorge Donn at the McAlpin Hotel. His room was large, but conspicuously devoid of charm. The most colorful aspect of it was Donn, who greeted me wearing a dark blue kimono and holding a long red cigarette holder. The twenty-five-year-old dancer wore his hair like a mane. His face suggested a leonine strength, but he was something of a tame beast as he reclined on his bed, saying that he had to rest for that evening's performance. We conversed in French.

"As a young child, I danced all the time," Donn began. "Whenever the radio played music, I danced. My mother was very musical. She had hoped to become a singer, but her parents were against it. She took me to dancing lessons at the age of four. This was in Buenos Aires, where I was born. My father was not very excited at the prospect of my studying dancing. But, at my mother's insistence, I was allowed to take one class a week until the age of seven. Then I entered the school of the Teatro Colón. I remained there till the age of sixteen, and eventually danced with the ballet company of the Teatro Colón. One day the Béjart company came to Buenos Aires. When I saw them perform, I was thunderstruck. Instantly, I asked Béjart if I could join. But there was no place for me."

Jorge Donn could not take no for an answer. He was mesmerized by Béjart, and determined to be a part of the freewheeling spirit and excitement of Béjart's choreographic concepts. Two months passed, and the sixteen-year-old boy borrowed money from friends and, alone, boarded a boat for Europe. He arrived in France practically penniless and unable to speak a word of French.

"When I finally reached Brussels, I immediately went to see Béjart. Luck was with me. Someone in his company fell ill, and I was asked to take his place."

I asked Donn what it was about Béjart that so excited his imagination.

"As a dancer, I felt I needed to find an inspiring teacher. I had the good fortune of finding Béjart. From the very beginning, I knew he would be my one great teacher. I also knew that if one found such a person, one would have to give oneself to him completely. I started in the *corps*, and little by little, went on to dance larger roles. All I know is that when you dance for Béjart, you are dancing for something important. It's not merely a matter of doing something with one's legs and feet, or to possess a pretty smile. Béjart is not only a great choreographer—he is a great philosopher. There are few people like that in the world. He has given his life to the dance, and he has raised the dance to new heights. But Béjart is not only a great teacher; he is a great guru. He has taught me so much about life itself. If one has found one's guru, one must not go looking for others. One must give oneself completely to such a person."

In effect, Béjart has made Jorge Donn a star dancer by creating roles for him and using him to fill the gap left by Paolo Bortoluzzi. But Donn is not interested in stardom:

"I am not interested in money or fame. What interests me most is to contribute something to the dance, and to be next to Béjart. It is true that Bortoluzzi was a bit of a star when he was with us. I am not like that at all. Also, I am not interested in ever joining another company. I am loyal. I consider Béjart's work the most important of the day."

Donn offers thoughts on how he approaches the role of Nijinsky:

"I did not do research on Nijinsky beforehand. I wanted to find the role internally. All I knew was that Nijinsky was a dancer, and I am a dancer. We were part of the same family. It was not until after I learned the role that I read Nijinsky's diary. It was then I learned that he was not merely a dancer, but a genius—a dominant being. It is very difficult for me to dance this role. I have to live the life of Nijinsky every night. The hardest thing for me is to find a renewed youth each night. The trick is not to fall into habits. Also, one must not show fatigue. I'm not speaking of physical fatigue. The dancing, as strenuous as it is, is the least of it. What takes the energy is finding something new within. A new inner strength."

The young dancer languorously lying on his bed shifts position. Jorge Donn drags on his cigarette holder and closes his eyes. He falls into silence. Suddenly, he opens his eyes and says, "The life of a dancer is very difficult. It's very simple. It's very full. But it's very short. Still, it's a marvelous life. There is a part of the dance that is also very spiritual. I would say that my religion is the dance. Because of the dance, I have learned about life. It is a discipline. It is a discipline of living. Yes, it is a religion.

"When I dance, I do not feel that I am dancing. It is not I who dance. It is a force that propels me. It is a force one does not understand. It is the mystery of the unknown. Sometimes there are vibrations. Often they come from the people who love you, or from the public. They make you do things that you never thought you were capable of doing. The whole thing is very mysterious.

"I do not go to see other performances. And I do not go to other cultural events. I feel that today people are entirely too well informed about things. There is too much bombardment from the media. I am sure that Michelangelo didn't go and see a lot of exhibitions. He stayed in the Sistine Chapel, painting, working. I like to stay in my own milieu. I like to be myself."

Martha Swope

SUZANNE FARRELL
and PAUL MEJIA

Her delicate face pale with powder, Suzanne Farrell sits in her dressing room at the Felt Forum, where she will soon dress for her role as Romola Nijinsky in Béjart's *Nijinsky: Clown of God*. In an hour or so, she will appear onstage transformed into the embodiment of Nijinsky's feminine ideal. She will dance as a figure removed from Nijinsky's private turmoil. A circumference of light will set her apart. Throughout the ballet, she will represent a positive, healing force.

But Farrell will also be set apart in other ways. She comes to Béjart as an American ballerina schooled by George Balanchine. If she is to portray an ideal, she will also emerge as a Balanchine ideal. Everything about Suzanne Farrell is a reflection of what Balanchine considers the perfect female dancer. Her physical appearance alone will instantly mark her as a Balanchine product. The endless legs and arms, the long neck, the small head—the general grace implying speed, agility, and controlled lyricism.

Suzanne Farrell was born in Cincinnati, Ohio, in 1945. After private training in her home town, she was granted a Ford Foundation scholarship to the school of American Ballet. In 1961, at the age of sixteen, she joined the New York City Ballet. She danced solo roles in Balanchine's *Serenade*, *Concerto Barocco*, and the lead in *Movements for Piano and Orchestra*, a role originally created for Diana Adams. In 1963, Farrell was officially promoted to soloist, and danced Titania in *A Midsummer Night's Dream*, among other Balanchine works. In 1965 Balanchine created his full-length *Don Quixote* especially for her. With her role as Dulcinea, Suzanne Farrell achieved star status in the company.

During her tenure at the New York City Ballet, she was Balanchine's special favorite. It is said he fell in love with her. Considering the attention he lavished upon the young dancer, there is reason to assume this may have been so. After the gala performance of *Don Quixote*, at the New York State Theater, a supper party took place in the foyer. When Farrell emerged, walking among guests and admirers, Balanchine could be seen trailing behind her—following her, seemingly in worship of the very ground she walked on. Clearly, Balanchine, like Pygmalion, had become transfixed by his Galatea.

But he had not counted on his Galatea falling in love. In the company at that time was a young soloist named Paul Mejia. He and Farrell had been seeing each other during classes and rehearsals, and the two became inseparable. Ultimately, in 1969, they were married and left the company. There is no question but that Farrell's departure caused Balanchine considerable anguish.

During my visit with Farrell at the Felt Forum, her husband was at her side. He, too, is now a member of Béjart's company, and this evening he will dance the Pink Clown, a role he alternates with that of the incarnation of *Le Spectre de la Rose*. An intense, dark man, Mejia wears his hair parted in the center, falling in short waves around his quite spectacular face. The nose is beaklike, giving his features a sense of constant alertness. Paul and Suzanne look at one another adoringly. At times they touch.

I learn that Paul Mejia was born in Lima, Peru, and arrived in this country as a child of ten. Almost immediately, his mother enrolled him in the School of American Ballet. Upon completing his ballet schooling, Mejia joined the New York City Ballet and danced in the *corps*. Within a short time, he was made a soloist, dancing such roles as the Cavalier in *The Nutcracker*, Oberon in *A Midsummer Night's Dream*, and one of the leads in *Jewels*. Mejia claims that when he and Suzanne Farrell married, George Balanchine would no longer allow him to dance.

"I was fired after we were married. We came back from our honeymoon, and I was fired—not legally, because you can't be fired for getting married. But I was taken off the payroll. The press wanted interviews. It would have looked bad for the company if word got out to the press. So, I was rehired and put back on the payroll. But still, I was not dancing. In fact, they offered to pay me for a whole year if I agreed not to enter the theater. Of course, I had to leave.

"Balanchine stated that I gave him ultimatums—that I threatened to leave with Suzanne if I didn't get to dance. But that is not true. We are not that kind of people. Balanchine doesn't really know what happened, because he would not talk to us. Everything was done through messages. First of all, this whole thing didn't happen overnight. And it certainly didn't happen over my demanding great roles. It was just that one year I had a lot of good roles, and the next year, I had nothing. Absolutely nothing. Everybody in the company noticed this. I sat in the wings for a long time, and I didn't say a thing. My dancing was going to pot, because if you don't dance, you don't improve. One blow came after another. Balanchine would never talk to me. If I tried to get to him, he'd go the other way. Also, I never said anything about Suzanne leaving. I only said that if I don't dance, *I* leave. So I left. It was Suzanne's decision to leave also. She did not want to stay there because it would not have been easy for her."

Mejia continued to relate how badly he and Farrell felt over the situation. They had worked all their lives to be in the New York City Ballet. They had achieved their goal and were beginning to mature as artists.

"I know that Balanchine liked me a lot. He gave me so much. He was like a father to me. The point is, I did not go after Suzanne Farrell because he was interested in her. I had fallen in love with her long before that time—as many other people fell in love with her."

Farrell smiles. Then grows serious.

"I believe it all started that night at the *Don Quixote* gala." She says. "It was the most exciting night of my life. Through the tears, and all. And George danced that night—he danced the Don, and it was so wonderful to dance with him. But until that time, we had just worked very hard. I did not know that this all was going to happen. I was a young girl who was just willing to do anything he wanted. It was all wrapped up in this full-length ballet—something he had wanted to do for many years. Finally he did it because of me. So, naturally, I was in heaven.

"We had this wonderful attachment, mostly because of our work, and because I believe in what Mr. B. teaches. I was always so happy when I would do some little thing right—something no one else in the world would notice, except him. It all started on that basis. We had this friendship, and I didn't know what else would happen."

Lowering her blue-eyed gaze, Suzanne Farrell falls silent. Then, extending her hand to Paul Mejia, she looks at him for several moments. She seems, silently, to seek an encouraging nod from him to go on with her story. He presses her hand.

"Well, I knew he admired me as a dancer," Farrell continues, "and, for some reason, I could make him laugh. He liked my sense of humor. But we would usually only talk about the ballet—or about his cat. I got a cat because of him. Actually, it was all silly talk, because I was still very much in awe of him. Then, I heard, via the grapevine, that this thing was happening. I said, 'Oh, no. It's not true!'

"Naturally, I more than liked him. I have to be very attached to the person I work with, because I really give myself to that person. But I can't say I was madly in love with George. I was very attached to him—and more than just as a choreographer. Anyway, this was all before Paul. Then, when Paul and I got married, I tried to talk to George about it. Well, he accepted the fact that we were married. I told him it wouldn't change my dancing, or the way I still felt toward him. But George always says that once a dancer gets married, you never see her any more. She goes off and has a baby, and doesn't want to dance any more. But I wasn't going to do that. I still wanted, and needed to dance—and to dance for *him*. So, he accepted the fact that we were married. But then he said Paul had to leave. I just couldn't believe it. I mean, I don't think Mr. B. will ever find two people who believe more in his ways—who really believed, and wanted to carry on his tradition. He'll never find two people who were more dedicated to him. It's so sad . . . I was really quite sick about it all. And then, one couldn't see him. He didn't appear. One day, after a performance of *Swan Lake* he came to me and said, 'Even though you're married, you still did the best *Swan Lake* I've seen you do.' And I said, 'See? See?! I'm still fine!' But I never could say 'we'—I could only say 'I.' What I wanted to say was 'We three!' Because the three of us believed so much in the same thing."

Paul Mejia sat listening to his wife, then added:

"When I decided to leave, Suzanne said, 'If you go, I go.' The fact is, she hadn't been happy in the New York City Ballet for quite a while. It hadn't been so easy for Suzie. For example, she never had had an understudy. It was something Balanchine insisted on. When she danced, he wanted *her* to dance, because he had made the dance for her, and he didn't want anybody else to dance what he had created for her. So all those years she had no understudy. Then, when this whole thing broke, she was asked to teach everybody else her parts. That is already an insult to her as a person. So it was things like that. . . ."

"And not talking to me after all those years we had been through," Suzanne Farrell added. "You just don't go through things like that very easily. But we still love him. We always will. I'm sure that if I hadn't left with Paul, I would have had a breakdown. I was beside myself."

I ask Farrell how the company reacted to her departure.

"I'm sure there were some people who were very happy to see me go. I know that for a fact. There were people who were happy to have my roles. It's only human. I hold nothing against them for that. I suppose Balanchine made some of them unhappy by paying so much attention to me. It was beginning to be embarrassing, because during an evening of performances he would leave with me after I had finished my part. I was concerned for the company; I knew how other kids felt when Mr. B. watched them. They get nervous. They die, but they dance for *him*. So it would be depressing for the other kids to see him walk out with me when they still hadn't done their performance that night. It wasn't nice. I wouldn't have liked it myself."

"On the other hand," says Mejia, "Suzanne couldn't refuse him, either. If she did, he would be sick the next day. That happened many times. She was absolutely tied to him. You know, it's funny, the ballet we are dancing for Béjart, it's as though we were dancing our own story. Diaghilev was such a great man, everyone loved him. Just as Balanchine is a great man, and everyone loves him. I know I would have done anything for Mr. B.—practically."

When Suzanne Farrell and Paul Mejia left the New York City Ballet in 1969, they gave numerous dance recitals and Farrell did a complete *Swan Lake* with the National Ballet of Canada. The two also vacationed in Europe. During one of Farrell's guest performances, she injured her knee and did not dance for six months. While she was recuperating, she received a telegram from Maurice Béjart inviting her and Paul Mejia to visit his company, which was performing in Montreal. The two went to Canada, and liked Béjart's Ballets du XXᵐᵉ Siècle.

"I certainly never thought that I'd find another Mr. Balanchine, but Mr. Béjart is very gifted. Fortunately, for us, his teaching method is very similar to Mr. B.'s. It's fast, and it's precise. Also, he is wonderful to work with. It's great for us. We were happy to accept his invitation to join his company. I like dancing in his works. His *Romeo and Juliet* is divine. It's a wonderful ballet. And I love the role I'm doing now as Romola Nijinsky.

"We've made our home in Brussels. We don't have a big season, like the New York City Ballet—we alternate with the opera—but we work all year long, because we travel. It's nice living in Europe for a change. The people are different there. I love New York, of course. And it's a real treat to come back and dance here and to see our families. But there is something so charming about Brussels. It's big enough to be amusing, and small enough to be private."

Asked whether the two young dancers would return to the New York City Ballet if George Balanchine asked them, Farrell answered in a tentative manner:

"Well, it's hard to say. It's not as easy as all that. I don't know. We would have to sit down and talk—the three of us. Also, I wouldn't want to go back if I were only going to dance once a week. Naturally, I wouldn't expect to have my parts back. And so it's difficult, because I'm a dancer who thrives on dancing.

"And Paul would have to get roles to dance."

Paul Mejia suddenly bristles at the thought of returning to Balanchine: "I won't go back! I won't go back!"

"What's so awful," says Farrell, "is that Mr. B. took a tremendous interest in Paul. He encouraged his choreographing. He sent him to a music teacher. Paul was the boy and I was the girl that Mr. B. pinned his hopes on. He was our god. It shouldn't have ended this way."

Suzanne Farrell's voice trails off. She is genuinely sad over her break with Balanchine and the New York City Ballet. I ask the dancer to speak about the dance—about her own dancing.

"I love to dance so much that I almost start to hate it. I dance . . . for God, because he gave me what I have to work with. Also, I will always dance for Mr. B. I dance for my husband. I dance for Béjart because I'm very attached to him. I'm a terribly sentimental person. And I dance for myself because I should get a little fun out of it, and because I put a lot of work into it. I dance for my partners. In this ballet about Nijinsky, I dance for Jorge Donn, because I like him so much. Sometimes I like to dedicate my dancing to other people. If it's one of my sisters' birthday, and she's in the audience, I dedicate my performance to her. Sometimes, when I am depressed, I wonder why I am dancing. But then I hear music by Stravinsky or Tchaikovsky and I feel happy again. They give me a reason for dancing. Mostly, I dance because I have to dance in order to be happy."

Contrary to all expectations, Suzanne Farrell did rejoin the New York City Ballet during its winter 1974 season.

AMERICAN BALLET THEATRE

Martha Swope

CARLA FRACCI
— guest artist

Ingres would surely have drawn her. Delacroix would have painted an impassioned portrait of her. The nineteenth century clings to Carla Fracci like an invisible mantle. When Perrot's legendary *Pas de Quatre* was revived in the late 1950s, she interpreted the role originally danced by Fanny Cerrito.

Indeed, Carla Fracci's aura, her look, and demeanor suggest everyone's conception of the romantic ballerina. Like her great predecessors, Taglioni, Grisi, Cerrito, she brings to ballet that particular Italianate tradition of bravura and indefinable sweetness. When Fracci dances the classics, she embodies innocence and a certain nubile sexuality. There is about her the sweet coquette, perennially waiting for the kiss that will transform her into a woman.

As a technician, Fracci combines lightness and fragility with a clearly articulated line that gives her movements a special tensile lyricism. The lustrous, steely technique that attends some of her contemporaries may not be part of her balletic vocabulary. Fracci has something else: it is poignancy elevated to a poetic degree. Her movements and her gestures have a translucent cadence and phrasing. She has, in short, a style that is her own—one that alters our response to whatever role she creates. The word "magical" has been applied to her performances countless times. Whether dancing in *Giselle*, *La Sylphide*, *Coppélia*, or Tudor's *Romeo and Juliet*, she injects her characterizations with a subtly modulated range of emotions. Fracci, above all, is an actress.

A product of the ballet school of La Scala, Milan, Carla Fracci was born in that city in 1936. Her father was a streetcar conductor; her mother, a housewife. She has a sister five years her junior. Most of Fracci's childhood was spent living in the country some miles outside of Milan.

"I am a country girl. Even today, I feel that way. And I want my four-year-old son to know the joys of living in the country. I will always be a country girl. People say that now I am an important person—a prima ballerina—a diva. This may be true, but one can never lose one's background."

Carla Fracci was in New York dancing with the American Ballet Theatre during the winter season of 1973. As always, her appearances were hailed by both the press and the public. Fracci has a large New York following, and her fans adore her. On a cold, rainy day in January I made my way to visit her. Sitting in the living room of a close friend, the producer, Joseph Wishy, she continued to shed the aura of a creature not of this century. Despite her up-to-the-minute chocolate-brown turtleneck, brown wool skirt, and smart brown boots, she was the essence of the romantic woman—pale, fragile, and mysterious. She wore no make-up. Her hair, with a classic center part, framed her beautiful face. It was difficult to believe that this renowned ballerina had had a rather inauspicious beginning as a young student at La Scala.

"When I was brought to the school—I was nine—I was put in the very last group—the group that the school wasn't at all certain about. When the teacher finally got around to us, he took a look at me and said, 'She is very thin and her legs are very thin. But she has a nice face. Let's take her.' So, I was accepted on very shaky grounds. There was a month-long trial period. I went through that, and then my studies really began. At La Scala we not only danced, but we also had regular schooling. The entire course lasted eight years. For the first few years, I was the least promising one. Then, when I turned twelve, I was chosen to be a 'super' in *Sleeping Beauty* with the English Royal Ballet, which had come to perform at La Scala. Margot Fonteyn danced Aurora. It was the first time I was ever on a stage. And it was the first time I had really seen a ballet, because in those years they did not give many ballets at La Scala.

"Well, when I saw Margot dance, it was a tremendous revelation to me. It was then I really knew I wanted to become a ballerina. I looked and looked at her. I studied her every move. I studied the way she played with her eyes. And I began to imitate her. That's when I really began to work very, very hard in my ballet classes. We must all be very grateful to Margot Fonteyn for what she has given to the dance in general. But for me, she was my great inspiration."

In 1954 Carla Fracci graduated from La Scala. She danced in operatic productions, and occasionally sang in the chorus. In 1957 she had her first great opportunity to prove herself.

"Violette Verdy came to La Scala as a guest to dance in *Cinderella*. For some reason, she had to go back to Paris, and I was asked to go on. Of course, it wasn't all that simple. The directors all thought I couldn't possibly carry a three-act ballet. But I went to them and said, 'Why not try me? Give me this opportunity. Give me one rehearsal on the stage, then decide whether I can manage it or not.' So they gave me a stage rehearsal, and I was told I could do the ballet. It was my first moment. I was a success. My partner was Giulio Perugini. On top of it all, it was New Year's Eve!"

Another great opportunity came when, at the age of nineteen, Fracci was asked to perform in Anton Dolin's *Pas de Quatre* at the Nervi Dance Festival. Dolin discovered the young dancer in the *corps*, and saw in her demeanor something of the legendary dancer Fanny Cerrito.

"When Dolin first saw me, he said 'Come and do some arabesques with me.' So I did, and he said that I would dance the *Pas de Quatre* together with Alicia Markova, Yvette Chauviré, and Margrethe Schanne. Dolin also told me that I would make a very good Giselle, and that I reminded him of Spessivtzeva. Dolin then invited me to come to a London gala. I went with Mario Pistoni, who was already a star at La Scala, and he and I did a Glazunov *pas de deux*. Then, in 1959, Dolin asked me to join London's Festival Ballet, which I did. I stayed with the company for six months. It was at the Festival Ballet that I did my first important Giselle. They gave *Giselle* three nights in a row. The first was danced by Alicia Markova, the second by Yvette Chauviré, and I danced it the third night. The reviews were really fantastic. They even said that the last *Giselle* was the best. It was in London that my international career began. I was invited by the Royal Ballet's second company to dance *Les Sylphides*. Again, the reviews were incredible. So that's how it all started for me."

Fracci's approach to Giselle has changed with the years. She finds it the ultimate role:

"I must say that these days, when I must do Giselle, it is a crisis. To bring life to it requires enormous effort. The more I dance it, the more I find new things in it. It is such a complete role for a ballerina, and it must never become stereotyped. It must change as you mature. Fortunately, I don't dance the role very often. There is space between performances. I can forget it, then come back to it fresh. I always try to put new things into it, and take things out of it. My aim is to enrich the role. Of course, so much depends on your partner.

"By now, I have danced with most of the great ones, including Vladimir Vassiliev. I have danced with Nureyev, with Attilio Labis, Flemming Flindt, John Gilpin, and more recently with Ivan Nagy, Ted Kivitt, Paolo Bortoluzzi. Of course, Erik Bruhn was the ideal partner. He was such an extraordinary dancer—and such an extraordinary person. What happened between us on stage was a kind of love. There are really no words to explain it. It was something we felt. We did not need words between us. Something happened when we danced. When he retired, it was a great loss for me. We danced his last performance together in Washington, D.C.—it was *La Sylphide*. Then he became ill. I think that it was his sense of perfection that made it so hard for him to continue. When he felt that something wasn't perfect, it just went to his stomach. He developed terrible pains. We talked so much about it. Finally, he came to me and said, 'Carla, I cannot go on like this!' But thinking back on our partnership, I can only say that every time we danced, something new took place. Everyone who saw this understood that there was a true love between us. He once told me that he would have stopped dancing earlier if he hadn't found me. We gave so much to each other, and, I think, to the public. There was never any competition between us—never.

"When I dance with Nureyev, I feel there is some competition. Of course, we are such different personalities. He is so aggressive—so strong. He comes on, and he is so much himself. But when Erik saw us dance, he said, 'Now that I have retired, I see you and Rudolf as the new couple.' Actually, it is difficult for us to be a pair. He is not with Ballet Theatre. He has so much work, and we are in different places at different times. These days I dance with Bortoluzzi. We are both Italian, and I think we look very well together. Something works."

Carla Fracci has been a guest artist with American Ballet Theatre since 1967. She has lent the company part of its glitter. She is part of its star system. I asked Fracci whether the appearance of Natalia Makarova at ABT disturbed her in any way.

"No. In a company like ABT, the more prima ballerinas they have, the better. Don't forget that the company travels a great deal, and America is a big country. The public needs to see other ballerinas—they would be bored to see *me* all the time. There is room for everyone and it makes

THE PRIVATE WORLD OF BALLET**

everything more exciting. Besides, Makarova and I are so different, and it's good to see that difference."

Eight years ago, Carla Fracci married the stage director and librettist Beppe Menegatti.

"Actually, I met Beppe when I was seventeen years old. I was at La Scala, and he was the assistant of Luchino Visconti. Visconti and he wanted me to dance in a ballet which I finally didn't dance in because I was not prima ballerina. Then, when they came again to La Scala to mount *La Traviata* with Maria Callas, Beppe walked into a studio, and there I was, in practice clothes which happened to be all red. They used to call me Little Devil. Beppe saw me, and he went to Luchino and said, 'Look at this girl. She would be perfect for the ballet in *La Traviata*.' Anyway, I was engaged and that's how Beppe and I came together. Now we have a nice baby. Time goes so fast. . . . I'm already old. . . . It's time to retire!

"I've done so much—although I have not danced any Balanchine except *his Swan Lake*—the second act. Actually, I don't think I'm right for his work. I mean, I adore Balanchine. I think he's a genius. But I need a story in the ballets I dance. That's absolutely necessary for me. By now, I am bright enough to see what is good for me and what is not good for me."

Carla Fracci is one of the few Italian ballerinas in recent history to have made an international career. I asked her to comment on the ballet scene in Italy.

"I can only say that ballet has become quite important in Italy. When they do ballet, the houses are always sold out—even without a name dancer. *Swan Lake*, with or without a name, is always sold out. Curiously enough, the opera is not so well attended. One doesn't hear too much about Italian ballet because we don't have a national company. The fact is, we have some excellent dancers in Italy—especially ballerinas. In Rome, in Milan, and in other cities, ballet thrives. If Italy wanted to, it could really create a fantastic national company. But the Italians, as well as the French, still cling to their operas. Despite evidence to the contrary, the powers that be won't admit that ballet has a great drawing power all its own. I hope this situation will change in time."

What does it mean to be a prima ballerina?

"The responsibility is so large. In a way, it was easy to arrive at my position. It's far more difficult to maintain it—to stay there. Dancing is not just nice or beautiful or a fairy tale. It is a profession that requires tremendous discipline. You finish a performance at night, and the next morning you are in the first position at the *barre*. I have danced a long time. What I try to do now is to communicate a role—to get across some feeling of what a character is all about. I try to be as involved as possible in whatever role I dance. I am not interested in being a good machine. Of course, you can communicate something with technique alone. But that is not *me* at all. For me, even an arabesque has to be in character. An arabesque in *Giselle* is quite different from an arabesque in *Romeo and Juliet*. The pirouettes are different—the facial expressions are different."

What will Fracci do when she stops dancing?

"I cannot think about that. I take everything day by day. I am ready to accept whatever comes tomorrow. If tomorrow I feel I must stop dancing, I will stop. If I stop, perhaps I will act. Let's face it, it is easier to act than to dance. Dancing is really quite unnatural. Whoever said 'You are born to dance' was lying. Ballet dancing is nothing one is born with. When I think about it, a ballerina cannot really enjoy life too much. You have certain satisfactions—you can have success. Still, when you really think about it, your life has been sacrificed. Oh, I am not feeling sorry for myself. I am a very lucky woman. I'm lucky that I have work that I like to do, and at which I've had so much success. Also, I have a life outside of the dance. I have a husband. I have a child. I never say I am a dancer first. I always say I am a woman first. . . . No. Actually, I say, 'Life first!' "

Kenn Duncan

PAOLO BORTOLUZZI
— guest artist

I am a Taurus—born May 17, 1938, in Genoa," said Paolo Bortoluzzi
as we began our interview in January 1973 at the Russian Tea Room. The
dancer was appearing as guest artist with American Ballet Theatre. He is a
small, surprisingly large-chested man. At first glance, he does not have the
exquisite look of the *danseur noble*, and yet when Bortoluzzi begins to
dance, his oddly proportioned body moves with near-perfect symmetry.
Technically flawless, he conveys both abandoned energy and poetry. At

times, he is given to an excess of mannerisms which may be attributed to his Italian exuberance as well as to his twelve-year association with Maurice Béjart's frenetic Ballets of the Twentieth Century.

Bortoluzzi does not have the supremely handsome face that one associates with the male ballet dancer. There is something of the peasant about it. But, again, his face transforms into princely sensitivity when onstage. What is interesting about Paolo Bortoluzzi is this capacity for transformation, because it goes beyond the expected metamorphosis of person to stage persona. In idealized roles, such as Albrecht, he seems refreshingly real—blood courses through his veins. He is both man and princely being —both peasant and poet. He projects a sense of drama and urgency within the confines of classical strictures. He masters all the dynamics of manly dancing without sacrificing the essential lyricism of any given role. He is, in short, a kind of rough-hewn, splendidly charged-up dancer, who is able to convey immediacy and "presence," who seems always on the brink of losing control, but never does. He is at once tough and refined.

His manner, in person, reflects these qualities. Bortoluzzi is direct, and almost defensively self-aware.

"My parents were not in the theater at all. My father was a businessman, and my mother was a housewife. When a new ballet school opened in Genoa, I took classes with the idea of just exercising my body. It never entered my mind to make dancing my career. Earlier, I had studied piano and composition. Anyway, when I began my classes, and I touched this thing called ballet, I suddenly felt completely happy. My parents were not completely happy. I nevertheless insisted . . . because I am Taurus. I continued to study for four years in Genoa, then went to Milan, where my Genoa teacher Ugo Dell'Ara, had a private dancing school. He formed a company with the members of that school which was called Compania del Balletto Italiano. I was twenty when I joined that group, and remained with it for two years."

Bortoluzzi related that when the company performed at the Nervi Festival, he met Léonide Massine. Massine had his own company, Ballets Européens, and Bortoluzzi joined it for six months. He danced in such Massine works as *The Decameron*, *The Barber of Seville* (with opera singers and orchestra in the pit), and *Choreartium*. The dancer recalled his experience with Massine:

"He was the most unusual person that I have ever known in my life. He was unusual to a point of making me afraid of him. I was frightened of his appearance and of his manner of speaking. When he spoke to you, you never knew what he was thinking. I never knew whether he liked my work or not. Still, he was a marvelous person, and my time with him was the start of my career. I danced only principal roles. In fact, from the very beginning, I never danced in the *corps*. It was also at Nervi that I met

Maurice Béjart. This was all in 1960. Béjart saw me dance and asked me to join the company he was starting in Belgium. And so, I left Italy thinking I would stay away for one or two years—but I stayed twelve years. Even while with Béjart, I made guest appearances at La Scala, dancing the classics. I danced *Sleeping Beauty* with Carla Fracci. I also danced *Swan Lake*.

"Of course, at Béjart we took classes all based on classical techniques. By this I mean that even when I danced very avant-garde works, I never left the classical traditions. The first ballet I did for Béjart was *Pulcinella*, with music by Stravinsky. Also, I did Stravinsky's *Jeu de Cartes* and *Le Sacre du Printemps*. I did a ballet called *The Swan*, which had Indian music. It was a kind of masterpiece for me. We did big works like Beethoven's Ninth Symphony. We did *Romeo and Juliet*. I did a ballet to music by Xenakis, which was a solo and lasted twenty-two minutes. To work on this sort of thing, you have to be very close to the choreographer.

"I learned a lot of things with Béjart. I was very young, and Béjart had a powerful personality. It was useful for me to work with him. I think he is a genius—a marvelous theater man. I especially liked his direct way of meeting the audience—the public. Generally, in ballet, dancers are very far from the audience. You don't really feel what happens. But with Béjart, you are directly connected with the people. It is the kind of thing that I personally try to bring to traditional ballet. I think there is a way to do it. One *can* dance the classics differently.

"Finally, I left the company in 1972. I discovered there were many other ballets I wanted to do. Béjart never did *Giselle* or *Coppélia* or *Swan Lake* or *La Sylphide*. I joined American Ballet Theatre because it has such a big and marvelous repertoire. It is possible that Béjart was unhappy when I left, but I explained to him why I had to leave. He understood very well. Also, Béjart had taken on Suzanne Farrell as his prima ballerina, and she was much too tall for me. We never danced together, and that was not very satisfactory. I was dancing solo parts all the time. Things came to a head when Béjart asked me to dance *Romeo and Juliet* with Suzanne. I told him she was too tall for me, but he insisted that she would be Juliet. I said, 'Look, Fracci and Makarova are waiting for me at ABT. Erik Bruhn has stopped dancing. Why stay here?' "

When Bortoluzzi joined ABT, he did indeed dance with Fracci and Makarova. He danced *Le Spectre de la Rose* and *Giselle* with Fracci, *La Sylphide* and *Pillar of Fire* with Makarova. He danced *Coppélia* with Eleanor d'Antuono, and soon established himself as a favorite with the public. Since Erik Bruhn's retirement, he has become Carla Fracci's main partner. Bortoluzzi expounded on the dance in general and on what he considers to be his particular style:

"I am extremely sensitive to movement. Every time I am sad or tired or nervous, I begin to move. This makes me happy again. I don't believe in limitation of movement. That is, movement could be ballet or modern dance or social dance. I am very happy when I go to a night club and dance and shake. It is wonderfully releasing.

"You ask about my style of dancing. I have a lot of friends who have seen me dance with Béjart. They cannot understand why I want to dance *Giselle*. Other friends who know me only as a classical dancer cannot believe that I did all these modern things with Béjart. The point is, I don't have one particular style. I prefer it when people say, 'He is beautiful in Béjart, and beautiful in *Giselle*.' "

We touched on the stigma attached to the male dancer.

"A lot of people still believe that all male dancers are homosexual. I will tell you why they believe this. It is because a male dancer, when he dances, must be very beautiful. You must move very softly. If you do *Les Sylphides*, you must have no sex at all. If you do *Le Spectre de la Rose*, you are neither a man nor a woman—you are a spirit. But, generally, when people see you moving gently and softly, they immediately think you're a homosexual. I think it's idiotic. One must accept a dancer as a dancer. You must look and see if you like his dancing, and if he moves in the right way for any particular ballet."

Paolo Bortoluzzi is married to Jaleh Kerendi—a dancer with the Béjart company. The two have a young daughter, Vanessa. "Our baby was born in July, she is a Leo. It's important for the character to know what sign you were born under. My wife still dances with Béjart, and although we don't see each other too often, we still manage very well. Every season I arrange to spend time in Brussels, where we make our home. My wife comes to see me perform whenever I dance in Europe."

Bortoluzzi claims that he never thinks when he dances:

"There are dancers who think how to do the steps. I never think. I choose a kind of liberty. Of course, I study very hard beforehand. But when I go onstage, I try to forget everything—to make my pleasure the dance, and to transmit my pleasure to the audience. I am not an intellectual dancer. At least, not for the moment.

"Sometimes I am asked by young male dancers what they must do to have a career in the dance. I always tell them that the first thing is to adore the dance. It is not enough just to love it or to like it. You really must adore it. Also, it is important to be very persevering, because ballet is very demanding. You must be very strong psychologically. If your mind breaks because of the training, all is finished. You must also have tremendous musicality. You must have a nice body, and a lot of intelligence. Intelligence is particularly important if you want to have a very big career. Because you must know how to choose your roles. You must understand where you can go and where you cannot go. Above all, a dancer must not listen to too many people. He must know what is right for *him*."

Does Bortoluzzi consider himself to be in the league of Erik Bruhn and Rudolf Nureyev?

"It may sound a little pretentious, but it has never been my aim to dance like Bruhn or Nureyev. I feel that I would like to combine the best qualities of both these dancers. I do not wish to imitate. I wish to be my own dancer."

Dina Makarova

NATALIA MAKAROVA
— guest artist

he Palm Court in the Plaza Hotel in New York has its old-world charms, but those charms are quickly dispelled when waiters rush to the table and ask us to leave. "The gentleman with you has neither tie nor jacket. No, we do not have a tie or jacket for the gentleman. I'm afraid I must ask you to leave."

The gentleman in question is Vladimir Rodzianko, a young Russian composer, who has brought ballerina Natalia Makarova for an interview. He is to be her interpreter, but, unaware of the Plaza's new-world regulations, he arrives wearing a sweater. I try to explain things to the head waiter: "This young lady is Natalia Makarova . . . you know, the Russian ballerina who defected to the West . . . in London, last September . . . a member of the Kirov Ballet . . . just like Nureyev . . . surely, you've read *something* about it." No response from the head waiter. "I'm sorry, but I cannot allow you to stay here if the gentleman has no jacket or tie," he says coldly.

I look helplessly at Natalia Makarova. She sits impassive, an icy stare upon her perfect features. The interpreter is dismayed and apologetic. He talks in Russian to Makarova. She whispers an answer and rises. Makarova is clearly put out. I think fast. No. Another midtown restaurant won't do. Then I recall that The Viking Press, which has published books by me, is located only two short blocks away. I ask Rodzianko to tell Makarova that they should follow me. More explanations to Makarova. She looks at me, and (at last) throws me a dazzling smile. She leads the way out of the hotel—a slight, compact figure in black boots and black coat, a long purple scarf, encircling her fragile head. There is purpose in her walk, but the chill December air makes all of us walk briskly. There is no conversation.

We reach The Viking Press on Madison Avenue, step into an elevator, and emerge, unannounced, hoping it will grant us a quiet spot for the interview. Receptionists, secretaries, and editors are marvelously obliging. We are ushered into an elegant, unoccupied conference room. The door is closed. It opens again only when sandwiches and coffee are brought in for our lunch. Makarova is pleased. The interpreter is pleased. I am immensely relieved.

Natalia Makarova is in New York as the newest and most controversial member of the American Ballet Theatre. In a few days, the Soviet ballerina will be making her debut with the company, dancing Giselle, a role that has catapulted her to fame in both Russia and Europe. Indeed, Makarova has been an established star of the Leningrad Kirov Ballet since 1961, the very year Rudolf Nureyev made his own spectacular defection from the company at Le Bourget airport in Paris.

The two had, of course, known each other while they were members of the Kirov Ballet, and there has been some speculation that Makarova's recent defection was largely prompted by Nureyev's great personal and professional success away from the company. But the ballerina's own version of why she defected does not emphasize Nureyev's flight.

"I was with him and the company in Paris at the time," Makarova says in Russian, as the interpreter translates. "It was my first tour abroad, and I was busy preparing to dance *Giselle*. I believe it was Nureyev's dramatic departure from the company that made the directors decide to let me dance *Giselle* in London. They wanted to put on a show which would offset, to some extent, the effect of his action. I must say, I wasn't thinking very much about Nureyev at the time, but only about the wonderful reception the London audiences gave me."

Makarova's extraordinary performances in *Giselle* and other classical ballets established her reputation. She is one of the most acclaimed young dancers in the world. In Russia, she was accorded star privileges, and, in purely material terms, she lacked nothing. Politically, she was uninvolved. Never a member of the Communist party, she chose to be judged solely on her abilities as an artist. The authorities never pressured Makarova in any way. On the contrary, in 1969 the Soviet Union awarded her the title of "Honored Artist of the Russian Federation." Yet on September 4, 1970, while the Leningrad Kirov Ballet was in London, twenty-nine-year-old Natalia Makarova applied to the British Home Office for permission to remain in Britain.

The Home Office granted her request. The defection was instantly publicized throughout the world, and the rumor mills began to grind: Makarova had defected because her second marriage to a young Soviet film-maker had ended unhappily in divorce, and she wanted to start a new life, away from bitter memories; she had defected because she was madly in love with a handsome thirty-four-year-old BBC announcer, John Touhey, and could not live without him; she had defected because the Kirov would not mount new ballets for her, chaining her to roles that would forever limit her artistic expression; Makarova had defected because she wanted fame, money, total stardom, and world-wide recognition.

In London, Makarova went into seclusion, letting the gossip do its work. Two weeks later she emerged and agreed to write a three-part article on the defection for the London *Sunday Telegraph*. The first of these articles, entitled "My Steps to Freedom," contained her reasons for leaving Russia and the Kirov Ballet:

> My decision to defect was certainly the gravest decision I have ever made in my short life. Why did I choose to make this leap into the West—into, if not the unknown, at any rate, into a great deal of uncertainty? The simple answer is: Because I wanted to be free—free to dance as I please, free to develop my art, free to work with whom I want to work, free to make the maximum use of all the talents nature has provided me with. . . . In the Soviet Union, there is no experimenting with new styles, new techniques, new choreography, such as there is in the West.
>
> I knew that if I wanted to go further, to develop my art, and to reach new heights—if I was capable of them—I would have to leave my own country. So long as I stayed there, I would be up against a brick wall. I would dance the old, classical rôles to the end of my dancing years, and that would be that. Some ballerinas are ready to accept that fate. For me, it was artistic death.

Natalia Makarova seems somewhat tense as she now sits in this handsome, indirectly lit conference room. She occasionally picks at her nails.

Her voice has an edgy, strained quality. Still, the grace of her body (she is five feet, two inches tall) and the limpid clarity of her face with its intense blue eyes (false eyelashes deepening their gaze), pert nose, high cheekbones, and long, long hair pulled into a bun, suggest a woman of enormous self-possession. During our talk, she smokes incessantly ("I cannot live without cigarettes!").

Through her interpreter I learn that she already misses Leningrad.

"I often have such contradictory feelings about it all," she says. "I miss my family—especially my mother—and I miss my city, Leningrad, which I love more than any other city in the world. And, yes, I miss the great Kirov Ballet, which has nurtured me, and which has given me my *grand jeté* into my career.

"I suppose I will learn to love my new life. I suppose I will even learn to love New York—I have been here before—but it is so immense, so confusing. I am confident that New York will satisfy me in the question of my art. I certainly hope so. I certainly hope that my one-year contract with the American Ballet Theatre will fulfill my needs for experimentation. What persuaded me to accept their offer was the company's artistic perspective. It has a most interesting repertoire. What is more important, it seems not to want to restrict itself to the repertoire it has. What I also admire about the American Ballet Theatre is that it combines this love for the classics with the new and the contemporary. It is the contemporary repertoire that I am pinning my hopes on."

I ask Makarova why she did not join London's Royal Ballet.

"That is a good question," she answers. "Frankly, I was not asked to join the company. I, myself, am not altogether sure as to why. I suspect it was internal politics—and, possibly, external politics." Makarova laughs when I tell her that I had read that the Royal Ballet would take her on over at least four dead bodies!

Does Makarova feel her presence in the American Ballet will upset or overshadow its leading dancers—Carla Fracci, for example?

"I haven't thought about it," she says. "My God, perhaps I should! But I must tell you that I constantly feel too much is expected of me. This worries me, because whenever one expects too much, one is bound to be disappointed. I simply hope to do my best. I hope to be happy on the stage."

Prior to coming to New York, Makarova danced with Nureyev for London television. They performed the *Black Swan pas de deux*. The ballerina was not ecstatic over the experience. "We had never danced a *pas de deux* together—and we did not have sufficient time to adjust to the question of our individual technique, manner, and character. But I would say Nureyev is a very good partner."

Makarova's defection has clearly been traumatic:

"It just came to me on the spur of the moment. And I realized that if I missed that moment, it would be a sin against my art. I *had* to defect—and I had to do it immediately. Of course, many strong feelings went through my heart. But I made my decision. Perhaps I have made a mistake, but I do not think so. I hope to do here what I could not do in Russia. But doing these things, I hope to help Russian art in general.

"Individual, creative talent does not have a chance in today's Soviet Union. Great writers are put in jail, and freedom of expression in all the arts is condemned and suppressed. One cannot fulfill one's creative needs in such an atmosphere. I certainly could never grow under such conditions. That is why I have taken my leap to freedom!"

The above was an interview which appeared in *The New York Times* on December 20, 1970. During the subsequent three years, Natalia Makarova's career burgeoned in this country. She was acclaimed during her period with the American Ballet Theatre, and American audiences took the ballerina to their hearts. Her astonishing technique, her personal magnetism, and her interpretative powers all combined to produce performances of rare brilliance. Makarova's great desire to work with contemporary choreographers was only partially fulfilled. While she danced some of the Antony Tudor repertoire, she did not succeed in having Tudor, Robbins, Balanchine, or other well-known choreographers create ballets especially for her. Makarova remained with American Ballet Theatre for two years, touring with them and dancing the classical repertoire, as well as such works as Tudor's *Jardin aux Lilas* and *Pillar of Fire*. She then chose to dance and live in Europe, making a number of appearances with London's Royal Ballet. She also agreed to make infrequent guest appearances with American Ballet Theatre. During its 1973 summer season, ABT announced only one performance in which Makarova would dance. It was a *Swan Lake* and it was considered a triumph by New York audiences.

During her various New York appearances, I had had the opportunity of seeing Makarova dance and of becoming better acquainted with her. Her English had much improved, and her constant regret was the lack of new ballets in which she could perform. On an icy January day in 1973, Makarova visited me for a brief interview for this book. She was so cold that she requested a shawl and some very hot tea. Once comfortable, she relaxed, and we began to talk. I had known nothing of her childhood in Leningrad. Makarova told me a bit about it:

"I was a peculiar child," she began. "My real father disappeared during the war—probably killed. I was just a baby. My mother remarried. I have a stepbrother. As a very young girl I had the desire to be an actress. I had very little interest in music, and did not think about dancing. I just wanted to express myself in any way I could. I remember that whenever my parents were not at home, I would stand in front of the mirror and try many different expressions in rapid succession, while remaining the same inside . . . I was about ten years old then. I would dress up, I would cover myself with a tablecloth or a bedspread. I had such a good time! Sometimes I would cry because it was impossible for the outside world to know the world inside me. I knew I could move. I was acrobatically inclined and double-jointed. Sometimes I frightened my mother when she would come into a room and find me with my legs wrapped around my shoulders."

I asked Makarova how she came to be interested in dancing.

"It was by accident. A girl friend and I went to an organization similar to your Girl Scouts. They gave ballet lessons. I was not very good. Anyway, my mother didn't want me to become a ballerina. It was fine with me. I didn't find ballet interesting at all. I thought it was boring. It was just fun for a little bit. However, the teacher at that ballet class advised me to go to the Leningrad ballet school. She said it would be better for me. And so I went. They gave me a physical examination. The director of the school liked me. By then, I was already twelve. I stayed for six years. Usually, it takes nine years to graduate. I graduated at eighteen, and I was fantastically successful. I remember that for my graduation, I did the *Giselle pas de deux*. It was the first time I ever received flowers. They were beautiful large lilies sent to me from a young boy who was mad about me. I felt it was the most beautiful time in my life. Then I entered the Leningrad Kirov Company. First, of course, they put me in the *corps de ballet*. I was terrible in the *corps*. I hate it when everybody looks like everybody else. I couldn't understand why I wasn't allowed to do what I wanted to do as an individual. There was conflict all the time. I think that's why they made me a soloist very soon. Actually, I wasn't ready. Six years' training is not enough. But I did all the solos. I did all the solos in *Sleeping Beauty*—even the Pussycat. Finally, I became principal dancer. I did *Swan Lake* and *Giselle*. Then, I did *Giselle* in London for the first time. It was 1961. I had great potential, but still, I wasn't ready. Every performance was wrong. Sometimes I would finish my variation in the prompter's box. Sometimes I would fall down. The public just waited. After a while, I became strong."

Makarova went on to tell me that she soon became an important member of the Kirov and led a very good life. In 1965 she entered the Second International Ballet Competition at Varna, Bulgaria, where she received the Gold Medal.

Makarova's defection in 1970 was still on her mind:

"I hate the word 'defection.' I just chose to remain here and work. Actually, while I was still in Leningrad I had the opportunity of working with a very talented choreographer who did very experimental works, but these works were never performed. I mean, a limited number were shown, but if anything is limited, it cannot flourish as art. Even the ballets that *were* allowed to be shown were altered or censored. It was hopeless. I wanted a new life, new work, new dances. I wanted to express myself completely. Unfortunately, I am still waiting. I still have not had this opportunity. Of course, I could not refuse to do the classical ballets. For me, the classics will always *be* ballet. What I try to do is to make them more contemporary. I don't change the steps, but I alter the feeling—the attitude."

Lingering on the classics, Makarova gave me some idea of how she prepares for them. We talked of *Swan Lake* and *Giselle*.

"I must do many things before I dance *Swan Lake*. I know that it is a technical ballet first, so I must prepare my muscles. Secondly, I must prepare my arms. I must make my arms as flexible as possible. Before going to bed I think of the new feeling that I must convey the next day. I never remember what I did in the last performance. I try to find something fresh. I think of my feeling toward my partner—an emotional state of mind must be found. Then comes the day of the performance. I prefer to be alone. If I am in the mood, I will go shopping and buy something exciting. Usually, I prepare myself very intensely. I am at the theater four hours before the performance. It allows complete concentration and preparation. On the day of the performance I prefer to warm up alone. I don't like to take class with anybody else.

"With *Giselle*, it is the same thing. I've done so many Giselles. The important thing is not to repeat myself in performance. It is a great effort. Sometimes a whole performance depends on a new nuance that has occurred to me, or that I have invented.

"When the orchestra begins, I stand in the wings. Sometimes I get very nervous and forget all the steps. Other times I am very calm. Recently, I have danced *Giselle* with Ivan Nagy. Sometimes I ask Ivan which Giselle he wants today. Of course, he doesn't answer, because he is losing himself in his part. So I decide by myself which interpretation to use. Often I decide I will do a Chekhov Giselle. These associations give me insight into the character. I get a mental picture.

"Then I step onstage, and suddenly my body, my head, my hands, and the music are all together. I never think about single details. I think of the full picture. My best and happiest moments are on the stage. It is then I feel completely natural and am myself. The role that I dance is not *on* me, but *in* me. I know that when I lift my eyes or my head or my hand and when it all feels comfortable, I am in my world. Those are the best moments for me."

I asked Makarova how it was for her working with Antony Tudor, whose style must have been so alien to her.

"I admire Tudor tremendously. When he coaches you, he himself transforms into the role he is showing you. He did not need to talk. I just had to watch him. I was delighted to do *Pillar of Fire*. I think it is the best Tudor ballet. When I was preparing for *Pillar*, I tried things out in my apartment.

Things did not always work when I was being coached in the studio. Schönberg's music is very difficult—and very beautiful. I decided that the whole role depends on how you walk on the stage. If you discover how Hagar walks, you discover the character."

How does Makarova feel after a performance?

"If I am happy with a performance, I feel very alive. When I am unhappy with a performance, I get very depressed. When I have an unhappy performance, it is terrible to have to smile and sign autographs. After a performance I like to go out and eat. Usually, I want to be with someone who has good taste and who will analyze my performance for me. I like that very much, because sometimes I don't remember what I did."

Prior to her defection, Makarova was twice married and twice divorced.

"I was in love with my first husband. He was my first love. But he was so much older than I. I grew up quickly, and he stayed the same. It was not interesting for me any more. With me, whenever things get boring, I just run away. Actually, it's not just boredom. It goes deeper than that. Anyway, later I married a man my age. He was a very talented film director. He was very intelligent. He was perhaps too complex. I found him very interesting . . . but it was not enough. I will tell you only that I never regret what has happened in my life. I try to forget the bad moments. Perhaps I am not yet a complete woman—because I do not have a child."

Makarova informed me that she was not any longer happy dancing with the American Ballet Theatre: "I am bored with ABT."

Was it because ABT could not persuade choreographers to create new ballets for her?

"I think so. I thought that being with the company, I would be like putty in the choreographers' hand—ready to be molded. Somebody told me that choreographers were afraid that I would be too demanding. That there would be too much pressure. But I am not like that. When I work with a choreographer, I try to help him. I give myself to him completely. Tudor knows that. Still, he did not create a ballet for me. It was my dream to work with Robbins. They said it was frightening to work with him. I don't believe this. But Robbins has not created a ballet for me. Balanchine won't work with me. He is more interested in creating a dancer. So it is all very frustrating.

"Of course, I believe that a choreographer should find *me*. It is not right that I should have to find a choreographer. What I am looking for is a masterpiece. I don't want to waste my time. I am tired of experiments. I want a new three-act ballet. I even know what I want. I want Dostoevski on stage. I want *The Idiot*. I want to dance Nastasia Filipovna. She is such a woman! A woman with so many aspects!"

The volatile ballerina sat up nervously. In a way, she seemed almost desperate. Time—any dancer's enemy—seems to be passing far too quickly for her. Makarova rightly feels that she is at the height of her powers, but that the range of her creative abilities has not yet been fully tapped.

Makarova continues to dance in many parts of the world, and continues to make headlines. During the summer of 1973, she danced with Rudolf Nureyev at the Paris Summer Festival. After their performance, Makarova held a press conference and announced to the world that she would never dance with Nureyev again—he was not a refined partner—he was rude and thoughtless. Nureyev, for his part, did not issue any statement. Clearly, Makarova recalls the era of the high-flown, temperamental ballet star. Were she less an artist, this might be dismissed as mere publicity-seeking. As it is, Makarova reigns as virtuoso dancer—a performer whose destiny, it would seem, is the quest for the one role that will create ballet history— the one work that will truly embody *her*.

"I have tried everything," said Makarova. "I have tried comedy, drama, lyrical drama, modern abstract things. I am ready for something very challenging. But nothing and no one has used me fully."

MIKHAIL BARYSHNIKOV
— guest artist

had my first glimpse of Mikhail Baryshnikov, the famed Kirov dancer, during an intermission at the New York State Theater, where the American Ballet Theatre's 1974 summer season had been in progress for some three weeks. By then, it had been approximately two weeks that the ballet world had known about Baryshnikov's defection in Toronto, where, during June 1974, he had been appearing as guest dancer with a touring section of the Bolshoi Ballet.

On that mild New York evening, flanked by ABT co-director Lucia

Chase and the company's associate director, the British choreographer Antony Tudor, Baryshnikov seemed a tiny, almost inconsequential figure. The three sat in the first ring of the State Theater watching a performance of *Coppélia*, in which another Kirov defector, Natalia Makarova, danced the leading role. As chance would have it, Rudolf Nureyev, the first and most spectacular of Soviet defectors, was on that very evening performing in a dress rehearsal of the National Ballet of Canada's production *Sleeping Beauty* at the Metropolitan Opera but a few steps away from the New York State Theater. (To round matters out, the character dancer Alexander Minz, a less-publicized 1973 Kirov defector, was also in the audience at the State Theater.) New York was playing host to four Kirov defectors, a coincidence as rare as it was heady.

But, clearly, the news of the moment was Mikhail Baryshnikov's first public appearance in the city. It was further abetted by a previous announcement to the effect that the dancer would make his United States debut with American Ballet Theatre, dancing three performances during July and August of the company's selfsame summer season. (The unusual sight of long lines circling the State Theater for tickets to Baryshnikov's appearance was literally the talk of the town.)

Blasé New Yorkers have, of course, grown used to the dazzlements of international ballet stars. Baryshnikov, however, was something else. His New York appearances were preceded by newspaper and magazine reports of his Toronto engagement with the Bolshoi. Critics and writers, ever on the lookout for new gods of the dance, flocked to Canada prior to Baryshnikov's defection. Their reports were nothing if not ecstatic.

A few days prior to his American Ballet Theatre debut, I talked to this young Russian phenomenon in a dressing room of the New York State Theater. Dina Makarova (a close friend, though not a relation to the Soviet ballerina, and a brilliant young photographer) was my Russian interpreter. Baryshnikov entered the room in his practice clothes. He had been rehearsing with Natalia Makarova, whom he would partner a few days hence.

In person, Baryshnikov does not produce the high-voltage offstage persona of a Nureyev. He is not a tall man, about five-foot-seven. His body, though muscular and compact, suggests frailty. Baryshnikov's face might be called angelic, with its large, deep-set, serene blue eyes, gently up-tilted nose, and softly pointed chin. Light-blond hair falls romantically about his head. His smile can only be termed as sweet. But as he speaks, a gamut of expressions cross his features. His sensitively shaped eyebrows rise or contract, as a stream of Russian flows forth. The voice is melodious, at times impassioned in timbre, at others melancholy in cadence.

Baryshnikov smoked incessantly during our talk. The publicity attending his defection and the supreme expectations of an eager New York public have clearly put him on edge. "I am terribly nervous. The public always expects too much!" he said, with a tense smile.

I learned that Mikhail Baryshnikov was born in Riga (Latvia), on January 27, 1948. He is the only child of an engineer and a fashion-house seamstress.

"My family had absolutely no relation to the world of ballet," he told me. "Oh, they liked music, and my mother loved going to the ballet. In fact, it was my mother who introduced me to it. She would take me by the hand, and we'd go to the Latvian Opera Ballet, which is still quite a good company. I was enthralled by what I saw. Immediately, I loved the ballet, and immediately wanted to study it. I was already twelve years old, which is an advanced age to begin ballet studies. But I was accepted into the Opera Ballet school, and made rapid progress. Before that time, I was just a very normal schoolboy. It was only *after* I began my ballet training that I became 'abnormal.' I became obsessed with dancing."

Baryshnikov remained at the Latvian Opera Ballet for some four years, studying and dancing tiny roles. When he turned sixteen, he and a group of school friends traveled to Leningrad, where Mischa (as he is called), tested for the Kirov school. He passed the rigorous examination, and entered the Kirov ballet school. For the next three years, he studied with one of the world's greatest ballet teachers, the late Aleksandr Pushkin, who, ten years earlier, had unleashed the marvels of Rudolf Nureyev.

At nineteen, Baryshnikov entered the Leningrad Kirov Ballet. His work was deemed so unusual that he was permitted to skip his apprenticeship in the *corps* and immediately made a soloist. He was but one week with the company when he danced the difficult Peasant *pas de deux* in *Giselle*. Among other solo roles were the *pas de trois* in *Swan Lake* and various parts in *Don Quixote*.

"I was a soloist for two years," said Baryshnikov. "I was very good, and the Kirov management was pleased with me. Still, two years is a long time. I felt I was being held back. I longed to do principal roles. After all, every soldier wants to be a general! But the directors did not see me as a principal dancer. I did not have the look of a *premier danseur*. I was short, I was very young, and I looked it. The Kirov tends to select its principals by their appearance, and I did not have that princely look.

"I could do or say nothing. I could not complain. But I showed what I felt with my eyes. Finally, while still a soloist, I was given my first principal role in the full-length *Don Quixote*. The role is a *demi-caractère* part, and, having danced it well, the management now saw me as a character dancer. I was being typed, and, again, felt frustrated."

In 1972, at the age of twenty-four, some of Baryshnikov's frustrations came to an end. He was made a principal dancer with the Kirov Ballet, and began performing in such princely classics as *Giselle* and *The Sleeping Beauty*. The impact of Baryshnikov quickly made itself felt. Word came out of Russia of a "new Nijinsky." Americans who had witnessed Bary-shnikov performances returned with words of disbelief. Anthony Blum, a principal dancer with the New York City Ballet, had been performing in Leningrad with his company.

"On one of our nights off, I went to see Baryshnikov dance," Blum said. "I was stunned. I simply couldn't believe what I saw. I mean, he would leap into the air and just stay there! He'd do incredible things, seemingly without any 'preparation' at all. You just looked in amazement at what was happening. I've never seen anything like it!"

Others echoed such wonderment. "He's a combination of Nureyev, Erik Bruhn, and what one has heard about Nijinsky," said another dancer. "A Baryshnikov comes along only once in a lifetime!"

Dancing with the Kirov Ballet held its rewards. Baryshnikov became a star of the first magnitude. The public adored him, and the management considered him their prize possession. He traveled with the company to Britain and the Netherlands. His reputation widened, and all indications were that a major comet had once again ignited the rich firmament of Russian dance.

As for Baryshnikov, the rewards of national fame held certain restrictions.

"You see, I have had incredible schooling. I carried this 'baggage' of unbelievable training on me, and it could not be properly 'opened.' I felt constrained. I was dancing the same things over and over again. The Kirov repertoire, while large, is basically quite limited. The authorities refuse to invite Western choreographers to create new ballets for the company. They feel it is unpatriotic to do so. Also, the Kirov is sadly lacking in new, first-rate ballerinas. I seldom had a suitable partner to dance with. This was a great handicap. Furthermore, the Kirov would not permit me to be a guest artist with Western companies. This would have been a wonderful and valuable experience for me. I'm sure I would never have defected had I been given the chance to be in the West for prolonged periods of time. In short, I began to feel I had no identity—no *true* identity.

"I became demoralized. I felt that working within the system was slowly killing my talent. I longed to dance in the works of the great Western choreographers—Jerome Robbins, Antony Tudor, Gorge Balanchine. I wanted to try new styles of dance. I wanted to enlarge the scope and depth of my art. I could no longer do so at the Kirov. More and more I realized how short is a dancer's life!"

When, in June 1974, Baryshnikov was sent to Toronto as guest artist with the Bolshoi group, the moment of revolt had come. With the aid of an American friend, Christine Berlin, the daughter of a Hearst executive, he defected from the Bolshoi—and thus, from the Soviet Union. Canadian authorities admitted and sheltered Baryshnikov—and the deed was done. The dancer went into seclusion in Toronto. During this period, ballerina

Natalia Makarova spoke to Baryshnikov, and persuaded him to make his American debut, partnering her in American Ballet Theatre's production of *Giselle*, later partnering her in ABT's *La Bayadère* (staged by Makarova) and *Don Quixote pas de deux*. To Makarova's astonishment and pleasure, Baryshnikov accepted. The ballerina telephoned her good tidings to Lucia Chase.

"I could not believe it!" Miss Chase told me, elated over the coup that had been scored for her company. "It was all Natasha's doing! It was the most incredible news. Of course, we were delighted to give this great dancer a home base. I think he will dance with us often."

Smoking his endless cigarettes, and twisting and retwisting a pair of new ballet shoes that had been handed him, Mikhail Baryshnikov talked briefly of his defection:

"I don't like the word 'defection.' Rather, I would call what I did a 'selection.' I *selected* to come to the West. Actually, I feel sad that it had to be this way. I am terribly sad not to be able to return to my own country. It should not be like that. Of course, I worry about my parents. But, you see, I *had* to take this step. I felt I owed this to myself."

Baryshnikov touched on his dancing:

"I cannot tell you what makes me dance the way I do. I think it is a combination of technique and a certain terror before I go onstage. Before every performance I am always terribly nervous, terribly scared. Then I go on, and something happens. I know one must hold the audience in one's hand. For me, each performance is like a card game. It's like playing cards with a partner—sometimes you win, sometimes you lose. And each ballet you dance is a different card game, as well. In a way, dancing *Giselle* is like playing solitaire. You are very much on your own."

And what of partners?

"Always, I seek a partner with whom I can have an emotional rapport. It must go beyond technique. It is the emotions that must be real. Every impulse, every movement must be sincere. There must be a great *giving*. The ideal partner is the one with whom you can dance with your eyes closed."

Baryshnikov looks to the future with hope.

"I wish to dance everything, and with as many different companies as possible. Of course, it would be wonderful if choreographers would create ballets for me, but I would be just as happy dancing in existing works by Robbins, Balanchine, or Tudor. They would all be new to me in any case."

For the moment, Mikhail Baryshnikov is free of personal ties or attachments. There are no romances, no love affairs.

"My romance is ballet," he said with a mischievous grin. "It is quite true! It is all I think about. Ballet is my water, my food, my light. It is what I live for."

CYNTHIA GREGORY

It is possible that Cynthia Gregory may emerge as this generation's first *bona fide* American ballerina to achieve international stature. In America, her performances in *Giselle* and *Swan Lake* have already been hailed as superb examples of interpretation, stylistic refinement, and technical bravura. Her presence on the stage is both imperious and dramatic. She is one of the tallest dancers extant. On *pointe*, she soars to a dazzling six-foot-one. Her *Swan Lake* has the nobility and poignancy of the best of the Russian tradition, but it achieves the added dimension of newness and freshness by virtue of an American buoyancy and technical cleanliness. Gregory makes of her Odette–Odile a creature at once vulnerable and steely. She infuses the dual role with an ecstastic drive and momentum which transforms it into a dynamic and brilliant tour de force.

Miss Gregory has been a member of the American Ballet Theatre since 1965. She joined the company in the ranks of the *corps*, and quickly moved to principal dancer. She has danced most of the ABT repertoire— from the classics to Eliot Feld. She was born July 8, 1946, in Los Angeles, California. Her father is a dress manufacturer, and her mother is a house- wife, who also assists her husband in designing clothes. Miss Gregory is an only child. She claims that as a very young child, whenever she heard music, she was propelled to dance. "My uncles would lift me to the ceiling, and I'd strike a pretty pose."

Gregory received her earliest training from Eva Lorraine, who ran the first California Children's Ballet Company. When Cynthia was six years old, Miss Lorraine put her on *pointe*. This is an extremely early age to be put on *pointe*, but it did not affect the dancer adversely. She remained with the Children's Company for approximately four years, training and per- forming in children's versions of *Swan Lake* and *Sleeping Beauty*. This early experience on the stage made the youngster feel very much at home in the performance situation. Following this period, she was enrolled in classes given by Carmelita Maracci and Michel Panaieff. She also studied with Robert Rossellat.

I learned more of Miss Gregory's career and something of her life when we met for an interview in August 1973. She made time between strenuous rehearsals and visited me in my apartment. She wore blue jeans and a pretty peasant blouse. Her hair was pulled severely back, setting off her splendid aquiline face with its prominent, chiseled nose, its large, dreamy blue-gray eyes, and flawless complexion. Her height is not as apparent in person as it is on the stage. Neither is the intensely dramatic quality she projects when performing. Indeed, in person, Cynthia Gregory is a rather shy and somewhat insecure girl. When speaking, she can be tentative, and seems somewhat ill at ease with words. Over some coffee, she extolled the qualities of her major teacher, Carmelita Maracci.

"When I first went to her, I was only nine years old, and I had difficulty in understanding much of what she was trying to tell us. I didn't get quite as much from her as I did when I was a little older. She had so much to offer! Just to listen to her talking about art and music was wonderful. It was from her that I began to appreciate the finer points of the art of dancing. She would give you very difficult technical things to do. I did them all, but I never understood *how* I did them. Actually, I still do that. I do things naturally, without knowing how I do them. When I go back to think about how I did something, it ruins everything. So I never think about it much."

When Cynthia was fourteen she was awarded a Ford Foundation scholarship to work with the San Francisco Ballet, headed by Lew Christensen.

"I studied for about a year, and was also an apprentice with the company. The Christensen school is fashioned very much after the Balanchine style. I loved it. It was good for me. With the company I did several Balanchine ballets. All along, I had been going to Catholic schools for regular schooling. Then, when I entered the San Francisco Ballet at the age of fifteen and a half, I had to quit high school during my junior year. I did correspondence courses for my senior year, and I received my high-school diploma. I feel bad I never went to college. I speak to people, and they seem to know so much more. Anyway, I stayed with the San Francisco company until I was nineteen. It was in the company that I met Terry Orr. Actually, he joined one year before I did. He was seventeen when we met. I was fourteen and a half. We were in classes together—we danced together in character class or in adagio class. I was nineteen and he twenty-two when we married. We've been married seven years now."

The two young dancers decided that they had gone as far as they could with the San Francisco Ballet. It was their ambition to come to New York and join one of the major New York companies. In point of fact, their hope was to join the New York City Ballet. When they got to New York, they attended several performances given by the American Ballet Theatre. They were thrilled by what they saw.

"It was really terribly exciting for us to see ABT performances. We loved their repertoire. We loved the fact that they were performing *Les Noces, Miss Julie, Petrouchka*, and Tudor ballets. We decided to audition for the company. The minute ABT saw Terry, they took him. I had to audition three times before I was taken in. They felt I was too tall to fit in with the rest of the *corps*. Finally, they found a place for me. Terry and I learned about twelve ballets in two weeks. We were both dancing in the *corps*. In 1966, I was made a soloist, and nine months later, I became a principal dancer. Terry is also a principal dancer now."

Because it is the policy of the American Ballet Theatre to engage widely acclaimed European stars, the American contingent of the company has for years had a difficult time making its presence truly felt. Miss Gregory, among other American members of the company, feels this to be a problem:

"In a way, I can't really blame the company. I think it's more the fault of the American public, because they still think that it's the foreigner who must be the better artist. Also, they were brought up to know that whenever you think of ballet, you think Russian—Ballet Russe. This has been something of a hassle. For example, when Makarova joined our company, the rest of us were pushed into the background. At least, for a while. I personally felt resentful. Later, I found that Makarova's presence among us was very good for us. It gave me that extra boost—that extra push. I've always been one for competition. I like it. When I saw such a beautiful dancer in our midst, I felt challenged. I felt it was either sink or swim. I could either say to myself, Well, it will always be this way, someone will always come in and be better, or I'm just going to have to make myself be as good as they are, if not better."

In 1972 Cynthia Gregory performed in a *Swan Lake* that had audiences totally enthralled. She was cheered again and again, and suddenly found herself in the front ranks of classical ballerinas. She was the recipient of ovations and fans clamored for endless curtain calls. At twenty-seven, Cynthia Gregory became a star. How, in effect, did this come about?

"About two years ago I began to somehow take hold. I was maturing. I did my first *Swan Lake* when I was twenty-one. I just sort of did it. I had two weeks to learn it, and I did it. As I would get more performances, I thought of more things to do with it. Of course, what always propels me is the music. Dance is moving to music. It is my inspiration. It is the same with *Giselle*."

Miss Gregory told me how she prepares for a performance of *Giselle*:

"When I have a full-length performance such as *Giselle* or *Swan Lake* or *The Tales of Hoffmann*, I do not have any rehearsals that day. But I like to get my body going, so I usually take a class, sometime around noon. I break in my toe shoes for that night. I try to rest. At around four P.M., I have a nice steak—salad, vegetables. For *Giselle* I like to get to the theater around two and a half hours before the performance. My face is not really a 'Giselle' face, but I try make-up that gives me a wide-eyed, innocent look. I'll do my eyes a little softer—more open. As I put on my make-up, I think about the role. Also, I have a tape recorder in my dressing room, and I listen to some music—usually Bach. I do my warm-ups about forty-five minutes before curtain. Then comes the bell announcing five minutes, which really means ten minutes. I get into my costume, and go to the stage to check out the scenery. I wish my partner good luck, and go on.

"I like doing *Giselle* because it starts you out with pantomime. There's not too much dancing at the beginning. You can grow into the character. You are onstage most of the time, so you're not distracted. You can really build within the first act. With *Swan Lake*, it's a different story, because you keep coming on and going off all the time. It's hard to keep up the continuity."

In the works of Antony Tudor, Cynthia Gregory brings a particularly contemporary look to her roles. She falls into the Tudor movements with as much expressiveness as she does in the more classical vehicles. But working with Tudor posed some problems. He is a difficult taskmaster and demands perfection.

"When I first joined the company, Tudor was reviving *Pillar of Fire*. I was one of the sexy girls in it. I was scared to death of Tudor. He's kind of a scary person. I would work with him, and he would humiliate me. I would cry. It was difficult. But I respected him so much. I wanted him to like me. For the longest time, he didn't really see what I had in me. It was because I would clam up when I'd be around him. I'd get very shy. I really couldn't give what I wanted to in front of him. Now, things are easier. I know what he's really like. Also, he's not as tough as he used to be—he's mellowed. Earlier on, I would always be able to do the technical things he wanted. He would tell me to do something, and I'd do it right off the bat. But he was never quite interested in that. He likes to see people struggle. He feels that with struggle, things come out much better. He likes to pull things out of you.

"But Tudor liked to sort of torture you, too. He would look at you and immediately know your weak spots. I remember his looking at me one time: he just saw into my soul. He has such uncanny perception about people. I'm looking forward to doing the role of Caroline in *Lilac Garden*. I've always done the 'other woman.' Recently, Tudor told me he'd like to see me do it." (Indeed, in early 1974, Miss Gregory's first Caroline met with great critical acclaim.)

When Gregory danced with Erik Bruhn in Birgit Cullberg's *Miss Julie*, one could feel Bruhn's effect on the dancer.

"I had to learn *Miss Julie* from a film with Toni Lander. It was a very dark film, and there was no music to it. When I continued to work on the role with Erik, he really made me *think*. He had the characters *so* worked out in terms of their psychological motivations. I was amazed at how he, himself, transformed on the stage. He became somebody you *really* could play to. When he threw me, he really *threw* me. He was so powerful! You couldn't help but react. I had never done anything that dramatic before, and it was a real lesson in acting. Of course, Erik was a marvelous partner.

"I've always had problems finding a partner tall enough for me. The company found Michael Denard, but he and I don't often see eye to eye. Recently, we've danced Peter Van Dyk's *The Unfinished Symphony*, and it worked very well, because it's an abstract work. But we've never really sat down to discuss things. He's never around enough, because he works so much with his own company—the Paris Opera. I wish I could travel all over the world to find myself the perfect partner."

I asked Miss Gregory whether her present star status interferes with her marriage to Terry Orr, whose status with the company is high, but not spectacular.

"Terry is a very, very realistic person. This thing that's happened to me is not a problem. He has found a place for himself with the company. He does a lot of character roles, and some classical roles. But he never aspires to be 'The Prince.' He's also very good at administrative work. He's a member of our company's rehearsal staff. He's a very diversified person with a lot of energy. Just to dance has never been enough for him. We video-tape most of our ballets now, and Terry is the head of that department. I think he's thrilled at my success. He's my chief critic. He gives me very good corrections. I have danced with Terry, but not very often."

Cynthia Gregory still seems somewhat astonished at her current success. Her basic shyness appears to stand in her way offstage.

"One of my problems is that I suffer terribly from shyness. Also, I'm very paranoid, and sometimes think that people don't like me. I'm not really open with people until I really get to know them. In that way, I really have a hard life. I am happiest onstage. When Terry and I are not dancing, we go off to the country. We have a house near Jacob's Pillow in Massachusetts. We have forty acres of land, and we just love to roam around in it. Most of our friends are in the dance world. I suppose one day, we will have children. I'd like a couple of them. But right now, I'm going to concentrate on just dancing. Actually, I don't know how dancers manage with children, because you can't really give your all to either them or your dancing."

Bil Leidersdorf

IVAN NAGY

A true prince of the ballet, Ivan Nagy has become Natalia Makarova's favored partner. He complements the ballerina's special fragility with his virility and charm. So superb is his partnering that Dame Margot Fonteyn has specially requested his presence on a month-long tour of Australia. There is about Nagy's dancing a particular manliness, tempered by a poetic and aristocratic grace. A member of the American Ballet Theatre since 1968, Nagy excels in the classics.

Ivan Nagy was born in Debrecen, Hungary, on April 28, 1943. He is the youngest of three children. His father is presently on the Board of Directors of the Hungarian Railroad. His mother had hopes of becoming a professional dancer, but family objections thwarted her career, and she became a ballet teacher instead. Ivan's mother was his first teacher. From the age of six through fifteen he studied at the Budapest Opera House ballet school, then joined its ballet company. In 1965 he won the Silver Medal as the best classical dancer at the International Festival in Varna. One of the judges at the Festival was Frederic Franklin, who promptly engaged Nagy for the National Ballet of Washington, D.C., with which he performed for three years.

Ivan Nagy invited me to visit him in his spacious apartment in the West Eighties in New York City. He lives there with his second wife, the former ballerina Marilyn Burr, and their two young daughters. As always, one is startled by the comparative smallness and compactness of someone who on stage appears far taller, far more imposing. But Ivan Nagy's stunning good looks are just as arresting offstage as on. Startling green eyes are set in a face of perfect proportion, and they look out at you with piercing, birdlike intensity. Nagy speaks English with a soft middle-European accent, and during our talk he kept searching for the right words to express himself. He began by telling me something of his childhood:

"I am my parents' prodigal son—because I am the youngest child, and I left them. My entire family stayed in Hungary, even during the revolution. Oddly enough, my mother wanted my sister and my brother to be dancers. Her plans for me were that I should become a doctor or a lawyer. As it turned out, it was my brother who became the doctor, and I became the dancer.

"It all started for me when I was three years old. We lived in a very big house, and my mother taught dancing to a lot of children. For some reason she never wanted me around, but I used to peek through the keyhole of her studio, and I just loved what I saw. One day the pianist came a little earlier and began to play something. Right then and there I began to improvise some dances. I was only three years old, but the pianist thought I was terrific. Eventually, my mother realized how very much I loved to dance, and, gradually, she began teaching me. Then I auditioned at the Budapest Opera House school, and was accepted. This was a school in which you learned everything, including dancing. We had a very hard life for nine long years. You had to stand at the *barre* at seven forty-five every morning. It was dreadful. I really had no childhood at all. I never played with children my own age.

"The first three years away from home were simply awful. Then, it became better. We learned music history, dance history, art history. We learned piano, fencing, folk dancing, pantomime. Unfortunately, they did not teach modern dancing, which didn't exist there. Anyway, my favorite teacher at the school was Irene Bartos—she was the one I liked the best, because she formed me. I also had the chance to work with Olga Lipichinska from the Bolshoi Theatre. She was the big rival of Ulanova, and she came to us as a guest teacher. I worked with her for two years."

Ivan developed into a brilliant student, and eventually joined the company. He danced with the Opera Ballet for five years. While with the company, he met and married his first wife, who was a company soloist. This marriage ended in divorce after one year.

"I had a very hard time with the company. My director did not favor me. He did not like me. He tried to push me down all the time. Nevertheless, he told me that I was to enter the Varna competition. He practically forced me into it. I did not want to go. But I went, and I won. It was in 1965, and it was the same year Natalia Makarova won the gold medal. Frederic Franklin and Erik Bruhn were on the jury. It was Mr. Franklin who invited me to come and dance with the National Company in Washington, D.C. It was very difficult for me to leave Hungary, because it was an Iron Curtain country. Finally, through the Cultural Minister I received permission to go. I was engaged as principal dancer, and I was thrilled. But when I came to America, I was quite miserable, because I did not speak the language. Also, I had been very spoiled. The theater we danced in in Washington, D.C., was unbearable. I could not believe it. Actually, I couldn't wait for my engagement to be over so that I could go back to Hungary. But when I got back, the Opera Director continued to treat me very badly. He cut my salary. He put me back in the *corps de ballet*, and it became impossible. He wanted me to sign a contract, but I refused. And so, the Director fired me."

Eventually, Ivan Nagy defected from Hungary, returned to America, and rejoined the National Ballet. He had in the meantime met and married Australian-born ballerina Marilyn Burr. In the spring of 1968 Nagy left the National Ballet and joined the New York City Ballet at the invitation of George Balanchine. The experience did not prove a happy one.

"The year that I joined the City Ballet was a very bad year for the company. Suzanne Farrell got married, and the atmosphere of the company was dreadful. But, more importantly, I soon came to realize that the repertoire was not very interesting to me. I danced *Symphony in C,* First Movement and *Brahms-Schönberg* and I rehearsed *Concerto Barocco* and *Serenade* with Suzanne. But I had no position with the company. It was just a contract. Also, I was earning very, very little money. Marilyn was pregnant. I couldn't pay the rent. She had already stopped dancing. We had to start completely naked in New York with two suitcases and a new life. We hadn't a stick of furniture. Marilyn started to work as a seamstress. I helped her sew on buttons. I was making a miserable salary of ninety-two dollars and forty cents a week at the City Ballet. This would not be so terrible if I had a happy life with the company. But I knew in my heart that even if I were given everything to dance, I would still not be happy, because, basically, with that company, you are just stage crew. You're lifting and supporting the ballerina. You are not a person. I felt that with Balanchine I could not develop a personality. Finally I talked to Mr. B., and I was very honest with him. I thanked him and told him that I must leave, because I had to find myself. I felt I wanted to do more classics. We shook hands, and Mr. Balanchine was very friendly—and I left. The very next day I joined American Ballet Theatre."

It was with American Ballet Theatre that Ivan Nagy seemed to find himself. He could dance the classical repertoire, he could dance works by Tudor, José Limón—he could dance *Petrouchka* and such modern works as *Monument for a Dead Boy* by Rudi van Dantzig. I asked Nagy to comment on the company.

"Well, the last thing I would want to be is in the shoes of Lucia Chase. Because you cannot please sixty or seventy dancers. Actually, I had a hard time getting where I am right now. Miss Chase never particularly singled me out. There was nobody behind me to give me a little push. I did my own work, which is very hard. I must say, I am proud of my own discipline about pushing myself. I do not spit in my face every morning when I look in the mirror shaving. Anyway, I am happy at ABT, and I do not mind the competition I have from other dancers—especially the ones who are invited from Europe, like Paolo Bortoluzzi. The competition inspires you, and makes you work better.

"Actually, the dancer who inspired me the most was Erik Bruhn. When he retired, I felt very empty—I lost so much interest in dancing. There was no one to look up to. I cannot tell you what Erik meant to me. He was the most intelligent dancer I ever met. He was absolutely fantastic from the *barre* to the stage. He was the most helpful in terms of my career with ABT. When he left, I was the first person to know it. When he told me that he was retiring, I just went to pieces. He talked to me, and I cried. I was lost. The trouble with Erik was that he was such a perfectionist. When a legend gets bigger and bigger, you finally feel that you cannot live up to the public's expectations. You almost become paralyzed. I think that was what finally made Erik decide to retire."

We turned to Nagy's assessment of his own particular style and technique.

"I feel I am technically limited. I have strong things and I have weak things. I know I have good leaps. I am strong. I am a good partner. I have line. But I also have things I cannot do. I have had knee trouble, and for years I was dancing with injections. I had a cast on my leg eleven times. I developed many complexes. I had a knee operation. I felt terrible that I couldn't do certain things, but I am not a machine that can do everything.

"A dancer's life is based on discipline. Without it, you are not a dancer. It's a short career, and you have to go out and dance no matter what. You may have a toothache, or a headache. You may have pulled a muscle. You may hurt all over. Still, you have to go out there and do a job. A couple of seasons ago I was doing a *pas de deux* with Cynthia Gregory. My back went out. I suddenly was paralyzed, and I had to be taken to the hospital in an ambulance. But exactly one week later I was back on the stage. You see, no matter what the agony and the pain, your mind *makes* you get on that stage and perform."

Would Nagy comment on his partnership with Makarova?

"I have danced many times with Natasha Makarova. We are very good friends, and we understand each other. People complain about Natasha not dancing with an American partner when she was with ABT. Actually, it has nothing to do with being American. It has more to do with the training Natasha has had. Her Russian training sometimes does not go with American training. I had the Russian school also. I know the Russian way of partnering. She has confidence in my hands. I know how to follow her. Also, we look well together. She has left ABT because, as she told me, she defected so that she could have a very free career. So she is accepting a great many guest engagements, and many times I fly to wherever she is dancing, because she feels comfortable with me."

What is the life of a dancer?

"I feel it is almost a religion, to be a dancer. But I will tell you something—I believe that basically every dancer hates it. It's just that nobody wants to admit it. I hate it also. But I go to the *barre* every morning anyway. I force my body until it hurts. It's not a very great pleasure. It takes such a long time to reach the stage. I am now thirty-one. I am not young any more, professionally speaking. Still, in private life I am a young gentleman. It's a strange feeling. I look at the younger dancers around me—someone like Fernando Bujones, who is so young. I think he is divine—a fantastic dancer. When I knew him first he was twelve years old, doing a guest appearance in Miami with a Cuban company. He was just a baby. He will be very big with ABT. I'm glad he had the good sense to join the company from the bottom. I'm glad he went into the *corps*. If they put you immediately at the top, it's very bad later on. It is important psychologically to be in the *corps* first, and work yourself up.

"I feel that our profession is not creative. We are just performing artists. The curtain goes up, and we do something. But we do not really create. I would like to go on dancing. I would like to try many things. I would like to try Béjart. I would like to work with Jerome Robbins. Now, I accept many invitations as guest artist. Don't forget, it is a short career. I have only a few years left. When it is over, I do not know what I will do. I like the idea of teaching, but somehow, I don't think I will be a teacher. I don't think I will be a choreographer. I think when the curtain goes down for me, it will be the end . . . I will be out of the dance world. Frankly, I don't know what I will do. Perhaps paint. But I don't want to think about that. Somehow, I will find myself again. I will wait and see what happens when the times comes."

Bil Leidersdorf

ELEANOR D'ANTUONO

Toward the end of American Ballet Theatre's winter season of 1973, Eleanor d'Antuono, partnered by Ted Kivitt, danced the *Don Quixote pas de deux*. The bravura and élan with which the couple performed elicited a tumultuous response. The two dancers took repeated bows, but still the audience would not let them go. After what seemed an eternity of bravos, d'Antuono and Kivitt decided to repeat the *pas de deux*. They did this despite the fact that it is against the company's no-encore policy. When it was over, they were chastised by the management.

During our interview shortly after the event, Eleanor d'Antuono brought up the *cause célèbre*:

"I was so angry about that. It was outrageous. All I know is that the reception of our *Don Quixote pas de deux* was incredible. The people started screaming, 'Once more! Once more!' We were taking our bows. The whole balcony was standing up screaming. I asked Ted, 'What are we going to do?' I was almost in tears. You know, I was having my problems with the company, so this was very special to me. Anyway, we did it again. It was not planned. Then, management came and said, 'How tacky and circus-y.' Well, you know, anything that's done with that kind of spontaneity is never tacky. You can say many things about me, but never that I'm vulgar, or without taste. But the management was very angry, and that made me very, very angry. They should have been proud. They should have been thrilled that it happened to two of their dancers. They let me down. I was very discouraged."

Eleanor d'Antuono has been with American Ballet Theatre since 1961, and was raised to the rank of principal dancer in 1963. She has been a steadfast, loyal dancer and has served ABT well. Her presence in the major classics assures brilliant performances—performances rich in technical brio and stylistic refinement. If d'Antuono can be faulted, it is in areas of subtlety. She is an all-giving dancer. One could say that her enormous generosity of spirit, her sheer love of the dance, and her dazzling technique have tended to overshadow some of the aesthetic considerations inherent in major roles. Still, as a maturing artist, she is beginning to find the ephemeral qualities of a *Giselle, La Fille Mal Gardée, Coppélia*, and *Swan Lake*.

D'Antuono was born in Cambridge, Massachusetts, and spent all her life there until the age of fourteen. Her father is a printer; her mother is a housewife who loved the ballet. There is a younger sister.

"I heard a lot of Verdi operas in my house—our Italian background. When I was four years old, I was exposed to ballet. The Ballet Russe de Monte Carlo came to Boston. I can clearly remember my first *Schéhérazade*. I was sitting in the first row. I can still see the curtain going up, and all the colors—the orange, yellow, amber, and blue. From that moment on, I kept asking my mother about taking ballet classes. I was not quite five when I was enrolled in a class given by Maria Papporello. It was the loveliest way to be introduced to ballet—through Madame Papporello. Not that she was an important teacher, or that she gave me such great training, but it was her *look*. She came from La Scala, Milan. She had a small, oval-shape head and wore her white hair tied back in a knot. She had sloping shoulders, and a little tiny waist—really not of this era. She may even have had a cane. Well, you can imagine. And she was born in October, as I was, and she wore opals. Of course, I immediately fell in love with her. I studied with her until I was nine years old."

From the age of nine through fourteen, Eleanor d'Antuono studied with E. Virginia Williams in Boston, and danced with her New England Civic Ballet. Miss Williams made it a practice to take some of her pupils to New York City. On one such occasion, Eleanor was taken to classes given by Tatiana Chamié, and Madame Chamié invited Eleanor to take classes with her. She found in the young girl a promising dancer. Indeed, she recommended her to Sergei Denham, who headed the Ballet Russe de Monte Carlo and who, at that time, was looking for dancers.

"When we got back to Boston, I received a call to return to New York and audition for Mr. Denham. I was fourteen. I was put on a plane, and landed in New York in pouring rain. I was two and a half hours late for the audition. Finally, I got there, did what I was asked to do, and flew back to Boston. A week later, we received a telegram asking me to come to New York right away. I had been accepted into the Ballet Russe, and a contract was waiting for me. Of course, my mother became terribly worried, because I was still only fourteen, but nothing would deter me. From the very first day, I never doubted for a minute that I wanted to be a ballet dancer. It never occurred to me that I would be anything else."

Eleanor d'Antuono entered the Ballet Russe de Monte Carlo on July 12, 1954. In the company at that time were such stars as Irina Borowska, Maria Tallchief, Yvonne Chouteau, Gertrude Tyven, Frederic Franklin, Leon Danielian, and Victor Moreno. Alicia Alonso and Igor Youskevitch also joined the company. In short, d'Antuono was exposed to great dancing. She was the youngest member of the company, and began the strenuous life of a touring dancer.

"Being in the Ballet Russe was like being in the Army. You were programed. You had no time to yourself. You got up. You took an eight A.M. class. You took a bus, and rode until three o'clock in the afternoon. Then you had an hour to get to the theater, eat, get your make-up on, and go to rehearsals until about six o'clock. Then you prepared for the performance. You had to dance three ballets a night. Usually, you got to bed around two o'clock in the morning. Of course, I was in the *corps*. I was one of the swans in *Swan Lake*, I did the Can-Can in *Gaîté Parisienne*. But from the moment I joined the Ballet Russe, I was in everything. I was made a soloist when I was sixteen, and I began dancing all the solo roles."

D'Antuono enjoyed the atmosphere of the Ballet Russe. She was a novice, and she kept her eyes wide open, learning from everything and everyone:

"I knew I could dance well, but I didn't understand why everybody else looked so much better than I did. I realized they were professionals and I was not. They all could do everything. They knew how to manage their lives and get themselves costumed and onto the stage. And they could rehearse steps that I hadn't seen in class. Right away, they *knew*. I worked

very hard. There were quite a few young people in the company. I quickly
had roommates, and we managed to stay up too late a few times. But we
were good—certainly by today's standards. I made a lot of friends. Everybody was very nice to me. The principals were a bit more removed in those
days, but they were nice to me, too. I so admired Frederic Franklin. He
was inspiring. And I loved Maria Tallchief because she had such a degree
of excellence."

Eleanor d'Antuono remained with the Ballet Russe for six years. She
was given every opportunity to develop, and danced numberless roles.
Ultimately, however, at the age of twenty, she felt she needed additional
training. She was also tired of touring and became aware of the fact that
the Ballet Russe de Monte Carlo would remain simply a touring company.
She came to New York and began study at the School of American Ballet,
as well as at the Joffrey School. At the same time, she continued her high-
school studies, and received her diploma. At one point, the Joffrey Ballet
invited her to join its company, and she accepted. She remained with the
Joffrey for the season 1960–61. That fall, she learned of an opening at
American Ballet Theatre, auditioned, and was invited by Lucia Chase to
enter the company as a soloist.

"At the time, ABT needed me. But I entered the company like a child
—that is, as far as they were concerned. I have the feeling they still think
that. When I joined, the company was still under an old system. They did
not have as many young people as they have today. Anyway, after two
years, I was made principal dancer. From the first, I wished that ABT had
given me support. I wish that from the beginning it would have let me
do *Giselle*. I would have had a much easier time—because I was obviously
suited for it. But in those days the only people who did *Giselle* were Lupe
Serrano and Carla Fracci—nobody else was supposed to do it. It would
have been better for me had the company pushed me at that time. It was
bad timing. More recently, I have gotten this opportunity. Of course,
Natasha Makarova came on the scene. And naturally, she was given preference. Natasha's coming didn't affect me too much. I felt that being
around good people only makes you better. But I must confess that I
resented it when ballets were taken away from me. I can't say that Natasha
was on a level above me. I felt we were equals. I resented Makarova's
doing *Giselle* first in New York. It was wrong. That's where ABT could
have backed me. Really, in America, we don't have a ballerina that has
been acclaimed as Giselle—an American ballerina. ABT should have said,
'This is *our* Giselle.' But they did not do that. I think that Lucia Chase is
thrilled at the idea that I'm good. But all companies are politically run. So,
what can I say?"

D'Antuono's feelings about ABT's policy of hiring European stars ex-
tended to comments on Carla Fracci:

"When Carla first joined the company, I found her even more annoying than Natasha. I don't feel that any more. Actually, I have a great deal of admiration for Carla, because she has done the maximum with her gifts. I think she's physically capable of much more, but she's given to not having a great deal of confidence. But I know her personally, and it's difficult for me to be objective. Still, she gives a very finished performance—she really does. She is also magical. I could tell that when Natasha first saw Carla, she didn't recognize that magic. That was a shortcoming."

What does d'Antuono expect from ABT?

"I would like the company to give me a push. I know the company is very fond of me—especially Lucia. They like it that I'm well received. But we are in conflict about what I think I want to do with my work, and what *they* would like. I'm interested in the next step. These are my best years. I won't get them back. I want the independence of being able to say '*This* is the way I want to do something.' I want that privilege. I want to see how much *I* can do. I want performances, and I want to be considered a real ballerina.

"ABT takes me too much for granted. A little of that is my own fault. I'm reliable, and there's nothing worse for an artist than to be considered reliable. I now will go out 'guesting.' Also, I need a ballet done on me. I need that desperately. People think of me as being technically proficient, but few people notice that I also dance well. Everybody is so surprised that I can dance well—people like Tudor and Robbins. They are amazed, and tell me so. But why should they say these things in a surprised tone of voice?

"You see, my one fear was always that I would be a fine dancer with no foundation. So I developed my technique to an extreme degree. Now, people just see *that* part of it. That's what bothers me most."

The vivacious, coquettishly pretty Eleanor d'Antuono continues to delight her audiences. If she can have her way, her future may indeed be spectacular. Her resources are phenomenal, and her qualities as a dancer bring the stage to life. She has developed a following, and the public adores her.

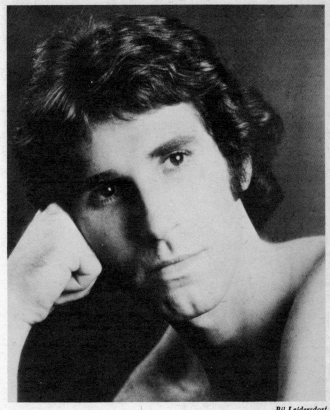

TED KIVITT

As a child living with his parents and brother in Miami, Florida, Ted Kivitt was an asthmatic. The youngster was so ill that the family thought of sending him to a special retreat in Arizona. Finally, doctors decided that dancing might help his condition, and when he was seven years old, Ted took a tap-dancing class. The asthma got worse. At the age of ten, his mother thought that perhaps ballet might be a better form of dancing, and for the next four years he studied with a local teacher. Miraculously, the asthma got better and finally disappeared altogether. Ballet was to become Ted Kivitt's life, but those early ballet lessons proved traumatic.

"I thought taking ballet was the sissiest thing to do, and I fought it tremendously. I made my family promise that it be kept a top secret, because if any of my friends found out, it would have been a disaster. I would go to classes only on the condition that the teacher would work with me alone, and that while he was working with me, all the blinds be drawn. I didn't want anyone else in the class. Anyway, after awhile, I started to like ballet. It was a big challenge to me. And, little by little, I discovered girls, and started to take full classes with everybody. Actually, I was the only boy. When I got into junior high school, it leaked out that I was studying ballet. I was beaten up, and I had to fight my way all through high school. Guys I thought were my friends turned against me. It was pretty bad. So I had a fairly lonely school life. But I didn't care, because I knew what I wanted to do."

Ted Kivitt, now a principal dancer with American Ballet Theatre, related all this as we sat in his sunny New York apartment one morning in January 1973. A handsome, boyish man with a face that continually breaks into sunny smiles, Kivitt is among the *danseurs nobles* of the company. Possessed of a spectacular technique, he brings to his classic roles a measured lyricism. His leaps are breathtaking, as are his turns. As partner, he presents his ballerinas with steely grace and charm. But Kivitt's special quality is his dynamism—a kind of supercharged exuberance that inflames the stage. There is whirlwind excitement when he leaps onstage, slashing space with razor-sharp precision.

In person, the thirty-year-old Kivitt is an easygoing, endearingly informal man. He loves to talk about dancing and likes to express his thoughts and feelings in a frank and candid way. His unpretentiousness and genuine charm made our session thoroughly enjoyable. Kivitt went on to tell me about his rise in the ballet world:

"When I was fifteen, I began working in Florida night clubs. The shows were at nine and twelve, and by the time I got home it was three o'clock in the morning. I would have to get up at seven o'clock, go to regular school, then take ballet classes, then go to the night club. It was awful, and I had to drop out of high school. I went to a private, professional school for my last year. My parents were always a hundred per cent behind me. There was never any conflict. Anyway, I took ballet classes with Alexander Gavrilov and Thomas Armour. After the night-club stints, I became connected with the Miami Ballet, and I danced in practically everything. However, they thought I should concentrate on character dancing. But I hated being put in a category.

"One time, the Miami Ballet traveled to Kentucky as part of the South-eastern Ballet Festival, and we performed there. The Ballet Russe de

Monte Carlo, American Ballet Theatre, and the Joffrey Ballet also performed. This was in Louisville. A big dinner was held one evening for all the companies. Our company was selected to perform at the dinner. Afterward, Lucia Chase, Bob Joffrey, and somebody from the Ballet Russe all offered me contracts. It was quite something. But my teacher told me that Ballet Theatre would be the best company for me. Anyway, I waited a year before deciding on anything. I was still very young—seventeen—and my parents were a little worried about my living on my own in New York. Then, ABT came to Miami, and I auditioned for them. Six months later, I received a very fat envelope from them. It was a contract. When I saw it, it was the most exciting moment of my life."

When Kivitt arrived in New York, he checked into a grim Broadway hotel. He began in the *corps* of ABT, earning about $85 a week, and eating at Horn and Hardart. He was very frightened as a new member of this prestigious company. During the very first rehearsal, he was too shy to use the boys' dressing room and changed in a small bathroom instead. In a short time, he began making friends, and became more relaxed.

"During my first year with the company—it was 1961—they threw absolutely everything at me. I was in every single ballet. There were wonderful dancers I could learn from— John Kriza, Scott Douglas, Royes Fernandez, Toni Lander, Lupe Serrano, Sallie Wilson. And there were European guests. The company was smaller in those years, and we were all very close. I remember that as a novice, I had to go through a company initiation. They put you through 'Goose the Moose.' They blindfolded you, turned you 'round and 'round, then told you to stick out a finger and 'Goose the Moose.' What they did was make you stick a finger in a jar of Vaseline. We were always doing some funny things with the new boys. There was one boy who couldn't get along with anybody. We glued down his make-up to the table, or glued his shoes to the floor—things like that. We had a lot of fun. The best things for me were the one-night stands. The idea of crossing the United States was so exciting. I thought I'd never leave Florida! When I joined ABT, all the boys seemed to be straight. Of course, there were one or two who weren't. I was never bothered. We had wonderful times. Everybody went out with the girls. We had parties. We had fun."

In 1964, the company toured South America. In the *corps* of the company was Karena Brock. Ted Kivitt fell in love with her. When the company returned to America, Ted proposed, and Karena accepted. After their marriage Ted began doing solo roles, and was also given the opportunity of dancing the role of Alain in *La Fille Mal Gardée*.

"Even though we had a lot of fun, ABT had a hard time of it. We didn't have rehearsal space, and we kept moving from one rehearsal hall to another. Once, in Washington, we rehearsed in an old church, and the facilities were awful. That's when Mr. Tudor came to begin staging *Lilac Garden* for the company. It was freezing cold, and we were all bundled up. We would take class, and the steam would be coming off our bodies because it was so cold there. In the early years, dancers worked under the most terrible conditions. And all those one-night stands, seven cities in a week. Getting on the bus and traveling four hundred miles a day. I don't know how any of us did it. We used to go on with injuries, with being sick. I guess we all lived through it because we were all much younger. If I had to do that today, I don't think I could survive."

Ted Kivitt was made a principal dancer in 1967. He dances all the classics.

"I really like the story-ballets more than the abstract ones. I did my first *Swan Lake* in Japan—in Osaka. Bruce Marks and Royes Fernandez were doing the dancing, but the demand for *Swan Lake* was so great they needed someone to relieve them. I began watching them. Every single night, I was in the wings watching it. I almost taught it to myself, although Royes Fernandez helped me very much. I just love that man. I always loved his elegance, and how he looked on stage. He and Dimitri Romanoff helped me on the miming. The dancing was easy for me, but doing the mime was difficult. I danced my first *Swan Lake* with Eleanor d'Antuono. I also danced it with Cynthia Gregory, and this was a highlight of my life, because she is such an inspiration to work with. I also did it with Lupe Serrano. I'm so sad she's retired."

Ted Kivitt told me what he feels when he dances:

"There's an electricity that builds up inside me. When I'm jumping, there's such a sense of freedom. Just taking off is so exhilarating. Standing still in the air is such a thrilling feeling . . . to hit a peak in the air. It feels like flying. You're suspended. You stay there. Also, with turns—when you go beyond five or six turns, the sensation is impossible to put into words. I have this power building inside me. If I don't release it, I would surely burst. It's a surge. Also, I get so involved, so wrapped up in the characters I dance. Siegfried or Albrecht or Franz—I really get inside them. I almost write a script for what I'm going to be doing onstage.

"Of course, I have to prepare myself. I do breathing exercises for endurance. You have to build up the lung capacity for breathing. Sometimes I catch myself holding my breath on stage—which is very bad. There must be a rhythm to your breathing to make the flow of the movements look even all the time. Then, there are nerves. Nerves can help, and can also destroy you at the same time. When I first started with the company, I was terribly nervous. I used to draw a lot of blanks onstage. Some dancers take pills for their nerves, but I don't believe in that. I have to work on my own energy and know my own body. I can't work on a false feeling."

I asked Ted Kivitt to speak about partnering.

"I've danced with almost all the ballerinas of the company. Each one is very different. At times, it was difficult adapting to them. Eleanor d'Antuono has to be partnered a certain way. She likes her foot pointed over, because she has a little difficulty there. She has to be partnered extremely forward. When I worked with Lupe Serrano—she was so on her leg, that I had a tendency to push her too far forward, and she didn't like that at all. When I partner Carla Fracci, I have to be very careful. I have to forget about myself. I have to try to make her look well. She has trouble with her calf muscles. They cramp on her. But my biggest problem came when Natasha Makarova joined the company. It was traumatic.

"When she first came over, we were supposed to dance together a great deal. For some reason, she didn't particularly like me. To this day, I still don't understand why. I've always been a gentleman, and I've always been very gracious to her. Well, we danced *Coppélia* and *Fille* together. We did the *Black Swan pas de deux* on the *Ed Sullivan Show*; we did lots of concerts together. But she never wanted to dance with me in the company. For two years, she put me down. I had a two-year depression. The situation took a tremendous toll on me, mentally. I discussed it with everybody except her, because I couldn't *talk* to her. It was always through an interpreter. I just couldn't understand it. She always liked to put the men down all the time. I'm not one to be put down. I never had any bad words with her, but she always wanted to dominate the situation.

"I think the big problem was that, when she came in, she insisted on changing all the choreography in the classics. I mean, I thought she defected from Russia because she wanted to break away from the old, and do something new. But she came over here, and refused to change anything. This caused a tremendous amount of problems for me. What was so awful, as well, was the fact that management said they were going to stand behind me. They told me emphatically that Makarova *had* to do our choreography or she wouldn't dance at all. They even told me that I should tell Natasha that I would not dance with her if she changed any of the choreography in *Swan Lake* or *Giselle*. Well, I stood up to her. I told her. But the company let me down. Management didn't stand behind me— which destroyed me. When it came to doing so, nobody knew what I was talking about. Finally, I had to adapt myself to her way of doing *Giselle* and *Swan Lake*. The company insisted. She scared the hell out of them. They wanted her. She was tremendous box office. I always thought she *was* a big asset to the company. But she fought me all the way; she's very temperamental. Needless to say, she was the hardest partner I've ever had. All the others have been super."

Kivitt shakes his head, still in disbelief of his experience with Natalia Makarova. We touched on the general subject of ABT's policy of engaging European star dancers.

"That's one of the sorest points with all the Americans in the company. Their presence has caused the Americans to take a back seat. Now, we're beginning to take a stand about that. I think they represent a tremendous amount of talent. But American dancers never get the right publicity. We never get the right performances, and we are never presented under the right conditions. We never get the proper rehearsals when all the Europeans come over. I have nothing against the *dancers*. I'm talking about management. They pit us against one another at times, which is very bad. Anyway, we're taking a stand. European dancers often leave the company in the lurch. They take off, and we, the Americans, are the stand-bys. We do all the work while they have concerts all over the world. Now, Ivan Nagy is taking off. I'm the only principal that does all the classics. I have to carry the whole tour. We have put our foot down. Cynthia, Eleanor, and myself have said that this has got to stop. We told them, 'You bring these Europeans in, you pay their transportation over, they get all the big salaries.' The company is just beginning to realize that these Europeans don't stick—they keep running off. Now, don't misunderstand. American Ballet Theatre has been my whole life. They've really been very good to me. But I resent it that every time someone new comes in from Europe, they get the big chances. The Europeans only want to dance in New York and Los Angeles. Recently, I have been given a raise. I think the company realizes it has overworked me tremendously. That is because the Europeans refuse to go on tour. Tours kill me. And then, the company doesn't let me dance in New York very much. They don't let me dance what I want to dance. This very week I've given up two performances of *Fille* and a *Coppélia* so that Michael Denard could get a chance to do them. They felt Denard didn't have anything to do. He was supposedly coming on tour to help out, but he's only coming to Houston for one *Swan Lake*, and that's it. I've told the company that now I only want to dance three times a week on tour. To do *Swan Lake* and *Giselle* and all those big ballets in a row is too much. That's why I started injuring myself. Last year, I tore a tendon in my calf muscle, and then, in Washington, I tore some fibers in one of my feet. All of that has taken its toll. When I do get a chance to dance in New York, I get little rehearsal—they give the new people rehearsals. A lot of my performances have not been up to my standard, and I'm my worst critic."

Despite all his complaints, Kivitt continues to dance superbly. In more ways than one, he embodies the present generation of American male dancers. He loves what he is doing, in spite of the varying hardships and frustrations that the profession entails. In conclusion, I asked Ted Kivitt what he would say to boys who wish to become ballet dancers.

"The main thing is hard work. You've got to dedicate your life to the dance. You can't just take one or two classes a week. You have to take class every single day, and really think about what you're doing. But the most important thing is finding the right teacher. My first teacher gave me a very bad foundation, and I had to relearn everything. There are so many quack ballet teachers around the country. I think one day I might form some sort of union of dancers to get all the quacks out, because they have ruined so many young kids. They're just in it to make a lot of money. Everybody starting out with a teacher should look into his background. That's very important. That's really all I have to say."

Bil Leidersdorf

SALLIE WILSON

Wearing black boots, a tweed skirt, a green blouse, and a gold chain, Sallie Wilson sat in my living room for our interview. Her face, while not classically beautiful, has a very special radiance. It is a face of awkward logic, reminiscent of early American portraits, and framed by a fall of lovely reddish hair. There is expressive subtlety whenever she moves her hands. When she speaks, her words reflect thought and consideration. She projects honesty and intelligence, and these qualities are mirrored in her dancing. Called one of the great dramatic ballerinas of her time, she brings a spare, lean yet unstudied precision to her roles. While she is emotional, her emotions are never aimlessly squandered. A specialist in the Tudor repertoire, she is the natural heir to Nora Kaye, whose performances of Tudor ballets were legendary. Miss Wilson does not emulate Nora Kaye but brings her own highly refined sensibilities to the Tudor style.

A principal dancer with American Ballet Theatre since 1961, she entered the company in 1949, at the age of seventeen. Between 1958 and 1960, when American Ballet Theatre suspended operations, she joined the New York City Ballet. She then rejoined ABT, dancing a variety of classical roles as well as Tudor works. Born in Fort Worth, Texas, she trained with Margaret Craske and Antony Tudor.

The flow of our interview was so natural that it is set forth below as it occurred:

GRUEN: How many in your family, Sallie?

WILSON: There are five of us. I'm the baby. My father was an architect. My mother is my mother. But before she was my mother, she played the violin with the Chicago Symphony. We all took music lessons. I play the violin and the cello.

GRUEN: When did you first think about dancing?

WILSON: I was always very athletic. I used to climb trees and jump out of them—and play Tarzan. There were all kinds of things I liked to do. But they were passing fancies. At the time, in school, in Fort Worth, I played the cello in an orchestra. We accompanied an operetta, and in it was a little ballet. My best friend danced in it. For some reason, they had to turn off the music-stand lights. We had to learn the music by heart. So I would play, and watch the ballet every time. Something went "click." Just by chance, at that time, my sister was associated with a children's theater group, and they had a ballet teacher there. My sister suggested I take ballet lessons, and it all coincided with that "click." From that moment on, I knew what I wanted to do. I was twelve. I worked with one particular teacher for only three months. She was inspiring, and very young. But she died. All of her pupils were given over to another teacher, and she was also good. Then came another teacher, Dorothy Edwards. I studied in Fort Worth for four years. When I turned sixteen, I came to New York.

GRUEN: Your parents approved?

WILSON: Yes. They helped me.

GRUEN: What happened when you got to New York?

WILSON: My mother found Miss Margaret Craske. We went and watched a class. We sat there, and Miss Craske walked in. The first thing she said to the whole class was, "Lift up your bodies." She's very English, and has this quiet little voice. The whole atmosphere of the class was incredibly beautiful. When I saw her, light bulbs flashed, and I knew *she* was my teacher. I lived in New York with a lady who rented me a room, near Carnegie Hall. I had not finished high school, but my mother said, "You'll never have a teacher like this again in your life." When I began my classes, I couldn't speak to anyone. I was so shy. I never lifted my eyes. The only thing that I did that was adult was to pursue my decision about dancing.

GRUEN: What did Miss Craske impart to you?

WILSON: She teaches you to know what you're doing. You just don't copy, and do exercises. She gives you self-reliance. I *know* what she has taught me. I can teach it to someone else. It's not just blindly put onto my body. It's intelligent—it's very fine. Her whole outlook on it was that you don't waste the motion, you don't waste the inner movement. It follows the principle of "less is more." She taught us to see the whole movement—the whole idea. You could aim at what the whole thing should be, rather than struggling through a mess of details.

GRUEN: How long did you work with Miss Craske?

WILSON: I was with her one year, and then I got into Ballet Theatre. Then, after one year, I was fired from Ballet Theatre. That year I was the girl Lucia Chase didn't like. I was too young and too shy. Then, Tudor came along and said, "Don't fire her. Give her to me." Tudor was going into the Metropolitan Opera to head the ballet. So, instead of just being dropped, Lucia gave me to him. I went into the Met company.

GRUEN: That must have been a terrible blow to you.

WILSON: It was hard, except that it was also the nicest thing that ever happened to me. I could study with Tudor, as well as with Miss Craske, because both taught at the Met. I should also add that I had studied for a while with Edward Caton. Anyway, I had five years of fine training at the Met with Tudor and Craske.

GRUEN: What was that like?

WILSON: Well, at the time, I studied with them equally, and I always considered Miss Craske my teacher. Tudor was something else. . . . He was an inspiration. His class was more choreography. Craske brought you back to the rules, and he broke the rules all the time. It was a wonderful combination. Tudor is a very special man. You adore him; yet you hate him. Right now, I could say terrible things about him, and yet, I love him.

GRUEN: Why so?

WILSON: He tinkers with people. He likes to get into their hearts, and break them, thinking that's making you a better person or a better dancer. With some people it doesn't work. I've seen some fall by the wayside, because they couldn't survive that. He toyed with people's emotions—with anyone he was interested in.

GRUEN: Did he toy with your emotions?

WILSON: I loved him. He could have told me to jump off a cliff, and I would have done it. He told me when it was time to lose my virginity. So I set about doing that. And I told him when I had done it. He gave a dinner party for me. Not that he *told* me to do it. He just said he thought it was time. I took the suggestion . . . but he knew I would.

GRUEN: How did Tudor prepare you for the roles you would eventually do?

WILSON: It was interesting. The first year I was with the Met, he took a group of us to Jacob's Pillow for the summer. There were eight of us. It was in 1951. We were called the Jacob's Pillow Company-in-Residence. Tudor did several ballets. He put on *Dark Elegies*, and he did two new things for us. It was a summer that affected the lives of all the eight people who were there. I am the only one who came out of it, really.

GRUEN: What happened?

WILSON: I think I learned most of what I know during that summer—not just about performing or technique or class. He woke us all up about being on the stage. Some of what we learned became very cruel lessons. I remember five performances of *Dark Elegies*. It was very difficult for us. We really were students. I could do all the steps, but Tudor showed me the difference between doing all the steps, and doing them right. But it never was established—what was right. It still isn't, because I am still doing the same part that I did then. What I mean is, if you do all the steps, it doesn't mean it was a good performance. Out of those five performances of *Dark Elegies*, I did one performance where I did absolutely everything wrong. I fell off *pointe*, and I was desperately unhappy. Tudor came back afterward and said it was my best performance. That shattered everything. I had to sit back and figure out what he meant by that.

GRUEN: You were probably more vulnerable to the character.

WILSON: It wasn't the character. It was the aura that had to be in that dance. You never quite know what it is—and that's what he wants. He wants you never to know, and be smug about it, and say, "I know how to do that." It's always some unknown thing, and that's what keeps it alive. That's what's so wonderful. I did *Pillar of Fire* for three years, and Tudor came back after one performance, after three years, and kissed me on the forehead and said, "*That* was your first *Pillar*." I was so upset, because I couldn't understand why *that* performance was better than the others.

GRUEN: You seem to be possessed by Tudor.

WILSON: I survived him by myself. He didn't help me to survive at all. If I were a different person, I wouldn't be dancing today. At one point I was really ready to walk in the other direction.

GRUEN: How did you survive?

WILSON: I don't really know. All I know is that he killed me and cut my heart out and ate it and spit out the pits. It didn't show all that much, but I suffered a lot. Then you have to make the decision that *he's* not doing it—that you're doing it . . . which is what he wanted. After the whole thing was over, he said to someone, "You see, I was right." He did it on purpose.

GRUEN: Was Tudor testing your strength?

WILSON: Yes. I might have died. I really was suicidal. I didn't know what I was going to do.

GRUEN: How did this all come about?

WILSON: You know, I've blotted a lot of it out. But I remember certain times . . . certain rehearsal periods. He didn't scream or anything. He quietly said something to me, and everyone in the rehearsal knew I was getting cut to shreds, and they disappeared in the wings. The whole stage emptied. He put on his coat and left. I was left standing alone on the stage, and they turned off the lights. I stood there paralyzed. One girl in the company waited for me. She had put on her clothes, had gone downstairs and waited, and kept me company. She saw that I got home, because I might not have.

I really can't tell you what he said to me. But he knew what would hit me. It probably sounded innocent. Anyway, the next day Lucia excused me from all the rehearsals. She said, "Sallie will be all right." When she spoke to me, it was in hospital tones. I'll never forgive him for it. But I know that he was right—whatever he did to me. At least, he thought he was right.

GRUEN: How does Tudor work on his ballets?

WILSON: He is very precise. Sometimes, he is wrong. He says that *Pillar of Fire* takes place in the South. But I don't see it in the South at all. It's in New England. Actually, it doesn't have to be anywhere. Anyway, I think he was mistaken about the South. But about his working methods, often when he starts teaching you something, he'll just start teaching you dryly the steps—and that will be that day's rehearsal. The next day it will be about interpretation. I remember one day he sat us down and talked about *Pillar*. He talked about the house we all keep going into—the house we live in. He kept talking about what the inside of the house looks like— what we do when we go in the door. He said it was presumably a Sunday morning, and they'd all come back from church. When the eldest Sister goes into the house, he asked, "What do you think she did first?" And people came up with answers. He said, "No. Don't you know, she went into the house, took her hat off, and put it in the hatbox up on the shelf in the closet. Then, she took her gloves off, and she laid them in tissue paper and put them in the drawer." He went on to say that inside the house— which no one ever sees—preparations are made for tea, because the gentleman caller is coming.

Tudor makes you aware of the fact that when you are stepping on the stage, you're not coming in from the wings, but from where you were. Everything is really a continuation of the action. You're not just making an entrance. Anyway, there's one moment in *Pillar* where the eldest Sister is being rejected entirely. When I do it, I go up to the back of the stage and I run forward. I do a movement, appealing to the other people, who reject me. One day at a rehearsal Tudor said he didn't like the way I was doing that. He said I was just doing the movement. He searched for an image to give me. At one point he said, "It's your baby. You need milk for your baby!" Then—and this is why you want to kill the man—the next year, I did that in rehearsal, and he said, "Why are you doing that as though you have a hungry baby?" He tried to put it back into technical terms. I wouldn't accept that. I think he wanted me to decide.

GRUEN: You stayed with the Metropolitan Opera Ballet for five years. What were the circumstances of your rejoining Ballet Theatre?

WILSON: Tudor arranged it. I got a note from him saying that I had an audition with Lucia Chase. He said it was time for me to leave the Met. He knew, of course, that Lucia didn't like me, so he took Lucia out to lunch before the audition. That was nice. He reported to me that the fad at BT was to wear black leotards, black tights, and black toe shoes—those were their practice clothes. So I ran and bought a pair of black tights and dyed my toe shoes black. Tudor told me that for the audition I was to hold my head up, and offer Lucia my hand. In her presence, I always used to duck my head. I got to the audition, and it was just Lucia and Tudor and me. He said, "What would you like to do?" He didn't offer any help at all. So, Lucia suggested something—*bourrées* across the room. Tudor never opened his mouth. Finally, Tudor said, "Do some pirouettes." So I did those. Then, Lucia said, "When can you sign a contract?" That was all I had to do. But she made me promise to let my hair grow. The reason Tudor wanted me to get back to Ballet Theatre was because he wanted me to do the sexy girl in *Pillar of Fire*, and Rosaline in *Romeo and Juliet*.

GRUEN: And did that all work out?

WILSON: The blow was, I got into the company, and I had dinner with Tudor, and he said, "Now you're going to have to fight me." And I said, "But I don't want to fight you." From then on, he never lifted a finger to help me. I went into *Romeo and Juliet* with no rehearsals. I did the Sexy Girl in *Pillar of Fire* with one half-hour rehearsal. Tudor wanted me in the company, and he wanted me to do those things poorly. After a short period of time, he said to Lucia, or to someone around, "She's no performer." Then, we just didn't speak. I never took his class. And we had been so close. He loved me, in a way. I mean, we could talk, or we didn't need to talk. He would ask me a question out of the blue, and I would know what he was talking about. It was almost like a game. And it was fun. Then he lowered the curtain. I realized I had to live without him, that's all. I simply got too close. And I believe he did *that* on purpose—and also for my own good. At least, I'd like to think so.

GRUEN: But why did you allow all this?

WILSON: I loved him. And I still do . . . but, not really. I can't explain it. I love his ballets. They are attached to what I love about him. And I've never seen anyone else work the way he did. Having him as the first choreographer I ever worked with has spoiled me for everyone else.

GRUEN: Why has Tudor stopped choreographing?

WILSON: He's very self-destructive. He thinks he can't top himself. But one of those little ballets he did at the Pillow—*La Ronde,* based on the play by Schnitzler, was really marvelous. He used music of Satie. Instead of ten episodes, as in the original play, he used eight. There are eight seductions. That is an interesting story. At the Pillow, I knew nothing about men—about seduction. But he cast me as the Seductress. She's a very worldly, defined character—entirely foreign to me. I had no confidence that I could do that. Well, it was so beautifully costumed—every detail was perfect. But in rehearsals I was so self-conscious and unhappy that I would just dribble . . . cry. He said, "All right. You go sit over there and I'll do the part." He did all my rehearsals for me. I just stood behind him and learned the steps and listened to what he said. He had a running dialogue. I mean, for every movement he had something to say. We rehearsed like that for a week. The ballet was a terrible problem for me. I would go to bed at night and cry, and pray. On the day before we had a stage rehearsal, everyone went off on an excursion. I didn't go. I went to the theater and solved the problem by myself. With his dialogue, and knowing his steps, I went over the whole thing—doing the character. When we had our stage rehearsal, I did what I had figured out. Afterward, Tudor pulled everyone together and said, "Obviously, one person has been working behind closed doors." He gave me credit for thinking. I must say, it was one of the best things I have ever done. From this experience, I really learned how to study a role.

GRUEN: Why was this ballet never done by a company?

WILSON: He never thought it significant enough for a company to do, except that it *was.* It was so delectable. It was delicious comedy, like no one else can do. Lovely laughs, beautiful movements.

GRUEN: Did you ever speak with Nora Kaye about Tudor?

WILSON: Yes. I think he hurt something in her. At one point, he and Hugh Laing took over her life—told her what to do, what to say, what to wear. I think she had a breakdown. But I only heard of it. Also, after a period, they lost interest in her. Tudor now acts as if he had lost interest in me.

GRUEN: But you are a true link to Tudor's work.

WILSON: He resents that. The last time we did *Pillar of Fire,* Makarova was also doing it. She did two performances, and I did one. Well, he suddenly gave me a full rehearsal. I think it was about his wanting to reassure me about it—that it was about him and me—and he said, "She doesn't really need a rehearsal. She knows more about this ballet than I do." But he said it very resentfully.

GRUEN: How did Tudor like Makarova in *Pillar*?

WILSON: He gave out ten versions of his opinion. Every time anybody asked him that, he thought of a good answer. The last one I heard was, "Well, it was interesting."

GRUEN: How did *you* like Makarova in *Pillar*?

WILSON: She asked to do the ballet, but those steps are very hard if you don't work on them. There aren't even that many steps *in* it. But they are of a particular style. The great joy is to work toward them. You have to go in a corner and figure them out, because they're not what you learn in class. Makarova didn't bother to do that.

GRUEN: After Nora Kaye left the company, were you chosen by Tudor to do *Pillar*?

WILSON: Tudor taught me *Pillar* against his will. Oliver Smith pushed that.

GRUEN: Do you still see Tudor?

WILSON: He comes around to rehearsals occasionally.

GRUEN: You have been called a great dramatic ballerina. What *is* a dramatic ballerina?

WILSON: I don't think the term is valid. Because, I think when you're doing the Swan Queen, that's a dramatic role. You either *are* it, or you're *doing* it. There are degrees of how that's done. Some people do it beautifully, technically, and some people make you sob hysterically—and you don't know why. They have become it, instead of exhibiting it.

GRUEN: Would you tell me something about your current position with American Ballet Theatre?

WILSON: Well, during this New York season [1973], I've been off nine days. I sent Lucia Chase a card saying, "Thinking of you is almost as good as being there." I hope she got the point. Actually, it's not all Lucia's doing. There's a turmoil in the company right now about people trying to take over directorships.

GRUEN: What about Lucia Chase's bringing in all the foreign stars?

WILSON: She didn't bring them all in. Sherwin Goldman brought them in without her even knowing. He signed Bortoluzzi without her knowing. He arranged the Makarova thing, which was all right. Lucia was delighted with that. We were not. We were, at first. We were perfectly happy to be friends with her, and help her. It isn't Natasha. It's the management, acting as if we didn't exist. Suddenly, she was wrapped in cotton wool and carried around and given everything. She just had to say what she wanted, and she got it. Cynthia Gregory, Eleanor d'Antuono, and I suffered a lot. We wondered who we were. We never felt that with Carla Fracci. Carla was a different thing altogether. Carla also makes up for something. She's warm.

GRUEN: Is Lucia Chase a difficult woman?

WILSON: Yes. It's like catching a butterfly. She has a wonderful blind that she can throw up—and disappear. The company walks on their staples, which some of us are. Eleanor is a staple. Eleanor and I get thrown in on two minutes' notice, and they don't even say thank you.

GRUEN: Between 1958 and 1960, you joined the New York City Ballet. What was that period like? How did you enjoy working with George Balanchine?

WILSON: I didn't like it at the time. I didn't appreciate him. But he was so dear to me, I couldn't believe it, because I didn't do anything to make him love me. I argued with him over so many things. No one else will argue with him. I mean, he says perfectly outrageous things to his dancers about ballet technique, and they all accept it. I recall one day his asking us to do a jump. He wanted everyone to land on half-*pointe*, and never put their heels down. It was a big jump. When I heard that, I backed away, and leaned against the *barre* and didn't do it. He stopped the class, came over to me, and made me do it. I tried, and nearly broke my ankle. I stopped and said, "Are you serious?" Everyone in the room gasped. He smiled at me, took me by the hand, and said, "If you do what I tell you, I will make you jump." I jumped higher than anyone in the company, and I always put my heels down when I landed. He never said another word about it. The point is, he loved the fact that I questioned him.

With the Balanchine company, I danced *The Cage*, *Symphony in C*, Third Movement, *Western Symphony*, *Stars and Stripes*. I also created the role of Queen Elizabeth in *Episodes*, Part I, which was choreographed by Martha Graham.

GRUEN: You performed the role of the Mother of the Groom in Jerry Robbins' *Les Noces*. How was it, working with Robbins?

WILSON: It's very exciting to work with him. Jerry is to some other people what Tudor is to me. I could work with Jerry happily and openly, because I didn't have that pressure. Some of my best friends have worked with him, and their lives have been blighted somewhat. I've seen him do his act with other people. He's insecure when he works. You could say a crooked word in rehearsal, and he'll suddenly hate what he's doing. We did at least forty versions of certain sections of *Les Noces*. I remember the sixth version of the boys' dance, which I was in. It was so beautiful that tears came to your eyes. We worked on it one day, and everyone was exalted. The next day, he threw it out. He changed it completely. I couldn't believe that he didn't see how beautiful that one version was. But I always got along with Jerry. I could go over and sit on his lap and call him "Dad" and pull his beard. Everyone would gasp, but he was always sweet and dear to me. Whenever I would do a performance, he would thank me afterward.

GRUEN: What would you say to the student of the dance?

WILSON: You have to read and observe everything. You have to get involved with more than just going to class. You have to have imagination, fantasy in you. Dancing is play-acting. You must read. I read every book in our house. I wept over them, and ran outdoors and re-enacted them. That's how you must involve yourself in dancing. *Swan Lake* . . . there are a lot of people who do *Swan Lake*. You admire their fantastic technique. Some do a beautiful performance, and you're not moved at all. Then, there is one who isn't technically perfect, but she believes it. You have to believe that legend. You have to believe that you have been transformed into a swan, or that it's possible. You have to be a child. Become a child, or be one. Retain, remember. You can't be a grown-up pretender. You must, must believe!

JOHN PRINZ

qually at home in *Swan Lake* as in such contemporary works as *Monument for a Dead Boy*, John Prinz epitomizes the total performer. Prinz, who has been a principal dancer with American Ballet Theatre since 1970, is one of the most versatile and personal dancers around. His own personality—while not distractingly obtrusive—dominates every role he assumes. His smouldering good looks give his characterizations a certain sensuality. Whenever Prinz dances, he exudes an aura of furtive sexuality. This quality comes across equally clearly when one meets him in person.

Prinz agreed to have a talk in the offices of ABT. Lucia Chase's office not being occupied, we spoke there one January morning in 1973. It was eleven o'clock, and Prinz told me he had just gotten up. "I woke up this morning, but I just didn't want to get out of bed for early-morning class. I'll have to take a noon class." Over some hot coffee, the dancer volunteered some information about his background:

"I'm from Chicago. My mother is from Yugoslavia. My father worked for the railroad. He was always at work. There was little communication between us. As a kid, I used to love to move and act all the time. I have a sister, a half brother and a half sister. My sister started ballet as a little girl, and I had to meet her after school and come home with her. I sat in on her class, and gradually I got involved.

"When I was seven, I was taken to the ballet at the Civic Opera House. They were doing *Giselle*, and I loved it. I saw Alicia Alonso and Igor Youskevitch. When I saw them dance, I cried. They had such a beautiful thing together on the stage. You could see a real love between them. Even at that age, I felt all the little delicacies, the little betrayals. When Youskevitch crawled at the end of *Giselle*, he had tears in his eyes. I haven't seen that since. Anyway, living in Chicago was tough. Chicago is a very insensitive city. But I was not insensitive. It seemed everyone around me had no feelings. That hit hard. When I began to take ballet lessons, my friends looked at me in a funny way. I was eight years old. But it didn't bother me. I didn't see anything queer about it. I thought it was very athletic and very beautiful. It was masculine and sensitive. Actually, I was a very tough kid. When I got older, I was in gangs. Also, I liked to play jazz—I played trumpet and piano. When I studied, I could do things immediately. I could do jumps and *double tours*. I could do a lot of pirouettes. I had a natural technique without having to think about it. Actually, this wasn't the best thing, but I found that out only later. I stuck with dancing. When I became an adolescent, I studied at the Ellis-Du Boulay School. Things became difficult, because I didn't know what to do about adolescence. All those problems came in. I almost tried to quit once, but I couldn't."

When John Prinz turned sixteen, he left Chicago. His mother drove him to New York, and the boy lived with an uncle.

"I had never been to New York before, and I had never seen anything like it. I lived on the Lower East Side. There were kids in the street; there was chaos all over the place. It was a jungle, but I loved it. This is what I wanted. I went to the Joffrey School and got a scholarship immediately. That was in 1963. It was my hope to join American Ballet Theatre, but it had temporarily folded. The only company around was the New York City Ballet. I went to see them perform, and it was a whole other thing from what I wanted to do. But I needed a job."

Prinz decided to go to the School of American Ballet for further study. Again, he was admitted on scholarship. Within a year, he was in the company. He was seventeen years old. He stayed with the New York City Ballet for seven years, rising from the *corps* to principal dancer. Prinz discussed his life with Balanchine and the company.

"Balanchine was incredible. The man is a genius. He is a man of his time—and beyond. He was very kind to me from the very beginning and gave me a lot to do. Of course, it was all up to me. Now I realize that, at the time, I was a very immature person. I had a lot of problems understanding myself. Of course, I was young. I had too many relationships. You see, it was an 'I'm going to live' type of thing. So I did. I met one girl in the company, and it got very, very serious. It was a big tragic affair. Well, we've all had those things. Then there was another girl. It was a situation. . . . I was like a volcano. In fact, everybody called me the 'Volcano.' I had all this incredible energy that always kept exploding. The thing is, I wanted to do *everything*. It just got worse and worse as I got more and more involved with more and more people in the company. I don't know how Balanchine put up with me. It got to the point where I couldn't do it any more. Then I met the girl I'm married to now—Nanette Glushak. It wasn't love at first sight or anything like that—it was just the first time that I was able to be friends with a girl—and have conversations. That's when I realized it would work. From that point on, things began to grow for me. I had really gone to the depths. All the way down. I had really reached the bottom. I knew what it was to want to die. Nanette was the foundation of my maturity. But what that meant was that I would have to leave the environment—the company."

John Prinz and Nanette Glushak, who was in the *corps* of the New York City Ballet, were married in 1969. They left the company and traveled to Europe. In Germany, both dancers were asked to join the Stuttgart Ballet, but living in Germany did not appeal to them. They returned to New York and in 1970 the two joined American Ballet Theatre.

"When we joined the company, everything seemed to fall into place for me. Nanette and I got into an incredible growing process with each other, and what we have is very real. I feel very much at peace.

"When I joined ABT, I was made a soloist right away. That's not their usual policy, but they needed a soloist to do the *pas de trois* in *Swan Lake*, and the Peasant *pas de deux* in *Giselle*. So I went in and did those. I was made a principal in 1972."

What does dancing mean to John Prinz?

"Dancing means you feel this ecstasy of warmth. But it's more than that. It's knowing exactly who you are as an artist. It's being on top of a situation professionally. It involves everything you have to give. I had to pull everything together in order to develop this thing. It's a complete understanding of what you're doing—the dancing, the acting, the timing. If you get close enough to these things, then you get that beautiful feeling . . . that feeling of oneness. It's like you're looking at yourself, and you're aware of everything around you. It's all these very complicated things happening at once. It's an incredible experience.

"Whenever I stood in the wings ready to go on, I had nerves. Now, it's the adrenalin working. You think you're so weak, but as soon as you hear the music, the strength comes to you. It's the adrenalin and it's your mind working together. Actually, I think your mind is in control of everything. Because that mental strength creates the energy."

Prinz discussed partnering and some of the ballerinas he has danced with:

"I was the first one to partner Natalia Makarova in Tudor's *Lilac Garden*. Natasha is very light and delicate to partner. She has wonderful placement, and a little extra something else. Finally, she felt more comfortable with Ivan Nagy, because their backgrounds were the same—their training. Americans are trained differently in partnering. European dancers like Makarova and Fracci have to be held in different ways. Their legs are in different lines, and you have to push them a little more one way or another. You have to adjust to each one. When you partner a prima ballerina, you have to do it with tremendous precision, because they've got big temperaments. I've found that the European ballerinas have tremendous emotion. They have to look you in the eyes. I love that, because then, you're not just moving, you have a relationship onstage."

John Prinz dances easily in all styles. He moves comfortably from *Les Sylphides* to *Fancy Free*, from *Petrouchka* to *Giselle*. To all his roles, he lends a personal, highly dynamic profile.

"I just go on and on. It's a constant development. I want to continue to grow as a dancer and as a person. And my wife is making wonderful strides also. She is now a soloist. We had never danced together before. Now, we do. The first time it was incredible, because I didn't know her as a partner. She gets fantastically into a role. Right now, I'm into things outside of dancing. I am aware of a lot of vibrations. I'm into reading an awful lot. I read a lot of Hermann Hesse. I'm also into people. I'm into psychology—and spiritual things. There's a lot of knowledge I've got to acquire. I'm putting the energy that I have in dancing into all these things. Right now, I can go in any direction. Nanette and I feel that we can do anything in the world. The whole world is open to us. But when it comes time to dance, I put all of the other things aside, because that comes first."

ANTONY TUDOR

The most fascinating, most enigmatic of choreographers is, without question, Antony Tudor. Born in London in 1908, he did not come to the dance until he turned nineteen, when he studied with Marie Rambert, Margaret Craske, and Nicholas Legat, among others. He began his dancing career with Ballet Rambert, remaining with it from 1930 to 1938. It was with Rambert that he also began choreographing. Tudor also danced with the Sadler's Wells for a period of two years. His first important choreographic effort was *The Planets*, composed for Ballet Rambert in

1934. This was followed by such masterpieces as *Jardin aux Lilas*, 1936, *Dark Elegies*, 1937, and *Judgment of Paris*, 1938. That same year Tudor founded the London Ballet, choreographing two works for it—*Soirée Musicale* and *Gala Performance*.

Antony Tudor came to America in 1940 to join Ballet Theatre, with which he danced and choreographed. He remained with the company until 1950, during which time he became director of the Ballet Theatre and Metropolitan Opera Ballet School. He continued to head the faculty of the Met school after Ballet Theatre withdrew from the Metropolitan. In April 1974, Tudor joined Lucia Chase and Oliver Smith as an associate director of the company, now the American Ballet Theatre.

While with Ballet Theatre, Tudor restaged *Jardin aux Lilas* under the name *Lilac Garden*. He also choreographed perhaps his greatest work, *Pillar of Fire*, in 1942. Additional ballets included *Romeo and Juliet*, *Dim Lustre*, *Shadow of the Wind*, and *Undertow*.

Tudor's works are in the repertoire of almost every great ballet company throughout the world. His style may be said to be innovative in terms of deep psychological probing and the invention of movements that subtly combine classical and modern dance technique. In point of fact, any Tudor ballet contains a magical and indefinable sense of mystery—a peculiarly haunting quality of reserve and containment. His characters are rooted in life, and their emotions develop out of life-problems. Tudor is a perfectionist. The most infinitesimal action must bear meaning. Every gesture, every stance, every movement must contain a true link with feeling and emotion.

It is an unhappy fact that Antony Tudor has not composed a major ballet in over ten years. While he and his long-time friend, the British dancer Hugh Laing, travel extensively to supervise revivals of his works, Tudor has not felt the urge or need to create.

In the winter of 1973, Tudor agreed to come to my apartment for a talk. He arrived wearing a dark suit and seemed nervous at the prospect of speaking into a tape recorder.

One first becomes aware of Tudor's eyes. Their gaze is piercing, and disquieting. He is a tall man who carries himself with particular grace. His nearly bald head lends starkness to his appearance. Speaking with a clipped British accent, he chooses his words carefully. Indeed, during our interview, there were frequent long pauses prior to his answering any question. The presence of Tudor is all-pervasive. He transforms any room he enters—the transformation manifesting itself in an odd, quite pleasurable tension. This is not to say that the choreographer puts one ill at ease. He is decidedly charming and communicative. Still, to be with Tudor is to feel a certain gripping apprehension. The following is a verbatim account of our talk:

GRUEN: Why is it that you have not choreographed a new work in some ten years?

TUDOR: The reason I don't choreograph is that so many other people are doing it rather well. It's nice for them to have the field to themselves. Also, it is incredibly difficult to find a score, where you're *not* dependent on the score. For instance, nearly every ballet I go to see that I rather like, I wonder how good that ballet would be if you took the music away. Last night I went to the Joffrey Ballet and saw Robert Joffrey's new work based on music by Wagner. I won't say what I thought, because I don't think one choreographer should talk about another's work. But I *did* find myself having the same thought: Take the music away, and where are we? With me, music must become a *partner*, and not the sole source of inspiration. But it is not merely a matter of finding a score.

I have not choreographed because my body is much older. When I choreograph, I like to show every movement that everyone does. Now, in *Pillar of Fire*, some of the movements I, myself, could no longer show. My knees would crack in a minute. I couldn't devise those movements any more on my own body. I really couldn't. I *have* to do my ballets like that. Other people, obviously, can do ballets without that. People like Martha Graham and George Balanchine have their dancers so trained in their own way of working that the movements can be described or just hinted at, and they take form. I have to feel everything through my own body, always.

GRUEN: But would there not be equally exquisite movements you could make at your juncture of age and life—perhaps of a more profound character?

TUDOR: There'd be much less movement. Actually, I haven't entirely discarded the idea of doing something—now that I'm really cleared of teaching. You see, when I taught, it was quite impossible for me to choreograph, because, if you are a choreographer your mind is straying around with you. Even in the street—you're daydreaming all the time, in terms of the ballet. If you're teaching, you're thinking in terms of class— your students. That occupies your mind. You're thinking up combinations for class. If you're doing a ballet, you cannot think in that sort of idiom, because you would stereotype everything into a ballet, which I wouldn't be any good at.

GRUEN: Getting back to finding a score: most choreographers tell me that it is the music which is the sole propelling element of their work. You said music must merely be a partner. Could you elaborate?

TUDOR: I'm not against having the music be the propelling factor of a ballet. The fact is, the general audience sitting out in front doesn't realize that it's the music that's sending them most of the time, and not the choreography. I mean, just go back to the thirty-two *fouettés* in *Swan Lake*. If Tchaikovsky had not written that very dull, repetitive piece of music, you can see thirty-two *fouettés* to a lot of different kinds of music, which doesn't work the same way.

GRUEN: How did you happen to choose Schönberg's "Verklärte Nacht" for *Pillar of Fire*?

TUDOR: The score impressed me because I felt it was not a completely satisfactory concert piece. It's a work that doesn't really complete itself. It seemed to me it might make a marvelous marriage with dance. Whereas, when I did *La Gloire* in 1952 for the New York City Ballet, I made the terrible mistake of choosing three Beethoven overtures. When you get all the bombast of all those drums going full blast, then how do you match up to it onstage? You just can't go in competition with it. You can't really make music the partner. The music must dominate. So, again, where are you without the music?

On *Jardin aux Lilas*, I had an idea of the story before I started, and I looked for a score that would fit it. I actually began choreographing *Jardin* to music of Fauré—the "Ballade for Piano and Orchestra." I rehearsed for a while with it, and it obviously wasn't going to work. It may have been the percussiveness of the piano. But, by then, I was into some of the characters, and into the beginning of the ballet. Then, I had to start looking for another score. It took me a long while before I got to Chausson's "Poème for Violin and Orchestra." The movements I had formulated for Fauré could go into the new piece.

GRUEN: Could you describe the birth of your ballet *Romeo and Juliet*?

TUDOR: Well, the birth of *Romeo and Juliet* was, very simply, that I heard a concert suite of the Prokofiev *Romeo and Juliet*. I think it was the first performance of it here in America. When I heard it, I thought, This is marvelous. I've got to use this music! Then, of course, the more I thought about the score, the less I wanted to use it. It went on forever, and for me, it didn't have Shakespeare as I saw Shakespeare. By then, however, I wanted to do *Romeo and Juliet*, but I wanted to do it *my* way. I wanted it in the feel of the Shakespearean theater—meaning, the feel of an open stage, like the Globe. Then, I had to look for music. I listened to all the other works on the subject—Berlioz, Tchaikovsky. But none of them fitted my concept. Then I felt that the gentle folk melodies that are sprinkled through the music of Delius were terribly reminiscent of a lot of Italian melodies, and I thought they also had the colors of the Italian painters of the period. I could never find anything that *really* satisfied me for the last scene. I had Sir Thomas Beecham, who was the great Delius authority, look with me; but we couldn't find anything that was absolutely right.

GRUEN: Your only commissioned score was the one used for your 1945 ballet, *Undertow*, composed by William Schuman. Were you pleased with it?

TUDOR: I was shocked by it. At the time, I was on tour, and I'd write Schuman letters, which I think he's still got, and which would louse him up, because they would tell him exactly what he didn't want to know. I mean, I wouldn't tell him anything about the story. I would just say that I wanted something reminiscent of a sunset over the Brooklyn Bridge. I'd give him pictures. I'd give him geographical and atmospheric things. But I wouldn't tell him what was happening on the stage, because if I had, he might start putting it in his music, and that, I didn't want. Well, a week later, I would get a couple of pages of music. It invariably was a great shock, because it was quite different from what I had expected. Still, everything functioned. The music obeyed the atmospheric demands.

GRUEN: *Undertow* strikes me as being one of the most accurate psychological depictions of a highly disturbed individual. How did you research, if at all, the story for this ballet?

TUDOR: For *Undertow* I amassed a library of books. There were thirty-four books on psychiatry alone. I worked on them because I didn't want to make any mistakes. I don't think I can be faulted from a psychoanalytic point of view. I worked six months on that.

GRUEN: Have you been analyzed yourself?

TUDOR: I tried that later, just to see what it was like. It was a disaster. I went for an interview with a highly recommended analyst. He asked me why I came. I said, "I thought you were supposed to tell *me*." I went about eight times. The analyst was in a state of total nervous breakdown himself. I discontinued going.

GRUEN: Dancers who have worked with you have told me that you have profoundly stirred and even changed their lives. When you and Hugh Laing worked with Nora Kaye at Ballet Theatre, for example, it was said that you transformed her completely.

TUDOR: Well, Nora did a lot, too. What you must do with dancers is to strip them of their superficialities. Strip them of their own conception of themselves, until you find something underneath. This takes time, patience, and occasional bullying. When you choreograph, there are two of you creating a dance. You've got to get the dancer to climb into the skin of the dance with you. For a while, there are two of you in the same skin. Then, happily, *you* get out of it, and leave the skin to the dancer—and she has to stay with it. If she goes back to herself, the performance won't be any good.

But about Nora Kaye . . . She was recalcitrant before I used her. The very first time I saw her was in a class. She was a girl who hit my attention. She was very strange. She had a drive. I remember the dance studio being very long and narrow. This one girl managed to keep getting right in front of where I was sitting. I thought this was rather pushing things a little, and I carefully evaded my eyes from her. It was as though I were never looking at her. Then, at one point, she settled again, right in front of me, and did five or six pirouettes on *pointe*, which I had never seen before. Of course, I made believe I didn't see it, and Nora stomped out of the class and into the dressing room. I think she swore she would never work for that so-and-so

Englishman, ever. Meanwhile, I put her on the list for my next day's rehearsal call. She came in like a lamb, and from then on, I had no trouble with her.

From then on, she would sweat blood and tears to get what she knew I wanted, and which she thought was probably true as movement. I will give you an example: When I worked with Nora on the Russian Ballerina in *Gala Performance*—this was before we approached working on *Pillar of Fire*—she had to appear downstage, backing the audience, and just walk to centerstage. It was just a simple walk that turned out not to be so simple. Nora could not get this walk. So she rented a studio for herself on Broadway just to practice this walk. She came back, and it still wasn't better. This was absolute torture for her. She cried over just this simple walk. Finally, she achieved it, and with it, got into the woman she was portraying.

GRUEN: How do you get your dancers to fully understand your movements and your portrayals of characters?

TUDOR: I will tell you another story regarding this. When I worked at the Royal Ballet on my *Shadowplay* in 1967, I had a rehearsal with Anthony Dowell. I walked into the rehearsal room, and said, "Well, I don't know what we're going to do. We'll just waste time." I asked Dowell, "Which corner would you like to come on from? Have you any preference?" He didn't know. I said, "Well, suppose we start by finding you in this corner—as though you'd already come on." I started him moving to the music—and we just moved. We improvised quietly. I made him walk to the place where he comes upstage—back to the audience—and I said, "Now I want you to look up, and I want you to see the tree." He asked, "Which tree? What tree?" I said, "There is a tree. Don't you *see* the tree? I'd like *you* to tell me what kind of tree it is." He couldn't tell me what kind of tree it was. So we left the rehearsal there. I mean, if he didn't know what kind of tree it was, what use was it doing the ballet.

On the next day, I was coming out of the tube and walking to the Royal Ballet School at Barons Court. In the window of a shop, I saw a fruit. I went in and bought that fruit. I took it to the rehearsal. Dowell and I got to the same point, where he was looking up at the tree. Again I said, "What kind of tree is it?" He did not answer. I said, "Put your hands behind your back." I slid the fruit into his hands. "Now you may look." And he looked at the fruit. It was a beautiful mango. He had never seen one in his life, and he was ecstatic. He suddenly looked up and said, "It's a mango tree!" At this moment, the tree came to life. He knew what he was looking at. That is very typical of the way I approach things. It's peripheral, but it's a way to go through all the wrappings until you get to the center.

GRUEN: Sallie Wilson has been a fine interpreter of your ballets, notably, *Pillar of Fire*. In talking with her, she made clear her strong attachment to you and your work. Do you consider her an outstanding interpreter of Tudor?

TUDOR: I've known Sallie from the word go. She became a devotee, and a great disciple. I really only got to work with her because she was in the *corps de ballet* at the Met, when I first worked there. That first summer, a group of us from the Met went to Jacob's Pillow, and I worked some things on Sallie especially for the Pillow. Obviously, I'm satisfied with her interpretations of my works. If I weren't satisfied, she wouldn't be doing them.

GRUEN: When working with such dancers as Carla Fracci and Natalia Makarova, did you find them suitable to the content and special movements of your ballets?

TUDOR: Fracci is terribly valuable, because she knows her theater so well. She has that sales pitch of hers. What she does with my works is not really quite my concept, but I think her concept is probably valid. She does my movements. She doesn't vary them. She gives them an intonation that, to me, is slightly operatic. I never felt I was doing what might be called operatic movements. But she is a star, and she knows her business.

There were quite a lot of problems working with Makarova. I loved working with her as a person. But she had astonishing moments where she couldn't do movements because the legs couldn't turn in. She felt excruciatingly unhappy doing a movement where the knees have to turn in to accomplish what I wanted. This was approaching something in her body that was against all her training. But she worked on it. Finally, she approached what I wanted. She is, of course, a great, great ballerina. I went to see her *Swan Lake* the last time she did it with ABT. Well, there were moments when she was so completely and totally of the moment—of *it*— that it was a totality of *being*. It was one of the greatest performances I'd ever seen.

GRUEN: So many major dancers wish to have a new Tudor ballet created on them. I know Rudolf Nureyev is desperate for a Tudor ballet.

TUDOR: We have constant conversations, Rudy and I. I haven't heard from him recently, and I sent a card to friends in England which said, "Rudy doesn't love me any more!" They answered, "Rudy *does* love you. Why don't you do a ballet for him?" You see, he's been harping on this for years. But you see, a lot of choreographers have done ballets for him, and not a one has been successful. I really would love to work with him, but the problem is getting him into that other skin. I mean, getting Rudy out of his *own* skin, because his *own* skin is already so very, very good. I really would love to work with him. But to get the right picture that I would want him to get into . . . it's very difficult.

GRUEN: This sounds as though something new might be stirring. . . .

TUDOR: No, no. Nothing is stirring. At least, I hope not. Because it's such a pain in the ass. You start getting an idea for a ballet, and you're up against all that nonsense of devising steps, and going through that whole torture again. Because it *is* torture for the choreographer as well as for the dancer. You can go out of your mind. You can go for three days knowing there's a movement you want, and you can't find it.

GRUEN: What kind of life are you leading now?

TUDOR: I lead a marvelous, indolent life. I think it's just gorgeous. I get up in the morning. I look for my glasses . . . where did I put my glasses? I look for them for two hours. Finally, I find them. I sit down with the paper. I make the coffee. Roughly that. A gorgeous wasting of time. Sometimes, I go to the library—the Dance Collection. You see, we want to revive *Dim Lustre* at American Ballet Theatre, because it's so gone to the dogs with the New York City Ballet, for which it was created. The City Ballet won't let me cast it. I've asked for rehearsals, and they won't let me know when I can have rehearsals. So now, the idea is to redo it with ABT. Also, I want to have a new set. The original was by Motley. But I don't want that set to come back. I want to fix up little things in it. The audience will not know the difference, but for me, it will be satisfying. The ballet is very hard to cast. I had originally wanted the Actress to be modeled on Luise Rainer.

GRUEN: Do you see a lot of dance?

TUDOR: Not particularly.

GRUEN: Do you admire the work of George Balanchine? Do you see him?

TUDOR: I don't see much of Mr. B. I never have. He's a sort of world unto himself. Of course, I think he's a great genius. There's no doubt about it. But, you see, the first ballets I saw of George's were *The Prodigal Son, Apollo*—and they bowled me over. I thought they were so wonderful. I don't think he's done anything really so much better than those. I love *Serenade*, but that's a long time ago. And *Agon*, which everyone screams about being a great masterpiece, is the third of a trilogy that began with *Apollon Musagète*. All it does is get more people on the stage, and makes the movements faster. But it's, to me, of the same physical background as *Apollo*—just varied.

GRUEN: Have you ever tried working in the area of totally abstract ballet?

TUDOR: No. I'm very interested, but I don't think I'd be very good at it. Also, I don't know what an abstract ballet is. If I see a human body on the stage, I don't see it as an abstraction. I see it as a body.

GRUEN: Could you talk about Hugh Laing as an exponent of Tudor ballets?

TUDOR: Laing was my leading dancer from almost my third ballet. It's funny about Hugh. He got to the stage where he could almost read my mind and do the movement before I'd set it. In the studio, he never looked as though he could make things happen. But in performance, he was amazing! He was so theatrical as a mover. He was always so infinitely better than I ever expected him to be. But he had this smell of the stage. Also, other people have been very good in roles I created for Hugh, but when he did them, he put every ounce of his being into them. He knew the way I worked, because he had been there while I was developing. And in the early days, while I was rehearsing all these things, he would sit down, and he would help. He'd help Nora.

GRUEN: In what way?

TUDOR: Well, I would work with the dancers, and I'd get them to do everything right. In a way, everything would get too well rehearsed—to a degree of perfection, where it really began to lose the breadth and the blood. Then, Hugh would move into the rehearsal, and manage, with his own enthusiasm and drive and emotionalism, to get the emotion back— everything I'd let slide.

GRUEN: Could you characterize your style—your body movements?

TUDOR: I always want the body to sing. Therefore, nearly all my phrases are as though they would be sung. That's why I'm against counting. No one can count if they're singing. Also, a singer has a breath for a certain phrase. Now, we don't actually do this in dancing. But I do create my phrases with that sort of innate thing happening. And so, I devise in phrases of movement, not in a sequence of steps.

GRUEN: What led you into choreography? Who were your influences?

TUDOR: I like the theater. I didn't think I'd make a very good actor, because I didn't have the voice for it. And even if I had become an actor, it would have been acting in English—and that would have limited my travels to the Western world. I wanted to see the *whole* world. Ballet dancers saw the world. I saw photographs of Anna Pavlova performing in a Mexican bull ring, or in front of the Sphinx, in Egypt, and going to all these gorgeous places. So, obviously, ballet seemed a much better area. But I also knew I would never be a dancer—at least, never a Nureyev. I knew I'd be competent enough, but not in an area that would satisfy me. The only other job I saw for myself was being a choreographer. So, since I wanted to be in the theater, and also see the world, I thought choreography would be the answer. It was a very practical decision.

As for influences. In those early days, when I was about fifteen up to nineteen, I went every day, whenever Diaghilev came to perform—two seasons a year, in London. I thought it was all marvelous.

GRUEN: One hears so many things about the ballet world, in general. That it is a closed and jealous world. That it is filled with intrigue and backstage politics. Is it all true?

TUDOR: Don't believe every word you hear. I think, of course, that it's a divine profession. I can't think of anything that's more fun. Just being able to move around—to feel your body in action—to get a certain amount of adulation, which is usually desirable. Ballet is a world unto itself. But so is composing.

GRUEN: Are there any young choreographers you particularly admire?

TUDOR: Yes. There are a lot of them. When I see Eliot Feld's *Intermezzo*, I'm moved.

GRUEN: I'm told that you are now deeply involved with Oriental philosophy and religion.

TUDOR: Yes. I'm involved. But in the area in which I'm involved, I'm a total beginner. Even after sixteen years! It's Zen. Of course, the longer you're with Zen, the less you know about it. Thank God.

GRUEN: Has your involvement with Zen taken the place of your creative activity?

TUDOR: Well, from movement, I went into nonmovement. In Zen, you just sit on a platform for hours on end, without moving. And I do that.

GRUEN: Is this fulfilling?

TUDOR: If it fulfills anything, it's failed . . . with everyone. Anyone who gets fulfillment out of Zen, hasn't gotten anything. You see, it's a system of stripping of the extraneous matter. It's a stripping of what you've got. You go into it to lose, not to gain. It's very hard to do this. It's very tough. Very challenging. And it's very nice. You really get no results from it. There are no rewards.

GRUEN: Being a perfectionist, have you ever seen a perfect performance of any of your works?

TUDOR: I think so. I saw one performance of *Romeo and Juliet* with Alicia Markova and Hugh Laing which was just perfect. And the first *Undertow*, with Laing, Alicia Alonso, Rosella Hightower, Nana Gollner, Diana Adams, and Lucia Chase, was perfect. I was enthralled. But, you see, if I see a performance that I like, it's as though I had nothing to do with it. I see the work as a work. It's there with a life of its own. It has it's own reason for being. Nora Kaye has given me some perfect performances of *Pillar*.

GRUEN: What was your relationship with Lucia Chase during the early years of Ballet Theatre?

TUDOR: Lucia was always very canny. Lucia is rather rare in that she never interferes, in any way, with anything. She allows the choreographer and the dancers to go into a studio, and she will leave them to their business. She was marvelous in the parts I built for her. I called on her acting ability—which she had.

GRUEN: Do you frequent dancers? Do you socialize?

TUDOR: I don't socialize any more. Not at all. I rarely see anyone. Even in the old days, I didn't. I went my own, lone-wolf way. I still do.

GRUEN: Some people have said that you are a cold, unemotional person.

TUDOR: Oh, yes. Speak to anyone, and they will tell you I'm the most cold-blooded son-of-a-bitch that ever happened. Well, I am. But my characters aren't.

ERIK BRUHN

█ magine a nine-year-old blond boy in a backstage dressing room in a Copenhagen theater, watching his mother combing the hair of a great stage actress, applying make-up to the actress's face. There he stands, wide-eyed, observing the transformation in the mirror. His mother deftly completes the hairdressing ritual. She is intent on her work. Suddenly, she looks into the mirror and sees her son staring. She abruptly turns around, tells him to leave the dressing room.

Startled, he rushes out and finds himself in a corridor lined with other dressing rooms, where other actors and actresses are preparaing themselves for that evening's performance. The boy—Erik Bruhn—wanders cautiously, peeking into dressing rooms whose doors have been left ajar. He is hypnotized by a world he has never known or seen before. He is enthralled by the magical ways in which ordinary people re-create themselves into strangely costumed figures that seem to have no relation to their true selves. At the same time, the boy still smarts from the cruel dismissal given him by his mother. After all, she had brought him along. Where was he supposed to be, if not near her. He knew, of course, that his mother had her job to do—she was a professional hairdresser, and she had to support him and his four sisters. Still, she could have been kinder.

The impact of the theater and the overwhelming short-tempered and critical personality of his mother were the two most powerful influences of Erik Bruhn's life. In time, this slight, frightened boy would turn into one of the greatest dancers of the twentieth century. In time, the name Erik Bruhn would be synonymous with all that was classically pure and technically accomplished in male ballet dancing.

For twenty-four years Erik Bruhn set the standard of excellence for balletic refinement and dramatic intensity. An Erik Bruhn performance would never be less than an event. The road to his particular genius was by no means an easy one, for it was fraught with psychological complication.

At the age of forty-three, Erik Bruhn retired as a dancer. His last performance in *La Sylphide*, in which he partnered Carla Fracci, took place at Kennedy Center on December 29, 1971. Bruhn's retirement was triggered by illness, but the illness was an indefinable one. In recent years, physical pain would come whenever he had to appear. When he did appear, the dancer continued to be flawless, but for days afterward he would be in agony.

Erik Bruhn came to have lunch with me in my apartment on a brisk, sunny April day in 1973. Sun-tanned, and surprisingly slighter than he had appeared on stage, he wore an elegant denim suit, with zippers everywhere, designed for him by Pierre Cardin. A dark blue sweater bought in Rome was worn over a striped shirt acquired in Cannes. The blond, blond hair framed an angular face illuminated by intelligence. Bruhn was in New York to supervise his versions of *Swan Lake* and *La Sylphide* which were currently being performed at the Metropolitan Opera by the National Ballet of Canada, with the leading male roles danced by Rudolf Nureyev.

Sitting with me for a prelunch drink, Bruhn looked dazzlingly healthy. He had been in retirement two years. Lighting a cigarette, he told me that these days he has been traveling throughout Europe, Canada, and America staging various versions of the classics.

"I would like not to give up ballet altogether," he said. "Actually, I have just signed a three-month contract to work with the Canadian Ballet —three months out of the year is just about the right time for me to spend with ballet. But I now want to pay more attention to some of my other interests. For example, I have always wanted to write. I have just finished a short story which needs reworking. I have also let it be known that it would interest me to do some acting. This fall I will go to Denmark to appear in *Rashomon*. Of course, I'm terrified that I will lose my voice. But I'll go through with it, because I need to keep busy."

We touch on Bruhn's retirement.

"Well, I will tell you something. It was a tremendous shock to me—a mental shock. But I will give you a little story. When I was fifteen and going to the Royal Ballet School in Denmark, I was singled out for demonstrations. Even the company would come and watch me. Major dancers would come and see how I did certain things. I had a natural facility, and I never knew exactly why I could do such things. All this came to the attention of the press, and I remember that at that early age I was interviewed. What came back to me was that at fifteen I told the interviewer that I would stop dancing—right then. You see, I became frightened of my capacities, and frightened of the responsibility of the talent I was apparently born with. Of course, I continued dancing, but that initial fear never left me."

Erik Bruhn was born in Copenhagen in 1928, and entered the Royal Danish Ballet School in 1937. Ten years later, he was accepted into the company. Soon hailed as an extraordinary dancer, he was allowed to make guest appearances throughout the world. His longest tenure as a principal dancer, however, was with American Ballet Theatre, which was the last company he danced with. (In August 1974, however, Bruhn made a notable New York guest appearance in the major character note of Madge, the witch in the National Ballet of Canada's production of *La Sylphide* with Rudolf Nureyev as James.)

"My real breakthrough as a dancer took place in America. When I arrived here in the late Forties, it was a revelation to me because I was exposed to so many different kinds of dancing. It was marvelous to become friends with people like Martha Graham and José Limón. I must admit, however, that as much as I wanted to join in some of their modern classes, I didn't dare, because I did not wish to break the classical discipline. One thing that the exposure to modern dance did for me was to make me go back and work even harder, with some of the modern dancer's awareness and consciousness."

Over lunch, Erik Bruhn told me of the trauma connected with his decision to stop dancing. It was a most detailed and fascinating account:

"I of course realized that one day I would have to stop. In the past four or five years I became more and more aware of this. But during that time I did not allow myself to give in to the physical weakness that takes place as a dancer matures. I kept asking more and more of myself. You see, by the age of thirty-five, the body reaches a certain peak, and muscles no longer develop. With me, it became a question of too much pressure. Also, I began to miss the challenge. I had already achieved a great deal, and I felt I could not give more. Then, too, when you become a box-office name, nobody dares to tell you anything. They don't realize that sometimes there is a need to be told that something is still working or that something is bad. You hear neither. I'm sure Rudolf never hears any criticism from anybody. The point is, fellow dancers are afraid to say anything. Even more so, directors or managers never say anything—as long as the house is full. So everything falls on you.

"The truth is, that because of the tension and the pressure of all this, I made myself ill. I think that I unconsciously prepared myself to stop. The whole thing was pretty painful. All along, I felt that it was my mind that was really destroying my body. On the other hand, the pain I felt was real, and overpowering. I thought that I could keep it in control, but two years ago I realized I could not continue.

"I developed pains in my stomach—unbearable pains. I went to doctors. They said I had a peptic ulcer. I think that most of the doctors felt they had to tell me it wasn't anything serious. I was always convinced that my illness was really all in my mind, and for that there are no pills. I woke up one morning in such pain that I couldn't face anything any more. Still, I continued for another year. Finally, I saw a woman doctor who told me that if I were not careful, I would actually induce a real illness out of my unconscious mind. I was just on the border of desperate illness when I made my decision. I announced my retirement, and it came out in the papers. It was good to see it in print. I felt a tremendous relief. The pains subsided. In fact, there were no pains two or three weeks after my formal announcement. Then, I began to travel around. I began to escape from one place to another. I rushed around Europe. At one point the pain caught up with me again. Only this time, I was on my own. There was no sympathy, no consolation. I did not miss being on the stage. Slowly, I began to make the transition. I began to write. I needed my mind occupied. I needed an outlet. That was a year and a half ago. I feel much calmer now, and I have almost no pain." (As it turned out, Bruhn was suffering from ulcers and was successfully operated on in December 1973 and January 1974.)

Erik Bruhn spoke with a slight Scandinavian accent. His voice has the cultured inflection of a man of the world. Eating slowly (the food he asked for had to be bland and mild, indicating a prescribed diet) and speaking slowly, he responded to some questions about his early life and about his family.

"I had a mother who, despite everything, was a fantastically inspiring example. She died when I was thirty-two years old, and it was only during her last years that I began to develop an admiration for her. Before that, I only knew a person who was called my mother. It was that kind of relationship. You might say that I hated her. My mother and father were separated when I was five. I had four sisters. We all lived with my mother. My sisters didn't like me very much because when I was little I seemed to have been my mother's favorite. The trouble was, she didn't hide it. She actually said so in front of all my sisters. When we were alone, my sisters would beat me up. I begged my mother to stop saying that I was her favorite child. She said, 'If you can't take it, you're not strong enough. You're just like your father.' The worst thing she could say to me was 'You're just like your father.' My father represented everything that was weak to her. Basically, I feared my mother. Only rarely did she show any love or affection. When she did, it was enough to keep me going for a few years. It was so strong that you never forgot it. Anyway, this was not a typical mother bringing up her children. None of us survived her strong character, and as a result of it I don't get along with my sisters. They are *still* jealous of me. And because of me, they don't even speak to each other. It's all very difficult.

"As for my father, I only got to know him later, when he was married to somebody else. He was a civil engineer. He was the one who had the education and the background. My father was a very nice man, but I was told that one of the reasons he left Mother was that he was jealous because she liked me more than she liked him. You see, my mother really didn't need anybody. She was unbelievably independent, and my father couldn't cope with that. He became a negative. That is, he stopped working, he spent her money. He gambled, he drank.

"My mother never stopped criticizing me. When I studied at the Royal Ballet, she never came to see me. She just assumed I was a big nothing. All my early life was one big criticism and one big opposition. As I grew, and as I finally developed into perhaps the most important dancer in the theater, she didn't care a damn. When I made my debut, she didn't come to see me. Then, at nineteen, the newspapers called me the greatest Danish dancer there ever was. When she read that, she called me up and said she wanted a ticket to come and see me. That's when I took my revenge. I said to her, 'You go and buy your own ticket. You go and stand in line with everybody else.' And she did. She had to get up at seven o'clock in the morning to stand in line for the box office to open at eight. I enjoyed that revenge. Of course, after she saw me she began to criticize everything, although she did admit that I could dance.

"I don't know how I managed to survive her. On the other hand, without her, I might never have been provoked into proving myself so much. I think every artist needs, not a mother like mine, but an element of opposition to push you into achievement."

Given this strong element of opposition, yet surviving it, and indeed achieving miracles from an artistic point of view, what kind of personality emerged?

"I was very much *me* as a dancer, and because of my youth and technical facility, I was a phenomenon. But I was not an artist or a mature dancer. In fact, people began to say that I was technically perfect, but that my dancing was almost *too* perfect. They began to say that my dancing was cold, distant, and aloof. In a sense I agreed with that, although I never had the idea that I was perfection. I worked for an idea of something that I only sometimes achieved the look of. I did not begin to 'open up' as a dancer until after the age of twenty-nine or thirty."

There is no question that Bruhn's achievement is one of unparalleled nobility of line and expressiveness. Bruhn claimed that he felt himself to be at one with all of his artistic powers perhaps five or six times during his dancing career:

"I don't remember exactly how it happened, or during which ballet. It may have been in *Giselle* or *Miss Julie* or *La Sylphide*. All I knew was that everything felt completely integrated. There was something special that went beyond technical matters. It was a feeling of totality, of total involvement. It is a chemical thing, a physical and mental phenomenon. I can't explain it. One thing I can say is that when this happened, I was a physical wreck afterward. For two or three days after, I was almost sick. I was burnt up completely. Then came the thought of recapturing that unbelievable state. You try to achieve the same feeling. You work for that, and you despair. You do a performance and you begin to know how to fake that essence. You feel untrue, dishonest—although you are true, perhaps, to that particular moment. Strangely enough, even when you're most dishonest, there's a certain way of being honest . . . because something honest is left floating around your performance. Don't forget, when you are a dancer and you go out and perform, you always take a chance. You know that the route can be different each time."

Among Erik Bruhn's many partners, perhaps the singular one in his career was the Italian ballerina Carla Fracci.

"Having danced with Carla was like the fulfillment of a love affair—a love affair that was consummated on the stage. Of course, I've had great satisfaction from dancing with ballerinas such as Nora Kaye, Rosella Hightower, Alicia Alonso. I've said that I've had many affairs that I never regretted. I've had these affairs that made me ready for *the* affair. I recognized that all the affairs were valuable and worthwhile . . . when Carla arrived. We did not recognize what we had when we first danced together in 1962. We did some excerpts from *La Sylphide* for television. We met. We danced. We parted. Then, two or three years later, we danced on the stage in Milan. But it was not until 1967 that we were both ready for what happened between us. The moment was there, and we were both prepared for it. We created something very special.

"When Natalia Makarova came to American Ballet Theatre, I danced with her. And if Carla had not also been there, Natasha and I would have

had something different, also something special. At any rate, I am happy
to have had the privilege and the luxury of having partnered these great
artists. I was also happy to have danced with young Cynthia Gregory.
Perhaps I was a little help to her—to make her breakthrough in her first
years. I got her to do things that Lucia Chase didn't think she was ready
for. I wanted her for *Miss Julie*—and we did other things. Of course, I was
much more mature than she was, but I think I was instrumental in bringing
something special out in her."

On the question of male dancers, Bruhn related that when he was
eighteen years old, he went to England and became deeply impressed by
Jean Babilée. He saw the French dancer perform the *Blue Bird* variation
and was overwhelmed. By that time Bruhn had already made remarkable
strides in his own dancing, and he arrived in London with the idea that he
alone was the best to be seen on the stage. This thought was quickly
shattered when he saw Babilée. He even went so far as to ask himself why
he was dancing at all. He became aware that there are other styles of male
dancing—that the Bournonville tradition that he had been trained in was
by no means the only valid one. From that moment on, he did not look
upon other male dancers as competition but concentrated on learning from
the very best of them and developing his own style.

"You know, a few years ago a journalist asked me which male dancers
had been the greatest competition to me, hinting that Nureyev might be the
one. I surprised him by saying that I didn't find any male dancer any
competition. That, if anything, they were an inspiration for me to continue. My only competition has been with my leading ballerinas—because
that's who you dance with. I remember telling Carla Fracci that she was
my greatest competition. She laughed because she thought I competed with
the boys. Anyway, I think that most people have thought that my biggest
competitor was Rudolf. Quite on the contrary. And I will tell you why.

"When Rudolf jumped from Russia he came to Denmark. I had not
seen him on the stage. I read of his escape. And I learned that he would be
coming to Denmark for study. At that time I was guesting in Copenhagen
and I saw him in class one day. He had seen me dance with American
Ballet Theatre in Russia. One day while we were in Russia our company
was invited to see a performance of *Swan Lake* danced by the Bolshoi.
Nureyev was also in the audience. He saw me sitting with Maria Tallchief,
but he was not allowed to approach us. The police were around. Rudy, I
later learned, had studied films that I had made with Ballet Theatre, and
his teacher had said that I was an unusual dancer—that I was the dancer
to watch and the one from whom he could learn something.

"At any rate, Rudy came to Denmark and I saw him in class and two or
three days later we began to talk. We began by arguing greatly about
certain technical things. At the time, his English was very limited and I felt
that the more I explained, the less he understood. But we looked at each

other, and we worked together. We could see that whatever we were talking about *worked*. So this was my first contact with him. In the meantime, I had been invited to guest-dance with the Bolshoi and they were negotiating a three-year contract for me to dance and live in Russia. Somehow, I couldn't see myself in Russia for three years. So we settled on one year. This all happened after Rudolf defected from the Kirov. In other words, I had made contact with Rudolf and I had also negotiated a one-year stay in Russia. In fact, I was to have left for Russia in two or three months. Anyway, because of a hotel shortage in Copenhagen, I told Rudolf that he could live in my house. Well, a few weeks passed, and one day I received a letter from the Bolshoi which I didn't understand. It was in Russian, but Rudolf translated it for me. The Bolshoi wanted me to postpone my appearance with them. Actually, it never occurred to either of us that we were being watched and that this all happened because he was staying with me, that we were seen together in the street, that we gave interviews together, and that we were working together.

"Of course, I was very upset, because I had mentally prepared myself for my Russian year. I replied to the Bolshoi that it was now or never. I did not, finally, go—and I never regretted it because I'm sure I would not have gotten as much out of dancing with the Bolshoi as I got out of working with Rudolf. After that, Rudolf and I managed to travel a lot together—to dance, see each other, and especially to work together. At the time, I was at the top. I was thirty-two years old, and I had reached a peak in Europe. I had reached that peak alone, I felt. There seemed to be no other dancer around. Everybody was looking to me. I felt alone. That was the first time I became aware of the whole establishment thing. I could get any booking I wanted. My name alone was enough. I felt isolated, and I didn't really know where I could go from there. If it hadn't been for Rudik—his drive, his inspiration, I would have come to a standstill. It was Rudik who kicked me onto a new period. He boosted my career for another ten years. If it hadn't been for Rudik I would have quit. I felt that dried up."

Bruhn spoke fervently, yet calmly, about his friendship with Rudolf Nureyev. His blue-eyed gaze seemed to conjure the image of his friend with pride and love. A flicker of concern could be noted as he touched on Nureyev's incredible dancing schedule.

"I have occasionally said to Rudik, 'Why don't you stop for a while? Stop working so much. Rest, then come back, renewed.' But he has not listened. Because I think he feels that a break will make him stop altogether. Actually, when I think about it, Rudik has overcome something incredible, because he has certain physical handicaps. But when he moves, everything comes into proportion. I must tell you a story that he may, perhaps, not have told anyone, and I don't think I'd be letting him down by relating it.

"When he came to the Kirov at seventeen from his little city in Siberia, having only done folk dancing and very occasionally having seen a ballet, he was so smitten by the classical dance that he went, under the most difficult circumstances, to audition for the Kirov. That he got in was not just a matter of drive, but a matter of life or death. That first year at the Kirov, people made such fun of him. They put him in front of a mirror and said, 'Look at you! You'll never be a dancer!' How he must have suffered. Because what he wanted to be, no one believed he should ever attempt to be.

"Some people have found it a little unlikely that two dancers in our particular position could be friends. They are only convinced when they see us together. Two years ago, two young dancers from the American Ballet Theatre came with me to see an opening night of the Royal Ballet. Rudolf was dancing. They had never met him. I had not seen Rudik for a long time, and I knew that I would not be seeing him again for a long time. When I went backstage, and into his dressing room, the two boys with me witnessed something that cannot be explained. When we left, they felt that they had been to a church. It was the intimacy of that moment that Rudolf and I had together that gave them that feeling. The closeness was in the air. Rudy and I don't even think about it. It's always there whenever we meet. It is something that doesn't happen very often in this profession, and it all stems from mutual respect."

Erik Bruhn danced two seasons with the New York City Ballet. This was in the early Sixties, and Bruhn recalls the period with mixed feelings. Basically, he felt that the trouble lay in his relationship with George Balanchine:

"As a working relationship it was a disaster. It was death. It was like a destructive force, generated by us both. Only once did Balanchine and I have a rapport. He was teaching me *Apollo* one Sunday—we were alone. There were no girls at the session. I had never danced *Apollo*. For years it was the one ballet I didn't do. It was probably one I should have done—but years ago. I was thirty-one or thirty-two when Balanchine taught it to me.

"To be with Balanchine alone was something incredible. During that session he said, "You are *the* Apollo!" I remember his coming into the studio with a very bad cold, acting as though he were falling apart. But within three or four hours, as we worked together, a transformation took place. I mean, he stripped off years in age. It was because he was being with that work again, that work that he had choreographed so many years ago. He was inside the music. He danced every part, too. And he showed me how to dance the Apollo part. I danced the *pas de deux* with him—and he was all the Muses. After working for hours he said, 'You've learned the part. You know it.' Of course, I almost picked up on him too quickly, and he was such a fantastic teacher. Anyway, this was Sunday. Monday was a dark night. And on Tuesday Balanchine scheduled me to dance *Apollo*—without a rehearsal. I was shocked. I went to the manager of the company and I said that I had had no rehearsals with any of the girls. I was told that I didn't need a rehearsal, because Balanchine had said I knew the ballet. Well, I thought it must be a joke. I told the manager that I would do *Apollo* on Tuesday night only on the condition that Balanchine would dance with me exactly as he had done in that rehearsal room. I was not going on that stage and see those girls for the first time. It was perhaps the worst situation between me and Balanchine. Now I look back on my period with the New York City Ballet as something funny. My longest period was with American Ballet Theatre, and there I had to deal with Lucia Chase.

"I am, in a sense, lucky that I survived her. It was not because of her that I survived, but in spite of her. She's a very strong lady. If you talk to her, everything is rosy and pink. But if you ever suggested anything to her, she would apply it in her own way, which is, of course, her prerogative. During the last few months that I was with the company, I became an unofficial adviser to her. For the first time, I found that she was listening. Then, recently, when I retired, she wanted me to be codirector. I turned her down because I felt that if I came in as codirector I would rock the boat. There were certain policies I couldn't stand for.

"During the last two years, Lucia has been writing to me—and in her own hand. She writes rather personal, intimate things, revealing what she's like. Last summer she wrote to me that she wanted me to come back. She wanted me to come and 'fit in.' Well, I wrote her back that you just don't 'fit in' like that. She understood this. We now have a very down-to-earth relationship. I will always be a friend of ABT. It has all worked out between Lucia and me, but there were times when it was a fight. I can only say that being with ABT, there was never a dull moment."

The future for Erik Bruhn remains tied to the dance, despite various excursions into writing and acting. He has requests from companies the world over to come and stage the classic ballets. He is thinking of creating some original works. If he has stopped dancing, films are still available to yield his artistry to those unfamiliar with it. For the rest of us, there remains the memory of a dancer who has given the words nobility and refinement a new and unforgettable meaning.

NEW YORK CITY BALLET

Martha Swope

GEORGE BALANCHINE

On November 20, 1972, George Balanchine was kind enough to appear with me on an interview series I held at the New School for Social Research in New York. I was most fortunate in securing Mr. Balanchine for the series. He rarely makes public appearances. That evening, the New School auditorium was filled with many people from the dance world. In attendance were such luminaries as Jerome Robbins, Tanaquil LeClercq, Alexandra Danilova, Felia Doubrovska, Muriel Stuart, Patricia McBride, Jean-Pierre Bonnefous. Also present were many members of Mr. Balanchine's company, the New York City Ballet, and students of his school, the School of American Ballet.

Coming onstage, George Balanchine looked, as always, extremely dapper. His face, with its fine-boned features reflected both pleasure and amusement. A slight touch of surprise crossed his features as he glanced into the auditorium. Balanchine is not given to making speeches or answering direct questions. Indeed, I had been told earlier by one of his close friends not to ask him any questions at all, but to let him simply tell any stories he wanted to. He is a fabulous raconteur, and is at his best when allowed to just talk and reminisce without anyone demanding definite answers.

When I told Mr. Balanchine that I *did* have a whole series of questions to ask him, he said, "Why don't you just ask them . . . ask all your questions at once, and then we will see what happens." Here, then, is an account of the New School interview with interpolated sections from a March 1972 interview in *Vogue* magazine.

GRUEN: What was it like working with Diaghilev? What was it like being in the atmosphere of the Diaghilev company? What were your first experiments in choreography? When did you know that you were a choreographer? How does music affect you? What does the dance mean to you? How do you communicate dance to your dancers? What was it like working with Stravinsky? What is a Balanchine dancer? What does he or she look like? Shall I go on?

BALANCHINE: Yes, yes, go on. Ask more.

GRUEN: Why do you like some dancers and not others? Why do you not have a star system? Why is Nureyev not dancing with your company? Or Makarova? Shall I go on?

BALANCHINE: Yes, why not?

GRUEN: You do not believe that your female dancers should marry. Why? After all, you have been married to five of them—or at least four of them. What about your early life?

BALANCHINE: You didn't ask me if I was born yet.

GRUEN: I'm sorry. I should have. But I think I know the answer. You *were* born. Your name was Georgi Melitonovitch Balanchivadze, born on January 9, 1904, in Saint Petersburg, Russia.

BALANCHINE: All right, I will tell you that I was nine years old and I started as ballet dancer. It took about eight years and I graduated. I started with Emperor Nicolai II, and we lived very beautifully. Our place of study was really fantastic. We lived there and we dressed in uniforms. We were sort of like pages. We were trained to music and drama. You could choose finally if you wanted to be actor or musician or dancer. I thought I had a good figure. At that time, I was a hippie, because I was the first person who had long hair. But when I went to school, they shaved me. It was disaster, because when I looked at myself, they called me "rat." I ran away from school, and I didn't want to go back. But they brought me back. Somehow, I was unhappy for about a year. There were a lot of examinations—very hard.

Then I saw, through a little keyhole, three dancers. They were working with my professor Andreyanov. One was Karsavina, the other was Bagonova, and the third was Gert. I looked through the keyhole, and I saw this working, and it was very interesting. It was like a little game. So since then, I decided that it would be very interesting to look at something like that. Also I danced because I was a born dancer. I am Georgian, and we all dance. Then came the Revolution. I can't tell you how terrible it was. Finally, I left. I left with my friends Danilova and Tamara Geva. We went to Germany for just a few weeks, then Diaghilev sent us a telegram to come to Paris. We went to see him in Paris. Misia Sert had a little place where we danced and Diaghilev said it was very good, that he had never seen anything like that. He asked us if we wanted to stay. We all said, "We will." He told me that I would have to choreograph some operas with the Monte Carlo Opera. He said, "Can you do it very fast?" I said, "Of course I can do it very fast." I was young. When you're young, you do anything. So I grabbed the opportunity, and that's how it started.

The first year, I had to do a ballet called *Le Chant du Rossignol*. Matisse was there. I didn't know who the hell he was. I didn't know the names of the people or the wonderful painters. I was absolutely stupid. I never read anything. Nothing. I just could see things. What I have, really, is that I see better than anybody else—and I hear better. Maybe that's a blessing. God said to me, "That's all you're going to have. It's not your business to think." I said, "Fine." Anyway, I couldn't speak a word of French and Matisse was there. He was making costumes and scenery. Then the next one was Utrillo. Then Rouault. Then Derain. Then was Braque. Picasso was around. I didn't know who anybody was. Then I met Ravel, too. He played for me his opera, *L'Enfant et les Sortilèges*. The first time it was produced, I did it. Somebody translated it into Russian for me. I staged that thing for Diaghilev. I did about twelve ballets for Diaghilev and hundreds of operas.

GRUEN: When you did *Song of the Nightingale* you must have met Igor Stravinsky.

BALANCHINE: Oh, I forgot Stravinsky. . . . It was the first time I met him. He started to play the piano and said, "That's the way it should be." I don't really remember that time. I remember my early days better. When I was nine. I was, for instance, able to remember *A Midsummer Night's Dream* in Russian. If you want, I can recite you the whole thing. But very little I remember from when I was grown up.

GRUEN: Let me remind you slightly. From 1925 until 1929 you were with the Diaghilev company. During those four years, you created *Le*

Chant du Rossignol, which was danced by Alicia Markova. You created *Barabau*, danced by Lifar and Danilova; *Romeo and Juliet entr'acte* danced by Tamara Karsavina and Lifar; *La Pastorale*, danced by Felia Doubrovska, Danilova, and Lifar; *Jack in the Box*, danced by Danilova, Tchernicheva, and Doubrovska; *The Triumph of Neptune*, danced by Danilova, Lifar, and yourself; *La Chatte*, danced by Lifar and Olga Spessivtzeva; *Apollon Musagète*, danced by Lifar, Tchernicheva, Doubrovska, and Nikitina; *The Gods go a-Begging*, danced by Danilova, Loubova, Tchernicheva, and Doubrovska; *Le Bal*, danced by Danilova, Doubrovska, Anton Dolin, Lifar, and Balanchine; and *The Prodigal Son*, danced by Lifar, Woizikowski, Dolin, and Doubrovska.

BALANCHINE: Yes. And Monteux was conducting, and Sir Thomas Beecham.

GRUEN: What was Mr. Diaghilev like?

BALANCHINE: He was a very nice man. Intelligent. Tall. Enormous head. And half-dark, half-white natural hair. He wore a monocle, because he couldn't see with one eye. And he wore perfume. . . . I remembered when he passed by, I smelled his perfume. You know, I give perfume to some of the girls in my company. Not because I like them, but because I like to know where they are. When I come to the theater, I already know. . . . Oh, there is Mazzo. I know everything that is going on there.

GRUEN: What was the sound of Diaghilev's voice?

BALANCHINE: First of all, he had false teeth. And he used to chew his tongue. I must say, he could have been President of the United States. People think he danced. He never danced. He was a pupil of Rimsky-Korsakov in composition. He was an expert musician. He played the piano. He did the lighting for the ballets.

GRUEN: When you arrived on the scene, who was the choreographer?

BALANCHINE: Bronislava Nijinska was there. Massine had been there, then he came back to do a few things. But I was the choreographer.

GRUEN: It has been said that Massine was very jealous of you.

BALANCHINE: He thought I was stealing something from him . . . his ideas. I did my ballet *La Chatte*, and I did several things that had never been done before. One day Diaghilev called me. He said that Massine was very angry because I stole his ideas. I asked him how I could steal his ideas. Diaghilev told me that Massine said, "I wanted to do that for a long time, and I never did it." Diaghilev told him, "Well, if you think people are stealing your ideas, then don't think!"

GRUEN: How did you come to choreograph *Apollo*? What was your inspiration?

BALANCHINE: First of all, I didn't know that it was going to be beautiful. Inspiration is not something that comes suddenly, like a stomachache. There is no such thing as inspiration. You have to work from childhood, and go through certain things, and sweat, and understand, and learn the métier. You have to learn how to cook, for instance. You have to know how to put together things. You will spoil everything if you don't.

GRUEN: The art of choreography is so mysterious. It involves the human body and telling somebody how to move, where to move, and then make it mean something. I'm sure that the general public must be totally mystified about the art of choreography. I'm sure they wonder how dancers remember all their steps. Some people have the idea that ballets are just done once and then forgotten. Mr. Balanchine, how do you choreograph?

BALANCHINE: You ask so many things. You ask about technical part. How do dancers memorize? From childhood, they have to memorize steps anyhow. It's part of that body ability, quickly to remember in time. How do the Lippizaner horses move? It takes fourteen years, I think. First of all, they are born black, and it's only when they get very old that they get white. They know exactly what to do, because they have been told what to do. . . . But, the trouble begins when we try to explain things that are unexplainable. We always want to know how much things weigh; how much things cost. It's impossible to speak about those kinds of realities. You cannot describe with words something for which there are no words. Poetry, art, religion—you cannot explain these things. There are no formulas. There is nothing that you could devise mathematically. You say, "That girl is beautiful." You say, "She is like a rose." But what *is* a rose? You say, "A rose is like a beautiful girl." You see what I mean? With words you never get anywhere.

GRUEN: You have a school—the School of American Ballet—and the training there is very traditional, which it must be from a technical point of view. But when young dancers finally come under your own supervision— under your own training—they are transformed. You give them a certain way of dancing and a certain "look" for which the company is often criticized. It has been said that the New York City Ballet has a homogeneous look. All the Balanchine dancers look alike—they are interchangeable—they have no soul. The girls are tall—all these things. . . .

BALANCHINE: First of all, this is my company. I started it. If somebody doesn't like it, he doesn't have to come and look at it. If somebody thinks they want small people, let them get small people. I like tall people. I'll tell you why I like tall people. It's because you can *see* more. With short people, you can see less. As for the soul. People think that the soul looks like something. It's a kind of nebulous thing—and yet, they have to know what the soul looks like. What happens is this: If someone wakes up in the morning, and their stomach works well—that's their soul. They feel good. That's how people judge art. People really want to see their personal lives when they look at art—their personal suffering. Someone will say, "I didn't like that because it didn't remind me of my own life." I say, "All right. If I do a ballet for you, what about your neighbor? The neighbor also pays money." So we'd have to dance several thousand times a variation to appease people's stomach. I don't think the soul exists. People have a bad stomach, but the soul doesn't exist. There's no such thing.

GRUEN: Mr. Balanchine, what does a Balanchine dancer look like?

BALANCHINE: The dancer that I like. First of all, I didn't name them Balanchine dancers. Somebody else did. Also, some people say that I am a pseudoclassical or neoclassical choreographer. They named it, not I.

GRUEN: I'm only repeating some of the things that are said. They say that Balanchine is a dictator in his company. What he says goes. Also, the dancers must always be there for him. Which leads us into the question of your dancers' private and personal lives. You prefer that your female dancers not get married. Why is that?

BALANCHINE: That's a good question. Of course, they can do what they want. But I like to protect their image. When a girl gets married, she's not *she* any more, she's *he*. Because she is Mrs. So-And-So, and it's over. For a female dancer marriage means the end of her individuality. Men don't lose this individuality. Take a promising eighteen-year-old girl. She is beautiful. She dances like a dream. Everyone wants to see her, to know her. She becomes a star. Suddenly, from being a star she becomes Mrs. So-And-So, married to a doctor. She runs around like mad being a dancer and being a wife—and, of course, it's all over. You cannot meet her any more, because she already belongs to somebody else. And all those home problems! All right, the husband would perhaps not mind her going to class once in a while, or to rehearsals once in a while. He wouldn't even mind her making a little money.

But I say, no. It won't do. It won't do because she must be here *all* of the time, just as I am here *all* of the time. I say dancers should have romances, love affairs, but not marriages. I have a few married dancers in my company. There's Allegra Kent, but she's an exception. She even has three children! Of course, she did not dance for six years, because each child takes two years.

GRUEN: I suppose the classic case was that of Suzanne Farrell, who left the company after she married Paul Mejia, who also danced with your company. They are now with Béjart. But Suzanne was truly one of your products—tall, beautiful, technically brilliant. And you created *Don Quixote* for her. It must have been a blow to you when she left. I'm told that they left because you did not give Paul Mejia any more roles to dance—that you were furious about the marriage.

BALANCHINE: He threatened me—he said he would leave with her if I didn't give him roles. How dared he think that I would be scared and say okay? Why should I have given him leading roles? I have Edward Villella, I have Jacques d'Amboise. And so, those two just left, and, of course, I became the villain. I don't really think Farrell wanted to leave the company. She never even came to me to talk about it or to explain. She just couldn't. Because she is so fascinated with him. It's one of those things. She likes him; and no matter what he does or what he wants, she'll be there with him. Of course, she would like to come back. She calls me and says, "We want to come back." And I say, "You are still *we*? How about you?" —because, you see, *she* is the one. Anyway, I hope she will be all right. Everybody will admire her. She is very tough, and she will be there with that technique of hers—and she will be marvelous.

GRUEN: Why *don't* you take them back?

BALANCHINE: No. We have a school—it's like a meatgrinder. We produce more and more and more new dancers.

GRUEN: Well, you don't approve of your female dancers marrying, and yet you were married to five of them—Tamara Geva, Alexandra Danilova (whom you didn't marry, but lived with as man and wife), Vera Zorina, Maria Tallchief, and Tanaquil LeClercq. Why is that?

BALANCHINE: I have never left any of my wives. They have all left me. But then, you see, I am an Aquarius and an Aquarius is not supposed to be a male at all. I am water and air—a spirit. These women I married— they were all Muses. They married Apollo who inspired them to make something of themselves. And they did. They became fabulous artists and fabulous people. And they learned a tremendous amount. Also, I may have made lots of mistakes. When you are young, you don't think. Now I feel I should not have married any of them. The point is, I am a cloud in pants. I am a workingman—a gardener. I was born that way. I am a servant—when I was married, I served.

GRUEN: You have stated that ballet is a woman. How so?

BALANCHINE: Yes. But look, I will tell you. Man is a better cook, a better painter, a better musician, composer. Everything is man—sports— everything. Man is stronger, faster. Why? Because we have muscles, and we're made that way. And woman accepts this. It is her business to accept. She knows what's beautiful. Men are great poets, because men have to write beautiful poetry for woman—odes to a beautiful woman. Woman accepts the beautiful poetry. You see, man is the servant—a good servant. In ballet, however, woman is first. Everywhere else man is first. But in ballet, it's the woman. All my life I have dedicated my art to her.

GRUEN: You prefer very young dancers for your company. I mean, you will take an exceptional sixteen-year-old. Generally, they are seventeen or eighteen. Anyway it has been said that when a dancer of yours reaches her thirties, you somehow tire of her.

BALANCHINE: Who has said that? How do you know I do that?

GRUEN: Well, one hears stories.

BALANCHINE: Well, well. I don't hear those stories. I will tell you. I am always very conscious of the children who come to my school. I like them to come early, and they appear in *Nutcracker*. Then they grow. We know each other a long time. The girls who are with me now, I have known them since they were eight. So we know each other for about twelve years already. And they are intelligent, in spite of what people say. Because people say that dancers are stupid. They may be stupid on this earth—but they are wise above the earth. This is a wonderful thing. They don't say anything, but they *know*; because it took a long time for them to learn. A dancer's body is a tool, and when I work with it, I make it for that particular person. Of course, woman is more flexible—she has a more ideal body for technique, for speed. Boys are made to jump or to lift a girl or to support a girl. But boys don't have speedy legs, because they are not built that way. I know what dancing is. I was myself a dancer, and I wasn't bad either. When I was twenty I could jump, and I was a good acrobat. I did everything better than maybe lots of people now. But I also know how to teach a woman. Almost nobody knows. I think Petipa and I were the ones. Because it's very difficult to stage for a woman. You can just kill them or spoil them—it's very dangerous. Yet it is possible to choreograph for them without injuring them. This is important.

GRUEN: In the innumerable ballets you have choreographed, you have preferred to stage plotless ballets. You are not in favor of story-ballets.

BALANCHINE: Again, somebody put those words in your mouth. I don't like bad stories—lousy stories that have nothing to do with dancing. Ballet is not intellectual, it's visual. Ballet has to be *seen*. It's like a beautiful flower. What can you say about a beautiful flower? All you can say is that it's beautiful. So to make a story in dance is very difficult. Always you have to sit and read the story—but it's wrong. You have to *look*, to *see*. I mean, it's boring that you have to know that in a first entrance it's the father entering. And the father and the son and the girl friend . . . No. Family relations are impossible to dance.

GRUEN: Another thing you don't believe in is the star system. Other companies trade on great names . . . Nureyev, Fonteyn, Makarova, Fracci, Bortoluzzi. I believe that Rudolf Nureyev wanted to join your company shortly after he defected from Russia—but you did not take him.

BALANCHINE: Oh, that. He came in to see me at that time—just to say hello. I invited him to the Russian Tea Room. I spent lots of money. I thought he was very hungry. I gave him vodka. He drinks vodka like I do. So I told him that anytime he wants, he was welcome. He said he wanted to come and dance *Giselle* and the full-length *Swan Lake*. I said, "No. We don't have those ballets. We don't have *Giselle* and never will have *Giselle* —and that's that." So he said he would go somewhere and dance *Giselle*, and then come back to us. I said, "No thank you." You see, his idea is not *Giselle*—his idea is money. He makes so much money. I never made so much money. He has a villa in Monte Carlo. He has a Rolls-Royce. He's a millionaire. So we can't pay him. No. Our dancers are not stars. The star system is for Hurok. He has to have a great name. What he does is to bring a company from Australia, and put in a great name—to make money. We don't do that. We have an enormous repertoire. We have about a hundred ballets. Supposing we sell tickets to see Fonteyn or Nureyev, and supposing they get sick. Then we have to put in somebody "uninteresting" like Pat McBride and Jean-Pierre Bonnefous. People will come and take their money back, and there will be an empty house. We don't advertise. I'm very smart. I don't say who is going to dance.

GRUEN: Clive Barnes, the dance critic of *The New York Times*, once wrote that the natural heir as director of the New York City Ballet would be Jerome Robbins. Did you read that?

BALANCHINE: First of all, I would like to ask Mr. Barnes *when* he thinks I should retire. One thing that he doesn't know about me is that I am Georgian, and Georgians live to be one hundred and thirty-four. Of course, I may look like hell—I am sixty-nine—but I am very strong—very strong. That is all I have to say.

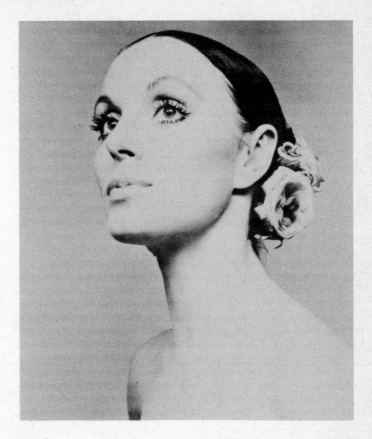

PATRICIA MCBRIDE

Patricia McBride defies the clichés of what a Balanchine dancer is supposed to look like. She is neither tall, long-legged, nor possessed of that exaggeratedly loose-limbed quality generally associated with Balanchine-trained dancers. Quite on the contrary. She is of average height, compact —even petite—both on and offstage. And yet, perhaps more than any dancer in the New York City Ballet, Patricia McBride perfectly embodies the Balanchine precepts of clean line, speed, and musicality. What is more, she adds an individual dimension to the Balanchine repertoire by infusing it with a special, almost abandoned poetry. Watching McBride dance, say, in *Brahms-Schönberg Quartet*, is to be in touch with an artist of radiant poetic gifts. Her fleet presence illuminates her variations in ways that transform both dance and music into a single, glowing unit. There is about McBride's technique the lustrousness that brings into play her intuitive musicianship. Even in the most staccato phrases, one discerns her innate lyricism.

McBride is a *bona fide* star in a company that eschews the star system. She may well be America's reigning prima ballerina. Her repertoire is very large and includes dozens of Balanchine ballets, as well as works by Jerome Robbins. During the fifteen years she has been with the company, McBride has created several roles, including Chinese Entry in *The Figure in the Carpet*, the leading girl in John Taras's *Ebony Concerto*, Hermia in Balanchine's *A Midsummer Night's Dream*, Columbine in *Harlequinade*. Jerome Robbins has created solos and *pas de deux* for her in *Dances at a Gathering, In the Night, The Goldberg Variations*, and *An Evening's Waltzes*.

In the winter of 1972, I visited Patricia McBride at her home not far from Lincoln Center. She lives there with her husband, dancer Jean-Pierre Bonnefous, also a principal with the New York City Ballet. At the time, the two were not yet married. The apartment was furnished simply and comfortably. It was clearly a home, with a large dining-room table, bowls of fruit, many plants, and, on the walls, prints and paintings of sensitive, excellent taste. Indeed, the McBride hallmark is one of simplicity and total lack of affectation.

We talked pleasantly for less than an hour. Because Pat McBride was due at a rehearsal, the interview was slightly rushed, and many of the points taken up were not fully gone into. It became clear that another interview would have to take place at a later date. This, as it happened, was accomplished a whole year later. Thus, in the winter of 1973, Miss McBride consented to come to my apartment after a performance of *The Nutcracker*, in which she danced the Sugar Plum Fairy.

She arrived wearing furs and holding a large bouquet of flowers that had been given her onstage. She still wore her stage eye make-up, lending great drama and beauty to her face. The performance had gone well, and McBride was elated. Over some food and wine, we began our talk.

Patricia McBride was born in Teaneck, New Jersey, on August 23, 1942. Her parents have been divorced for many years, and Patricia and her brother, Eugene, lived with their mother. Mrs. McBride had always loved the ballet. At one point, she was a great jitterbug dancer. McBride explained that her mother had never decided what her daughter's life should be. Pat was always given a sense of independence. "Mom didn't care whether I became a dancer or not. She just wanted me to be happy."

When Patricia turned seven, her mother thought it might be nice for her to take some ballet lessons. Mrs. McBride attended several local dance recitals near Teaneck, and found Ruth A. Vernon's to be the most outstanding. Thus it was that Patricia was enrolled in Miss Vernon's classes.

"Miss Vernon died many years ago," said McBride. "But she was such a wonderful teacher. I went to her when I was seven, and stayed until I was twelve. I took tap and acrobatics, besides ballet. My brother also took acrobatics for about a year, but then switched to the piano. Eugene now teaches the piano and is involved with some avant-garde music groups.

"In Miss Vernon's classes, there was never a pianist to accompany the lessons. Miss Vernon had an old player piano, and she would put in old piano rolls, and the piano would play by itself. She also used a stick when she taught us. Anyway, when I got to be twelve, she said to me, 'If you're serious about becoming a professional dancer, you must go to New York. I don't want to waste your mother's money.' So, she forced a decision. I said, 'Yes. That's what I want to be—a dancer.' So she sent me to New York."

The young student arrived in New York at the age of thirteen. She enrolled in a school headed by Sonia Doubrovinskaya, which is no longer in existence. Her mother would drive Pat into New York two or three times a week, after her regular school. Pat stayed with Miss Doubrovinskaya for some eight months.

"Well, first of all, it was a shock to have a live pianist in the room. Also, the competition was much greater. In Miss Vernon's school in Teaneck, there were only two of us who were sort of the best in the class. So, suddenly, I had real competition. But it's always good to have people around who are better than you. That's how you progress. Miss Doubrovinskaya was a very warm and wonderful teacher. She gave Russian classes. She made you aware that there were other things besides just acquiring a technique. She gave you a real feeling for music.

"I don't think I was so special at the age of thirteen. I had to work very, very hard, because I always felt I wasn't good enough. I concentrated on getting strong. In those classes there were a lot of older pupils—singers and actors who wanted to take some dance training. One of these people came up to me one time, and said that I ought to audition for the School of American Ballet. At that time, I was very thin and long-legged and growing fast. It seemed I might develop into a typical Balanchine dancer. Actually, I never really grew much more. I've stayed about the same. In any case, my mother listened to the suggestion that I audition at the Balanchine school. I didn't really want to leave classes. I was happy there. But Mom saw it was time to leave."

Now fourteen, Pat McBride went to the School of American Ballet, then located on Broadway near Eighty-third Street. She walked into a classroom and was asked to do a short *barre*, then came to the center. She was very nervous. Still, she passed the audition and was placed in Division B.

She began taking classes from Anatole Oboukhov and Pierre Vladimirov. She worked with Antonina Tumkovsky, Muriel Stuart, and Felia Doubrovska.

"I was really scared of Mr. Oboukhov, but he gave the most remarkable classes—so inventive. And there was Mr. Vladimirov—a dear man—very quiet, very sweet. There was Madame Tumkovsky, who was very warm, very open, and full of vitality. And there was Muriel Stuart, also warm, but in a different way. She was so precise. She had such style. And Madame Doubrovska! She was something else. It was beautiful to watch her . . . just the way she entered a room was extraordinary! That's what's so wonderful about the School of American Ballet. You take a little from every teacher. Things seep in almost unconsciously. Oh, yes, I also had Madame Hélène Dudin. But very rarely, because she mainly taught the younger students. Later, I studied with Stanley Williams and Alexandra Danilova, who had not been at the school when I began there. Two of my fellow students were Carol Sumner and Gloria Govrin. We started together.

"The first time I saw Mr. Balanchine at the school was when he was rehearsing the company. I was so in awe of him. I thought he was so handsome, so full of energy. He looked so young. He was a beautiful man! One time, he came into one of my classes. Mr. Vladimirov was giving class, and he made me do a step. Well, I was so nervous and embarrassed. I'm sure I did everything wrong. Anyway, when I turned sixteen, I was chosen to be an apprentice with the company. In the end, it's always Mr. Balanchine who decides who he wants in the company."

The young girl found her apprenticeship exciting. There were six girls chosen from the school, and each girl was placed in the *corps* for the Fourth Movement of *Symphony in C*. This has been a tradition for years. When Pat made her debut, dancing in that movement, her mother, brother, and her former teacher Ruth Vernon were in the audience.

"I happened to be the first girl in the first row. We do a complicated step, with a lot of *tendus*, and with the arms moving all the time. Well, I got on the wrong foot. My foot was going out while everybody else's was going in. Throughout the step, there was that one foot always sticking out. You can imagine how I felt. I thought, This is the end of my career! I was sure I would get fired."

Patricia McBride continued to be an apprentice for one year, then, in May 1959 (she was sixteen), she was taken into the company, dancing in the *corps*. The principal dancers at the time included, among others, Melissa Hayden, Diana Adams, Patricia Wilde, Allegra Kent, Nicholas Magallanes, Francisco Moncion, Jacques d'Amboise, Roy Tobias, Edward Villella. Pat remained in the *corps* for a year, then, circumstances hastened her promotion to soloist.

"There was a dancer in the company called Judith Green, who was twenty years old and had just been made a ballerina. During a performance, she tore something in her knee. It was a terrible tragedy, because she never danced after that. It was so sad, because she was a wonderful technician. She could do anything. Well, when this happened, I went into a lot of her roles, and was made a soloist. Before that time, Mr. Balanchine created his ballet *The Figure in the Carpet*, and he did a leading role on me, which I danced with Nicky Magallanes. It was such a shock for me, because I was still in the *corps* when that happened, and only seventeen. The next year, I was made a principal dancer."

All along, McBride was taking company classes from George Balanchine.

"Mr. B.'s classes have changed over the years. When I first took his class, we weren't performing as much at the old City Center. We would do two-hour classes. They were extraordinary. When he was teaching in those days, he had to start from the beginning with his dancers—on technique. You see, at that time, none of us really knew precisely what he wanted or expected from us. Later on, dancers who had been formed by him, like Diana Adams and Suki Schorer, already knew what he wanted and could impart this to the new students. But when I started, Mr. B. had to sort of start from scratch, because to dance his ballets requires a very special technique. First of all, *speed* was terribly important. You couldn't be lazy or sluggish. Mr. B. liked to see people moving quickly. Well, he would spend a lot of time on the mechanics of doing a special step. For example, he might spend fifteen minutes just showing you the way to do a *glissade*. Well, you were never bored. There was a rhythm to his classes. In the old days, he would give an hour of *barre*. And he would take time to explain each position. We'd start off with *grands pliés*, and if we didn't go down just the right way, he'd stop us. He likes to talk. You always got stories with his instructions. We *still* get them. What was so wonderful was that Mr. B. would make you think. He always wanted you to pick up on things very quickly.

"On the other hand, he's the most patient man. He doesn't insist you take his class, but you are made aware that he'd like you to take his class. He's so amazing. He always knows exactly what any particular dancer can do. He understands the possibilities inherent in any one of us. He's especially sensitive about working with women. Sometimes a male choreographer doesn't always know how a woman can stand on *pointe*. Balanchine knows so well what she can do on *pointe*. You have complete confidence in him. And he always gives you things that are good for you. You may hate to do them, but ultimately you know that they will help you.

"When Mr. Balanchine choreographs, he dances every part. When he choreographs something especially for you, he shows you so well—he brings the best out in you. If you look at the dancers now dancing in our company, you can see what he's done for them. Another amazing thing about Mr. B. is that sometimes in class he may not correct you very much.

Or he may not spend time with you in that way. But what he *will* do is to put you in certain ballets that will correct things in your technique. You learn and progress by being in the ballets he assigns you. They form you. They teach you so much. Just think of what he did for Allegra Kent when he did *Bugaku* on her. Or what he did with Suzanne Farrell. He used her so beautifully. Also, he allows you freedom. He will set something, but he'll leave you a little freedom to do what *you* want. He never tells you to do something *exactly*. He doesn't say your head must be here, your arms must be there. He wants you to do these things naturally—the way you feel them."

I asked Patricia McBride to describe the working methods of Jerome Robbins.

"The first time I worked with Jerry was when he came back to the company to do *Dances at a Gathering*. Mr. Balanchine invited him to come and work with us, and we were all so excited. *Dances* really started as a smaller work. It started with a *pas de deux* for Eddie Villella and me. Then, Jerry added Kay Mazzo and John Prinz. Mr. B. kept coming in and saying to Jerry, 'Make it larger . . . use more dancers!' So, it finally became a ballet with ten people, and lasting about one hour. I just adore working with Jerry. It's very different from working with Mr. B. With Jerry, everything has to be absolutely exact. Jerry explains more. Jerry changes more than Mr. B. does. Jerry always finds many more possibilities. I mean, the ideas and inventions that we *didn't* use could make a whole other ballet. When Jerry choreographed *In the Night*, it was initially done on Melissa Hayden. Then I came in and did the role. I love to do that ballet. After that came *The Goldberg Variations*. Helgi Tomasson and I do that last *pas de deux* in it. Jerry has made several changes since we first did it. He's changed our *pas de deux* several times. He always wants to make things a little better. Last year, Jerry did *An Evening's Waltzes* which he did on Jean-Pierre and me. I think it's a beautiful, beautiful ballet—and the music is so lovely. Our entrance is like *Romeo and Juliet*—I guess it's the Prokofiev score."

In 1970 Jean-Pierre Bonnefous, a leading dancer with the Paris Opera Ballet, joined the New York City Ballet. The event was a joyous one for Patricia McBride, who had met Bonnefous some five years earlier.

"It was through our late friend Christopher Allen that Jean-Pierre was invited to the United States for a guest appearance with the André Eglevsky company. He performed with Violette Verdy—it was in Newark, New Jersey. On that occasion I danced with Eddie Villella, and there was also John Prinz and Marnee Morris. Jean-Pierre and I met. We began to date. When Jean-Pierre went back to France, we corresponded. Then John Taras suggested Jean-Pierre for the title role in *Apollo*, which Mr. Balanchine was staging in Berlin. That is how Jean-Pierre met Mr. B., and that is how he eventually came to join the New York City Ballet. We then began living together. Mr. Balanchine likes Jean-Pierre very much. He has choreographed that beautiful Stravinsky *Violin Concerto* for him, and *Cortège Hongrois*."

Considering George Balanchine's reputed dismay over his ballerinas' marriages, I asked Pat McBride whether there were any repercussions when Bonnefous and she were married in 1973.

"Oh, no. You see, Mr. Balanchine was never in love with me. I mean, from the very beginning, it was never anything like that. He's like my father. He's somebody I look up to. He is very happy about Jean-Pierre and me. There are no problems."

Patricia McBride had an extraordinary wedding. The invitation I received read: "PATRICIA LEE MCBRIDE/JEAN-PIERRE BONNEFOUS/REQUEST THE HONOR OF YOUR/PRESENCE AT THEIR MARRIAGE/SATURDAY, SEPTEMBER 8TH/AT THREE O'CLOCK/CHURCH NOTRE DAME OF LA CLAYETTE/LA CLAYETTE/SAÔNE-ET-LOIRE." Face aglow, McBride recounted the events of her wedding day:

"Jean-Pierre was born in a very small village near Lyons. In the years we've known each other, we've been there several times. It's the most beautiful town I've ever seen, with only three hundred people in it. They've known about the wedding for years. I was known as *l'Américaine*. The people there aren't used to Americans at all. Of course, Jean-Pierre is a very big celebrity in France. He's done a lot of television there, so everyone knows him. The town prepared for the wedding months in advance. We wanted it to be held in September, which is a time when the weather is very beautiful and warm, and all the flowers are out. We invited a lot of our friends and members of the company. Unfortunately, it all coincided with the company's being in Berlin filming a series of television programs. But a few friends came. John Taras. Carol Sumner. And some others. Mr. Balanchine couldn't be there. Of course, my family came, and a more beautiful day I couldn't have imagined.

"We were treated like royalty. The whole town was there. All the shopkeepers brought chairs, which lined the streets. We rode in a car driven by Jean-Pierre's uncle. As we went by, everyone was waving. We stopped at the Mayor's office, which was in a tiny square. We entered a tiny little room, and we signed our wedding certificates. Then, we drove to the church, and there were hundreds of people waiting. Some of them couldn't even get into the church. The church was the one in which Jean-Pierre's father and mother were married, and in which he himself was baptized. I was so very happy. There was a sense of tradition. So, we were married. And when we came out of the church, a horse and carriage were waiting for us. It was decorated with beautiful flowers. The whole thing was out of another period. Yves St. Laurent designed a dress for me of crepe Georgette. It had beautiful lace, which came up around my neck. Alexandre sent a man to do my hair in a sort of 1900s style. Jean-Pierre led the horses. He looked so beautiful, wearing a Lanvin suit. The whole town followed our carriage. We went to the Château La Clayette, which is simply beautiful. There was a reception, with caterers bringing the most delicious food from Lyons—which is considered the gourmet capital of France. Well . . . there was wine and champagne, there was dancing, and it all lasted until five o'clock in the morning. It was the happiest day of my life."

Patricia McBride closed her eyes, recapturing the day. Returning to the present, we talked about the future. Would she not like to expand her dancing horizons? Would she not like to dance the great classics—*Giselle*, for example?

"I'd love to dance *Giselle*. I've thought about it for many years. But I would have to study it. You have to think of that ballet as an actress. They say Balanchine dancers can't dance the classical ballets. I disagree. We are all so well trained. It's just a matter of studying the roles. You have to prepare yourself for them, mentally as well as physically. One day, I will dance *Giselle* with Jean-Pierre."

What does McBride want to tell a young dance student who may wish to grow up to become a Patricia McBride?

"I would say that when you're a young girl and going to ballet class, you must simply learn everything there is about dancing. You have to become technically proficient. You have to become very strong. Later on, you must learn that there are other things one needs. You must look around you. Look at the world. You must grow as a person. This will make you grow as a dancer. Life-experiences influence your life as a dancer. The more you see, the more you are aware of things, the more you *feel* and the more you absorb. You have to be open to everything. You have to be open to people. Perhaps the most important thing I can tell young dancers is to have faith and confidence in themselves."

Martha Swope

EDWARD VILLELLA

For Villella, dancing seems a healthy athletic release. His formidable technique and truly magnetic presence combine to give his performances a uniquely American dazzle and bravado. And those who consider the male ballet dancer somewhat less than male have in Edward Villella the living and dancing proof that virility is as much a part of the art of ballet as of any other art form.

There is about Villella's dancing a directness and immediacy—an openness that instantly communicates the joyous sense of freedom that the act of dancing implies. His every movement is possessed of freshness and brashness. Villella cannot be said to be the subtlest of dancers, nor does he always project psychological profundity. These qualities seem alien to his basically sunny nature. His movements generally tend to emphasize strength, speed, and simplicity. But within these poles exist the possibility for high drama and a natural theatricality. Villella in *The Prodigal Son* or *Watermill* or *Pulcinella* makes this brilliantly clear.

Still, the bravura elements of his technique are what ignite and enthrall the audience. Always, Villella's dancing suggests a great generosity of spirit. Villella does not show off—he *gives*. Like all superb dancers, he makes the complicated seem easy. But with him, the added stimulus is to make the complicated exhilarating. Villella will throw himself into leaps, jumps, or turns with the sort of braggadocio that is not merely thrilling to the spectator but is equally, if not more, thrilling to him.

Edward Villella is probably the best-known American male ballet dancer. One of the most popular members of the New York City Ballet, he has made countless guest appearances on television, throughout the country, and abroad. Handsome in the extreme, with dark, burning eyes, a shock of black hair, a rakish, mischievous smile, Villella is clearly the ballet world's matinee idol. He is also something of a "heartbreak kid." The girls adore Eddy Villella. Indeed, Villella knows his worth, and understandably capitalizes on his art as well as on his looks. To him, ballet dancing is not merely a profession but a business. In recent years, Villella has become a corporation. His business acumen is such that a generally underpaid profession has, for him, been a lucrative one.

Villella's life-style is commensurate with his position as a major ballet star. He lives in a town house which he and his ex-wife, Janet Greschler, a former dancer with the New York City Ballet, have transformed into one of New York's most elegant residences. It was here that Villella received me for our interview. I was ushered into a paneled living room with coffered ceilings, a brass chandelier, books, paintings, comfortable couches, and several handsome period pieces. These days Villella lives there alone, and he seems to revel in his elegant surroundings.

"I guess I've worked hard to get all this," Villella told me. "There were things that I wanted. And one of the things that I wanted most was to live in a house. I don't like apartment living. To live in a house in New York gives you a very special feeling. For example, I like being in this room alone. Especially at night. I close the shutters. This wood-paneled room becomes very quiet. There are sliding doors, and I can close them. I put music on and lean back in my chair. I dim the lights and put some candles on. I drink a beer, listen to the music, and just let it all hang out! There's a garden downstairs. I was married when we bought the house, and we planned it in a very special way. We wanted it to be a very quiet, warm place. Downstairs are a dining room and kitchen which have an English country feeling to them. The bedroom upstairs is Art Nouveau. The front sitting room is eighteenth-century French. It just works so beautifully. My ex-wife now lives in her own town house on East Sixty-eighth Street."

For a typical American lower-middle-class boy, born and brought up in Bayside, Long Island, Edward Villella has charmingly learned the ways of sophisticated living. We began by discussing the early days.

"My mother wanted very much for both my sister and me to have those things she never had. She wanted us to have the best education, and to give us a feeling and taste for culture. Our background was certainly not that. As mothers do, she took my sister to a local ballet school in Bayside. One day, while my sister and mother were at the school, I was playing baseball and I was hit on the back of my head and knocked unconscious. When my mother came home and found out about this, she was so upset that she insisted upon my going along every time she took my sister to her ballet classes.

"Naturally, I was very unhappy to be taken away from my playtime. But she dragged me along, and I had to sit and watch this very, very strange activity. At one point, my mother asked me whether I wouldn't like to take some ballet lessons. I said, 'Absolutely not!' I couldn't possibly do it—it would ruin my entire social life. I was eight at the time. But Mother insisted, and so, I took a few classes, and actually liked it. One thing about me, I could never sit still. I would never walk any place, I would run. I wouldn't reach for anything, I would jump for it. It's strange, but my little boy is like that. His name is Roddie, but I call him 'Mr. Half-Toe,' because he's always standing on half-toe. He's three years old. Anyway, I took to dancing. And I must say that I was very lucky, because I also enjoyed a typical childhood."

Villella went on to say that his mother's ambitions were really directed toward his sister, Carolyn. In fact, she had pinned all her hopes on her little girl becoming a ballerina. She brought the child to the School of American Ballet, where Carolyn was given a half-scholarship. Again, she dragged young Eddy along, and off-handedly let the school know that her little boy was also taking dancing lessons. The school, always eager for male dancers, asked Mrs. Villella to allow Eddy to audition as well. This done, the boy received a full scholarship. Villella was ten years old when he began training at the School of American Ballet. The year was 1946. Among his teachers were Anatole Oboukhov and Pierre Vladimirov, Muriel Stuart, Felia Doubrovska, and, very early on, Elise Reiman. The boy was particularly impressed with the classes given by Oboukhov.

"Oboukhov was a fantastic person. He verged on being a character. He was a great disciplinarian. Also, his classes were the most inventive. He would give you a very basic technique—one that was very structured, and one from which he would never deviate. But within that structure, he would never give the same combination twice. It was absolutely incredible.

I studied with him the first five years, and again, for another four years, later on."

While Villella took his ballet classes, he went to the High School of Performing Arts. There, he also took dance training. His schedule was more than hectic, since he was also obliged to return home to Bayside every night, and insisted on continuing his boyhood friendships, which meant playing baseball and other sports. In fact, Eddie was named the Most Valuable Player of his home town's athletic club. And so it was that both Villella children seemed on their way to becoming full-fledged dancers, each working steadily and hard at the Balanchine School.

As it happened, a dramatic turn of events interrupted the seemingly smooth course of their early training. By the age of sixteen, Carolyn Villella decided to stop her training.

"When Carolyn decided to stop, it was a terrible blow to my mother. You see, my mother was, in essence, living vicariously through my sister. The ambition was really my mother's, and less, my sister's. Actually, Carolyn could have become a very, very good ballet dancer, but she never had that burning desire—that almost masochistic drive that most of us have. She also sensed that the pressure came from my mother, rather than from an intrinsic need in her. So, when this happened, my mother said, 'This is the end.' She told *me* that I would also have to stop my training. My father was never terribly happy about my taking ballet. He had always wanted me to go to college, because no one in our family had ever been to college. This was an awful blow to me—I was now fifteen and completely enthralled with dancing. I thought of nothing else. It was going to be my life, my career, and my business. I never once thought of going to college. Actually, I only spent one year at the High School of Performing Arts, and then went to Rhodes Prep, so that I could graduate earlier. I did high school in three years.

"Anyway, my father was adamant. I was terribly upset. I remember the day that my father drove me to college. I went to the New York State Maritime College at Fort Schuyler. I walked through the arch with a bag in each hand, believing I would never ever dance again. And I *didn't* dance again for almost four years. For four years, I never did a step. I went through college preparing for an officer's career in the Merchant Marine and/or the Navy. The Maritime College prepares you for admiralty law, naval architecture, marine engineering, import/export, and cargo. I got my B.S. in marine transportation. When I got out, I gave my father the diploma, and I said, 'Here it is. I've done what you wanted me to do. Now I'm going to do what I want to do. I'm going to give myself a chance to see if I can still become a dancer.' By this time, I was nineteen, and I hadn't danced a step in four years."

Villella settled in New York, but was reluctant to return immediately to the School of American Ballet. He was, as he put it, ashamed because neither he nor his sister had ever informed the school that they would not show up again. The Villella children had simply walked out. He thus enrolled in another school, Ballet Arts, with the thought of getting himself back in shape. After a while, he presented himself at the desk of the School of American Ballet, and announced that he was back, and could he continue taking classes. He was told that an Oboukhov class was about to begin in five minutes. He ran into the dressing room, changed, and for the next four years, completed his training.

In December 1957, Edward Villella entered the New York City Ballet. He was placed in the *corps*, and within two weeks created the role of the Faun in Jerome Robbins' *Afternoon of a Faun*. Villella recalled the occasion:

"It's an amazing story. It seems I inspired Jerry to create the ballet in the first place. He and I were in the same late-afternoon class at the school, and Jerry told me that he had observed me leaning against the *barre*, standing in a shaft of warm sunlight . . . I was just lazily leaning there, waiting for my group to be called, and I just began to stretch. He saw me doing this, and this visual thing gave him an idea that eventually turned into *Afternoon of a Faun*. That was really the beginning of my career."

It was clear that in Edward Villella the New York City Ballet had a potential star. He was soon dancing solo roles in a wide variety of ballets, including *Interplay, Symphony in C*, Third Movement, *Western Symphony, Stars and Stripes, Agon*. By 1960 he was a principal dancer, and gained particular stature with his performance of the title role in Balanchine's *The Prodigal Son*. I asked Villella to describe how this came about.

"Well, *Prodigal Son* was, of course, first created by Mr. Balanchine for Serge Lifar in 1929. Then, when Mr. B. started the New York City Ballet, he revived it for Jerry Robbins. Then, Hugh Laing danced it, and, later, it was danced by Francisco Moncion. I had never seen the work. I knew nothing about it. It had been taken out of our repertoire. One day, I was standing in a classroom when Diana Adams came up to me and said, 'Oh, congratulations. You're doing *Prodigal Son*. In fact, we're doing it together!' Well, I fell on the floor. It was fantastic. For that time of my life, it was really amazing to be asked to do a role of that size—my first dramatic role! It was an enormous challenge.

"Actually, no one remembered the ballet very well. Vida Brown, who was ballet mistress for a while, was brought in especially to put this thing together. She barely remembered it. Oddly enough, Mr. Balanchine was not really interested in staging it, because it's a very tedious piece to stage. But somehow, we got it all put together, even though it was a little ragged around the edges at first. Mr. B. taught me the opening in about twenty minutes, and he taught me the closing in about twenty minutes. He showed me the *pas de deux* in about half an hour. That was about it. He said, 'Okay, here it is. Now do something with it.' At one point, I remember his telling me to think of Russian icons. That's what finally gave me the basis from which to build. I looked at books of icons, and I studied the gestures, the tilts of the heads. That's how I found the way."

Edward Villella was acclaimed for his performance in *The Prodigal Son*, and his career flourished. While it would seem that the dancer might have developed a close and highly personal relationship with George Balanchine as a result of this success, the opposite seems to be true. Indeed, Villella is among the few leading City Ballet dancers who do not take company classes with Balanchine.

"Well, let me say first of all that I think Balanchine is a genius. But somehow, I can't take his classes. I can't even *tell* him I can't take his classes. I mean, you can't argue mathematics with an Einstein. You can't argue music with a Mozart or Stravinsky. But, you see, I don't take his classes because my body had to be reshaped, due to the fact that I stopped dancing for four years. My muscle tone is like no one else's muscle tone. My muscles were let go. When I came back at nineteen, I sort of shocked my body. I tried to come back much too quickly. Slower would have been quicker. But I did the reverse. This left me with a very tight and tough muscle tone. Well, Mr. B.'s classes are basically to build quickness and strength. I *have* a great deal of quickness and a great deal of strength. So, to take them would only be putting that on top of what I already have. What's difficult about the classes he gives is that they are structured in a way that doesn't give one enough time to warm up. I need a long time to warm up, for my body to function properly. So I take classes with other people.

"About a personal relationship with Mr. B. . . . Well, you know what sort of person he is. He keeps a lot of dancers close to him. I never really got close to him. There are a number of reasons. One is that I'm in such awe of him. I'm scared to death of him, but in the best possible way. I just respect him beyond belief. Also, my character is very different from his. My background and my experience are different. There was also the matter of the four-year gap—I didn't have the continuity of knowing Mr. B. the way other dancers did. In a strange way, I didn't really feel part of the company when I entered. I felt slightly uncomfortable, and I didn't quite know how to make the adjustment. Those four years away at college didn't exactly prepare me for the very esoteric and specialized life that's part of ballet dancing. The manner of behavior, the way people live as ballet dancers was alien to me. Oh, there were times when I have been close to Mr. B. But we've also been distant at points.

"I know that Mr. Balanchine has this small, familial group of dancers around him. I know that when he has a small, loving, appreciative audience around him, he can be fantastic. He's congenial, and a great story-teller. I was never drawn into this small, familial group. I suppose the basic problem between us is that I haven't taken his class in years and years. I don't think he forgives me for that. I think he never will."

When Villella joined the New York City Ballet, he met Janet Greschler. At the time, she was dancing with the American Ballet Theatre. Their first meeting was in an adagio class at the School of American Ballet. Later, Miss Greschler left ABT and joined the New York City Ballet. The two were married in 1962.

"Janet is a very attractive girl. She stopped dancing, which was too bad, because she had a very lovely body for dancing, and she was very talented. But, like my sister, she never had that kind of burning desire. For Janet, everything was too easy. Anyway, we have a son—which is great. We have been divorced for about a year and a half. But we're very, very good friends. We have a common interest in our son. Now Janet has made a whole other life for herself. She's a very special individual. She has a great sense of fashion and style."

When Jerome Robbins choreographed *Dances at a Gathering*, one of the most ravishing set of variations was done on Edward Villella and Patricia McBride. Later, Villella was chosen by Robbins for one of the choreographer's most controversial ballets—*Watermill*. Villella talked about working with Robbins:

"I've known Jerry for years and years, but was never really close to him until I joined the company. Then he left. He was doing his Broadway thing. It wasn't until *Dances at a Gathering* that we really got close. Pat McBride and I were the first two people he worked with on *Dances*. I came early to the rehearsal. I warmed up, and I saw Jerry walk in. He was an absolute nervous wreck. I walked over to him and said how exciting it was for us to work with him. Inside of an hour, Jerry really got into it. He did most of our *pas de deux* in that first rehearsal. He's a very slow worker. He tries to be verbal at times, but I think he's much more successful just demonstrating.

"In choreographing, he is the exact opposite of Mr. Balanchine. I mean, Mr. B. won't have thought of a step until he walks into the room, has the mirror, the piano, and the body. Naturally, he's digested the music so well that he knows patterns and groups—he knows what he wants to do with those. But I think Jerry prepares everything very carefully. He does all of his homework. I'm sure he tries all the steps himself. Anyway, that's the way he begins to work with you. He starts to put things on you. Then, he's constantly changing them. He's famous for doing Version 'A,' 'B,' 'C.' It's a very difficult way to work. Also, Jerry expects you always to dance full-out. That's also very difficult, because if you're in a repertoire of forty-odd ballets, and you're dancing that night, and possibly eight times in a week, and you have other rehearsals, plus your classes, it's very difficult to work three to six hours a day on one particular role, and do it full-out. Also,

Jerry is famous for bringing in other people to come in and look at what he's done, to get their reactions. You're always doing a full performance in rehearsal.

"Sometimes Jerry treats people a little roughly. These dancers often resent that sort of treatment. They will not be uncooperative, but their attitude will display a reticence. Actually, every time I've worked with Jerry, I've gotten along with him very well. I think my most single extra-ordinary experience with him was working on *Watermill*. The whole thing was collaborative. Again, I had to rehearse everything full-out, and I must say, that after the first couple of weeks, I finally told Jerry I simply couldn't do it full-out any more. The ballet requires such concentration that it was absolutely maddening to maintain it when it was not a perfor-mance. I like rehearsing to the point where I know the role, but I'm not a person who likes to rehearse. I like the spontaneous feeling you get during a performance. I don't like the idea that absolutely everything must be square and placed and exact. I like the excitement of things going on during a performance.

"My attitude about *Watermill* was that this was a unique challenge for me. It was not my business to decide whether the ballet had great artistic merit or whether it was pretentious. To this day, I don't want to hear opinions about it, because it's too close to me. I cannot take a stand on it. All I know is that to dance in it is absolutely mind-blowing. If I feel my concentration slipping, I have to work like crazy to get it back."

I asked Villella why Jerry chose *him* for the part.

"I think it came about from *Dances at a Gathering*. When he was doing that, he found a piece of music which was exactly what I'm mostly about —jumping, flying around, bravura. Then, at one point, Jerry said, 'You know, I'm going to find another piece of music for you, because I think there's something else in you that I'd like to explore.' It turned out to be the opening variation to *Dances*, which is stillness and serenity, and a kind of quiet drama. I think that was probably the thing that propelled him toward thinking about me for *Watermill*. I was very happy because it brought out another side of me. It gave me another dimension—another look."

What does dancing mean to Edward Villella?

"Complete and total pleasure. It's a complete and fantastic physical and mental sense of yourself—of your body, of your mind. Dancing shows who you are—your temperament, your sensitivity, your musicality, your dra-matic qualities. Everything about you is there. You're completely and totally naked. You really can get to know a person when you watch him dance. My background, being American, and not having been brought up in the nineteenth-century-romantic style of dancing, has given me the at-tribute of *sensing* dance. I sense dance, rather than portray it. A lot of people like to portray dance. I simply like to *do* it—to experience it. When

I'm throwing myself around the stage with complete abandon, yet complete control, I feel totally honest. I cannot lie. I think dancing is so much more honest than talking about something. When you talk, you can't be totally honest—I mean, *completely* honest. When you're talking, you tend to add things, you tend to use certain inflections, your mind does things. When you're there just dancing—that's *you*."

Villella has seen in the dance a way of making it a lucrative, as well as fulfilling, business. In what is certainly one of the most underpaid professions, the ballet dancer does not ordinarily become rich. But Villella has proved to be the exception to the rule:

"People tend to think of dancers as superartistic individuals who are happy to dance for nothing at all. They are thought of as being beyond the mundane financial aspects of life. Dancing in the New York City Ballet won't make you rich. We have a popular-price ticket, and we have a popular-price salary. I always say that I dance *outside* so that I can afford to dance *inside*. In a way, I am subsidizing my own art. It's so fantastic to dance with the New York City Ballet. I will never leave the company—it's just too great a source of inspiration. But I want to be a complete dancer, a complete artist. I do so many guest appearances because I want to broaden my horizons.

"Anyway, for anyone entering this profession—especially the men—I would like to say to them that there's a damn good living to be made of it. That's very important to know. Of course, we have to face the problem of age. There are some people who go on dancing until they're fifty. I don't intend to do that. But there are very good ways of making money in the dance world, even when you stop dancing. There is teaching. There is choreographing. There is television, movies. Also, universities now have major dance departments. I am on the President's National Council on the Arts. And being on it, I've learned a very extraordinary fact. I've learned that dance is the single most popular art form in the country. In the last five years or so, it's grown by about six hundred per cent. Well, that's unbelievable!

"As for the stigma attached to male ballet dancers, that's passing very quickly. There are lots of male ballet dancers now, and lots of damn good ones. The male dancer in this country has acquired a strong American quality. By that I mean it's sharp, linear. It has an attack to it. It's less overly poetic. It's efficient. So, for a boy to become a ballet dancer is really a very challenging and a very masculine thing. It's no longer anything to be ashamed of."

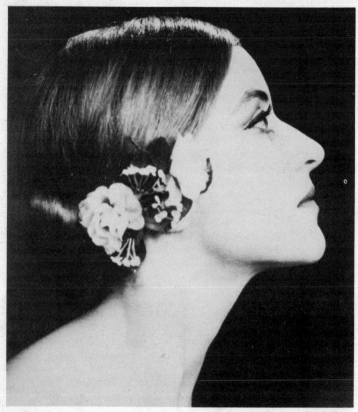

VIOLETTE VERDY

Her New York City apartment in the West Seventies is a small corner of Paris—old Paris, at that. The furniture is massive, solid, stable. Chairs and couches are ornate, covered in rich velvets. There are large and small oil paintings—some by Old Masters. There are wall-hangings, chandeliers, antique lamps, many *bibelots* and heavy drapery. There is even an old French mother about—a charming, warm presence that completes this Old World ambience.

It is this handsome European woman who has greeted me at the door, saying that her daughter, the ballerina Violette Verdy, has been slightly delayed at a rehearsal with the New York City Ballet. In the most cordial manner, I am shown around the apartment and offered some tea.

Presently, Violette Verdy arrives. That same electric something that marks her appearances on stage makes itself felt instantly as she enters the room. Indeed, the vivacity, alertness, intelligence, and *brio* of her performances are as tangible offstage as on. Her generosity of spirit, her sincerity —the spontaneity of her reactions, her quickness and wit, all give truth to the fact that being with Miss Verdy is as intoxicating as several glasses of the finest champagne.

Just now, as we sit and begin our talk, she helps me in describing her appearance:

"Your eyes are blue. . . ."

"No. They are blond . . . like oysters. They change with the weather. Actually, they are gray-green. They are like the sea in Brittany, where I was born, and which is not a peaceful sea."

"Your face is without make-up. . . ."

"It is totally make-up-less . . . washed out by practice."

"You are wearing glasses."

"That's my schoolteacher look."

"Your hair is blond."

"Mousy-blond."

"You have taken your shoes off. . . ."

"To clear my brain."

It is an endearing fact that Violette Verdy, in person, does not present the image of the glamorous ballerina. That image is reserved for the stage. In person, she eschews the expected trappings of the star. Her clothes are invariably sensible—no fancy, flowing gowns, no overtly elegant accessories, no glittering jewels. Verdy's effervescence is her glamour. She is, of course, an international star. In January 1973, the French government awarded her the Order of Arts and Letters for her contribution in perpetuating the French arts all over the world. Miss Verdy is the only performing dancer who has ever received this award, which carries with it the rank of Chevalier.

"My story is a long story. You don't want the whole thing, do you? I'll make it as brief as possible.

"I was born in Pont-l'Abbé-Lambour, a small city in the south of Brittany. My mother was a schoolteacher. As a very young child, I was frail and nervous. The family doctor recommended that I spend my time in a harmonious way. He suggested any form of gymnastic exercise that my mother would choose. Mother immediately declared that ballet would be the epitome of harmony and discipline. Mind you, she had never before seen a ballet. And so, I began dance lessons. I must add that my father died when I was still very young. It was Mother and I from the very first."

Violette Verdy was at first known as Nelly Guillerm. At the age of nine, mother and daughter moved to Paris, and discovered the ballerina Carlotta Zambelli, who suggested that Nelly begin working with Madame Rousanne. This she did, for some two years, becoming something of a child prodigy. Soon, she attracted the notice of Roland Petit, who had formed his Les Ballets des Champs-Elysées. Petit invited the gifted child to join his company. She made her debut as the girl acrobat in *Les Forains*, a role created especially for her by Petit. Her success was such that Petit offered her a five-year contract. The year was 1945.

"It was an exciting time. We toured, and Mother was able to come on tour with me, having also been given work by the company in the publicity and wardrobe departments. In the company at that time was Leslie Caron, who became my roommate on tour. Leslie was an enormously interesting girl. She could draw, sew, and she could dance beautifully. At any rate, around 1949 a German movie director began a search for a young girl to star in a film called *Dream Ballerina*. They auditioned many girls. I was chosen for the lead."

The film was among the first to use the subject of ballet as part of its plot. It was an elaborate French production, boasting special choreography by the German dancer and choreographer Yvonne Georgi. It was at this moment that Nelly Guillerm became Violette Verdy. *Ballerina* was seen by Jean-Louis Barrault. He was then casting a play by Montherlant starring Madeleine Renaud. He needed a thirteen-year-old girl, who would play his mistress. Violette, at sixteen, landed the part. Throughout, she continued studying the dance. Her second teacher was Victor Gsovsky, who had become ballet master of Les Ballets des Champs-Elysées. It was with Gsovsky that Verdy learned the full-length *Swan Lake, Giselle, Sleeping Beauty*, and *Coppélia*. Gsovsky felt that one day Violette would be dancing these ballets.

"He taught me these works without any particular date set for performing them. It was a planting of the seed, without any particular date for blossom or harvest."

Roland Petit disbanded his Les Ballets des Champs-Elysées in 1948, and in 1953 formed a new company, Ballets de Paris de Roland Petit. Violette continued to dance for Petit, creating her first international success—the role of the Bride in *Le Loup*.

"*Le Loup* was my first important dramatic role. It was the role that brought me to the United States shortly after its premiere in Europe. Our company was asked by Hurok to appear in a Broadway theater. Also in the repertoire was Roland Petit's famous *Carmen*, which he created for his wife, Zizi Jeanmaire, but on that trip to America, Zizi was not with us.

Carmen was danced by Colette Marchand, Leslie Caron, and by me. It was a wonderful part. Roland told me that I was the best Carmen, after Zizi. It was very demanding to dance, because of that beautiful cruelty and anger that had to be projected. I mean, Carmen was being bled like a bull. It was really the arena. It was marvelous. But mainly I was dancing *Le Loup*. Hurok was very impressed. He told me that he would always think of me if he ever needed a dancer. We did a small tour, and then Leslie Caron, who had already made films in Hollywood, was asked to return there and star in two films. Roland Petit would supply the choreography, on the condition that his dancers appear in the films. So I went along, and I participated.

"Actually, I only stayed for the first film, because Hurok called me and asked whether I would be interested in joining the London Festival Ballet on its sixty-city tour of the United States. They needed a ballerina to dance with John Gilpin. I accepted the offer. This brings us to 1954. Once the tour was over, I returned to France, and made guest appearances in England and in Italy. I danced with Ballet Rambert in London, and at La Scala in Milan. With Rambert I did my first full-length *Coppélia* and my first *Giselle*. My work with Victor Gsovsky was bearing fruit."

Violette Verdy was acclaimed for her European and American performances, and her name caught the ear of Lucia Chase, codirector of the American Ballet Theatre. She invited Verdy to dance with her company for the 1957–58 season. It was with ABT that Miss Verdy created one of her most sensational roles, that of Miss Julie. She also danced her first Balanchine ballet, *Theme and Variations*. At the end of the season, Lucia Chase temporarily closed her company. Verdy was left at loose ends, and did not really wish to return to France. Fortunately, George Balanchine and Lincoln Kirstein had seen Verdy dancing with the American Ballet Theatre. When Ballet Theatre closed, they invited her to join the New York City Ballet. She quickly danced principal roles, notably in *Divertimento No. 15*, *Symphony in C*, First Movement, *Stars and Stripes*, *Apollo*, *Western Symphony*, *The Figure in the Carpet*, *Liebeslieder Walzer*, *Episodes*, *A Midsummer Night's Dream*, among others.

The New York public fell in love with Violette Verdy. She brought a special piquancy to the Balanchine repertoire—a quicksilver excitement that lent brilliance and intensity to the ballets in which she appeared. Her European training and her considerable experience prior to joining the City Ballet added a particular depth and symmetry to whatever she danced. Her *bravura* technique, her musicality, and the intelligence at the core of her work gave further clarity, logic, and spark to choreography already singular in its inventiveness.

Both Balanchine and Jerome Robbins love working with her. In 1973, Robbins created *Four Bagatelles* for her, to piano pieces of Beethoven. In 1969, she premiered his *Dances at a Gathering* and in 1970, *In the Night*.

In 1972, she danced in the Balanchine/Robbins revival of Stravinsky's *Pulcinella*. But, whether dancing Robbins or Balanchine, Verdy consistently retains her own special presence. In a sense, and by her own admission, Verdy is not a *bona fide* Balanchine dancer. Indeed, while with the company, she made countless guest appearances throughout the world, and has danced the classics with such renowned companies as the Royal Ballet.

Lighting a cigarette, Miss Verdy told me something of her long association with the New York City Ballet, George Balanchine, and Jerome Robbins:

"Balanchine and Robbins call on everything I have to offer. The demands both these men have made on me have revealed my true identity. If they have not used the *complete* me, they have nevertheless used that which is the *true* me. I have come to know myself better as a dancer through them.

"My contact with Balanchine has always been on an artistic and professional level. To me, Balanchine was always a great master. He always will be. He will hate my saying this, but I do not see him as a semifather, semigod figure. I have always held my distance. It would never have occurred to me to be casual, pal-like, with Balanchine . . . to tease him, to pull his leg, to joke with him. This is something that a young American artist could do more easily, because in America, one is more chummy. Actually, at the beginning, I *did* think of him as the god, the creator, the provider. Now, finally, I can think of him as a man. I can give him that human respect. That's more or less my personal relationship with him. Lately, we have become a little more colleague-like, because he knows that I'm interested in teaching, in students, in choreography. Very often he talks to me about his dancers, about some of his problems, some of his projects, some of his frustrations and disappointments. Now that he is getting a bit older, he seems to be unifying everything. Philosophy has recently become his *modus vivendi*. Balanchine knows that I am also very interested in philosophy. So we have music, philosophy, and work as the basis of our relationship."

Verdy, speaking quickly in her charming French accent, related her thoughts on Balanchine's teaching methods:

"At this moment of his life, Balanchine goes beyond teaching. To describe his teaching is impossible, because it is not simply teaching. What he does is on such a high level that it is virtuosic, in the best possible sense. What he tries to communicate to us are the formidable possibilities that only the greatest interpreters, technicians, and creative artists have achieved. The conditions to which he submits us in class can best be described by saying that he wishes us to cross the fire and not be burned, to walk on water and not sink. Your emotions are shaken, because his demands, in terms of speed and precision, are so inventive that often your body revolts. Anyway, we dancers must remove ourselves from the incredible treasures that he reveals to us in class every day . . . remove ourselves only in the sense that we might have a performance that night, and we must conserve our energy.

"I have been with Balanchine for fourteen years. I can tell you that he is the kind of man who will push you to the last frontier of your own choices. It goes far beyond the level of what a psychiatrist could do for you. That is what I mean by the last frontier. I have been there, and at this moment, I'm floating in a no man's land. When I joined the company, I joined it with my eyes wide open. I was going on a visit, and I was going to be a good tourist. In this long voyage with the New York City Ballet, I have measured all the possibilities that were open to me. For some reason, I have not been able to give myself completely and entirely to Balanchine. I have wondered what it was that has prevented me from going all the way with him. It is a question of man and soul—body and soul. If you think of Balanchine as a man, you may only want to give the body. If you think of Balanchine as creator, you want to give much more than the body. You want to give everything. What I'm trying to say is, that you cannot give to Balanchine what is for God. The demands he places on you are almost tribal . . . tribal in the sense that he wants you to belong to him like a sort of willing soul. But, you see, you cannot give him your soul. He is, after all, only a mortal. He is close to being a God . . . very close, but there is that last margin of self-preservation which not all of us are able to relinquish.

"I will be quite frank. I feel that my place is not just with one company, not just with one man. Also, Balanchine needs many more people than just me. He has many things he needs to accomplish that don't always include me. Therefore, I need to continue to be what I am. I have found places where what I have to offer is needed. I go to many places, and I perform. I have had success. Still, what Balanchine has done for me is unbelievable. I mean, what he did for me in *Pulcinella, Jewels, La Source*. He found my true identity. These things he did for me did not come very often, but they were perfect when they came, and entirely worth waiting for. No one else has done for me what he has done for me. Even the people who love me, who promise things, and who have done things for me, have not equaled him. In the meantime, I have come to a point in my career where I am needed to do things for others.

"But you ask me also to speak of Jerome Robbins. He is probably the most intelligent man I have ever met. He is fantastically smart. He needs so much to know, to know, to know. Also, he needs to be reassured. In order for me to speak about Robbins, I must use Balanchine as an example. Balanchine is still the criterion. You see, when Balanchine sets out to do a work, and when that work is done, then it is not Balanchine any more. Balanchine leaves the work to the dancers. The work has its own existence. It assumes its own continuity. It is gone from Balanchine's hands. His hands are now free for the next work.

"When Jerry does a work, he does not seem to be able to cut the umbilical cord. He cannot cut it from the work, nor can he cut it away from the dancers who are supposed to take the work from his hands. Once the work is born, and has already started to live, Robbins is never entirely separated from it. Because in his mind, there still seems to be a question, and a need for reassurance or for re-evaluation. He will remanipulate the dancers. He will redistribute their energies and approaches. In other words, he will disturb the whole work all over again for reasons which I cannot completely understand. What I do understand is his desire to be undyingly linked with everything he has accomplished. Jerry is never separated from his past. He has an incredible sense of possession. Always, with him, the ambition for the new is not yet stronger than his desire for possessing the accomplished."

Verdy offers a dazzling smile. "Does this make any sense to you?" she asks. "I love words. I adore them."

We turn to Verdy's own dancing.

"I try to find the measure of what is required for the moment . . . for the particular performance that I am doing. With me, this measure has always come with the preparation and the evaluation of what precedes the moment. I do not try for an overcharged personal comment. I seek a sense of measure, proportion, symmetry, and harmony. This is a very French thing to do. I exercise judgment.

"Because of my work with Balanchine, music has become the propelling factor in my dancing. Music takes care of me. It gives me the courage to accomplish certain difficult technical things that I might be in doubt of, otherwise. It soothes me. It keeps me from being overexcited. On the other hand, it pushes me if I am shy. The music is my marinade, like a herring. More and more, music is my sustenance as a performer. I have this from Balanchine. It has always been our meeting ground."

Violette Verdy's brief marriage to Colin Clark ended in divorce.

"It was an interesting failure. Really, I had no business getting married whatsoever. I was not even that young. But I was young in the sense of knowing about relationships with men. I had no idea of the meaning of compromise. With my obvious idealism about dance, it was insane to pretend that I was ready for a compromise in another area of my life. So, I have now resigned myself, with a certain sense of humor, to a certain formula of living. I have decided that I am not available for romance— except for accidents, which sometimes happen, and which are very amusing or very frightening or very disturbing. No. My romantic life is nothing. There is very little.

"But I have a lot of marvelous friends, thank God. I have discovered friendship! It's the most incredible thing to discover. Friendship is one of the most difficult relationships to maintain. But it's a relationship that can almost encompass all the others. It is something in which I am now, finally, rolling and scratching my back, like a dog on a thick carpet. I love it. I still amuse myself with the idea that something else may happen. Basically, I have resigned myself to the fortunes of the traveling salesman. For a long time, I was confronted by a cliché confusion. I kept telling myself that I was not a complete person, that I have to have a physical, sexual life like every other human being—otherwise, I'm going to be incomplete in my dancing. Well . . . there is probably more to my private life than I would want to say . . . but in life, one *must* make one's choices."

HELGI TOMASSON

To watch any performance of Helgi Tomasson's is to be in touch with a dancer of superb discipline and steely lyricism. His movements have the staccato and coiling propulsion of a brilliantly manufactured precision instrument. This is not to suggest that Tomasson dances mechanically—far from it. But there is a special bristling dynamism at work in even his most fluid gesture—a kind of intense momentum, registering a tantalizing sense of pressure and release. Helgi Tomasson attacks and challenges space with compelling drive. He is very much a dancer's dancer.

I visited Tomasson and his wife, the former dancer Marlene Rizzo, in their East Seventies apartment in the winter of 1972. The Tomassons live surrounded by simple, modern furniture and the clutter made by two young sons—Kristin, age six, and Eric, age one. Tomasson met his wife while the two were dancing with the Robert Joffrey company. They were married in 1965. Mrs. Tomasson, a vivacious and exceedingly pretty young woman, tended to her youngest child as Helgi began telling me of his own childhood in Reykjavik, Iceland.

"When I was a young boy, we lived on what is called the Westman Islands, in the south of Iceland. My parents were divorced, then my mother remarried. I have a stepfather and a half brother. One time, the Royal Danish Ballet came to the Islands—they had been touring Iceland. They gave several performances at a local theater. I was brought to see them, and, as my mother tells me, from that moment on, I would continually listen to music on the radio and improvise dances. As this went on, someone in my family suggested to my mother that it might be fun to put me in a ballet school. So I was sent to a local school, run by two ladies. I was also going to regular school, of course, and I had a hard time with my schoolmates. They teased me a lot because I was attending a ballet school. But I'm very stubborn—it must be an Icelandic trait. The more I was teased, the more determined I was not to give up my ballet lessons. It was a matter of pride."

When Helgi was seven, his family returned to Reykjavik. It was at that time that the National Theatre was being constructed in Iceland's capital. A Danish couple began to teach ballet at the National Theatre, and Helgi enrolled as a student. His teacher was Eric Bidsted. By then, he was ten years old. One summer, Bidsted and his wife took Helgi with them to Denmark. He became their young protégé. For three months, he took classes at the Tivoli Pantomime Theatre in Copenhagen, and he was exposed to the many performances given there and at the Royal Danish Theatre. During subsequent summers, he would return to Copenhagen for further study. In the meantime, he continued his training in Reykjavik, while also completing his formal education. At fifteen, Helgi was engaged as a dancer in the *corps de ballet* at the Tivoli Pantomime Theatre.

"Suddenly, I realized there were boys my own age taking classes every day. It was the first time I sensed that I had competition. In Iceland, I was really the only boy studying ballet. There were a few younger fellows, but basically, I was the only one . . . I had never encountered competition. At any rate, it was during this time, in Denmark, that I decided that I wanted to become a dancer. Something clicked. I studied for two or three years, improving my technique and learning at a furious pace."

Having completed his training at the Pantomime Theatre, Tomasson was invited to participate in a production of *My Fair Lady*. Just prior to this engagement, he returned to Iceland for a visit with his family. While there, he read in the papers that Jerome Robbins' Ballets: U.S.A. would be dancing in Reykjavik. Helgi went to every performance and was thrilled by what he saw. He also had occasion to meet Jerome Robbins. Someone suggested to Robbins that he take the young boy into his company as an apprentice, but Robbins explained that this was not possible, since he was not certain whether his company would remain together. However, he promised to keep the boy in mind should something turn up for him in New York. The following spring, Helgi Tomasson received a letter from Jerome Robbins telling him that a scholarship had been arranged for him at the School of American Ballet.

Tomasson, overjoyed, arrived in New York in September 1960. He had very little money, but managed to pay for room and board, and to take daily classes at the school. All too soon, his money ran out. Finding a job would entail work permits, which, at the time, were difficult to come by. The young dancer had no choice but to return to Denmark and continue dancing with the Pantomime Theatre. He was determined to come back to America, and to that end began saving his money.

While in Copenhagen, he made the acquaintance of Erik Bruhn. Bruhn dispatched two letters—one to Lucia Chase at the American Ballet Theatre, another to Robert Joffrey. There were no posts available at ABT. But Robert Joffrey had a spot open. In 1961, Helgi Tomasson returned to America and joined the Robert Joffrey Ballet. He remained with the company for two years.

"It was a wonderful experience for me. The company was like a small family. We worked very, very hard. We toured a great deal. During layoffs, Bob Joffrey kept me going somehow. During the Seattle World's Fair, he took me along. Part of his company performed there. Mr. Joffrey was very nice to me. Also, I met Marlene. She and I often danced together. This was the period when the Joffrey company was sponsored by Rebekah Harkness. Then, suddenly, in 1964, the association between Mr. Joffrey and Mrs. Harkness was dissolved. Bob found himself without a company. A number of Joffrey dancers went with the Harkness Ballet, including Marlene and I. We were married at that time."

The Harkness Ballet made several world-wide tours. Tomasson became a principal dancer, appearing in such ballets as George Skibine's *Daphnis and Chloë* and *Sarabande*. He danced in Alvin Ailey's *Feast of Ashes*, Brian Macdonald's *Time Out of Mind*. At the time, the company's director was George Skibine. Later, it was Brian Macdonald. Later still, the company directors were Lawrence Rhodes and Benjamin Harkarvy.

"There were an awful lot of directors while I was dancing with the Harkness. I danced with the company for six years. I never really knew Mrs. Harkness, but she was always extremely nice to her dancers. In fact, it was Mrs. Harkness who suggested I enter the International Ballet Competition in Moscow in 1969."

The International Ballet Competition, held in Moscow every four years, is to ballet what the Olympics are to sports. It is a grueling, nerve-racking event in which some ninety dancers from all over the world compete in various categories, in the hopes of being awarded a silver or gold medal. Helgi Tomasson entered as a representative of the United States in the solo category. The experience became the highlight of Tomasson's early career. With shining eyes, he told me what it was like:

"The one stipulation I made about going to Moscow was that I wanted my wife to come along—and so, we went. On the day we arrived, confusion reigned. Naturally, there was an interpreter. I met a lot of Danish and Swedish dancers, some of whom I had known, and we were all put into one group. The competition, I learned, would be in three stages. On the application, it stated that those entering as soloists would have to prepare five solo dances. Actually, there was some confusion, because at one point someone told me that the jury expected *six* solo dances. I assumed that this meant one had to repeat one of the solos—which would bring it to six. Anyway, I figured that most of the entrants in the solo category would arrive with a lot of variations from the well-known classics. *I* decided to prepare things nobody ever heard of."

Tomasson was finally asked what solos he was going to perform. He announced that he had prepared a solo from *Variations for Four*, one from *Dances at a Gathering*, one from Balanchine's version of *Sylvia*, one from *Romeo and Juliet* by Norman Walker, and one choreographed by Brian Macdonald. He had not prepared a sixth solo. Tomasson had assumed that he was the only American entrant, but he learned that there were also a couple from Milwaukee who were competing.

"The first stage took four days. I made my first appearance on the third day. There were some absolutely terrific dancers including the Russians, Vladimirov and Baryshnikov. They had the best from the Leningrad and the Bolshoi ballets competing. The age limit, incidentally, was between eighteen and twenty-eight. I was very nervous. It was a terrifying experience. When my turn came, I began with my solo from *Variations for Four*. It begins with a walk across the stage without music. Well, that was one of the longest walks I've ever taken in my life. The Bolshoi stage is enormous. Anyway, I walked across and took a position. As I danced, I could see some of the judges. They were all sitting in the first row, with little tables in front of them. There were twenty of them. Some of the biggest names were there, including Ulanova and Plisetskaya. I felt I did very well. I felt I danced that solo better than I had ever danced it before. When it was over, I got a good hand from the audience. In the meantime, the two Americans from Milwaukee had been disqualified. I remained as the only representative from the United States. We were still at the first stage, and I had more solos to perform. By the fourth day, I still didn't know whether I had made it to the second stage.

"Nevertheless, I began preparing for round number two. It continued to be a madhouse. I mean, one had to stand on line for everything: to find out if you could have this or that studio, this or that rehearsal time, this or that accompanist. I should add that a lot of the dancers brought along their ballet masters and their own accompanists, and, in some cases, their own partners. I had to fend for myself and manage everything on my own. In any case, after the fourth day, we all had to gather in a big hall and a man read off the names of those who had made it to the second stage. I was among them. I think that out of ninety competitors, forty were left.

"When I heard that I had made it to the second stage, I really went to work. We all had a day off, but I used it to work. I took class with the Danes, who had brought along a teacher. I had also brought along a tape recording with a class on it. I kept warming up to the tape recorder. Some of the Russians had never seen one. They kept staring at that magic box. I don't remember anything unusual happening during the second stage of the competition. All I knew was that the pressure was tremendous. The only sad thing about it was that some really marvelous dancers just fell completely apart. They were not used to those circumstances. At the end of the second stage, I was told that I had made it to the third stage. I couldn't believe it. Of course, I was delighted.

"At this point, some official came up to me and asked what my sixth solo would be. I would have to perform it during the last stage. I looked at him. I told him I didn't have one—that I had thought only five solos were required, and that one could be repeated. He said I would have to do a brand-new solo. I got together with Marlene and some of the Danes and we decided I would dance the solo from the *Black Swan pas de deux*. I was frantic. I had never danced it. I sort of knew it, by watching it. I remember Erik Bruhn dancing it, and other people. I only had a day and a half to prepare it. I remember asking my friends a thousand questions about the way Erik had done it. Did he have his arm that way or this way? Did he do this or that? So, I finally managed to pull it together, and I rehearsed it over and over again. It then turned out I would have to have an appropriate jacket to dance in. More red tape. Finally, through special permission from Ulanova, I was allowed to borrow a 'classical jacket' from the Bolshoi wardrobe. I also had trouble in getting an accompanist. They were all frantically busy. Anyway, with one thing and another, I got ready for the third and final stage."

Tomasson, as it turned out, had already become a popular favorite with the audience. The young Icelandic dancer representing America gained confidence, although the outcome was still far from certain.

"On the day of the third stage, I first danced the Balanchine *Sylvia* solo. It met with quite a bit of success. But then came the real test—the *Black Swan* solo. I went out on stage in my borrowed jacket, and simply did it. The competition was over. We waited and waited for the judges to make their decisions. Very early the next morning, I received a telephone call from my interpreter. She said, 'Congratulations! You have won the Silver Medal.' Well, it was fantastic. I couldn't believe it. On the following day, there was a big gala, during which all the winners had to do a dance. It was also the moment of the presentation of the medals. There were many speeches. The Russian Baryshnikov won the Gold Medal. There was no Gold Medal for a female soloist that year, but Vladimirov and his wife won the Gold Medal in the *pas de deux* category, which was in fact split with a French couple. The Silver Medal for a female in the solo category was won by a Cuban girl. Anyway, I had won the prize for America."

It will be remembered that when Van Cliburn won the famed Tchaikovsky Piano Competition in Moscow in 1958, he returned to America in triumph. There was a ticker-tape parade on New York's Fifth Avenue. Fame and glory came to the young Texan. No such glory attended the return from Moscow of Helgi Tomasson. The reason was simple, if unfair. Tomasson was not American-born—nor had he become an American citizen.

"When I first arrived in Moscow, the *New York Times'* Moscow correspondent called me. I had just made it to the second stage. He said, 'How exciting! You're an American citizen, of course.' I said, 'No. I'm Icelandic. But I'm a resident of the United States, and I'm competing for America.' There was a long silence. Finally, he said, 'Well, good luck.' And that was it. I never heard from him again. Even the dance magazines gave me very little coverage. There was a small article in *Dance News*. The only nice thing that happened was that Marlene and I were invited to an evening at the home of the American ambassador in Moscow. That was nice. Actually, I don't think the Americans realize how important this competition is. When I got back to the States, I did a few radio shows, and I got on the *Today* Show. The whole thing boiled down to the fact that I wasn't an American."

Helgi Tomasson returned to dance with the Harkness Ballet. When the Harkness temporarily disbanded, the dancer went to talk to George Balanchine about joining the New York City Ballet. Balanchine took him into the company. The year was 1970. Tomasson's wife, who had been dancing up to this time, gave up her career in favor of motherhood.

Tomasson then told me about what he did next:

"I was delighted to join the New York City Ballet. I had traveled so much with the Joffrey and with the Harkness that the idea of settling in one place was very attractive. Also, I love the atmosphere of the City Ballet. I was made a principal dancer, and Jerry Robbins immediately put me into *The Goldberg Variations*. Mr. B. put me in *Le Baiser de la Fée* during the Stravinsky Festival. It was a good beginning. I enjoy taking Mr. Balanchine's classes. I have made friends in the company. Jean-Pierre Bonnefous and I share a dressing room. We get along fabulously. There's

Peter Martins, another friend. Considering the brief time that I've been with the company, I've gotten a very good repertoire. I think I've done well. The public seems to know me now. I dance in *Symphony in C, Donizetti Variations, Tchaikovsky Pas de Deux, Tarantella, Theme and Variations, Dances at a Gathering, Stars and Stripes, Four Temperaments, Symphony in Three Movements*.

"Mr. Balanchine is very easy to work with. He's extremely fast. But he doesn't really make you nervous. He gets the most out of you. I have a very good relationship with Jerry Robbins. After all, he was the first person to enable me to come and study at the School of American Ballet. We have a very good rapport. Really, I have no complaints. I think my career is going in the right direction. I have no complaints."

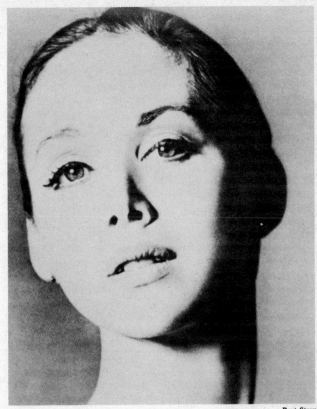

Bert Stern

ALLEGRA KENT

It may have been the fact of my visit, or it may have been the kind of day it was—a cold, wet January afternoon in 1973. But Allegra Kent seemed slightly harassed as she greeted me at the door of her hotel apartment, and led me through a series of charmingly cluttered rooms in which her three young children were busily at play. All around was the special confusion of family life—a life in which very young egos need individual attention, the more so, in the presence of a stranger. Soon, Miss Kent had the situation under some control. She explained to Trista, aged twelve, Susannah, aged eight, and Bret, almost six, that she was giving an interview and that everyone would have to be quiet and keep themselves occupied. As it turned out, all three children made no effort to disperse, but huddled around us as we talked. Bret, Miss Kent's unusually handsome son, paid me the compliment of sitting on my lap. Some further feeble attempts on Miss Kent's part to shoo the children out of the way proved a failure. And so, the five of us, nestled on a large couch, settled down to a conversation which found the children as attentive as I was.

Allegra Kent has been separated from her husband, the photographer Bert Stern, for some two years. Lately, she has adjusted her life to include some truly superb dancing and renewed appearances with the New York City Ballet, of which she has been a member since 1953. Her life has not been particularly easy during the past few years, what with her husband's illness, a trouble-fraught separation, and the fact that she had been forced on several occasions to be away from dancing. Still, Miss Kent had now determined to regulate her life in ways that would allow her a maximum amount of dancing, while also enabling her to raise her family.

It is, of course, unusual for a ballerina to have three children. It is perhaps more unusual for such a ballerina to have deepened her art in the face of great struggle and emotional upheaval. Allegra Kent is clearly a survivor. She continues to project a look of fragility and sensitivity. Her light gray-blue eyes suggest an untroubled, childlike innocence. It is in talking with Miss Kent that one realizes what lies beneath this surface serenity.

"I'm back out of a bad time," she told me. "I couldn't work because of several bad episodes in my marriage. I'm just coming back to myself as a dancer, and as a person. I've simplified my life. I've discovered how little I need. It's awful to say, but I had been trying to get out of my marriage for almost the whole time that I was married. I left six weeks after I was married, but my mother encouraged me to go back. I was so *much* under her influence. Anytime she suggested something, I did it. I was always doing things that other people told me to. Eventually, I stopped that.

"Last year, I really had to make ends meet. I had to sell things to live. Sixteen years ago, I met an artist—Joseph Cornell. He made a box for me—one of his beautiful boxes. But he never gave it to me, until fifteen years later. I did treasure it, but I had to sell it. That box kept us alive last year. I had to support the children. This year, I'm getting into concerts. The salary at the New York City Ballet is not enough."

The children listened quietly. Their mother has kept nothing from them. Miss Kent spoke freely. I asked about her beginnings.

"I was born in Los Angeles in 1938. I'm the youngest of three. We were always traveling. My father was like a traveling salesman-gambler. He may not like that, but it's true. He supported us by playing gin rummy. My mother divorced him very fast, because it was just impossible. I was sent to boarding school. They gave us folk dancing. I suddenly thought I loved dancing. So I started jumping around in boarding school. Folk dancing really got to me. I kept embroidering on it. I wrote my mother and told her I wanted to be a ballet dancer. I wanted to do that although I had never seen ballet dancing. And so, my mother took me out of school and I started studying with Nijinska's daughter. I think her name was Irina. She was very good. I studied with her in L.A. Working with her was very strange, because you didn't learn anything. You got to her class, and you started jumping and turning. You didn't analyze anything. What she gave you was spirit and strength. I *still* had never seen ballet. I was already eleven. Finally, I suggested to my mother that we go and see a ballet. She took me to the Ballet Russe. I hated it. I thought, I hate ballet. It's horrible. I saw *Schéhérazade*, I saw *Gaîté Parisienne*. Now I appreciate these ballets—think they're funny. But then, I thought they were hideous. The one thing I saw that I liked was *La Sonnàmbula*, which in those days was called *The Night Shadow*. I found it very interesting. It was a Balanchine ballet. I didn't know it was Balanchine at the time. Then I was taken to Ballet Theatre. I saw Nora Kaye dance. She struck me as phenomenal."

Being exposed to ballet performances, Allegra Kent developed the desire to study more seriously. She went to work with Carmelita Maracci. She also took classes with Bronislava Nijinska.

"With Madame Nijinska, it was the same as with her daughter. You danced, you jumped, you just did it. It was marvelous. With Maracci, it was different. She was unbelievable. She was just brilliant, as a dancer and as a person. She taught us to do everything in the most exaggerated way. With her, everything was done to the fullest, to the most extreme. Actually, I think that if you're doing movement, it *should* be extreme. It should be unusual. In the classical things, movement has to be done in the traditional way. But in the works of Balanchine (those that are not classical) you have to have that leeway—to overstretch. That's how you do *Agon* and *Bugaku. Bugaku* was done on me by Mr. Balanchine."

Allegra Kent studied with Carmelita Maracci for two years. Her mother then brought her to New York City. Allegra applied for a scholarship at the School of American Ballet. She was accepted and studied there for one year. At the age of fifteen, Allegra Kent was made an apprentice with the New York City Ballet.

"I got into the company at sixteen. Then, when I turned seventeen, my mother felt that I should leave the company and go to college. She felt that I wasn't leading a normal life. Of course, it was too late for something like that. Nevertheless, I followed her advice. I returned to L.A., and enrolled at UCLA. It was a joke, because after three weeks, I knew it was ridiculous. I wasn't interested. I continued taking dancing lessons while going to school. My mother then decided I wasn't living the right kind of college life. She decided UCLA was the wrong kind of college for me. She thought of sending me to the University of Utah. I went to Utah. For me, it was the bleakest, dreariest place. I got terribly depressed. I knew I had to get out. All I did there was listen to Bach—all day long. It was listening to Bach that got me out of my depression. Bach has never sounded so beautiful to me as it did while I was in Utah. Anyway, I was in such a state that I got on a plane and flew back to New York to rejoin the New York City Ballet. I started getting better parts right away. I went on tour in Europe, and I got all the jumping parts. Those were the days when I could really jump. Now, I've lost my jump. With every child, I went a little down.

"When we got to Denmark, Tanaquil LeClercq developed polio. It was really awful. The company went back to New York, and Balanchine stayed there. It was horrible for him. It was horrible for Tanny. The next season, Francisco Moncion did a ballet for me called *Pastorale*, with music by Charles Turner. Then, the next year, Mr. Balanchine created *The Seven Deadly Sins* for me. I wish it could be revived. It was about fourteen years ago that I did *The Seven Deadly Sins*. It really wasn't a ballerina part. It was just pure movement and acting—which I really feel is what I do best. I don't feel like a classical ballerina, in any case. The other day, Mr. Balanchine criticized me for wearing my crown too far back in one of the classical ballets. I wore it as far back as possible. I don't like the regal bit."

Allegra Kent was made a principal dancer at the age of nineteen. This occurred at a time when the New York City Ballet toured Japan and Australia. Miss Kent learned some thirty new roles on the tour. Dancing during that period were Diana Adams, Patricia Wilde, and Melissa Hayden, among others.

"I did everything in those days. Ballets were thrown at me all the time. Maria Tallchief had left to have a baby. Diana hurt her foot. There were just the three of us—Melissa, Pat Wilde, and me. We did two ballets a night, and four on the weekend. I couldn't possibly keep up that kind of pace any more. But then a lot of things began to happen to me. A lot of things that distracted me from dancing. I had the children. I had a lot of trouble with Bert. Everything threw me for a loop at different times. I've taken a lot of time off.

"Also, from the age of nineteen to twenty-five, I was Mr. Balanchine's favorite. But every time I had a child, he got upset. Of course, I couldn't blame him. Still, in spite of having an unfortunate marriage, I always wanted to have children. It was one of those things. I wanted to have everything. Then I sensed that Mr. Balanchine wasn't paying attention to me. Suzanne Farrell came along. I didn't know how to handle it. I felt a certain amount of jealousy in being displaced. I think if the same thing had happened now, I would have handled it much better. But at that time, I was thrown. I couldn't understand it. I mean, I like Suzanne's dancing very much, but I couldn't handle the situation. . . . Now I don't get involved with the company as much. It's more abstract for me. I no longer think about how other people are dancing, or how they are not dancing. I just try to do the best that I can.

"I don't know how Mr. Balanchine feels about me these days. But I know that I was once his favorite. He's a remarkable choreographer and teacher. When he did *Bugaku* on me, it was a fantastic thing. He just sort of threw it together. He doesn't spell out what he wants exactly. He indicates. Then, suddenly, you can embroider and add to what he's indicated. With something like *Bugaku* you can do that, because he just gives you the outline. Mr. Balanchine trusts his dancers. I do it differently now than when I first did it. In fact, I now feel as though I'm getting back again to where I once was. It's a wonderful feeling. I like taking class, because you sweat, you work hard, you use all your energy. You can forget about everything. You can do your steps with more intensity, and you feel sort of purified and ready to face the world. I'm just starting to do all of that again. I think I'm dancing well these days."

Allegra Kent onstage offers an image at once feminine and austere. She is one of the purest dancers in the New York City Ballet. In works such as *Bugaku, Agon, Orpheus, Apollo, Episodes, La Sonnàmbula,* among other Balanchine ballets, her movements conjure a fervent, ecstatic, often poignant sense of drama. Her cleanliness of line is such that any ballet she appears in is suddenly charged with a fresh and exquisite tension. In *Bugaku,* she seems to define the Balanchine aesthetic. What is more, in this essentially ritualistic work, she injects a consummate delicacy into even the most convoluted of gestures and variations, transforming the work into a highly personal statement. By the same token, Kent can project overt sensuality—as in *The Seven Deadly Sins*—coupled with a tremulous vulnerability that is never less than magical.

"I think that I give the illusion of flexibility. I think I move unusually. When I was away at boarding school, I used to love to swing. It's that movement of being carried very high on the swing—that feeling of running fast that I love. I love the animalistic pleasure of running and jumping and climbing mountains. Still, I'm one dancer that never encourages anyone to dance. It's a lot of work, a lot of labor. It's always been hard for me to get back into condition. But I've come back. Last year, I was in a terrible funk. I couldn't get out of it. Then, Eddy Villella called me. He asked me to do a concert with him. I knew I had to pull myself together and do it. And Jerry Robbins was terrific to me last year. There I was, sitting at home. I had mononucleosis. I got over it, but I couldn't get back to class. I was just sitting around, wondering what I should do. I got depressed. It was literally paralyzing. Then Jerry Robbins called me up and told me to come back and work. That helped. So, Jerry helped, and Eddy helped. Jerry put me in his *Dances at a Gathering.* Then I did *Dumbarton Oaks.* Jerry only got upset with me when he thought I really wasn't trying. He is really fantastic. Of course, there are still times when I can't turn off the outside world. I'm still not legally divorced. Anyway, when it's all over, I will never get that involved again. I now go to a woman doctor. She is helping me. She is good.

"Right now, right this minute, my state of mind is good. But I still get into depressions. I get depressed thinking that I can't dance, and I'm not going to be able to do a season. I think everybody gets depressed. Right now, at this very moment, I feel good. I think I'm going to be able to dance well again. . . ."

ANTHONY BLUM

I am from Alabama . . . from Mobile," said Anthony Blum. "My mother was an actress in New York in the Twenties, but she was dragged back to Alabama kicking and screaming, because my grandfather, who supported her, didn't think it was right for a young lady to be an actress. So she remained in Alabama, still kicking and screaming, until nearly the end. When she brought me to New York, we lived together."

Anthony Blum, one of the New York City Ballet's most enigmatic principal dancers, sat in my living room sipping some wine. The twenty years he has been living in New York have erased the Southern accent, but not the brooding sense of drama and shadowy intensity that sensitive, troubled Southern boys à la Tennessee Williams often communicate. At the same time, there is a sweetness about Tony Blum—a warmth that endeared him to his fellow dancers and to the general public. He is very much a loner—a person difficult to know—someone possessed of myriad ambiguities and contradictions.

"My father was a character, also. He was an only child, a very spoiled child, from a very wealthy family in New Orleans. His father died when he was twelve, and the estate wasn't well managed. By the time my father reached college, the fortune was lost. Still, he remained totally spoiled and undisciplined. He was a medical student, although he never wanted to be one. When he graduated, he tore up his diploma and never practiced medicine. He never really held a steady job. The only stable person in my family is my older brother, who became an engineer. My parents were very unfocused. There was no focus or discipline in my upbringing at all.

"When I was a kid in Mobile, I took acrobatic and tap lessons. It was very easy for me. I enjoyed it. It was fun to do. Not that I had any goal in mind, but the acrobatics and the tap dancing all came very naturally. I never completed high school. I'm one of those. I lived at home—it was a dream world. I spent too much time in my house. I got hung up on it. It was a little sick. I was living out my mother's dramas with her. I was interested in flowers, and things. I lived in my own dream world. My father would sort of appear and disappear, in and out of it.

"Both my parents were great fighters. They made great scenes . . . lots of scene-playing, game-playing. Great struggles and strifes. Very exciting. My brother and I fended for ourselves. Often, we had to make do with peanut butter because my mother couldn't cope. I didn't mind. I was perfectly happy. I never complained. Now my parents are gone. Each one died very tragically, very dramatically. I loved them both. My mother was gorgeous. She was beautiful. Of course, she never grew up. It was difficult for her to adjust to growing old. She never made the adjustment. Then, when I had already joined the company, my father committed suicide. I understood, and forgave him for it.

"Actually, I only knew my parents very superficially. They were such interesting, crazy characters. They had a lot to give. I hadn't been told about my father's killing himself until weeks after it happened. Nobody told me. Anyway, I used this event for my own drama. I remember going to class that day. I was in shock, I suppose. But the way my mind works, it became a total fantasy. An extremely glamorous fantasy. I mean, a suicide! How incredible! So I went to class that day, and the whole day was a performance. I didn't realize it then. I performed at getting sympathy, and I got my fulfillment that way. If I had admitted it then—as something real—oh, God, how much I would have known today! How much further I would have gone!"

When Anthony Blum was fifteen, he and his mother came to New York for a two-week vacation. She thought it would be good for him to see the city. Some young friends of Tony's had also come to New York in order to study ballet. Tony had no such intentions, but, knowing no other people in New York, he hung around with them.

"My mother and I rented an apartment on East Eighty-third Street. When we arrived, and came out of Penn Station, I couldn't take it all in. I had never left Mobile. It was a traumatic experience. Everything happened so fast. Anyway, instead of staying two weeks, we spent the whole summer in New York. My friends said, 'Why don't you take some classes?' I said no. But they were insistent. So I went to the Ballet Theatre school, and took come classes with, I think, William Dollar. That was in 1953. I walked into the school, and I told them I had four years' dancing experience—which was a lie. They put me into a professional class. I was terrified out of my wits. I didn't even know how to put a dance belt on. I didn't even know I was wearing my dance belt backward. Needless to say, they soon put me into a lower-level class. It wasn't as difficult as I thought it would be. Actually, it was amazing. I caught on very quickly. I had a natural talent. But everything was too easy. If they showed something, I just did it. But I never learned *how* to do it, so I never developed discipline or a technique.

"Anyway, I decided I wanted to stay in New York. So my mother said, 'Fine. We'll stay.' So we did—we took an apartment in a hotel on East Fifty-eighth Street. My mother thought I should also be going to high school. I enrolled in the High School of Performing Arts—in the Dance Division. At the same time, I took classes outside. I studied with Aubrey Hitchins. I studied for about a year, and then cut loose. I had a job immediately. I auditioned for Rod Alexander, who was choreographing a summer show at the Jones Beach Marina. It was called *Arabian Nights*. I auditioned, and I got the job. I was sixteen. I have never been out of work since."

Blum and his mother remained in New York. He continued taking classes in modern dance, as well as ballet, but abandoned high school. At one point, he went to the School of American Ballet and asked for a scholarship. He auditioned and was accepted.

"After the audition, I was standing around the class, and I overheard Muriel Stuart saying to someone, 'Darling, he'll never make it. His arms are much too short. . . .' I'll always remember that. Now, of course, I adore her; I love her. Anyway, I got into the School of American Ballet, but I took classes erratically, for which I was often reprimanded. I studied with Pierre Vladimirov, Felia Doubrovska, Elise Reiman, and Anatole Oboukhov. Oboukhov was the only teacher that I was ever able to work for. Somehow, I wanted to. I hated working, but I enjoyed working for Oboukhov."

While he was still at the School of American Ballet, Lucia Chase, codirector of American Ballet Theatre, offered Anthony Blum a job with her company. She invited him to join as a soloist. Blum was dissuaded, being told that it would be far more advantageous for him to work with someone like George Balanchine. The dancer followed this advice with somewhat mixed feelings:

"Of course, I was aware of Mr. Balanchine. He was the director of the company. He was important. Actually, he was very encouraging to me while I was at the school. I'll never forget one conversation between us. He told me that if I worked hard and really applied myself, he would turn me into the greatest male dancer this country has ever had. He said, 'You have all the possibilities—more possibilities than anyone I've had in years.' Well, my ego was immensely inflated. I went out into the sunshine. I sort of basked in that. But I was very young—sixteen or seventeen. I just took it as a compliment. I heard what Balanchine told me, but I didn't really listen. I took what he told me too lightly. Somewhere, the message got lost. In a crazy way, I formed a bitterness toward him, which I can't explain. I became very arrogant. Balanchine would tell me something, and I would think that I knew more than he did, which was ridiculous. I should have realized that he was only out to help me. He certainly wasn't there to hurt me. I can't explain the bitterness that I felt. I think the main problem was that I didn't take Mr. Balanchine's classes. I listened to other people who told me that his classes wouldn't really teach me anything. And I listened to them. It was an ego thing. I was very full of myself. Of course, I was wrong. Now, more and more, every single day, I've come to realize that Balanchine knows more about telling people how to dance than anybody. He knows how to tell people how to move. I was so wrong. Still, I never took a class of Mr. Balanchine's."

In December 1958 Anthony Blum joined the New York City Ballet, becoming a member of the *corps*. George Balanchine was not in New York during that time. His wife, Tanaquil LeClercq, had contracted polio, and he remained with her in Europe.

"I was taken into the company because I was needed at that time. Also, I was good. I was fabulous. I *must* have been. I mean, I was young; I was pretty. I was fresh, and full of energy. And I was around. When I heard they were taking me into the company, a terrible fear came over me. Immediately, I had a foot injury. But I got into the company anyway, and suddenly, I was dancing in everything. At the time, there were about fifty-five people in the company—which seemed enormous to me. In those days we were dancing at the City Center. We worked so hard. We had three ballets every night. All of us in the *corps* worked like dogs. I don't know when it happened, but very quickly, I was given solo roles. I learned fast.

Things were thrown at me like mad. It was all great fun, and I didn't take any of it seriously.

"When Mr. Balanchine came back, I was totally indifferent to him. And he, of course, acquired an indifference toward me. I remained in the company but I still refused to take his classes. What's so awful is that somebody should have taken me aside and said, 'Look here. Work with him. Be more assertive.' But that didn't happen. Nobody took me aside. I think the truth of the matter is that I was scared to death of Mr. B. In all these years I've been in the company, I've never had a conversation with him. It's incredible to look back and see how arrogant I was. I don't know what he must have felt. Finally, he must just have felt that I was useful. He must have said to himself, Well, if he's not going to become what I want him to become, at least he can be useful. I was a fool. Anyway, I was being used, and thrown into things at the last moment. I acquired most of my roles in this fashion. Naturally, because of my attitude—I had become more and more bitter—no ballets have ever been created on me. I was only being used, never being chosen. Oh, there were three small things done on me by Balanchine—something in *Don Quixote,* a *pas de deux* I did with Suzanne Farrell in *Clarinade* [a ballet which is no longer in the repertoire], and something else.

"One of my best memories was dancing with Maria Tallchief. She had been out of the company, and then came back to us. It was Maria who chose me to do *Scotch Symphony* with her. It was the first time I had ever been *chosen* for something. I was given rehearsal time, which was unknown to me. I don't know why Maria chose me. Earlier on, she had mostly danced with Jacques d'Amboise. But when she came back, she was not on friendly terms with him. Maybe he was just a little too brash for her. Maybe his pace level was not what hers was. Anyway, Maria was incredible. I would love to go and see her dance, because her level—her pitch—was not something constant. That's the kind of artist I am, too. Watching Maria you would never know whether she was going to be on or off. That's very appealing to me. It makes a performance so much more exciting. Maria must have sensed something in me that appealed to her. Of course, I was terrified. To me, Maria Tallchief was *the* ballerina, and I was in total awe. I was afraid to touch her. But I did very well. We responded to each other beautifully. I mean, when she would turn to me and smile, my heart would pound. I would really be lost onstage. I went through incredible fantasies about her. Actually, I never got to know her very well at all."

If Anthony Blum did not take Balanchine's company classes, he nevertheless attended all rehearsals supervised by Balanchine.

"Working with Balanchine is, of course, incredible. He shows what he wants, and he talks, and, somehow, you instinctively know what to do. Actually, his working methods are very intangible. What I mean is: You have to *experience* Balanchine in order to know him. I've had times with

him when everything clicked. I felt at one with him. I felt myself responding to the emotions he was responding to, and I felt comfortable and
wonderful and right. I felt involved. I was on his plane. I related to him.
But it's happened very rarely."

A principal dancer with the City Company for nearly a decade, Anthony
Blum's repertoire is large and diversified. At his best, Blum projects a
feline strength—a sinuous, emotion-charged energy that gives dynamic
pulse and contour to whatever role he dances. Blum seems to inhabit
movement psychologically. He seems continually in search of that which
lies behind the gesture, the movement, the step. His dancing suggests a
question rather than an answer. A fascinating sense of struggle can be
observed. This struggle is seldom a technical one. It is an emotional one.
It is as if Blum were in a continual process of wishing to free himself from
the bounds of his questioning nature: thus, the urgency of his movements—
the darting, dashing quality of his encounter with space. In works such as
Dumbarton Oaks, Robbins' *Dances at a Gathering*, *In the Night*, and *The
Goldberg Variations*, a more lyrical, freer aspect is present. Blum seems to
respond to the austere poetry of Robbins' movements—their sense of con-
temporaneity, their easy flow, their gay, subtly abrupt changes. An innate
elegance comes into play, and Blum seems to have personally solved the
meaning of why he is dancing.

Blum described working with Jerome Robbins:

"I wish Jerry had discovered me earlier. There are a lot of things I
admire about Jerry, just as there are a lot of things about him that I don't
admire. He's a strange and crazy guy. There's a side of Jerry that I don't
like at all when working with him. During our association in *Dances at a
Gathering*, things got a bit rough. Early on, I gathered strength and told
him exactly how I felt. It happened in the middle of a rehearsal. A moment came when I felt very uncomfortable. I just couldn't work under the
kind of pressure he was putting me under. I told him that if I was going to
work with him, I would have to have some pleasure. If it was going to be
all misery and unpleasantness, I would rather not work with him. I really
wanted to work with Jerry—I wanted to enjoy him and respond to him.
But there were moments when things became too pat, too calculated and
contrived for me to relate to. There were moments that were so unreal and
so unnatural. . . . Of course, they may have been very real to Jerry.
Anyway, our relationship changed, and I worked very well with him.

"I'm afraid to get too close to Jerry. I've seen situations where people
let themselves be open to him and respond to him on an emotional level—
beyond working with him. I saw what they were going through. I just
didn't want that to exist between us. So, we had a very dry relationship
during *Dances*. The work went very quickly. God knows, I never worked
like that with anyone. It was the first time the work didn't seem like work.
The discipline I never had came out, because, somehow, I was able to

totally respond to what he was doing. *In the Night* was even easier. Jerry and I would have our little moments. We had our little spats. I would become arrogant and aggressive, and forget to be just assertive.

"I was also going through some difficult times in my personal life. I had reached the age of thirty. I was questioning everything. Suddenly, it hit me that I had been in the company for a very long time. I was realizing that I had had so many opportunities which I had neglected—which I didn't take advantage of. I could have done so much with my career—but I didn't. I allowed my emotional life to take over, and to influence me. I have a negative and self-destructive streak. Eighty per cent of me is negative. I'm one of those dancers who goes onstage thinking that I'm going to fall on my ass—that I'm not going to be able to do it—that it's going to be terrible. Then, another voice in me says, No. You're going to go out there, and you *can* do it. You've done it before. It's going to be fine! Then, the other voice comes back and says, No you're not! I've had so many years of this. It's with me all the time."

Anthony Blum, by his admission, leads a very secluded life. He does not have close friends in the company. His personal involvements exist outside of the company. Blum is not married.

"Marriage has never been in my thoughts. I mean, I think of marriage as something other than a ring, a piece of paper, and a vow. Marriage is not appealing to me. Anyway, I'm too unstable for it. *I* want to be taken care of. If I were married, I would have to do the taking-care-of. Oh, I suppose I could get married and also be taken care of. . . . I'm glad that I'm involved in living at this period, because things are loosening up. I just wish I were younger now. This is a fantastic period to be young in. The morals and the viewpoints are changing. Anyway, I have my own life outside the company. The people in the company don't really know me. I'm not into talking about dancing. I do my work, then go off on my own. At the moment, my mind is sort of nowhere. I'm thirty-five. I'm going through lots of learning about life. I used to be a fantastic technician. I'm not a fantastic technician any more. It's sort of scary. When I go out onstage and dance, things aren't as easy any more. I go out, and I get into a lot of faking. It's sincere faking. It's honest. I'm doing it the way I have to do it. But the technical level is gone, and it frightens me. When I stop dancing, I will only have one regret: that I never got to dance Balanchine's *The Prodigal Son*. It will have been the ego-blow of my life. I guess, of all ballets, *Prodigal Son* is my favorite. To me, it's the complete ballet. I think I would have done it well. Now, it's too late. It will never be given to me. It's been too much associated with Eddy Villella. To tell you the truth, I somehow gave up when Eddy happened—when he came into the company. It somehow made me want to work even less. I don't know why. I admire Eddy so much. We get along very well. But when Eddy happened, I somehow gave up."

KAY MAZZO

Fingers working quickly and deftly, Kay Mazzo sat in her dressing room at the New York State Theater, sewing on elastic and ribbons to several pairs of toe shoes. In an hour or so, Miss Mazzo would dance the Sugar Plum Fairy in the New York City Ballet's holiday production of *The Nutcracker*. Peter Martins would be her Cavalier. At various intervals the loudspeaker in the dressing room announced the passage of time and signaled the various activities taking place in preparation for the performance. One could hear the orchestra in a brief rehearsal of a section, and the general bustle of an elaborate, full-length ballet getting under way.

Through it all, Kay Mazzo sat calmly, attending to her work, unperturbed by the fact that she would presently be executing a role that demands enormous skill and concentration. But then, the dancer has been dancing the Sugar Plum Fairy for several years, as she has been dancing any number of roles in the large Balanchine and Robbins repertoires. A principal with the company since 1970, Mazzo is a product of the School of American Ballet, which she entered at the age of thirteen. The Balanchine traits are evident at a glance: long legs, long arms, high neck, small head. Miss Mazzo is considered a poetic, lyrical dancer who infuses her roles with a romantic, yearning quality. Throughout the years, she has developed a more bristling and linear thrust—one that is more in character with the Balanchine style, and comes into perfect play in such works as *Violin Concerto, Duo Concertant, Scherzo à la Russe*, among other more or less abstract works.

A splendid technician, Mazzo is extremely musical—perhaps one of the *most* musical dancers in the company. Her presence on stage is not precisely riveting, but she is possessed of a rare sensitivity that lends a special poignancy to whatever role she undertakes. What is finally interesting about Mazzo is her innate classicism—the natural affinity for transforming even the most complex set of variations into a lyrical unit that seems continually to hark back to the traditional. This quality makes her dancing unique.

A soft-spoken girl, Mazzo told me something of her background.

"My father is Italian, and my mother is Yugoslavian," she began. "I was born in Evanston, Illinois. I lived there till I was eleven, when my parents moved East. For me, it all began when I was six years old. I happen to have been a very sickly child. My doctor said, 'You've got to get her built up—give her ballet lessons.' My doctor was a balletomane. So my mother took me to a little studio in Evanston, and I enjoyed it a lot. I loved the ballet. I had a very good basic teacher. She was very academic. She put me on *pointe* when I was eight—which is very young, and could have been a bad thing to do. But she was very careful about it.

"Then, when I was nine, *The Nutcracker* came to Chicago. It was *this Nutcracker*, of the New York City Ballet. Thousands of kids auditioned for it. I was among them, and was taken in as one of the children. I performed in it for about a month—and I loved it. Maria Tallchief danced the Sugar Plum Fairy. Tanaquil LeClercq danced Dewdrop. Diana Adams was in the company, and André Eglevsky. I just loved the company so. Well, I was nine years old, and for me, to be with the New York City Ballet was a thrill. From that moment on, I wanted to be in this company. When I was about eleven, my father, who was in the paper business, was transferred to Massachusetts. For two summers, I came to New York to study at the School of American Ballet. Then, when I turned thirteen, my mother and I came to live in New York and I began to attend the school on a regular basis. I was very happy at the school."

Mazzo was particularly fond of Anatole Oboukhov.

"I had never studied with a Russian person in my life. But he was wonderful. He used to give the most beautiful adagios. They used to go on and on. He did not demonstrate a lot, but just by looking at him and at the way he held himself, you'd be inspired. It's very hard to get inspired in class, but Oboukhov inspired you. I also studied with Antonina Tumkovsky, who gave us marvelous character classes in the summer. She also remembered many of the Russian variations that she had learned, so we'd do things from *The Hump-Backed Horse*, and beautiful, beautiful little variations. I wrote some of them down because I wanted to remember them. I remember one summer being taught by Melissa Hayden, who was pregnant at the time. She was like no one else. She knew the Balanchine method, because he had taught it to her, and it was quite a shock to suddenly move quickly and know where you're putting your feet. Muriel Stuart was a wonderful teacher, because she was different from everyone else. She tried to make you remember that you not only dance with your feet but that you must dance with the rest of your body as well."

At the age of sixteen, Kay Mazzo was made an apprentice with the New York City Ballet. Very shortly thereafter, Jerome Robbins held a series of auditions for the company he was then forming—Ballets: U.S.A. Mazzo was among the girls chosen to join the Robbins company.

"That was a shock, because I didn't even know who Jerome Robbins was, and I really wanted to be with the City Ballet. I went to Mr. Balanchine and asked whether I should go with Mr. Robbins—I impressed him with the fact that I wanted to enter *his* company. Mr. B. said I should go with Jerry, because it would be good experience. Well, he was right. It was a good experience. Ballets: U.S.A. went to Europe. It was the first time I had ever been on a plane. It was the first time I had ever been out of the United States, and I was still only sixteen. The very first thing I danced in was *Afternoon of a Faun*. I did it with John Jones, who was a very good dancer. I was supposed to dance *Faun* in Spoleto, where the company first performed, but I came down with food poisoning and was sick for two weeks. So, I danced my first *Faun* in Paris which was incredibly nerve-racking."

Thus it was that Kay Mazzo made her first professional appearance in a major role. Jerome Robbins was extremely considerate of the dancer, since she was the youngest member of his company. When Mazzo danced in *Faun* for the first time, he asked everyone not to stand in the wings that night, knowing how nervous she would be. Mazzo also appeared in Robbins' *Interplay* among other works.

"Jerry treated me beautifully. I would hear him yelling at other dancers —but he would never yell at me. Actually, his temper has gotten much, much better. I think he still gets tense, but that's just a part of his personality, and it will never change. Anyway, that first experience with Jerry was extremely valuable. I learned so much."

When Mazzo returned to New York, she danced a New York season with Ballets: U.S.A. She was dancing leading roles. When the season was over, she returned to the New York City Ballet and happily entered the *corps*. The year was 1963. With the company, she did Robbins' *Faun*, but little by little, solo roles came her way, and within three years Kay Mazzo became a soloist. The dancer told me something of working with George Balanchine, as well as with Jerome Robbins:

"I've always taken Mr. Balanchine's classes. When I first entered the company, I thought of myself as a lyrical dancer. I never thought of myself as someone who could move very quickly and acquire that whole swift look. But in order to dance in Mr. B.'s ballets, you have to be able to move with great speed. Mr. Balanchine is amazing. He knows how everyone dances. I'm always so surprised that our dancers get flustered when Mr. B. is in the wings. There is no reason to be flustered—this man knows each dancer so well. Mr. B. stands in the wings because he wants to watch a performance, not because he wants to make us nervous. When he choreographs, he's amazingly fast. He will do something so quickly on you that you come in the next day having practically forgotten what he's taught you. Still, it's your job to remember. But he does throw so much at you.

"When Suzanne Farrell left the company, I had to take over a lot of her roles. This was extremely difficult, because no one had ever understudied Suzanne. I had to learn Stravinsky's *Movements for Piano and Orchestra*. No one had understudied this. After Suzanne left, nobody knew it at all. Luckily, they had a film of it. That's how I learned it. Of course, it's different when Mr. B. does a ballet on you. You see him working things out, and counting exactly the way it should be done. Mr. B. always counts with the music, which, in a way, is easier, because if you want to go back to something, you can look it up in the music.

"The difference between dancing Mr. Balanchine's ballets and Jerry Robbins' ballets is that Mr. B. always allows you a bit of freedom. With Jerry, it's quite different. He knows exactly what he wants to see. He has very good taste, and he'll always know what is right and what is wrong in a ballet. The only thing is, I don't think Jerry realizes that when you're out onstage, you just might not want to bend a certain way. If you've done a part for three years, you might want to do it a little bit differently. To him, this is not a good thing. He wants it exactly the same all of the time. I sometimes dance some of Jerry's things a little bit differently, but he never mentions anything about it. He's been awfully good with me."

It is said that Kay Mazzo is among George Balanchine's special favorites. She is occasionally seen in his company, and, indeed, at one point in our talk, Balanchine entered her dressing room, asking her to join him for supper after the performance. Some guests from Monte Carlo had arrived, and Balanchine wanted Mazzo to meet them. As it turned out, the dancer turned down the invitation, explaining that some cousins would be in the audience that night, and she would have to be with them. Balanchine seemed mildly disappointed, and left the dressing room. Mazzo smiled, telling me that Mr. B. would no doubt recover very quickly.

"I guess I know him pretty well. He's just a very good human being. He's very generous and gracious, with no pretensions at all. He doesn't like anyone who's pretentious. I think he feels very comfortable with me, and I feel very comfortable with him. Of course, it doesn't happen just like that. Sometimes, it takes years. I remember when I was first in the company, I would see Mr. B. and wouldn't have enough nerve to say hello to him. If he didn't say hello to *me*, my day would be ruined. I think Mr. B. is actually a very shy man. If he doesn't say hello, it's because he's a little shy."

I asked Miss Mazzo to describe her attitude toward the dance, and what dancing means to her.

"I don't think it's possible to dance mechanically. I have heard people say that our company is very mechanical, that we're just machines—that we all look like robots. I get very perturbed when I hear this. You cannot dance mechanically. I think what our company has is youth, energy—we *move*. We listen to the music. We give a different feeling to every ballet we perform.

"For me, the feelings change all the time. When I do the Stravinsky *Violin Concerto*, the feelings are very specific. I have three movements in it. The first movement is rather fast. When the curtain goes up, I have to start moving very quickly, so I have to pull myself together for that. When I come out for the *pas de deux*, I change my outlook completely. It's a very slow, lyrical *pas de deux*. My personality changes, somehow. When I dance, I have to put all my mind on what I'm doing. That's one of the most difficult things to do—to concentrate. It's hard to block everything else out. But the point is, once you get onstage, everything changes. Your adrenalin starts going. What's so amazing is that you prepare and prepare for a role, but the minute you're onstage . . . you are lost. You are lost in what you are doing.

"For example, all day I've been preparing myself to do *Nutcracker*. I'll be doing it shortly after you leave. And here I am, sewing all my shoes, having the whole thing in my mind. I can think and think about how it went the last performance, but I can only tell you that when I go out there onstage tonight, it will be different. The point is, you know what it's going to be like; but you don't know the outcome. Also, doing a performance can change your emotions. Sometimes, before going on, you can feel terrible. Then, afterward, you'll get offstage and you'll be feeling so uplifted. That's what's so marvelous about dancing. It gives you such elation.

"Actually, it's very hard for me to put things into words. I mean, dancing is such a completely visual thing. It's something that I find extremely hard to be verbal about. I can't really tell you what I feel when I'm out there. I just know that I've prepared myself very hard, and I hope that what people see is something that will give them pleasure."

Martha Swope

PETER MARTINS

█ was brought up by women," said Peter Martins. "I had no fathers, no brothers, no uncles. It was all women. Amazingly enough, I'm still not tired of them."

The tall, handsome, Danish-born dancer smiled, and leaned back on a large modern couch in his elegant apartment in New York's West Seventies. He wore an open shirt, worn-out jeans. This concession to the American look did not overshadow the Nordic aspect of his appearance and personality. There was the slight Danish accent, the strong, healthy fea-

tures, suggesting Scandinavian vigor and well-being, and the shock of light
blond hair, lending the final touch to his flamboyant good looks.

A product of the Royal Danish Ballet School, Martins has been a principal dancer with the New York City Ballet since 1969. Inured to the
Bournonville tradition, he retains the classic mold in even the most convoluted or bizarre choreography. In recent years, his princely line has been
modified, enabling him more easily to encompass the Balanchine and Robbins vocabularies, which often veer dramatically from the rigid "classical"
precepts. Indeed, when Martins first made his appearance with the New
York City Ballet, his dancing seemed curiously mannered. His movements
contrasted with those of his fellow dancers in ways that were slightly
jarring. Still, Martins offered superb proof of his technical abilities. Like
his fellow Dane Erik Bruhn, he combined masculine elegance with a lyrical, flowing line. The lean, sinuous stretch of his body produced a refined,
almost silken line. Leaps and jumps were negotiated with ease, and his
partnering was never less than secure, attentive, and suave.

Peter Martins was born in Copenhagen on October 27, 1946. His parents were divorced while Peter was still a very young boy. He has two
older sisters.

"I never really knew my father. I had never met him until about a year
ago. He is an engineer. He has designed many of the bridges that cross the
four little islands that make up Denmark. My family has some background
in ballet. One of my aunts was once a prima ballerina at the Royal Danish
Ballet. I, however, never had any wish to become a dancer.

"But one day, when I was seven years old, my mother decided to take
my two sisters for an audition at the Danish Ballet School. It happened to
be a Sunday, and it would entail having to stay at the school all day long.
My mother didn't know what to do with me, and so she took me along.
The school didn't take my sisters. They took me. They already had too
many girls. When they saw this little white-haired boy in the waiting room,
they just grabbed me, gave me an audition, and, the next thing I knew, I
was a member of the Royal Danish Ballet School. I really resented it! I
knew, even at that early age, that it would take up an awful lot of my time,
and that I wouldn't be able to go out and play with my friends."

Martins' first two years were spent under the guidance of Erik Bruhn,
who had already established himself as one of the world's leading dancers.

"I was just lucky, because Bruhn was dancing everywhere and seldom
returned to Denmark. But he was there during my first two years. I wasn't
very good at all. I had a tough time of it until I was fifteen. Of course, the
training is strictly Bournonville, although Vera Volkova came to the
school about twenty years ago and completely revolutionized the Danish
Ballet. She added the Russian tradition. We had character classes, mime
classes, music classes.

"At the age of fifteen, you become what is known as an 'aspirant.' You then have to go through some very tough examinations. The director of the company, the ballet masters, the conductor, and some critics all sit at a big green table. You do a whole class—the *barre*—you come to the center, and you do a variation. That's when you are judged. That's when they let you know whether you have a future in the ballet or not. I passed the examination. It was Stanley Williams who got me through it. Mr. Williams, as you know, is now a faculty member of the School of American Ballet, but he was my teacher in Denmark during my most important years—from twelve through seventeen. When you pass the examination, you are called a ballet dancer."

Martins entered the *corps* of the Royal Danish Ballet, and performed in such classics as *La Sylphide, La Fille Mal Gardée, Napoli*.

"I was really a slob in the *corps*. I would be off the music. I would do the steps differently. Finally, they took me out of the *corps*, because they realized that I could dance better alone, rather than in a line. Almost immediately, I was given principal roles. My first principal role was in a ballet called *Garden Party*. The music was by Glazunov. It so happened that this ballet had three leading roles—two boys and a girl. When the day of performance arrived, the other boy got sick. I had to take his part. My part was filled by Erik Bruhn—he was once again in Denmark. Well, you can imagine what a thrill it was for me to be on the same stage with Erik Bruhn. It was thrilling, and also frightening."

When Martins turned twenty, he was made a principal dancer with the Royal Danish Ballet. While he was given leading roles, he was not as yet permitted to attempt the major classics—*Giselle, Swan Lake, et al*. But he would dance in other classics, as well as in works mounted for the Royal Danish Ballet by visiting choreographers such as Frederick Ashton, John Cranko, and Kenneth MacMillan. On several occasions, these and other choreographers would invite Peter Martins to dance with their companies. The Danish Ballet did not grant him permission to leave.

"It got to a point where I had to turn down too many offers. I became extremely frustrated. The company wouldn't let me go anywhere—they wouldn't let me expand. Well, I decided that if they wouldn't let me go, I would just take off on my own. I mean, I was receiving invitations from Germany, England, France, and Canada. Finally, I went to the directors, and after much struggle, they allowed me to take a leave of absence. But even that was binding, because they had the right to call me back at any time. The biggest fight I had with the company was when I was invited to dance *Apollo* in Edinburgh. Balanchine was staging it. At last, they told me I could go, and I went for a week and came back with fantastic reviews. This all happened in the fall of 1967. I danced *Apollo* with Suzanne Farrell. Balanchine seemed to like me, and he invited me to be a guest with the New York City Ballet. I came to New York several times as a guest artist, but, of course, I would always have to fly back to Denmark.

The situation became absurd. I wanted to be a free man. I wanted to be free of the Royal Danish Ballet and its strict policies. I was told that if I left, I would lose my pension. Well, as a twenty-year-old, you don't think about pensions. I felt that if I became a success, I wouldn't need their pension. I decided to take my chances and leave the company."

Martins flew to New York and entered the New York City Ballet as a principal dancer.

"I had a difficult time making the adjustment. For some reason, I could not cope with Mr. Balanchine's classes—my body could not cope with them. There is no preparation. I was used to preparing myself with a forty-five minute *barre*. I kept going to Mr. B.'s classes, then I would stop going, then I would try again, then I stopped altogether. But I took classes with Stanley Williams, and they were great for me because he had been my teacher in Denmark."

During the first year or so of Martins' tenure with the New York City Ballet, the Royal Danish Ballet invited him to return as guest dancer. Martins accepted these invitations, absenting himself on frequent occasions from the City Ballet. George Balanchine was not pleased and whenever Martins returned, Balanchine would make him realize that it wasn't a good idea to leave the City Ballet too often.

The dancer described some of his early frustrations with the company:

"Twice, I almost left the company. It all began with the fact that I always thought that ballet had to be beautiful—in a very square, traditional sense. I couldn't stand to be told *not* to go into fifth position. All sorts of things like that. Finally, I went to Mr. Balanchine and told him I didn't know what I was doing wrong. He told me I was stubborn and didn't want to listen to him. He told me that if I *listened* to him, I would have a future with the company—but, if I didn't, I might as well go to American Ballet Theatre and be a 'classical dancer.' By this time I had already been with Mr. Balanchine for three years. Things weren't working out. In his classes I didn't want to give all the way. There even was a point where Mr. B. would take me out of ballets.

"One day, while he was creating *Tchaikovsky Suite No. 3* on Karin von Aroldingen and me, he humiliated me in front of the entire company. He made me do a certain run. I began to run in the way he told me to, which made me look horrible. He was really making fun of me. Sometimes, he just does that. Everyone laughed. I was mortified. On the next day, he told me that he couldn't use me in the ballet. There were other things. I went to Lincoln Kirstein and told him that I wasn't being used in the company. I told him that I had tried to please Mr. Balanchine in every way I could. I said I was wasting my time and might just as well leave. I told him I was fed up. Mr. Kirstein told me to be patient—that Mr. B. had things in mind for me. Well, it didn't take a month before things happened. First, I was put into *Chopiniana*, which was staged by Madame Alexandra Danilova.

Then came the Stravinsky Festival, and Mr. B. choreographed *Violin Concerto* and *Duo Concertant* on me.

"After the premiere of *Duo Concertant*, Mr. B. was really pleased with me, and even said so. By that time, I had, of course, pulled myself together. I began really to listen to what he was saying in his classes. I began to attend them regularly. When he choreographed *Violin Concerto*, I still had the tendency to make everything look 'beautiful.' Mr. B. would deliberately make everything look 'ugly.' He would make me turn in. When he would do a crazy movement, I would be a little embarrassed, and laugh. But Mr. B. would say, 'That's it!, *Do that!*' So I began to understand what he wanted. I became aware of the fact that he wanted to break up the whole body, and that I had to put it back together in interesting ways. What I came to understand was that you weren't going to his classes to feed his ego. You really went there to learn, and you had to *be* there one hundred per cent. Mr. B. has taught me so much. He has made me *look* at choreography—which I had never really done before. Basically, he has made me aware of the fact that I am a dancer."

Martins discussed working with Jerome Robbins:

"Jerry fascinates me. His craftsmanship is amazing. I, for one, love to work with him. It's such a challenge. At one point, Jerry was the only one who kept me going in the company. I had been having my difficulties with Balanchine. But Jerry helped me through those times. I danced in his *In the Night*, and *The Goldberg Variations*. He's extremely professional. He has a wonderful eye. He wants things to look good. I have seen many people fight with Jerry. I've never fought with him, but he certainly drives his dancers."

What does the dance mean to Peter Martins?

"Dancing is something very personal to me. I don't talk about my inner feelings to other people. But I believe that those inner feelings come out when I'm dancing onstage. I don't know, maybe they don't show that much. But somehow, when I'm dancing, everything that's inside of me is expressed. To me, dancing is a total expression of myself. In these last few seasons, I have become aware that I'm not just a ballet dancer. That's become a superficial term to me. I look at dancing differently now. I just see myself as a *dancer*."

At the age of twenty, Peter Martins was married to Lise La Cour, a dancer with the Royal Danish Ballet.

"The marriage didn't work out. We are divorced. We have a six-year-old son. I see him whenever I go to Denmark. I also see my former wife. We still have a very good relationship.

"At the moment, I'm not in love with anyone. To tell you the truth, I don't know what love is. I used to understand love so well. I used to be able to define it. Now, I've forgotten what it is. I have been hurt. I think the more you get hurt, the more you hurt other people. Anyway, I consider my private life as something very serious. Actually, I think I'm too serious. I should be more devil-may-care. But I can't be. I try to compromise, but that just doesn't work out for me. I can't play games. I can't play with other people's feelings.

"I'm very concerned just with dancing. Five years ago, I wanted to be the greatest male dancer in the whole world. I don't want that any more. After all, what is the greatest dancer in the world? Is it the one who can turn most, or who makes the highest leaps, or the one who gets the greatest publicity? There is no such thing as the greatest dancer. All I want now is to give *something* to the public, something that will satisfy *me* and that will satisfy *them*."

KARIN VON AROLDINGEN

On January 17, 1974, Karin von Aroldingen and John Clifford danced the world premiere of George Balanchine's ballet *Variations pour une Porte et un Soupir*, to a score by Pierre Henry. In his seventieth year, Balanchine had composed a work to sound, rather than to music. Henry's score was of the *musique concrète* variety—a taped mélange of sounds in which agonized, torturous breathing alternated with the creaking, squeaking, and scraping of a door. This hugely amplified score served as Balan-

chine's subject matter. Symbol-fraught in every way, the agonized breathing sections were danced by John Clifford, while the ominous door was
danced by Karin von Aroldingen.

The choreography suggested the eternal male-female struggle—in this
case, the female's rapacious, devouring character and the male's resistance
and final capitulation. Given its cliché situation, Balanchine's choreography was as inventive as it was controversial. Clifford gave extraordinary
drama and urgency to his role as victim, while von Aroldingen—imperious, menacing, seductive—performed with icy brilliance. Her role was
abetted by the presence of spectacular costuming by Rouben Ter-
Arutunian, who devised a transparent black skirt which progressively filled
the stage, rising in huge, billowing whorls to create a gigantic, all-encom-
passing silken trap which, at the work's end, ensnared both victim and
aggressor.

Von Aroldingen, in a cruel short black wig out of the Twenties, recalled
the male-destroying female of Jerome Robbins' *The Cage*, although in
Balanchine's hands she became a more impersonal figure, and thus, perhaps, more awesome and terrifying. In *Variations pour une Porte et un
Soupir*, the two dancers never touch. In casting von Aroldingen in this
fierce virtuoso role, Balanchine, as usual, made perfect use of the inherent
personal and balletic characteristics of his chosen dancer.

If von Aroldingen is not, in reality, the male-consuming female of Balanchine's ballet, she nevertheless projects a strikingly imposing image. One
of the tallest and strongest principal dancers of the New York City Ballet,
she is built along Teutonic lines. Her legs are long and muscular; her torso
radiates strength. Her arms flow in sinuous precision. Her face could be
called glamorous, in a high-cheek-boned, deep-eyed, European film-star
way. Her stage presence is at once steely and impassive. She is one of
those dancers people either love or hate. Her admirers adore her singular
and secure technique, her unusual flexibility, her control, her sharp and
precise line. They revel in her majestic aloofness, and applaud her aplomb.
Her detractors find her cold, overly developed, and harsh. They find her
dancing too aggressive and calculating.

The polarity of these viewpoints does not take into account the fact that
Karin von Aroldingen seems to represent the perfect instrument for
George Balanchine's more recent choreography. The dancer's so-called
impersonality serves as a crystal-clear vehicle for Balanchine's eye for
abstract composition and movement. Von Aroldingen's work in the Stravinsky *Violin Concerto*, for example, makes clear her stunning capacity
for the complex gesture, the coiling and convoluted movement. There is
nothing her body cannot do, and do with austere grace and dazzling speed.

Karin von Aroldingen and I talked in her stylish, sun-drenched duplex
apartment on East Ninety-second Street in February 1973. A certain diffi-

dence or shyness became apparent as she greeted me at the door. In person, von Aroldingen does not seem the towering figure she becomes on stage. Like most dancers, her body reflects a tense delicacy. Von Aroldingen wore a floor-length, sleeveless dress bearing Aztec designs. Her brown hair fell to her shoulders. Her eyes are gray-green, her complexion is pure white. We sat near a huge window overlooking a large garden. We were surrounded by abstract paintings, some executed by the dancer.

Karin von Aroldingen was born in Greitz, Germany, in 1941. When Karin was three, her father died. She has two sisters. As a child of nine, she was taken to Berlin, where she began school and ballet lessons. Her principal ballet teacher at the time was Tatiana Gsovska. She remained under her tutelage until the age of seventeen and was then made principal dancer with the Frankfurt Opera Ballet.

"I was a very ambitious student. I remember, when I was ten or eleven years old I fell sick, and I couldn't attend ballet school. I suddenly realized how much I missed going to class. From that moment on, I knew I wanted to be a dancer. Anyway, at seventeen I was engaged by the Frankfurt Ballet and danced in several works choreographed by Tatiana Gsovska. I also danced in Balanchine's *The Seven Deadly Sins*. Lotte Lenya sang in that production. It was Lenya who spoke to Balanchine about me. I had seen his company perform in Berlin. I was very taken with it, and my dream was to be able to come to the States and study at the School of American Ballet.

"I auditioned for Balanchine when he came to stage an opera in Hamburg. He had never seen me perform before. He thought I was terrible. He said he couldn't take me into his company. Well, I never expected to enter his company; I just wanted to study at his school. But a few weeks later, I got a letter from Betty Cage inviting me to join the *corps de ballet*. I was absolutely flabbergasted—and thrilled. I had another year to go at the Frankfurt Ballet, and I had great difficulty in getting out of my contract. The only way I could do it was to say that I was getting married, or that I was going to have a child. And so, I made up a story that I was going to America to get married. Of course, it wasn't true. But, as it happened, I *did* get married in America in 1965—three years after I got here. I married Morton Gewirts. He is in real estate. We have a little girl—Margo. She is six years old."

When Karin von Aroldingen joined the New York City Ballet in 1962, she could not speak a word of English. She had difficulty adjusting to Balanchine's classes, and it would take over a year before she would be able to feel at home and comfortable in the company.

"I had to unlearn everything when I joined the company. Balanchine's technique is very different. You have to be willing to give up what you are accustomed to. I remained in the *corps* for five years, and I was a soloist for five years. I have been a principal for one year. By now, I have danced in most of the repertoire. I am not really suited to the more classical things—like *Symphony in C*. I don't have the ordinary look of a dancer—the small little girl. I'm like a horse . . . I have to run a race."

Von Aroldingen is among the few City Ballet dancers who have developed a personal friendship with George Balanchine.

"Yes, we are friends. We have many things in common—especially a love for food. He taught me so very much about cooking. In fact, I think about food a great deal. Every time I go onstage, my first thought is: what will I have to eat afterward? Of course, we have a tremendous rapport about dancing. It's wonderful working with him, because he's very open. He's like a father. He's very protective. If you have problems, you can talk with him. He's always there.

"I feel very much a part of this company. People say that we all look alike, that we all dance the same way. Well, it's not true. The beauty of our system is that you have a chance to prefer one dancer over another. I think of our company as a big garden with many flowers. Some have less smell or color than others, and one can like one or the other. There is room for everyone. There's hardly any jealousy between us. There is no *one* star. Everyone gets his or her chance. It's up to you to succeed. Balanchine always says, 'It's all up to you!'

"I cannot analyze my dancing for you. I just dance. It's second nature to me. Once you have the technique, and once you can control it, you don't have to think about particular steps. You have learned your lesson. A dancer is like an animal. Animals don't question what they are."

In recent years Karin von Aroldingen has been seen to exuberant advantage in such works as *Firebird, Tchaikovsky Suite No. 3, Serenade, Cortège Hongrois, Liebeslieder Walzer, The Goldberg Variations, Who Cares?, La Sonnàmbula,* and *The Prodigal Son*, among others. Being a wife and mother does not interfere with the dancer's career.

"Balanchine was not in the least bit upset when I got married. As for my husband, he knew what he was getting into when he married a dancer. He accepted this fact, and he would never stop me from dancing. When I became pregnant, I danced until I was in my sixth month. I finished the spring season, then the company went on tour for the summer. I had my baby, and was back for the winter season. It was good timing.

"At first, I felt a little guilty leaving Margo. I don't any more. I feel that if I had stopped dancing just to be a wife and a mother, I would have taken it out on my husband and my child. Everything has worked out for the best. My little girl wants to become a dancer. Of course, I would only send her to the School of American Ballet.

"I have not given any thought to what I will do after I stop dancing. I suppose I will teach. I would impart all my knowledge to my students. A dancer learns from other dancers. I would show; I would not talk much. It is very difficult to talk about the feeling of dance. As soon as you talk about feelings, they're not feelings any more. Actually, dancers shouldn't be that verbal about dancing, because they have nothing to say, really. At least *I* have nothing to say. That's my nature. I don't think about dancing. I dance."

JEAN-PIERRE BONNEFOUS

His face is straight out of Matisse. Just now, he leans back in an easy chair, hugging Archie and Oscar, two Yorkshire terriers. The small dogs are excited over the attention lavished upon them, and soon nestle quietly in their master's lap.

Wearing a brown turtleneck sweater and brown slacks, drenched in a shaft of sunlight, Bonnefous offers the princely image of a *danseur noble*. This image is accented by a small, gold earring worn in his left ear. An aristocratic elegance makes clear Bonnefous's European background. I learned that he was born not far from Lyons in 1943, where his father was a tax official. There is a twin sister—the actress Dominique Arden. Both children were enrolled at the Paris Opera ballet school at the age of eight. When Bonnefous's sister turned seventeen, she discontinued her ballet training in favor of a career in the theater. Jean-Pierre remained with the Paris Opera, ardently pursuing a career in the dance.

"Everything was made easy for me. I never had one single problem about being a dancer. My parents were extremely encouraging. I remember my big moment, when I entered the *corps de ballet*. I was fourteen. All along, the director of the ballet company had been Serge Lifar, and everybody loved him. He was really a very important force in Paris society. He knew everybody. All the dancers were excited about having Lifar as their director. But when I turned sixteen, Lifar left the company—a new regime took over. The new director was Michel Descombey. Anyway, I remained in the *corps de ballet* for six years—which was an unbearably long time. But that was the system. Finally, I became a soloist, and then, only after having taken very difficult examinations which were held on the Paris Opera stage in front of an audience. Luckily, I passed, and remained a soloist for one year.

Then, Michel Descombey began to take an interest in me. He took me to Germany to dance in one of his ballets. It was my first experience dancing outside of Paris. At the Paris Opera, I was given many roles. I remember dancing Balanchine's *Four Temperaments*. Béjart came to do *Damnation of Faust*. I danced the Soul of Faust, which was a beautiful role and very important for me. Roland Petit came, and I later danced in his ballets. It was all marvelous experience. After a year of being a soloist, I was made a principal dancer. Then, a fantastic opportunity came my way. I was invited to dance in Russia. I danced *Giselle* with the Bolshoi, and *Swan Lake* and *Giselle* with the Kirov Ballet. I had success. I loved dancing the classical repertoire. I was intent on becoming a true classical dancer."

Jean-Pierre Bonnefous began to be noticed by the European press, and invitations came from companies all over Europe. One invitation came from America.

"About five years ago, I met a wonderful American man named Christopher Allen. He became a good friend. He was the sort of person who loved doing things for people—and, of course, he was crazy about the ballet. Anyway, Chris Allen thought that it would be interesting to bring a French male dancer to New York. It so happened that André Eglevsky was mounting a series of *pas de deux'*. Chris arranged that I come and do a *pas de deux* with Violette Verdy. Well, I came. Also on the program was Patricia McBride. You see, if it weren't for Chris, I might never have met Pat, nor would I have ultimately joined the New York City Ballet. And so, I came and I danced with Violette, and I met Pat. Then I had to go back to Paris because I was under contract to the Paris Opera. After awhile, another lucky thing happened to me. John Taras, who is a wonderful choreographer and a ballet master with the New York City Ballet company, recommended me to George Balanchine, who was coming to Berlin to stage *Apollo*. Taras thought I would be good as Apollo—which I had already danced at the Paris Opera. That is how I met George Balanchine.

"I worked with Mr. Balanchine on *Apollo* for four days. They were the best four days of my life. It was extraordinary working with this man. Being exposed to Balanchine, I suddenly knew that I wanted to break with the Paris Opera. I asked Balanchine if he would take me into his company in New York. He said that it would be possible only if I were willing to dance in all his repertoire. I agreed right away. That was in 1970. When I arrived in New York, I immediately began taking classes with Mr. B."

Bonnefous did not, in fact, make a complete break with the Paris Opera when he joined the New York City Ballet. To this day, he continues to make guest appearances there, and he is considered one of France's leading dancers. But his home base now is New York, and Bonnefous is among the less than a handful of New York City Ballet dancers whose training has been exclusively European.

"Of course, the adjustment was not easy. I had a difficult time when I began taking Balanchine's classes. I was not really used to his teaching methods. The rhythm of his classes is very different—very fast, very difficult. The *barre* is very short. But, more than that, I had to concentrate on getting closer to the Balanchine style. The first ballet I danced with the company was *Swan Lake*—with Pat McBride. Then I danced *Raymonda Variations*. I did *Tchaikovsky Pas de Deux*. I was supposed to have danced it with Melissa Hayden, but ten minutes before curtain time, she couldn't dance, and so, again, I danced with Pat. Little by little, I began to do more ballets."

Jean-Pierre Bonnefous adds a unique presence to the New York City Ballet. In the mold of a European *danseur noble*, he has assimilated the Balanchine style in ways that are often at pleasurable odds with the expected Balanchine approach.

A powerfully built dancer, Bonnefous's dominant quality is one of fluid lyricism. His arms and hands are particularly expressive, and his line has a princely thrust. He negotiates turns, leaps, and jumps with a *brio* that is exhilarating, and he makes of partnering something that is secure, gracious, and always felt. Perhaps his most salient quality as a dancer is his ability to inject a romantic aura into even the tersest of the Balanchine or Robbins ballets.

"When I entered the company, my aim was to be a really clean dancer. Always, I wanted to strike a perfect classical attitude. This seemed very important to me. I never wanted to leave anything to chance or improvisation. With me, there was never an in-between. Everything had to be just-so. But in the years that I have been with the company, I have changed this point of view. I have tried to get much closer to the music. I think I have become a much more musical dancer, because, when you dance Balanchine, musicality is everything. And so, this has made me freer, looser."

Recently, Bonnefous has created several major roles for the company. He dances important solos and *pas de deux* in Balanchine's *Violin Concerto* and *Cortège Hongrois*. Jerome Robbins has created *An Evening's Waltzes* and *Four Bagatelles* on him, making splendid use of his innate warmth and lyricism. In Stravinsky's *Violin Concerto*, Bonnefous executes a sinuous, beautifully articulated *pas de deux* with Karin von Aroldingen. In it, he lends to Balanchine's so-called abstract choreography a very human, even passionate dimension.

I asked Bonnefous whether entering the company as a principal dancer had caused any hackles to rise among the other male principals.

"Of course, it was difficult for a foreigner coming into the company. I would be taking away roles. It could have been unpleasant. But, as it turned out, I was treated very nicely. Jacques d'Amboise was very friendly, and Eddy Villella said 'Congratulations' and 'Welcome.' Eddy's saying that really made me feel happy. It was important to me.

"I don't see too much of George Balanchine—socially, that is. Occasionally we will have a conversation. He likes to speak French—his French is very good—and so I think he likes to speak French with me. Mr. B. is very accepting of my marriage with Pat. Really, we are like his children. There are no problems there. In fact, at this moment in my life I have pretty much what I want. Of course, I want to continue dancing the classics—and I can do that when I go out and guest. One day, I would like to dance *Giselle* with Pat. But dancing with the New York City Ballet has made me very, very happy. It is a great company. And Mr. Balanchine is a great, great choreographer—and a great man. With him, I have grown as a dancer and as an artist."

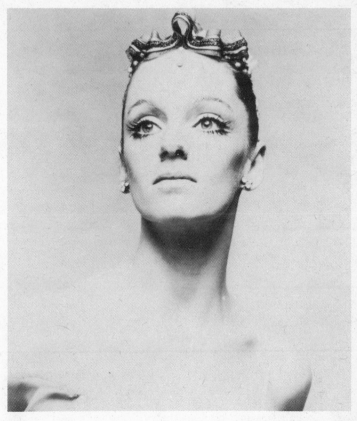

SARA LELAND

Her friends call her Sally. She is a lithe, unusually nimble and fleet dancer, built in the Balanchine mold. Watching Sara Leland in *Liebeslieder Walzer* for example, one is instantly struck by her expressive, windswept, ecstatic movements. Her attack has the singular effect of being at once terse and poetic. As Dulcinea in Balanchine's *Don Quixote* she makes clear her dramatic abilities, her technical precision, and delicate sense of nuance. A delightful *brio* and freshness is seen to equal advantage in such works as Balanchine's *Jewels, Tarantella, Tchaikovsky Suite No.*

3, Concerto Barocco, Ashton's *Illuminations*, and Robbins' *The Concert, Dances at a Gathering, The Goldberg Variations*, and *An Evening's Waltzes*.

When I approached Sara Leland for an interview, she seemed hesitant. For some reason, she did not wish to discuss her close professional association with Jerome Robbins. The dancer has become an expert in Robbins' choreography, and has assisted him in the staging of his ballets for other companies. Finally, however, she agreed to have a talk.

Leland met me at her apartment door with a bright smile and a paint-brush in hand. She was not at work on a canvas but on the woodwork of her newly acquired apartment. Her blond hair was in pigtails. She wore green slacks, a black shirt, and, in bare feet, led me through her large apartment on New York's West End Avenue. She introduced me to her cat. "And this is Gordon. Gloria Govrin gave him to me. He's the greatest company. Forgive the way I look, but I'm painting kitchen cabinets and doors. I've just moved in. I used to have a roommate, but I've decided to live alone. This is a co-op apartment. I asked Mr. Balanchine if he would come and see it. He came on Thanksgiving Day, and brought over some champagne. He thought I had made a good choice. He's very protective of his dancers, you know."

Offstage, Sara Leland does not present the image of sophistication and dramatic elegance apparent in her performances. In person, she has a vivacious prettiness, with eyes full of a sparkling, mischievous gaiety. Like most dancers, she is informal and unpretentious. We sat on a comfortable couch and she talked about her background:

"My father was Leland Harrington—a professional hockey player and coach. He played with the Rhode Island Reds, Montreal Canadiens, and the Boston Bruins. He's in the hockey Hall of Fame. He died some years ago. So, my real name is Sally Harrington. I always thought Sally Harrington was a good name for a dancer, but my ballet teacher, Virginia Williams, thought I should change it to Sara Leland. At that time, I was very malleable. Whatever my teacher said to do, I did.

"I was a very late child. My mother was born in 1905. I was born in 1941, in Melrose, Massachusetts. I have a brother, who's twelve years older than I, and a sister, who's three years older. Neither of them is in the arts. My mother wanted to take ballet lessons when she was a child, but, at the time, it wasn't the proper thing for young ladies to do. Her mother wouldn't let her. So she became a frustrated dancer. She always wanted my sister and me to study ballet. My sister quit when she was about thirteen. I seemed to show a talent for it and continued my lessons. Actually, I never really thought that I wanted to be a dancer. It was certainly not my burning desire. I think dancing was imposed on me. I started when I was five."

Mrs. Harrington, currently one of the directors of the Boston Ballet, encouraged her youngest daughter in her lessons. Sara's teacher, E. Virginia Williams, had started the New England Civic Ballet Company, which is now the Boston Ballet. She, too, encouraged the youngster and paid special heed to her budding gifts. Still, Sara was undecided about making ballet her life. Her high-school work was exceptional, and her father was anxious for her to go to college.

"I really didn't know what to do. I couldn't make up my mind. Anyway, I stayed with Miss Williams until I finished high school. By that time, I had finally decided to become a dancer. For a while, I danced in Miss Williams' New England Civic Ballet. At one point, Robert Joffrey came to teach the company. He saw me, and wanted me to come to New York and dance with him. That was in 1959. Just about then, my father died.

"It's funny, but I think I substituted Mr. Joffrey for my father. Mr. Joffrey pampered me a lot. I wallowed in it. It was the kind of thing that Virginia had also done. I worked like a dog, and I loved it. I would say that the one year I remained with Robert Joffrey was the most valuable year I've spent in my whole career. I think he fixed the things that were wrong. He got me to a point where I became like a Balanchine dancer. If Mr. B. had seen me the year before I went with Joffrey, I doubt he would have liked me. I had been very weak and mannered. Joffrey really concentrated on strengthening me."

Sara Leland entered the Joffrey company at a time when the Robert Joffrey Theatre Ballet had not yet merged with Rebekah Harkness. The company was small and consisted of some ten dancers, including Marie Paquet, Paul Sutherland, Françoise Martinet, Rochelle Zade, and Gerald Arpino. Sara was the youngest member of the company. The group made cross-country tours by bus, and these proved exciting and instructive to the young dancer. They danced three ballets every night, including such works as Joffrey's *Pas des Déesses*, and an abbreviated version of *La Fille Mal Gardée*. Leland danced in these, as well as in Francisco Moncion's ballet *Pastorale*.

During a vacation period, Sara Leland was in Boston visiting with her family and again took some classes with Virginia Williams. Fortunately, George Balanchine was on a cross-country tour in search of scholarship students. The Ford Foundation had made funds available to the School of American Ballet for scholarships.

"Miss Williams called me up and said Balanchine was coming to her class. She asked me to be there. I told her I didn't think Mr. Balanchine would be interested in me. Still, I arrived in class. When Balanchine saw me, he offered me a scholarship. Actually, I didn't *want* a scholarship, because by that time I had already become a professional dancer. I had been dancing for a year with the Joffrey. I didn't want to go back to the classroom. In fact, Virginia Williams also suggested I turn down the scholarship, because she felt that Balanchine would probably take me into his company without the benefit of study at the School of American Ballet. And that's exactly what happened. Three months later, the New York City Ballet called to say they needed a girl. I went right into the company."

Sara Leland entered the New York City Ballet in the summer of 1960: "I was ecstatic. I just couldn't believe it. I hated leaving Mr. Joffrey. It was a real wrench for me. But it was something I just couldn't turn down. I think Mr. Joffrey felt a little sad, because he had put a lot into me. I think he realized, however, that it would be good for me to go to Balanchine. I still have the best relationship with Bob. Anyway, I joined the *corps*, danced in *Symphony in C, Stars and Stripes*, and many other ballets. To begin with, it was shocking to enter such a great big company. Nobody paid much attention to me. It took me about a year and a half to adjust. I didn't want to take Mr. B.'s classes. I didn't like them. It wasn't the kind of class I was used to. I was lonely in the company, because I went into it so suddenly. I didn't know anyone. I was afraid of Mr. B. I was very shy."

After Leland's period of adjustment with the New York City Ballet, she began to fit into it with greater ease. In three years, she was made a soloist. She did solo roles in most of the Balanchine repertoire. She was given special help by John Taras, one of the company's choreographers and ballet masters. Taras created roles for Leland in his *Jeux* and *Ebony Concerto*.

In the spring of 1972, Sara Leland was made a principal dancer: "I had been a soloist for nine years. When I was made a principal, everybody said, 'It's about time!' "

During the Stravinsky Festival, held in the summer of 1972, George Balanchine choreographed *Symphony in Three Movements* for Sara Leland. He had also created a *pas de trois* for her in the Emeralds section of *Jewels*, and a solo in *PAMTGG*. Leland talked about her life in the company:

"I have attained a certain security now. I don't get nervous very much any more. When I dance, it's such a wonderful feeling—it's a fantastic high. When I first did 'Don Q,' I thought I would never get through it. The role is such a responsibility. But in later performances, I really felt I was dancing it well. Now, I just concentrate on it, and it's as if I'm suspended in the middle of time. Of course, 'Don Q' was created for Suzanne Farrell.

"I must confess that I was not sorry to see her go. While she was with us, there was practically nothing left for anyone else to dance. The way Mr. B. felt about her destroyed the morale of the company. It was the lowest it's ever been. I loved Suzanne's dancing. I adored it. From the minute she did her first solo, I felt Mr. B. was right about her. I thought she deserved to be one of the leading dancers in the company. I thought she was fabulous. But it was very, very hard on the rest of us. Mr. B. didn't seem to *see* the rest of us at all. At the time, I was a blossoming soloist, and I needed a lot of help, going into things like *Liebeslieder Walzer*. I needed coaching and rehearsing. But Mr. B. was not interested in anybody except Suzanne.

"Well, I suppose Mr. Balanchine is an incredible romantic. Actually, he's wonderful to all his dancers. I think he likes me a lot. I think the company is fantastically lucky to be headed by somebody like Mr. B. I don't have a rapport with everybody in the company. It's so big. I have my own special friends. Kay Mazzo and I are very close. I share a dressing room with Gelsey Kirkland. But Gelsey is so much younger than I am. She's darling. She's a doll. But with Kay, and also with Karin von Aroldingen, I have a greater rapport because we can talk about things that interest us. Kay and I have the same problems, because we're both single."

What goes through Sara Leland's mind as she dances?

"Well, I think about the first step. When the first step is over, I think about the second step. I think constantly about what I'm going to do next, and how I'm going to do it. Then, certain other things flash through my mind. Is it a good night or a bad night? Am I enjoying what I'm doing or not? You think about your partner. You think about how maybe he should have pushed you a little more forward in this or that pirouette. I suppose the best partner in the company is Conrad Ludlow. He's fantastic. You don't have to do anything. You don't even have to be able to dance, to dance with him. He does it all. All you have to do is stand on your toe, and he does it all. I also like to dance with John Clifford. He's fun.

"John and I are very close friends. We argue all the time. We have discussions about what I call 'digging into dancing.' We talk about what the art means, what we're trying to do . . . what's ethical to do, and what's not ethical. What's artistic, and what's not artistic. John and I always correct each other. He coached me on 'Don Q' when I first did it. He helped me a lot. He gave me some fabulous ideas. He has a very theatrical eye—sometimes, a bit too theatrical. Anyway, we sort of watch out for each other."

Despite her reluctance to speak about Jerome Robbins, Sara Leland did touch on their relationship.

"As a matter of fact, I should put something in here about Jerry. I went through a bad period in dancing for about two years. I had been a soloist for five years, and I didn't seem to be getting anyplace. I felt I didn't look good. I got depressed. I got fat. I didn't take company class. I was very unhappy. Mr. B. didn't give me anything very much to dance. I danced, but I don't know how I did it.

"Then, Jerry came along. Jerry started to choreograph *Dances at a Gathering*. I went to the management and told them that if Jerry needed anybody to fill in, I'd be happy to do so. Jerry didn't know me at all. I knew he wasn't going to use me in *Dances*, but I needed something to do, and he fascinated me. So I started working with him, and he gave me a very hard time, naturally. I didn't look good at all. He would never tell me whether I was going to be in the ballet or not. It really didn't matter. I just wanted to work with him and see how he would affect me. As it turned out, I did get into *Dances*, and, after that, Jerry put me in *The Goldberg Variations*.

"Through Jerry, Mr. Balanchine looked at me again. He took a second look. That's when things started to change for me. I don't think I've ever told Jerry this, but he really did that for me. He took me out of my crisis. I thought I would leave the company. I was terribly unhappy. I would cry before class and after performances. I guess it was a sort of growing-up thing. So it was Jerry who pulled me through. It was after Jerry that I decided that there was nothing I wanted to do more than dance, no matter how hard it was, and no matter how many problems I had. Later, Jerry took me to London, and I helped him on *Dances* when it was done by the Royal Ballet. I was like a liaison between Jerry and the Royal dancers, because Jerry can be very hard and demanding. I sort of relaxed them."

Sara Leland told me something about her private life:

"I suppose I would want to get married one day. The fact is I've had a lot of growing up to do. You see, ballet dancers are a special breed. They are undeveloped in many ways, because they spend all their early years concentrating on one thing. They don't learn anything about life. At least, I didn't. I came to New York when I was seventeen, but it was more like thirteen. I had hardly ever been out with a boy. I never thought about anything outside of dancing. Now, I spend more of my time living. But the company is my home. It's where I belong."

Jack Mitchell

JOHN CLIFFORD

He is the impish zephyr of the New York City Ballet. He darts and dashes across the stage as though propelled by lightning force. In *The Nutcracker*, he has for years been thrilling an army of children who can't quite believe the speed with which he repeatedly jumps through his hoop. Indeed, John Clifford adds wizardry and wit to the art of ballet. His small, intense frame, the electric gleam in his eye, the nervous restless nature of his personality convey unique dynamism.

There is nothing haphazard about Clifford's technique or style. He is superbly trained, and knows what he's about. If he is occasionally accused of "selling it"—of striving for undue attention—more often than not, it is his unbridled energy that prompts the criticism. In point of fact, John Clifford is uniquely equipped to lend *brio* and éclat to the balletic vocabulary.

When Clifford is required to project a more austere or slow-paced statement, he will do so with dignity, although beneath the measured elegance of his movements, a mock-seriousness and a glint of humor invariably shine through. He is too much the open, light-hearted dancer to permit the intrusion of heavy emotionalism.

In the fall of 1973, John Clifford was made a principal dancer of the New York City Ballet. He had joined the company in 1966, entering the *corps*. He was soon given solo roles, and eventually promoted to the rank of soloist. Clifford is one of the few City Ballet dancers who is also a choreographer.

Clifford is intensely verbal. He gave me a nonstop account of his peripatetic beginnings and ultimate arrival on the New York ballet scene.

"I'm a Gemini—June 12. I was born in 1947, in Hollywood. I went to Hollywood High. My family was in the theater. My mother was one of the lead singers in Earl Carroll's *Vanities*. She used to sing light opera. Hers was a 'class' act. My father was part of an acrobatic team—Park and Clifford. I was in their act when I was five. I didn't do anything tricky, really—a few headstands—things like that. But I always knew I was going to go into the theater—musical comedy, I thought.

"I didn't start dancing lessons until I was eleven. My parents were divorced. My mother has had a few other husbands—I'm proud of her. Anyway, my first teacher was Katherine Etienne. When I first went to her, I thought I was learning classical ballet. Actually, what I was learning was a strange mixture of ballet and Isadora Duncan. Miss Etienne was a very dizzy lady. She used to come into class in full make-up and regalia. She was fun. Immediately, she put me out onstage. She did a lot of little concerts. It was very good for me. It got me over the stage-fright period."

At the age of fourteen Clifford began to do television work. His mother was then married to an actor, who introduced John to his agent. There were appearances on the *Donna Reed Show, Death Valley Days*, and the *Dinah Shore Show*.

"All that running around, and all that performing could have gone to my head. Luckily, it didn't. People didn't rave about what I was doing—which is a good thing. Anyway, there I was, doing TV shows and getting a lot of good experience. Of course, I didn't get to do much schoolwork. I never got to school before noon. I just couldn't get up in the morning. My schooling was very haphazard."

All the while, Clifford took classes from Katherine Etienne. He next went to Carmelita Maracci, one of the best ballet teachers on the West Coast. He had not, in fact, decided to become a ballet dancer. He adored tap, could sing and act. At one point, he went to study at Eugene Loring's American School of Dance in Los Angeles, on scholarship.

"My scholarship included having to wash the bathrooms. Loring was very strict. Also, I wouldn't call him fair. But he probably thought I needed the discipline. So, I was there, washing the johns, taking class, and really messing up my schoolwork. I stayed for nine months. But I became irresponsible. I was doing too many things—running around like crazy. Mr. Loring finally took me off scholarship, because I was missing classes. I quit the Loring school. The best thing that happened to me there was working with June Morse. She taught me to move fast, to turn fast. She was fabulous.

"I next went to David Lichine's school—I had studied there a few times before. My teacher there was Irina Kosmovska. Just about that time, Mr. Balanchine had a big bash in L.A. with the Ballet of Los Angeles. Allegra Kent came, and Maria Tallchief, and they did *Swan Lake*, then *Firebird*, with the Los Angeles dancers as *corps de ballet*. When Balanchine left, he put Kosmovska in charge of teaching company classes. She allowed me to take them. They were impossibly difficult—two and a half hours each. But they turned me on, and I began to study a little more seriously. Irina was encouraging. She also encouraged me to choreograph. Of course, that finished me for high school. I never got my diploma."

John Clifford, by now eighteen, had had enough training to convince him that he *could* become a ballet dancer. But he saw no future for himself with the Los Angeles Ballet. He came to New York City, having made some money dancing on the *Danny Kaye Show* in Los Angeles. He had read in *Dance Magazine* that two of the best ballet teachers in New York were Hector Zaraspe and Valentina Pareyaslavec. He took classes with both these teachers. He also applied, and received a scholarship to the School of American Ballet. At the school, he took classes with Pierre Vladimirov, André Eglevsky, Stanley Williams, and Antonina Tumkovsky.

"My favorite teacher at the School of American Ballet was Antonina Tumkovsky. She was the most demanding, the toughest, the strongest of all my teachers. She was the best."

It was now the winter of 1966. Clifford remained at the American Ballet School for some four months. His money had run out. More importantly, he was not given a chance to perform. He decided to return to Los Angeles, and continued his ballet studies with Irina Kosmovska. He also resumed dancing on the *Danny Kaye Show*.

Fate now intervened in the form of the great Soviet ballerina Maya Plisetskaya. The Bolshoi Ballet had come to perform in Los Angeles. John was allowed to take company classes, one of which was taught by Plisetskaya. She singled out the young American dancer, and often kept him after class, working with him on jumps and *chaînés*. She instilled confidence in him and proved an inspiring teacher.

As it happened, Anton Dolin had also made a visit to Los Angeles, mounting his *Variations for Four* for the Western Ballet. Dolin met John Clifford during a Plisetskaya class. He observed and admired the dancer's unusual technical facility, and offered to write letters of recommendation to Lucia Chase of American Ballet Theatre, as well as to Robert Joffrey, suggesting that Clifford be hired.

Clifford returned to New York. Both the Joffrey and the American Ballet Theatre seemed interested in him. In fact, his dream was to enter the New York City Ballet. He went to see Barbara Horgan, George Balanchine's personal assistant, and told her of his wish to join the company. A few days later, he was called and told that he could continue his work at the School of American Ballet on scholarship. He would also be given more money. There was no mention, however, of his joining the company. Balanchine wanted Clifford to develop as dancer and choreographer. Young dancers were made available to him, and he soon began to compose ballets in workshop.

"I did lots and lots of ballets at the school. I just whipped them out. I also continued taking classes. One day, Balanchine said he wanted me to do Hoops in *Nutcracker*. I still wasn't in the company. So I did Hoops. Within a week, I joined the *corps* of the New York City Ballet."

As a member of the *corps*, John Clifford began to learn the large Balanchine repertoire. He was asked to understudy any number of solo roles. Soon, he was dancing them. The *New York Times* dance critic Clive Barnes began to notice John Clifford, and wrote favorably about him in his reviews. In the meantime, Clifford continued to choreograph. He created *Stravinsky: Symphony in C* in 1968, and *Fantasies*, to music of Ralph Vaughan Williams in 1969. Both these works entered the City Ballet's repertoire.

By 1969, John Clifford had been made a soloist. He also began work on a new ballet. He had found Leonard Bernstein's "Prelude, Fugues, and Riffs," and decided to use this music for a work in which he would dance with Allegra Kent. It was at this moment also that Jerome Robbins returned to the New York City Ballet. The choreographer was invited by George Balanchine to mount a new work for the company. This became *Dances at a Gathering*. Robbins asked John Clifford to be in the cast of *Dances*. The dancer was delighted, although he realized that his rehearsals with Robbins would conflict with his own work on *Prelude, Fugues, and Riffs*.

"Well, that whole episode was too much! Ever since I was fifteen years old, I put Jerry Robbins on a pedestal. I had seen *West Side Story*, and at the time, that sort of intense, dramatic side of choreography was very impressive to me. When I came to New York and entered the company, I only liked Jerry's ballets. I was crazy about *Faun*, and screamed about the greatness of *Cage*. In those days, I didn't really care that much for Mr. Balanchine's ballets. Of course, that's all changed now. I think Balanchine is a genius.

"Anyway, when Jerry came to do *Dances*, I had him on this pedestal. When he started to choreograph, we worked beautifully together. Jerry has these periods when he's really into somebody. I was the lucky one, for about two months. Everything I did was perfect. He would let me rehearse some of his stuff—I was like his assistant. I knew everybody's part in *Dances at a Gathering*. Jerry would say, 'John, Eddy Villela isn't here. Would you do that?' Or, 'Tony Blum isn't here. Would you do that?' Actually, Jerry choreographed almost all of Eddy's things on me.

"It was hard work, but I didn't mind it. We all worked hard. He had just come back, and we wanted to please him. Mind you, I didn't know Jerry from Adam—I just loved his choreography. Then, the disenchantment set in. He got so intense in rehearsals that he didn't think of people as people. Well, I got affected. Almost everybody got affected. There were bad vibrations. At one point, Jerry got this thing in his head that I was getting upset because I wanted to do Eddy's part. It wasn't so. It was clear from the beginning, that I was just filling in for Eddy, and I had my own part. Anyway, it was getting near the premiere of *Dances*. Jerry became more and more tense.

"In the meantime, I was trying to finish my own ballet, *Prelude, Fugues, and Riffs*. *Dances at a Gathering* would have its premiere about two weeks after my own ballet. Then we got word that the company was staging a benefit, and that both our ballets would be on the program. The Gala Benefit Preview took place on May 8, 1969. The actual premiere of my ballet would be on May 15, and Jerry's premiere would be May 22. It so happened that Allegra Kent was in my ballet and in Jerry's. Of course, Allegra had rehearsed my ballet for weeks, and she loved doing it. Well, came the benefit, and Jerry wanted Allegra to dance only in his ballet, and not in mine. I got hysterical. But Jerry had his way. I danced in my ballet with Linda Merrill. I was very angry. Mr. Balanchine kept telling me, 'You're young. You can be flexible. Don't worry.' But I was very hurt. I guess those are the breaks."

John Clifford turned to some thoughts on his own dancing.

"There are two things about me in performance. One is good; the other is bad. I'm at my best, as a dancer, when I'm not really thinking. By that I mean, when I'm just in total control of my body, and am unaware of myself as 'performing.' For example, when I do Balanchine's *Valse Fantaisie*, I just hear the music, and the body almost unconsciously does the rest. The bad things have to do with my being too conscious of what I'm doing. When I do Mr. B.'s *Four Temperaments*—I do the Melancholic section—I sometimes think I'm doing an act. That's bad. Also, I'm very applause-oriented. A lot of people think I'm very tacky and Hollywood for being that way. But even if everybody in the audience were mongoloid, my aim would be to make them happy, to move them, somehow. Plisetskaya did that to *me*, and that's what I want to do to an audience."

John Clifford has become an important and valuable member of the New York City Ballet. His performances in such works as Balanchine's *Stars and Stripes, Brahms-Schönberg Quartet, Danses Concertantes, Symphony in Three Movements*, among others, and Jerome Robbins' *Dances at a Gathering, The Goldberg Variations*, and *An Evening's Waltzes* prove consistently exciting. In January 1974, George Balanchine created a new ballet, composed for John Clifford and Karin von Aroldingen—*Variations pour une Porte et un Soupir* to music of Pierre Henry.

Clifford has choreographed several works for the company. After his *Prelude, Fugues, and Riffs* of 1969, he composed *Reveries* to music of Tchaikovsky. In 1971 came his *Kodaly Dances*, and in 1972, *Symphony in E Flat*, to Stravinsky, which was given its premiere during the New York City Ballet's one-week Stravinsky Festival. He has not recently choreographed for the company.

Does John Clifford have a life away from the dance?

"I'm a loner. Not by choice. But my life is really in the company. I'm there all the time. It's safe. When things go wrong at the theater, it upsets me more than anything. As for personal relationships . . . I don't seem to trust many people. It's probably my background—my parents . . . I've never had a commitment to anybody. I've never lived with anybody. Well, I've had roommates, occasionally. But I've never had a permanent attachment. I would like to have one. It's lonely. I mean, it would be nice to come home to somebody, especially if you've given a good performance. I keep thinking I don't need anyone, because I've got the company. But when I've really given a good performance, and made a lot of people happy, it feels awful traipsing home alone . . . that's when I start feeling sorry for myself."

It came as a great surprise to all followers of the New York City Ballet when, following the spring 1974 season, John Clifford announced his departure from the company. He returned to this native Los Angeles to assume the responsibilities of Artistic Director of the newly founded Los Angeles Ballet Theatre. His continued loyalty to his "parent" company was demonstrated, however, when he appeared with the New York City Ballet during its Los Angeles season in the summer of 1974.

Richard Lescsak

CAROL SUMNER

Carol Sumner, one of the most vivacious, endearing and enduring dancers of the New York City Ballet, has been a member of that company for some fourteen years. Her rank is that of soloist. Unlike some of her contemporaries in the company, she has not as yet been made a principal dancer. She may be said to represent that special phenomenon in the dance world: the dancer who continues to dance because she must, and not because the ephemeral rewards of stardom are just around the corner.

As dancer, Sumner offers innumerable pleasures. She has an exquisite body, she is light, fast, has a beautiful extension, moves with extreme grace, and is lovely to look at. Her appearances in such works as *Western Symphony, Illuminations, La Source, Concerto Barocco, The Nutcracker, Stars and Stripes,* among many others, invariably insures zestful, often enchanting performances. She has a particular poignancy onstage. It is something in her look. As she dances, her face assumes an expression of gaiety, sweetness, and intoxicating surprise. One senses her own delight with the dance—and this delight instantly translates into an innocent and guileless desire to please.

Carol Sumner lives alone in a small apartment in New York's West Fifties. This is where we met. Over a drink, I learned that she was born in Brooklyn, New York, in 1940.

"I'm just a plain ordinary Brooklyn girl. I'm an only child. *Because* I'm an only child, I've always had animals around."

As if on cue, two friendly cats made their presence known. One jumped on my lap, the other on Miss Sumner's.

"As a little girl, I was so inhibited and shy that when anybody would say hello to me, I'd run to my mother, scared to death. I was really a mess. My mother thought that when I reached school-age, things would get better. Not at all. They got worse. I never opened my mouth in class. I never raised my hand. When the teacher called on me, even though I knew the answer, I'd stand up and shake my head, saying nothing. Finally, some neighbors of ours suggested that I be sent to ballet school. It might rid me of my shyness."

Carol was thirteen years old when she began ballet lessons. She traveled to Manhattan to study with a teacher named Eileen O'Connor. The ballet school happened to be on the same block as the stage entrance of the New York City Center—West Fifty-sixth Street.

"I kept seeing all these people from the New York City Ballet. I was just fascinated by their comings and goings. I remember seeing Nicky Magallanes, and developed a tremendous crush on him. When I was four-teen, my mother took me to a performance by the company. I remember *Western Symphony.* I thought, My God! How terrific! My inhibitions were getting better. I loved working with Miss O'Connor. She encouraged me: she told me I had a very good chance of becoming a dancer. And I was so grateful, because, at last, I had found something in my life to which I was suited. One day I went to audition at the School of American Ballet—they accepted me."

Sumner studied at the School for three years. Her teachers included Anatole Oboukhov and Pierre Vladimirov, Antonina Tumkovsky, Muriel Stuart, and Hélène Dudin. At the age of seventeen, she was taken on as an apprentice with the New York City Ballet.

"I think it may have been a little too soon for me to enter the company. You see, I began fairly late. It would have been different if I had begun my studies at the age of eight, and not at thirteen. It was a big rush thing for me. I was not as strong as everybody thought I was. I did almost everything on will power, with very little technique. I did it because I wanted to dance. Finally, I began to build some muscle strength. I began taking Mr. Balanchine's classes.

"For years and years, I couldn't do a thing in Mr. B.'s class. When I couldn't do something, I used to get upset and go hang on the side of the *barre*. I wouldn't even try. I'm sure Mr. B. thought I was disagreeing with what he was saying to us. But it wasn't that. I was simply incapable of doing what he wanted. I had no power at all. Finally, after several years, I pulled myself together and got to be strong. Mr. B. has tremendous patience. Once you realize this, you get more relaxed in his classes."

Like most young dancers first encountering George Balanchine, Carol Sumner was in total awe of him. She thought of him as a god, and found great difficulty in even saying Hello to him. As time went on, however, the dancer and Mr. B. developed a friendship.

"I became much more secure in my dancing, and I could express an opinion about it, whether he thought it right or wrong. Anyway, I was able to converse with Mr. B. on this level. Gradually, we became friends on a social level. We talked about life in general—about philosophy. Because I became more relaxed with him, I think, I began to dance better. I began to understand him more in class.

"Mr. Balanchine, by the way, is not in the least bit temperamental. If he is temperamental, he shows it in such a subtle way that it's almost frightening. He will not scream at you. But he will give you the feeling that you're making your own bed, so go lie in it. That kind of thing."

From the vantage point of fourteen years, Miss Sumner is in an eminent position to discuss the development of a company that has almost consistently been called cold, mechanical, and remote by its detractors.

"Well, of course, that's total nonsense. First of all, Balanchine is a Russian, and Russians have lots of personality. They're very warm. They have lots of heart and lots of feeling. They love to suffer, and they love to be melodramatic. You have only to see George Balanchine dance to know he is filled with feeling and with soul. Now, obviously, that's what he wants from his dancers.

"But Balanchine is very canny. He doesn't tell his dancers to dance with soul, because they'll suddenly be pretending to have soul, and that's not what he wants. What it boils down to is: Mr. Balanchine doesn't want you to pretend to be a dancer but to *be* one. A subtle point to be made is that Mr. Balanchine would rather see a dancer just use her technique, rather than *pretend* she has soul. If she has it, it will show."

We turned to Miss Sumner's present status as a soloist.

"Yes, I've been a soloist for years. I would love to be a principal . . . I would love it. Naturally, it's what every ballet dancer works for. But I don't want to think about being a principal, because that only defeats you. The only thing you can do is, when you are given a principal role to dance—and I am given principal roles—be a principal *then*. Look, if Balanchine were to make me a principal, and give me things that I would not be good in, it would just mean that I'd be a principal, and not a very good one. Being a soloist and being given principal roles I can do well are much more important, certainly from an audience's point of view."

In a wistful mood, Carol Sumner described her life as a dancer:

"I don't have that many close friends in the company right now. Gloria Govrin is a good friend—we share a dressing room together. But my dearest friends in the company were Richard Rapp and Nicholas Magallanes. Neither of them is in the company any more. Richard Rapp is now on the faculty of the School of American Ballet. Nicky has retired. Anyway, it was Richard and Nicky who taught me how to be happy in a ballet company. You know, being a dancer is not an easy life. There are all sorts of depressions you fall into. Whatever you do, it never seems to be good enough. It's such an irregular, imperfect art. It's a big strain, and it's a twenty-four-hour-a-day job. It's not something you forget about when you go home. It's a very constricted world. You really have to *work* at meeting other people. It's good for you to talk about something other than ballet once in a while. And yet, you *have* to talk about ballet, because in that way you can analyze, think about, and improve your dancing.

"Of course, I've gotten up-tight in the company—over situations. I mean, you've wanted to dance something for years, and someone else gets to do it. You can drive yourself crazy that way. The best thing to do is to realize it's not all that important. It may be important at the moment, but in the long run it doesn't matter that much—eventually something good will come to *you*. That picks you up.

"I never made it into *Dances at a Gathering*. I have understudied for Jerry's ballets, but I have never been in them—at least, not the new ones. Way back, I was in his *Interplay* and *Fanfare*. Of course, I get to dance in many of Mr. B.'s ballets. I dance Sacred Love in Ashton's *Illuminations*, which I love very much. And I'm thrilled to dance Mr. B.'s *Concerto Barocco* and *Western Symphony*. I really dance in lots and lots of ballets. During the Stravinsky Festival, Mr. B. choreographed a beautiful variation for me in *Le Baiser de la Fée*, and I dance in *Danses Concertantes* and *Divertimento No. 15*.

Carol Sumner was willing to discuss some of the more personal aspects of the ballet world:

"Most of the girls studying ballet are very attractive. I'm sure they have men chasing them all the time. I know they often get tired of this. I do. I get tired of it. For that reason, it is very pleasant to spend time with men who don't want anything from you. Of course, if you want something from *them*, it's too bad. Then you suffer. But I think most of us girls in the ballet world are so well adjusted to the gay scene that we know when not to overstep our boundaries. We are able to accept Platonic relationships. For myself, I couldn't ask for better friends. They really care about me— and I care about them. They offer true companionship, which is something I have never been able to achieve with a straight man. I mean, I'll go out with straight guys, we'll spend a pleasant evening, we'll have a pleasant conversation, and you think it's going to be just *that*. Then, suddenly, they want to force themselves on you. It can be dreadful.

"It sounds as though I'm against men. I'm not. Actually, I'm in love right now, but it's a torturous situation—which has been the story of my life. I always fall in love with the wrong people. Maybe my problem is that I'm always giving advice to the people I love. That's not what they want. I tend to be too outspoken about my feelings. People are afraid to listen to people who come right out and show their feelings. Well, I jump right in, with both feet. Most of the time, I wind up getting burned. Actually, I have never wanted to get married. It was never important to me. It still is not important. What I want is to be with someone I love—someone I can rely on."

Many ballet dancers regret the fact that their careers have deprived them of a complete formal education. Indeed, it is rare to meet a dancer who has attended college. Carol Sumner, in her forthright way, has no such regrets:

"Did I miss not having gone to college? Heavens, no! I *hated* school. I couldn't wait to get out of school so that I could just dance. My father wanted me to go to college, but I got into the company in the nick of time. If I had taken a course in philosophy, I don't think I would have learned more about life than what I have learned just being a member of the New York City Ballet."

Carol Sumner summed up her feelings about her own dancing:

"In the beginning, the only thing that went through my mind was, Am I good enough? Am I going to make it? Will Mr. Balanchine give me another part? I kept remembering what Mr. B. asked us to do in class. I did this on the stage. I kept wondering, Will he notice? Or, Do I look pretty? Am I doing my best? All this went through my mind when I first began dancing with the company.

"Recently, I have changed. What goes through my mind now is, You're going to go out there, and you're going to make the audience happy. You're going to make the audience like you. They've paid their money, and no matter how you feel or how nervous you may be, you have to give them a performance. Going out with that attitude, you suddenly find that you're enjoying yourself tremendously. You find there's nothing to be afraid of. You find you've been wanting to do this all your life, and you're doing it! So you must enjoy yourself.

"Of course, I get nervous. I have nerves, all right. But when the chips are down, I'm always completely calm. I think it's the way I would face death. I think I would think about a death for a long time, ponder over it, be depressed about it, and finally, reconcile myself to it. That's how I feel about a performance. I'm nervous and I can't sleep for a week before dancing *Illuminations*. It's a nerve-racking part. But when the time comes, you just go out there, because there's nothing you can do about it. Whatever happens, happens.

"For me, dancing has never been a torture. In fact, I love it more and more. The longer I dance, the more I love it. In all these years of dancing, I have developed more control over my body and my mind. In short, I've learned how to be a professional."

Martha Swope

MELISSA HAYDEN

In May 1973, Melissa Hayden announced her retirement from the New York City Ballet. The city and her company honored her with awards and festivities. She had served them both royally, giving some twenty-three years of her life to the City Ballet, and bringing pleasure to countless audiences who, for an equal amount of years, were exhilarated by her performances. As a member of a company that does not believe in the star system, Melissa Hayden achieved total stardom.

On the evening of May 16, the New York City Ballet staged a Gala for Milly (as her friends call her)—a gala that, while also benefiting the company's production fund, served primarily to pay homage to the dancer. The occasion proved singularly touching. George Balanchine had created a new ballet for her, *Cortège Hongrois*, and Mayor John Lindsay presented the ballerina the Handel Medallion, the City's highest cultural award.

The New York State Theater was filled to capacity that night, and when Miss Hayden appeared in front of the gold curtain to accept her award, she received a standing ovation. "It's the most exciting night for me, to be honored by the city I love, and for the dancing I love," she said, visibly moved.

When the ballerina reappeared to perform in *Cortège Hongrois*—a somewhat kitschy romp in the style of Petipa to music from *Raymonda* by Glazunov—Hayden once again demonstrated the wide range of her artistry. At fifty, she seemed in her prime.

As she danced, the years fell away, and a rush of images telescoped her career. One recalled Hayden, crisp and cocky, in Balanchine's *Stars and Stripes*, staccato-perfect in his *Concerto Barocco, Symphony in C, Serenade*, poetic in his *A Midsummer Night's Dream*, and audaciously delicious in his *Scotch Symphony* and *Allegro Brillante*. One remembered her as the sexy and seductive Profane Love in Ashton's *Illuminations*, dangerous and cruel in Robbins' *The Cage*, and romantically abandoned in his *In the Night*. Melissa Hayden, with her secure technique and wonderful bravura, would leave in glory, fixed in the memory of her countless admirers.

Several months prior to the gala, I visited Melissa Hayden in her large apartment on Central Park West. She lives there with her husband, Donald Coleman, and her daughter, Jennifer, age eleven. Their son Stuart, age eighteen, was away from home. At the time, the dancer had already made her decision to retire from the New York City Ballet, and, as we talked, a note of wistfulness entered her conversation:

"Look, I consider myself an ancient lady in our company. It's a youth-oriented company, and I happen to be one of the charter members. I'm the only female left, of that beginning. Hundreds of dancers have passed through the New York City Ballet in the time I have been with it. When my contemporaries began to leave, I felt very alone, and very sad. Each time one of them departed, a part of me was departing as well. It was the strangest sensation. I'm not sentimental at all—I hate sentiment—but when that began to happen, something was lost, for me. In a way, I've outlived them all. Now, it's time to go."

We were talking in Miss Hayden's large living room, with its wall of books and many objects and paintings collected throughout the years. Hayden had brought us some Scotch. She sat curled up on a couch, look-

ing young and beautiful in a pair of boy's corduroy jeans and a turtleneck
sweater.

Melissa Hayden's career has been well documented. She was born Mildred Herman, April 25, 1923, in Toronto, Canada. She began her ballet
training at the age of twelve under Boris Volkov. At seventeen, she came
to New York and studied with Anatole Vilzak and Ludmilla Shollar. To
support herself, she obtained a job in the *corps de ballet* of Radio City
Music Hall. In 1945, she joined Ballet Theatre, and nine months later,
became a soloist. When, in 1948, Ballet Theatre discontinued operations
for one season, she joined Ballet Alicia Alonso. Hayden toured Central
and South America with the Alonso company, and, after one year, received an invitation from George Balanchine to come and join his newly
formed New York City Ballet. The year was 1950.

With humor, and a touch of nostalgia, Miss Hayden recalled those early
years.

"Back in Toronto, my parents were not given to exposing their children
to the arts. But my two sisters and I managed to fall in love with the arts
anyway. I was very responsive to music, and I studied piano for eight
years. At that time, one didn't see that many ballet companies. However, I
remember the arrival in Toronto of the Ballet Russe de Monte Carlo. That
was a thrill. Another time, Ballet Theatre came. Mostly, however, my
mother took us to see lots of vaudeville shows. They gave me my first taste
for the theater.

"As a youngster, I was something of a loner. I didn't make friends too
easily. My nose was always stuck in some book or other. I got tremendously emotional about reading. I would read, and I would cry. Along
with that, I was always very physically active, and belonged on the swim-
ming team at school. Then, when I turned twelve, came the ballet lessons.

"When I got to New York, I had to find a job to pay for my lessons with
Vilzak and Shollar. I landed one at Radio City Music Hall. Actually, I
only stayed there for five months. Then I got into Ballet Theatre. I was put
in the *corps*, and I was scared stiff. Suddenly, I was on the stage with
Alicia Markova, Anton Dolin, Alicia Alonso, Paul Petroff, Nana Gollner,
Hugh Laing. There was Antony Tudor, who directed the company at the
time, and, of course, Lucia Chase. It was Tudor, by the way, who told me
to change my name. He said, 'You'll never become a great dancer with a
name like Mildred Herman.' I said, 'Okay. Come up with something.' He
came up with Melissa Hayden—and that was it.

"Right away, I was given solo roles. I did the Little Bird in *Peter and
the Wolf*, which had been danced by Alonso and Nora Kaye. Then I was
one of the four little swans in *Swan Lake*. Of course, I was a very green
kid. And, I want to tell you, I never met so many dancers with so many
problems. I mean, it was the pit of neurosis. I was always a by-stander.

Everybody thought I was much more experienced than I actually was. They thought that because I always kept my mouth shut. I looked like the little girl who knew *so* much. Anyway, the two and a half years with Ballet Theatre was my growing-up period."

Just before Ballet Theatre temporarily suspended operation in 1948, Melissa Hayden had occasion to work with George Balanchine. He had come to the company to mount his *Theme and Variations*.

"I loved those moments spent in rehearsal with Mr. B. I felt that creative force as he worked with us. I had by that time worked with other choreographers. But I was terribly attracted to the uniqueness of this man. And, I liked the feeling I got from the kind of movements he gave. There were an awful lot of steps to the music, which was something quite new. So, from the very beginning, I sensed Balanchine's energy and force.

"While I was dancing in Alicia's company, Nicky Magallanes came to join us. He had come from New York, and he told me that Balanchine was forming a new company and needed dancers. I was intrigued, but I didn't think I'd want to join. I mean, Ballet Theatre was reopening, and my allegiance was to it. Anyway, Nicky left Alicia's company, because he had decided to join the New York City Ballet. I kept thinking of what Nicky told me, and just to test him, wrote him a letter asking if Balanchine still needed dancers. Almost immediately, I received a telegram from Balanchine himself, asking me to join the company.

"I was in Buenos Aires at the time, and when I got Mr. B.'s telegram—he'd arranged for a plane ticket—I flew straight to New York. Of course, the first thing I did was to go and see Lucia Chase at Ballet Theatre. She wanted me back in the company. I said, 'What have you got to offer me?' She told me. I thanked her, and walked out. I went to see Balanchine, and told him about my conversation with Lucia Chase. He asked me if I wanted to stay with him. I said yes. I didn't know what was in store for me. It was a new company. I just started from scratch, on this marvelous adventure."

Melissa Hayden joined the ranks of the New York City Ballet in the fall of 1950. Dancers in the company at that time included Maria Tallchief, Tanaquil LeClercq, Diana Adams, Janet Reed, Nora Kaye, Jerome Robbins, Herbert Bliss, Francisco Moncion, Todd Bolender, William Dollar, and Harold Lang. In that year, Hayden appeared in William Dollar's *The Duel*, Robbins' *The Age of Anxiety*, Ashton's *Illuminations*, Cranko's *The Witch*.

"I danced in ballets by all these choreographers, who seemed to love my dancing. They created all these roles on me. The only one who *didn't* create roles for me was Mr. Balanchine. I would dance in his ballets, but only after, say, Maria Tallchief. She would teach me the steps. I was learning the Balanchine repertoire from other dancers. I only worked with Balanchine himself at rehearsals. Naturally, I kept wondering about Mr. B. not creating anything on me. He kept telling everyone that I could do anything. Well, by 1953, I still wasn't creating Balanchine roles, and I got into a snit. In the meantime, new dancers were coming in. I was frustrated; I felt threatened. I mean, I didn't feel my position was threatened. I had no position. I was just a dancer—I was a soloist, as we were all called in those years. But I wanted to dance every night. I wanted to be in everything. I began questioning the artistic direction of the company. I asked a lot of questions, but I got no answers. And so, I left the New York City Ballet in a temper tantrum."

Hayden returned to Ballet Theatre. She remained with the company until 1954. While with them, she met and married Donald Coleman.

"The way I met my husband was a real fairy tale. I had heard about him while I was still in the New York City Ballet. At the time, Donald was a lawyer. He was very attracted to dancers. He would meet a lot of dancers in different companies and take them out. I remember going into the *corps* room of the City Ballet and hearing the girls talk about this man. One day, I got to be the lucky one. He called me and asked me for a date. I said, 'No, thank you. You've taken out every *corps de ballet* dancer of this company, and I don't want to go out with you.'

"When I left the company, he was after me again. I remember, sitting in a restaurant with friends. He appeared and just sat down with us. It was the first time I had actually seen this guy. Again, he asked me to go out with him, and this time I did. Then I flew to London with Ballet Theatre. When I returned from the tour, there was Don to meet me at the airport. I was very flattered. All along, he had been telling me how dissatisfied he was being a lawyer. Well, the next thing I knew, he had talked himself into being an assistant manager with Ballet Theatre, and he went on tour with us. Don and I became engaged. Our engagement lasted five days. On the sixth day we got married, and I immediately became pregnant. That was nineteen years ago.

"While I was waiting for my baby to be born, I went to have a chat with Lucia Chase. I told her that, as much as I loved Ballet Theatre, it really wasn't the company for me. I knew by then that I was committed to Balanchine. Lucia was very understanding. Soon after my son was born, I called the New York City Ballet office, and told them that I would like very much to come back. They thought about it for a few weeks, and allowed me to return. I thought it was very gracious of Mr. Balanchine to take me back, although I can't say that my codancers were all that pleased when I reappeared."

In 1955, George Balanchine choreographed *Pas de Trois (II)* for Hayden, Patricia Wilde, and André Eglevsky. In subsequent years, he created roles for her in *Divertimento No. 15, Agon, Stars and Stripes, Episodes* (II), *The Figure in the Carpet, Liebeslieder Walzer, A Midsummer Night's Dream*, among others.

Although Hayden's presence in these works made clear her special affinity for the Balanchine style, she did not, in effect, serve as Balanchine's ideal instrument.

"In all the years that I've been with the New York City Ballet, Mr. B. has choreographed very little for me. You see, the final attraction for him is to mold a dancer. I was not molded by him. But I am extremely grateful for what he did for me. What's so wonderful is that when he uses you, he's giving you a gift. You treasure that for life. My position with the company was somehow based on the fact that I was in on its beginnings. I was in on the pioneering spirit, on the blind forceful energy of its early formation. I danced ballets that were entirely new to me. It was another kind of dancing. I always leaned toward the more dramatic ballets, where my imagination could come into play. When I came into this company, I realized that I didn't have to use imagination to cover up for the steps. I just had to use the body. My mind worked in relation to the music. The movements I was asked to do contain enough drama for me not to have to add anything— you know, in a 'mugging' sense.

"I'm grateful for all those early, poverty-stricken years with the company. There was always a kind of desperation then, because we didn't have big financial backing. No one knew from one season to the next where the money would come from. Many of our ballets had to be danced in leotards and tights because there was no money for costumes. Of course, today, many of our ballets have no costumes. But that is because Balanchine realized the beauty of seeing full movement without the distraction of costuming.

"As for my personal relationship with Mr. B., I can only say that we have communicated very little. It was like that from the beginning. Somehow, I always seemed to say the wrong thing to him. I never got a straight answer. He never answered me directly. Until recently, I was always disappointed, or rejected, or negated.

"To tell you the truth, I've always felt that Balanchine never understood the English language and its subtleties. I don't think he understands English as English. I really reel that he thinks in Russian—that he translates the English that he hears into Russian—and then retranslates it into English. A lot can get lost that way. Anyway, I've never got a direct answer from George Balanchine—about anything. Perhaps it's his personality. Perhaps it's mine. I'm a very outspoken, very direct person. Well . . . who knows?"

Hayden related that things changed for her when the New York City Ballet moved from its old home at City Center to its elegant new quarters at the New York State Theater in 1964.

"The move was very dramatic for us all. Suddenly, from a caterpillar, the company turned into a beautiful butterfly. It sort of happened overnight. There was no transition. Suddenly, Mr. Balanchine, through his school, had a whole new crop of beautiful young dancers to choose from.

In fact, when the company moved, there was nothing he did not have at his fingertips. I think he must have looked over the entire picture and decided to have a brand new company for his brand new theater. We used to be fifty dancers. Now, we are ninety!

"When the move occurred, I felt Mr. Balanchine's attitude toward me was changing. It wasn't anything obvious. It was subtle. I had an instinctive reaction to little signs. I began to feel rejected. But then, that passed—I realized that ours was a repertory company, and I still had ballets that I danced in. Also, I realized that with so many new people in the company, they had to be given their opportunity. What kept me going was my love of dance and my commitment to the company.

"I've been with the company so long! It's the right time to leave. I've had a great, marvelous, unforgettable time with Mr. Balanchine and the New York City Ballet. I feel that if I stayed one minute more, I'd be overstaying. I have no regrets. I enjoyed every moment, even the sad ones.

"I feel that I still want to dance. But I must leave, because I am part of the ballets that *were*, not part of the ballets that *will be*."

Taking a long sip of Scotch, Melissa Hayden fell silent. She closed her eyes, then, banishing whatever troubling thought may have passed through her mind, she opened her eyes again and produced a dazzling smile. If her dancing career was coming to an end, her life in the dance would by no means be over.

On September 1, 1973, Miss Hayden joined the faculty of Skidmore College in Saratoga Springs, New York (the summer home of the New York City Ballet), where she would be artist-in-residence. She and her husband have a home in Saratoga; they would live there, and Hayden, still at the top of her form, would become the inspiration to numberless young students. Through Melissa Hayden, they will, no doubt, discover the varied riches of a life in the dance. They will learn of its disciplines, its rigors, its rewards.

But being in touch with Hayden will mean far more than that. She is, after all, living testimony to the fact that a career in ballet need be neither short nor circumscribed. Hayden has been artist, wife, mother—and star. She has seen the world. She has danced on the great stages of five continents. She has performed in a vast repertoire. She has worked with most of today's greatest choreographers. She has also demonstrated that a prima ballerina need not be temperamental to have temperament. Onstage or off, people have loved Milly for her high artistry as well as for her high good spirits, her friendly accessibility, her good nature. The world of ballet has been enriched by her indelible, luminous presence.

CITY CENTER JOFFREY BALLET

Louis Peres

ROBERT JOFFREY

Abdullah Jaffa Anver Bey Khan, or Robert Joffrey, was born in Seattle, Washington, in 1930. His mother was Italian and his father was Afghan. Both parents worked in a restaurant which they owned. Robert's mother was the cashier, his father ran the place, and his uncle was the chef. Above the restaurant was a music school. It was in this school that Robert Joffrey first became acquainted with music and with dancing. As a very young boy, he recalls running up to see and hear what was happening. He became intrigued by the different instruments and by the sounds that they made. His parents always knew that if he was not in the restaurant, he was upstairs.

Because he was asthmatic, Robert was advised by a doctor that he do certain relaxation exercises. The doctor suggested dancing. And so, at the age of seven, Robert began taking some lessons with the local teacher. These were tap-dancing lessons. The boy had heard that ballet was for sissies, and would have nothing to do with it. As time went on, his teacher introduced him to a bit of *barre* work and to Russian folk dancing. Without his realizing it, he was being introduced to ballet steps. Robert enjoyed these classes more and more and soon abandoned his tap dancing, although Fred Astaire and Gene Kelly remained his dancing heroes.

One day, Robert Joffrey attended a performance by dancers who were studying with a teacher named Mary Ann Wells. The boy was very impressed by what he saw, and wanted to study with Miss Wells. He was, by now, twelve years old. Miss Wells accepted the boy and trained him for the next five years. During a summer vacation, Robert traveled to New York, and took a summer course at the School of American Ballet. There, he worked with Pierre Vladimirov and Anatole Oboukhov. He enjoyed the complex technical combinations that these two Russian teachers taught him. When he returned to Seattle, Joffrey continued private study with Mary Ann Wells.

"Miss Wells was an extraordinary teacher," Robert Joffrey recalled when I visited him in December 1972 in his office at the American Ballet Center, the official school of the Joffrey Ballet. "She was the teacher of Marc Platt, who was the first American to join the Ballet Russe. She produced William Weslow, who danced with the New York City Ballet, and dancers such as Thomas Wall, Richard England, and Françoise Martinet, who now teaches at my school. And, of course, Gerald Arpino, whom I met in Miss Wells's classes and who is now my codirector. Miss Wells was a tremendous woman because she gave you tremendous respect for the dance. She thought all dancing was important. We had to do modern dancing with her, and when a Spanish company came, they gave a Spanish class. We had all the classical training besides."

At the age of seventeen, Robert Joffrey graduated from Mary Ann Wells's school, and his teacher urged him to move to New York.

"Ever since I was eleven years old, I wanted to have a company of my own. I remember telling that to Miss Wells and she said, 'You've got to dance first. You've worked so hard.' Of course she was right, and I did work hard. Miss Wells used to throw me out of the studio because I would take every class. I took the children's class, I took the baby class, I took the eurythmics class. I would go in the morning and I would leave at the end of the day. Anyway, I came to New York and again studied at the School of American Ballet. I also had private lessons from Alexandra Fedorova, who was a very, very fine teacher. She taught me variations from the classics, which were very important for one's background. I also took classes from May O'Donnell and Gertrude Shurr, who taught Graham technique."

In 1949, Roland Petit's Ballets de Paris visited New York. It was their first American tour, and Petit auditioned a number of dancers to appear with them in New York. It was a three-day audition which was narrowed down to three people—Robert Joffrey, Gerald Arpino, and another dancer. Finally, Robert Joffrey was selected to dance with the company. He danced in *Carmen* and other ballets in the Petit repertoire. The Petit company scored an enormous success in New York City, and Joffrey, a soloist with the company, was invited to go on tour when its New York engagement ended. The boy did not wish to leave New York. He had only just arrived. He left the company and accepted a teaching job at the High School of Performing Arts. It was his first encounter with teaching and the job paved the way for his very special involvement with teaching in general. He remained at Performing Arts for five years. All the while, Joffrey continued his studies at the School of American Ballet and with Madame Fedorova.

"I opened my own little school in Greenwich Village," Joffrey told me. "I lived in a small apartment behind the school. That was around 1951. I also decided that I wanted to do a ballet. I had my own students and some students from Performing Arts. I composed a ballet called *Persephone*, and Mr. Arpino danced the lead in it. John Martin, the dance critic of *The New York Times*, came to see it, and he told me, 'Keep working.' Once, we were invited to Jacob's Pillow, and I composed two more ballets. Around 1954, I did some concerts at the YMHA. My little company did two programs. We had about twenty dancers by then. In 1955, I was invited to go to London by Marie Rambert. She asked me to do a ballet for her company. I staged my *Persephone*. I lived in Marie Rambert's house, which was quite an experience. She asked me to do another ballet which turned out to be *Pas des Déesses*, which I had also done at the YMHA. But, to be honest about it, my experience with Rambert was not all that happy. It was my first time in Europe, and I was always being told what to do. I had always worked with my own people, and here, things were too confusing. I mean, Kenneth MacMillan was there at the time doing a ballet, and I was doing a ballet, and dancers were torn between one rehearsal and another. It was all very difficult for me."

When Robert Joffrey returned from Europe, he had made up his mind to establish a major ballet company—one that he could run his own way. The Rambert experience taught him that he did not enjoy working for anyone else. In 1956, he began with a small company of six dancers. He sent them on tour while he stayed behind teaching and raising money. The six dancers that went out in a station wagon were Gerald Arpino, Glen Tetley, Brunilda Ruiz, John Wilson, Jonathan Watts, and Beatrice Tompkins—names that would eventually assume importance in the dance world.

"That was my first company. And it was a difficult time for everybody. The dancers performed one-night stands, and took care of everything from pressing costumes to putting up lights. I had choreographed most of the ballets, accompanied by tape recordings and a piano which John Wilson knew how to play. Later, we were able to expand the company. We also managed to round up a little orchestra. And so we danced and toured until 1962, when we met Mrs. Rebekah Harkness.

"Our company was invited to go to Spoleto, Italy, for the Festival of Two Worlds. But we didn't have the money to go and I wanted to take everybody. I didn't want to divide the company. Someone told me that there was a wealthy woman, Mrs. Rebekah Harkness, who might be willing to sponsor us. So, we went to an audition which we held at the old Phoenix Theatre on Second Avenue and Twelfth Street. We did excerpts from all of our repertoire. Sitting out in front were Gian-Carlo Menotti, who ran the Festival, and an attractive young woman. I never realized that she was Rebekah Harkness. I had imagined her to be short, with gray hair, and wearing a black lace dress. And so we danced, and afterward Mrs. Harkness said yes, she would help us."

As it turned out, Robert Joffrey's company did not go to Spoleto. Mrs. Harkness, to be sure, had agreed to refurbish the company, providing it with new sets and costumes. She would send them all to Italy, give them ample paid rehearsal time, and, indeed, offer them the "best of everything." Upon seeing the cost of this venture, which would culminate in only a few performances in Spoleto, Joffrey decided that the money ought to be spent on a creative period for his company—a period where all the dancers would be paid, where choreographers could be invited to create new ballets, and where ample rehearsal time would be allowed. Joffrey suggested to Mrs. Harkness that instead of going to Spoleto for one short week, the company might be put up at Mrs. Harkness's summer estate at Watch Hill, Rhode Island. Mrs. Harkness agreed to this suggestion, and Joffrey and his dancers moved to Watch Hill. His benefactress built studios and arranged for living accommodations for the young company.

"It was a very disciplined existence, and a marvelous period for all of us. Mrs. Harkness was, herself, a composer, and she took ballet class with the rest of us. She got up very early in the morning, worked very hard at her music and her dancing. We were all very busy. I asked Alvin Ailey to come and do a ballet for us. He had never done a ballet for another company, and he choreographed *Feast of Ashes* for us. I invited Brian Macdonald to come, and he did a ballet called *Time Out of Mind* for us. Gerald Arpino created *Incubus*. And I did *Gamelan*. We had these four new ballets. Donald Saddler also came to work with us. I felt that it was important to see what these ballets all looked like and so we held an evening at the Fashion Institute of Technology in New York. We performed only twice before an invited audience and we danced the ballets in practice clothes. It was the first time my company had ever performed in New York, although we had been touring the forty-eight states for some six years. At the time, my company was called the American Ballet Center Company."

During the Harkness period, Robert Joffrey was engaged by the New York City Opera to stage opera ballets. His dancers were engaged to dance with the City Opera, which kept Joffrey's company alive. In 1962, the Joffrey company was given a government tour of the Near East. They traveled to Jordan, Syria and Damascus. They gave command performances for the Shah of Iran and King Hussein. When Joffrey came to Afghanistan, he had a reunion with some of his cousins. It was an exciting tour. The company traveled to India, where it stayed for seven weeks and sold out every night. Nehru came to see them dance. The repertoire included *Feast of Ashes, Time Out of Mind*, Balanchine's *Pas de Dix*, and *La Fille Mal Gardée*, among others. The dancers in the company now included Lawrence Rhodes, Paul Sutherland, Brunilda Ruiz, Helgi Tomasson, Marlene Rizzo, Finis Jhung, Elisabeth Carroll, Françoise Martinet, Lone Isaksen, and Nels Jorgenson. The company returned in the spring of 1963, the tour having lasted sixteen weeks. The following summer, Joffrey and his dancers returned to Watch Hill under the aegis of Mrs. Harkness. It did not take long before the Joffrey company received another State Department invitation—this time to travel to Russia. The tour included five cities, Leningrad being the first, and Moscow the last.

"We opened at the Kirov Theatre," Joffrey recalled. "I can remember Sergeiev, the director of the Kirov, and his wife, Dudinskaya, its leading teacher, looking at us onstage. They said, 'How nice you're here. When is the rest of the company arriving?' We told them that's all there was—just twenty-two of us. Christine Sarry was then a member of the company, and most of the dancers I mentioned. At any rate, we opened in Leningrad, then traveled to Karkov and Donetsk, and Kiev.

"I remember that after opening night in Kiev, we all assembled for dinner, and a man came into the restaurant and told us that Kennedy had died. We thought he meant Kennedy's father, who was ill at the time, and we did not think too much about it. Then, toward the end of the meal, people came to us again to say that President Kennedy had been assassinated by a German Fascist. We were all stunned. Our girls began to cry. We didn't know what to do. We canceled the rest of our programs, and went into official mourning. The Russians opened a church for us. We had a service for President Kennedy. Hundreds and hundreds of people came. We could barely get in. They had brought little flowers, and handed each of us a flower saying how sad they were. Later, we watched the funeral over Telstar television—it was the first time anyone was allowed to watch television directly. We did not dance for two weeks. Then, finally, we left Kiev and went to Moscow, where we finished our tour."

Robert Joffrey was now anxious to present his company in New York City. He asked Mrs. Harkness to sponsor ·a New York season. It did not happen.

"Things became strained between us. It may have started over a ballet that Anna Sokolow had done for us, which Mrs. Harkness did not like. I wanted to take the ballet to Russia, but Mrs. Harkness said no—that it didn't fit. Anyway, things began to get difficult. Basically, the problem had to do with the fact that there can never be two artistic directors for one company. Only one person must be responsible. Only one person must have the final word. You can't have two people doing this. Well, we clashed, and one morning I woke up with nothing. I had to start all over again. Mrs. Harkness kept certain dancers, and certain ballets we had commissioned. I was out. I had no ballets, no dancers, no costumes, no sets. I was glad this all happened while I was young enough to start all over again. I just had to work harder, and I learned an awful lot. It's amazing how much can disappear so quickly. Luckily, I had a school with some very talented students, and some of these became the nucleus of my present company."

The final rift between Rebekah Harkness and Robert Joffrey occurred in 1964. By 1965, Joffrey had formed a new company—the City Center Joffrey Ballet. It became the official resident ballet company of the New York City Center. It is among the youngest of the American ballet companies, run with Napoleonic drive by its founder and by his assistant director and choreographer, Gerald Arpino. The young love the Joffrey. The reason is simple—it caters to them. It is an "all-star—no-star" company, numbering some forty dancers. Every member of the Joffrey Ballet gets the opportunity to dance major roles. By the same token, everyone must also take minor parts on any given evening. The dancers are young, energetic, and technically proficient. Today, its repertoire veers from revivals of short classics to ballets drenched in multimedia razzmatazz. The company loves to jive, rock, swing, bump, and grind. Lights flash, music blares, scenery moves, wind machines blow, and both stage and dancers vibrate and gyrate to electronic devices and music.

At its best, the Joffrey produces the sort of excitement that comes with the boundless release and joy of dancing. Such Arpino ballets as *Kettentanz, Confetti*, and *Trinity* usually leave the audience in a state of euphoria. Often, the company tries almost too hard. It attempts to combine such classic revivals as Massine's *Le Beau Danube, The Three-Cornered Hat*, and *Parade*; Fokine's *Petrouchka*; and Jooss's *The Green Table* with such "now" works as Joffrey's *Astarte, Jackpot*, and *Sacred Grove on Mount Tamalpais*, in the hope of showcasing the greatest variety of dance.

At times, the results prove negative, for his young dancers do not always have the stylistic maturity to master the classics, and, more often than not, tend to sacrifice artistry for the sake of "selling it" in the more bouncy, contemporary works.

While the company's chief choreographer, Gerald Arpino, composes many of its major ballets, the Joffrey also invites outside choreographers to work with them. Ballets by such diverse talents as Alvin Ailey, Eliot Feld, Jerome Robbins, Ruthanna Boris, Twyla Tharp, John Butler, and Stuart Hodes are represented. A number of the Joffrey dancers are first rate. Starr Danias, Francesca Corkle, Rebecca Wright, Charthel Arthur, and Donna Cowen are great favorites with the public, as are Dennis Wayne, Gary Chryst, Tony Catanzaro, Paul Sutherland, Glenn White, and Christian Holder.

Despite the company's insistence on being "groovy" and "with it," there is no question but that Robert Joffrey is genuinely interested in shaping a company of depth and quality. "I feel that the Joffrey Ballet should reflect our time. But we must not forget our past—the traditions handed down to us, and the wonderful works that were created in those earlier times. To me, dance is everything that's good, everything that's beautiful, everything that's difficult. I couldn't exist without dance. It's my whole life."

Louis Peres

GERALD ARPINO

There is something mystical about Gerald Arpino. He exudes an aura of the other-worldly. He talks of reincarnation—of the unknown—the unknowable. A trim, compact man, Arpino has a delicate look. His words spill with an almost obsessive speed—as though he were afraid to lose the thread and inner meaning of what he is saying.

We met in a restaurant, not far from the American Ballet Center, the official school of the Joffrey Ballet, where Arpino is codirector, teacher, and chief choreographer. It was a cold December day, and Arpino wore not one, but two heavy sweaters.

"I dress very warmly," he told me. "I do so, because I find the base of the spine and the top of the neck to be the two most injurious places to a dancer. I'm very, very strict with my boys about dressing warmly. I will bring my own shirts for them to change into during a rehearsal. I look after them."

Over coffee, I learned that the choreographer was born on Staten Island, New York, and is the youngest of eight children. His parents came from Italy. His father was something of a gambler, working in real estate, owning a chain of shops, then losing everything during the Depression.

"My father's family owned hotels in Italy, and he was used to the very best," Arpino recalled. "Father was accustomed to the best of wines, the best of foods, the best of servants. I remember his wearing a fantastic coat lined with mink, and he wore spats and a derby and a cane. He looked like Diaghilev. Even when we lost everything, the table had to be set impeccably. For his dessert, father would always have his peaches in wine. We were all brought up on strict European manners, with great respect for the family.

"Of course, being Catholic, the stage and dancing were considered very sinful. But all my sisters loved to dance, and I had an uncle who was an opera singer who loved all the arts. I remember his taking me to the Metropolitan Opera. My introduction to the arts really came through opera rather than through dance. It never occurred to me that I would become a dancer—never. In school I was put in many plays and musicals, and I sang in the choir of our church. So, basically, it was music that got to me first. Anyway, I grew up in Staten Island, and I went to school, and later, entered Wagner College on a scholarship. World War II was on, and all my family began signing up. I also wanted to sign up, and one day, without my mother knowing it, I enlisted in the Coast Guard. I was seventeen. I will always remember the horror in my mother's eyes when I told her what I had done—the Italian tears and screams and the pulling of the hair. It was a real Anna Magnani scene."

Gerald Arpino's time in the Coast Guard was spent in Seattle, Washington. It was in Seattle that he met Robert Joffrey, who was then studying ballet with Mary Ann Wells.

"I met Bob, because my mother and his mother were friends in New York. When I learned he was in Seattle, I looked him up, and I came and watched him taking class with Miss Wells. I used to jump ship—go AWOL—to go to those classes. One day, I got to the class and learned that Mary Ann was doing a children's play. She said she needed someone to read voices, and asked me to do it. So I did boys, girls, witches, goblins—everything that was required. Then Miss Wells told me to take adult beginners classes at night. I told her I couldn't do that. But she said

'Try!' So I took my first lesson in my Coast Guard outfit. She was a fantastic teacher, and I was exposed to the classical techniques without knowing it."

When Arpino finished his time in the Coast Guard (he was twenty), he settled in Seattle, and concentrated on becoming a dancer. He and Robert Joffrey continued studying with Mary Ann Wells, then the two friends came to New York, and enrolled in the School of American Ballet.

"Actually, I didn't want to go to New York. Bob did. I wanted to go to London and work with Marie Rambert. Finally, it was Bob who ended up going to Rambert, which was so weird. Anyway, we did go to New York, and we did study at the School of American Ballet. There, I studied with Felia Doubrovska, Antonina Tumkovsky, Vladimirov, Oboukhov, and Muriel Stuart. I remember Miss Stuart saying to me, 'You have something special! But you must lift up and drop down!' I'd end up in a figure 'S'—but I loved it. Miss Stuart had a plasticity about her movement that I appreciated.

"In those days, you would also take classes elsewhere. I was with May O'Donnell and Gertrude Shurr and Martha Graham. I also studied with Leon Fokine's mother, Alexandra Fedorova. I would go to Ballet Arts and study with Tudor. I used to dance in everybody's works. If anybody asked me to dance, I would dance—and for nothing. I did years of free dancing, which is part of your training. Of course, I've danced Balanchine. He was a big influence in my choreographic works.

"I love Balanchine because of the allegro in dance. I believe the faster you move, the better a legato dancer you are. I think the faster you go, the more control there is. I always believed in a sense of control. I love him for that. I love Balanchine for his structured pieces—and for what he has done with the American body. And I respect Tudor. Well . . . Tudor touched my psyche. He touched things in me that I didn't know could be touched. He immediately wiped out all the old stereotype ideas of dance . . . dance that's filled with idiosyncrasies and mannerisms. I hate that form of ballet. I think ballet can be very dangerous if it's not left open. Ballet is the greatest art form there is—when it's honest. In order to be a great artist, one must have a very honest, open pelvis. You can't have a dishonest pelvis. It's got to be open, free! And so it is with the torso. I love the Leningrad school for the torso. Anyway, with Tudor it was the psychological thing that I loved, and with Balanchine, it was his allegro and fabulous use of the legs, and dimensional style—the musicality."

When Robert Joffrey began his ballet company in the early Fifties, Gerald Arpino was one of its principal dancers. I asked Arpino what kind of dancer he was—or wanted to be.

"I wanted to be a combination of Hugh Laing, Youskevitch, and a smidgen of Erik Bruhn—plus myself. I wanted a combination of all these, and something that had to do with the American male. Now, in my teach-

ing and choreographing, I want to unleash the American male dancer—
show him in his true form. I don't think he's been tapped. But he's coming.
The Messiah of American dancing is coming. He's on his way . . . and I'm
going to provide the way for him. I know the American male dancer has it
in him to outshine the European dancer. We've been so puritanical, inhibited. We have a hard hill to climb. But we'll do it. We'll do it, because
dance is now becoming part of our nature, part of our background. For the
first time, the male dancer is being accepted in America. He's no longer
considered effeminate. And he's coming. Of course, the Messiah of American dance could also be a woman. But I don't know whether she's formed
yet. I think the male must lead in American dance. Balanchine has brought
woman. Tudor has brought woman. But nobody has brought the man. So
we, in America, must discover him. The minute he's discovered, then
American dance will take its big stride."

What, in effect, is Arpino's relationship to his dancers? Members of the
Joffrey company have been rumored to take drugs, their dalliance with pill-
popping, etc., at times causing tension within their ranks.

"I try to negate this problem in the company," says Arpino. "I try to get
them to take a trip on their own artistry—through their own imaginations.
That's what I aspire to. But my relationship with our dancers is very close
and yet very far. I'm so close, it serves as a distance. I'm so close that one
more step would be the wrong step. I temper that so carefully. Strangely
enough, I attract a certain kind of dancer. I love the rejects. I think it's an
unconscious thing. When I find this kind of dancer, I unzip his soul, and I
get in there. When I choreograph, it's a play between us. I'm very aware of
the needs of my artists. So we play. I will tell them, 'Today this will be a
playground' and we'll experiment. Or I'll get very philosophical, or I'll just
get on technique, or movement *per se*. I might start teaching rather than
choreographing. I might concentrate on the pelvis—then the torso must
follow. I'll go over that until I can't stand it any more, and until I'm ready
to wipe the floor with them, or they're ready to tear me apart. Then I
might say, 'Okay, you've had me and I've had you. Let's look at the
movement for what it is.' There's a freshness that comes into the room. All
of a sudden the movement exists—all of a sudden we all understand what
we've done. Out of this great, great discipline of teaching and analyzing—
out of the tearing until we're all ready to cry—the movement is discovered! It's been there all the time. It was just waiting to be discovered. . . .

"My own choreography is always colored with a human quality—a
quality of compassion, of humor. If we examine ourselves and really look
at ourselves, we're beautiful. The *being* is beautiful. That's what I'm concerned with. This, in dance, is my first step. To *be* is very important to me.
I translate *being* into dance. And I relate this being to the time in which we
live. But it's all movement. To breathe is to move. To live is to move.
Action is life. When there is no action, there is death."

In qualifying the special quality of a Joffrey dancer, Arpino says:

"The Joffrey dancer is more exposed to life—and he's exposed to all forms of dance. An experience with Jerome Robbins, Eliot Feld, Anna Sokolow enriches their scope. All the choreographers love our dancers because Bob Joffrey and I direct them to keep their blinders off. That is our function. I think my own influence on them is very strong. I keep my blinders off, too. I'm very influenced by where I live, the people I'm with, the experiences I'm having. I love people. The other day, I walked down the street and I saw this man who was very run-down. He just looked at me. I went into my pocket and took a quarter out . . . he didn't say a word. He didn't ask for money. But that look just seared me. I was burned. That look I will always remember. So when I want my artists to feel or to experience something, then I will recall my own experiences and try to communicate them to the dancers. In that way, they will learn to discover the passion of dance.

"But, you know, I believe we've danced many times in our lives—the thread of dance continues in all of us. I see it revealed through my students. I see it as we work together. There is this interplay between creator and artists. Then, suddenly, the work emerges, and we become as channels for this work to take place. I think that the perfect ballet is the unity of all these elements—of movement, music, and the imparting of one's soul to the work so that it can breathe and live. It emerges with all of us taking part. I don't think there is one particular creative directive. One must think of many different forces coming together. I believe that the great moments come when the self, the ego, is out of the way, so that the creative thing can happen. It's like great moments in sports or drama. It's simply there. Those inspirational things come from life. You have to be constantly open, constantly aware, constantly in touch with life."

REBECCA WRIGHT

One of the most enchanting young dancers of the Joffrey Ballet is Rebecca Wright. On stage, her pixie face and smile express boundless joy—a sunny delight over her capacity for making dance an act of exuberant release. Miss Wright is not possessed of the long-legged, flowing dancer's body; her proportions are squarish and compact. But the quality of her movement transforms her body into a singularly lyrical instrument. In motion, her compactness dissolves into a fluid, clean, poetic series of unbroken gestures. Her repertoire includes the Ballerina in *Petrouchka*, and she is featured in such works as *Kettentanz, Pineapple Poll, Grand Pas Espagnol, Interplay, Moves,* and Ashton's *The Dream.*

On November 8, 1972, I visited Rebecca Wright in her tiny Greenwich Village apartment. That morning, a deluge of rain nearly drowned the city. Upon opening her door, she found a totally soaked interviewer who had left his house without an umbrella. Miss Wright was full of solicitude. She gave me a towel, made me some hot tea, and invited me to take my shoes off so that they might dry more quickly. I feebly began admiring her small and cozy apartment, as well as the outfit she was wearing.

"Shall I describe this apartment?" she said. "As you see, it's quite bare. It has neither a couch nor many chairs. I just have a bed, and when people come over, everyone winds up sitting on the floor, which I think breaks down certain barriers. You cannot put on false airs when you're sitting on the floor. I'll also describe how I'm dressed. I'm dressed like a girl who would be watching television by herself, in maroon corduroy jeans. I have a checkered blouse on, and a suède vest. It's a very casual outfit."

Sensing that I would not be particularly comfortable sitting on the floor, she invites me to sit on her bed.

I learn that Rebecca Wright was born in Springfield, Ohio, and trained at the Dayton Civic Ballet. She studied with two ballet teachers who happened to be sisters—Josephine and Helene Schwartz. She began her studies at the age of six, and gained dancing experience by performing at a very early age with the Dayton Civic Ballet and in various regional ballet festivals. When she graduated from high school, she came to New York and became an apprentice with the Joffrey Ballet. By eighteen, she was in the company.

"Mr. Joffrey had known me since I was a little girl. I was something like ten years old. That's how I finally came to be in the company. My mother never pushed me toward a career. She was not a ballet mother. In fact, she always thought that my life in the dance would amount to a series of unhappy moments. That's exactly what it ends up being. Only one quarter of a dancer's life can really be called dynamic—a climactic experience. Being a dancer is terribly difficult work. You start early in the morning. You finish late at night. When you come home, the only thing you're able to do is to wash out your dance clothes, sew the ribbons on your *pointe* shoes, maybe read a book. It's very limiting, actually.

"When I first came to New York in 1966, I was really quite happy. But then, as the years passed, New York became a very ugly, distorted place for me. It's a dirty city. It's very corrupt. I guess it has the heights of good and the depths of bad. I don't know how much longer I can tolerate the pace here."

It took three years with the Joffrey before Rebecca Wright was given important roles. She claimed that she was very nervous on the stage, and that her performances seemed exaggerated:

"I needed time to be comfortable onstage. Both Mr. Joffrey and Mr. Arpino gave me that time. I was progressing slowly. In the meantime, I met and fell in love with someone. This was some three years ago. Then, an event took place that changed my life. The man I was very much in love with—an architect—asked me to marry him. Just before we were to be married, he was killed in a fire. It was from that moment on that I really plunged into my dancing career. I started gaining roles. I had to go deep into work, because such a terrible thing had never before happened in my life. I was lucky in that my parents always taught me to be a problem-solver. I tried to solve my problems in the most logical and rational way I could."

I ask Miss Wright how she assesses the Joffrey Ballet.

"The Joffrey is a very vibrant, young company. I like its energy level. It's sort of superdynamic. Lots of vibrations. It's very different from the New York City Ballet, which does not appeal to me at all. The dancers there don't have a warm, human quality. They don't seem to be aware of all the possibilities that life presents. Joffrey, on the other hand, is small and warm and human. Mr. Joffrey is a very great teacher, I think. And Mr. Arpino a very gifted choreographer. Sometimes I think his work is a little affected, but it's not entirely his fault. He gives the dancers tremendous responsibility, which sometimes emphasizes their idiosyncracies to an ex-aggerated point. Anyway, I feel that one of the weakest aspects of our company is that it can't keep a great percentage of its dancers. In the last few years we've lost young dancers at the point when they were becoming artists. I'm not sure whether it's a political problem that the dancers have with Joffrey and Arpino. I've always been treated very well by both of them.

"Because it's such a small company—only forty dancers—half the company is overworked. The other half doesn't work much at all. This puts a strain on some of us who must dance all the time and maintain a consistent level of excellence. Also, we need more good ballets—*really* good ballets to add to our repertoire. I think we have ballets that rely too much on gimmicks. I wish Mr. Arpino would go back to simple things—like *Valentine, Viva Vivaldi!, Olympics*, or *Incubus*. I think the moment you start working with lots of props and too much costuming you get into dangerous areas in the dance. Dance is a physical and poetic art. You want to see body movement. It's bad to cover it up."

Rebecca Wright went on to say that the Joffrey Ballet gained much of its success through Robert Joffrey's *Astarte*. She feels that as a result, the company got a reputation for being sensational:

"The kids are now getting disappointed with us. They don't think the company is as exciting as it used to be, because we're not doing as many rock things. I feel our young audiences do not respond well to the truly good things we have—the Massine revivals and some of Mr. Arpino's ballets. This depresses me. Also, the company is changing. Mr. Joffrey is not able to keep his older members. Some of the new, young dancers lack respect for the older members. You don't find the young dancers growing. They're thrown into leading roles. They don't go through a system—a growing system. I think the Joffrey Ballet needs a system. Of course, I don't believe that it's good to be in the *corps de ballet* for years and years. On the other hand, there ought to be a sense of gradual achievement. I feel that some of our men are weak. This holds back the girls. But on the whole, I would say that we as dancers are very close to one another. We wish each other well.

"But what bothers me especially is that dancers tend not to be people. Perhaps it's the time-consuming element that dance requires. But I feel so strongly that it's more important to be a person than to be a dancer. One has to be a person first. It's important to get out and see things and experience things. Dancers are so closed-in. They've got to have life-experience before they can express themselves as artists. That's a limitation.

"Finally, I don't see myself as a performer for many, many years. I think I might like to become a dance critic. I'd like to go to college and study certain things. I would love to teach. Sometimes, when I'm on the stage, dancing, I feel a little resentful. The audience doesn't care how you're feeling—if you have a bad back or personal problems. Not that I blame them. I would want to see the best that a dancer can offer. But sometimes, onstage, for a split second, I ask myself, What am I doing? What does this mean? Is this important? Is this all valid? I would say that three quarters of my dancing career has not given me the opportunity of saying much. Maybe one quarter says something. But most of it has been frustrating, depressing, heavy on my mind. I suppose I should be grateful for that one quarter that *is* fulfilling me—making me aware that my body can create something. I suppose the realization that I've been able to put into movement something beautiful should be enough. And the fact that people get pleasure out of seeing that. Anyway, that's how I feel right now."

DENNIS WAYNE

Whenever Dennis Wayne performs John Butler's ballet *After Eden*, the stage is ignited by his potent sexuality. This elaborate *pas de deux* charts the emotional and sensual awakening of Adam and Eve following their expulsion from the Garden of Eden. Wayne, partnering Starr Danias, contrives to give a smoldering yet terse interpretation of the guilt and desire that assail Adam. The choreographic images depicting this primordial battle of the sexes are marvelously drawn, at once starkly austere and erotically convoluted. Danias and Wayne dance the work with superb artistry, but it is Wayne who lends *After Eden* its ambivalent passion and intensity.

After Eden was danced on a chilly November night during the Joffrey Ballet's 1972 season at the New York City Center. When I met Wayne afterward for our interview, he seemed particularly exhilarated by his performance and was in splendid spirits. Blond, curly-headed, blue-eyed, Wayne has the typical look of an American teen-ager. Rash, impetuous, and driven, he seems restless and a little dissatisfied with himself. There is always *more* he wants to give, *more* he wants to do, but a touching self-questioning seems to bring his ambitions up short.

Dennis Wayne was born in Saint Petersburg, Florida in 1945. His parents were vaudeville and circus performers. They wanted Dennis to follow in their footsteps, and the boy was put to work studying acrobatics, etc. He was also encouraged to study dancing, because it was their hope that Dennis might join them in a night-club act. This goal was not achieved, although dancing continued to play an important part in the boy's early life. In 1948 the Wayne family moved to New York and settled in Brooklyn. Dennis attended the High School of Performing Arts in Manhattan. During the summers he won scholarships to continue his dance studies at Utah State University, where he gained considerable stage experience. At the time, his interest lay in modern dance. During his senior year at the High School of Performing Arts his class gave a year-end performance attended by dance critic Walter Terry. In his review Terry singled out Dennis Wayne as a promising young dancer.

Wayne recalled those early years:

"I was forced to take dancing lessons. I hated the thought of it. I thought dancing was just for homosexuals. But I liked Performing Arts—I liked the atmosphere. The first two years, all I did was enjoy myself. It wasn't until my third year that I began to take dancing seriously. Then I began getting scholarships to Utah University during the summers. Gertrude Shurr and Norman Walker were part of the dance faculty, and we did modern concerts. During my last year at Performing Arts, I danced in pieces by Norman Walker, Doris Humphrey, and David Wood. I loved the modern dance. It gave me a chance to express myself. I left Performing Arts just before graduating—I auditioned for Donald Saddler, who was putting on the musical *To Broadway with Love* at Santa Fe, New Mexico. It was Stuart Hodes who introduced me to Donald Saddler. Anyway, I passed the audition and went out to Santa Fe. After that, Donald Saddler took the job of assistant director with George Skibine at the Harkness Ballet, and he asked me to come with him and audition for the Harkness. He thought it would be good for me to join a ballet company.

"I'll never forget that audition. I had been playing baseball in Central Park, and took the audition in my baseball uniform. Mrs. Harkness was there, and Leon Fokine gave the class. Well, I'd never taken ballet, really.

But I always had a high jump. I remember thinking at the *barre*, Wait till we get to the center—I'll show them! But the *barre* destroyed my legs so much that when I got to the center, I couldn't jump. Still, I passed the auditions. I made it. I thought I'd get to be a principal in a week—or, at the most, two. Mrs. Harkness invited us to her estate, Watch Hill, in Rhode Island, where the company took class and rehearsed. I drove up there on my motorcycle. When I looked into the studio, I saw Larry Rhodes, Helgi Tomasson, Finis Jhung, Elisabeth Carroll, Brunilda Ruiz, and Lone Isaksen. I saw them take class, and I said, 'I want a release from my contract.' The point being, I was the worst dancer in the company. For one year, whenever anyone was carried or lifted or thrown, I was the one doing it. It was in my second year at Harkness that I started to do things."

Dennis Wayne joined the Harkness Ballet in 1964. His first opportunity to show his gifts was in a work choreographed by Norman Walker in which the principal dancers were Lawrence Rhodes, Finis Jhung, and Wayne. When the company danced in New York, the critics again singled out Dennis Wayne as a dancer to watch. Wayne told me something about his six-year period with the Harkness Ballet.

"I believed in the company. Joining the Harkness was the best thing that ever happened to me. I'm convinced that if Rebekah Harkness hadn't made that decision of closing her company when she did, and firing all those dancers, it could have been a fantastic company—a company comparable to American Ballet Theatre. Actually, Mrs. Harkness is very nice. . . . She treated her dancers extremely well during the six years the company existed. She made wrong artistic decisions, but she was very good to us. She saw to it that we were well treated when the company traveled. One time, we danced in Egypt, and the theater was so dirty, so unsanitary—there was shit on the walls—that she came in and told the American Ambassador that either they clean the theater, or the company wouldn't perform.

"When she closed the company, it changed my life. I remember—it was May 15, 1970. I haven't been happy since that day. That's where I had met Bonnie Mathis. We danced together in the Harkness. We had been together for six years. The company broke up in Europe, and Bonnie stayed there, but then joined ABT. I came back to the States right away. Bob Joffrey wanted me in his company. He called me. I had been making a good salary at Harkness. He offered me less. But it was good enough. So I joined his company. I've been with the Joffrey for two and a half years.

"During my first year at Joffrey, all I did was fight. I fought Gerry Arpino, I fought Jim Howell. I don't know what's going to happen to my relationship with Bob Joffrey. I had established myself as a principal dancer with the Harkness, but I had danced in a lot of shitty ballets. I've insisted that each year Joffrey bring in a ballet for me. *After Eden* was one; Stuart Hodes's *Abyss* is another. But each year, it's a fight. Bob is very shrewd. He knows the kind of person I am. He knows I have a reputation for being difficult. I got into a lot of trouble in the company because I said what I felt. I mean, I resent some of the things that are going on there, like one human being telling someone else to shut up. It's unnecessary. Gerry and a lot of other people say, 'Shut Up!' 'Do this. Do that.' It bothers me. But I got to dance in a lot of nice ballets and received good reviews. Reviews are very important to Bob Joffrey. And I'm proud of the dancers we have. My only objection to the company is that it doesn't have a feeling of permanence. It's a very transient company. You can't be there for any long length of time. Joffrey doesn't really want mature dancers because he can't handle them. Also, Bob doesn't encourage people in his own company to choreograph. They don't encourage people to stay on as teachers or ballet masters. I, personally, can't wait to choreograph."

We turned to Wayne's thoughts on the dance and on what kind of dancer he thinks he is.

"When I dance, I just think about dancing. I'm not thinking of the problems I have as a human being. When I dance, I don't think about *what* I'm doing, but about *why* I'm doing it. That's when I do my best performances. What's so wonderful about dancing is that you can never recapture the moments you've had on the stage. What I did tonight in *After Eden*, I will never duplicate. Tonight was one of the performances where I didn't think of *how* I was doing it, but *why*. I like to captivate the audience with my emotions. I'm not the most perfect dancer in the world. My feet don't point so well. My legs don't straighten all that well. My shoulders are up a little bit. I can kick my leg, but holding it is another story. Still, I'm happy with myself, and Bob Joffrey is, too. He once told me that I had the chance to be one of the better dancers in America."

With the Joffrey Ballet, Dennis Wayne dances in such works as *Secret Places, Sea Shadow, The Still Point, Le Beau Danube*. In each of these, he makes clear his versatility and that special emotional thrust that gives such intensity to his performances.

"I want to be my own dancer. I want to be the kind of dancer you look at. Basically, I'm not a Joffrey dancer. I would like to join American Ballet Theatre. But only if they offered me the contract I want. I want to come in as soloist, or as principal. But Lucia Chase insists that if I joined her company, I would have to go into the *corps*. I shouldn't have to do that. I'm not a *corps* dancer. I've been in the *corps*. I've put in my time. If she's going to bring in Paolo Bortoluzzi or Michael Denard from Europe as principal dancers, she can do the same for American dancers. I can say without being egotistical that I can do Tudor's *Romeo and Juliet* better than it's being done. I can do *Dark Elegies, Miss Julie, The Moor's Pavane*. ABT offered me a contract to dance with Cynthia Gregory. They needed me. But they said I would have to enter the *corps*. I wouldn't be in the *corps* for one single day. What a policy! If I were French, I'd come in as a principal.

"I think I'm a Tudor dancer. I want to dance his ballets before I die. He's a genius. I want to do *Romeo and Juliet* so badly. That first entrance . . . that balcony scene! His work contains so much reality. Dancing should be real. It should be natural. I hate so many of those romantic ballets. You know . . . someone is in ecstasy, and he does a *double tour* to the knee. When you're in ecstasy you don't *do* a *double tour* to the knee, you *show* it. You *feel* it. Tudor says what he has to say with such economy.

"I feel I still have a lot to learn. I was very happy when I was with the Harkness because I was naïve. I was in Europe. I was making money. I didn't think. I was eating great food. I was listening to great languages, and seeing great culture and art. Now, I'm with Joffrey. I've gotten older. I like Bob. I really do. I respect certain things he does, but I would not run a company the way he runs it. I would deal with people on a human level. He is a little ruthless. He is afraid. I mean, you could be fired and not know about it. But I enjoy Bob. I'm the only person in the company who calls him Bob. Everyone else calls him Mr. Joffrey. When I first joined the company, I was told I had to call him Mr. Joffrey. I said I would do that only if he called me Mr. Wayne."

In his amiable, rambling way, Wayne offered more thoughts about his life, his career, his inner feelings:

"I've always been told what to do. I've always been yelled at and reprimanded and criticized for being outspoken and self-centered. As a child, I lived in a very competitive family. It was very important for me to be on top of situations. But the thing that's happened is that I don't know who I am. I have no identity. I just know that something inside of me is not making me happy. I don't have the drive I used to have. I used to have ambition. I'm only twenty-seven! I was going to have this and that— material things. There is an uncertainty in me. I don't know about my future. I want to dance until I can no longer dance. I think I only have another five years left. I think what I'd like most of all is to have a company of my own. I want to be a director. Oh, I could do it. I work well with people. I feel I have something to say artistically."

STARR DANIAS

If the Joffrey Ballet is an all-star, no-star company, Starr Danias is nevertheless among its special luminaries. In performance, she displays wide dancing experience, and seems to be possessed of a subtlety at times absent in other Joffrey dancers. Though not a bravura performer, she can imply a strength she may not necessarily possess. Miss Danias's individuality is felt more in her cleanliness of execution and her personal radiance. In works such as *After Eden*, Arpino's *Reflections*, *Sacred Grove on*

Mount Tamalpais, and *Chabriesque*, she dances with exhilaration, musicality, and instinctive elegance.

Starr Danias and I met for our interview at the Russian Tea Room. Her dark brown hair, parted severely to one side, sets off a face of poignant delicacy. Her dark brown eyes are very large, her nose is piquantly turned up, her mouth is small and sensitive, her skin, white and flawless. She has the look found in Persian miniature painting. In point of fact, Starr Danias was born in New York City of Greek parents. When she speaks, her voice is that of a little girl. Wearing a silver satin blouse and black velvet skirt, she sat facing me in a prim and proper attitude.

"My mother had always wanted to be a dancer—so I took after her," she began. "Mother is not a balletomane, but she has a good eye, enjoys the ballet, and is very glad I'm a ballet dancer. I didn't begin my serious training until I was thirteen. Before that, I had done the once-a-week-type class—half acrobatic, half ballet. Anyway, one day a girl friend took me to a studio in the West Fifties where an old Russian teacher taught class. Her name was Natalia Branitska. She had danced in the Diaghilev company. It was Madame Branitska who introduced me to classical ballet. During the summers I took classes from her twice a week. She was a marvel. She would talk to us about the olden days—about Massine, Danilova. . . . I adored it. She is still around, and she helped me immensely."

Danias studied with Branitska for several years. But Branitska told the young dancer that if she wanted to become a professional, she would have to study every single day. She enrolled in the High School of Performing Arts and also won a scholarship for study at the School of American Ballet. All along, she continued to take classes with Madame Branitska. At the School of American Ballet she became a favorite of Alexandra Danilova, with whom she took variation classes.

"Madame Danilova really took me under her wing. I adored working with her, and she took a very special interest in me. Just the other day, she came to rehearsals of Massine's *Le Beau Danube*, which we are doing at the Joffrey, and she did the Street Dancer as though she had only done it recently. She was incredible! By the time I was seventeen, I was ready to join a company. Of course, I wanted desperately to go with the New York City Ballet. But Mr. Balanchine was never very fond of me. You see, I was very, very tiny, and I looked very childish. I still hadn't grown completely. I was only about five-foot-one-and-a-half. Mr. B. was very fond of tall dancers. So, such was life. He told me that if I waited one more year, perhaps he would put me in his company. This sounded very vague to me. Along with this, Madame Danilova was dying for me to go to London. She wanted me to join the London Festival Ballet Company and dance the classical repertoire."

As it turned out, Starr Danias was invited to join the Festival Ballet. But the dancer was reluctant to leave New York, her friends, her family. She turned down the invitation at first, but reconsidered six months later.

"It took courage. But I decided to go. This was in 1969. I joined the London Festival Company, and remained with them for two years. I danced the Sugar Plum Fairy, the *Blue Bird pas de deux* and other marvelous roles in the classics. I lived in a little flat in Kensington, with a roommate—a Spanish girl. It was very, very cold. There was no central heating. I never got used to that. Two years in London, and I couldn't take it. I became quite ill and had to come home. Still, it was an invaluable experience. We performed almost more than we took classes. You see, the Festival Ballet is the touring company of England, and they all go around the world. We went to Japan, the Canary Islands, Spain, France, Italy— we went all over. That, in itself, was a great education. But I couldn't stand the English weather, and I was still very, very homesick for New York. I missed being in an American company—and an American dancer in it. I decided that two years abroad was enough experience."

While Starr Danias danced with the Festival Ballet, Robert Joffrey came to London and took an interest in her. At that time, however, he did not invite her to join the company. When Danias returned to New York, she took company classes with Joffrey. Finally, Robert Joffrey asked her to join his company. The year was 1970.

"Well, it was thrilling to work with the Joffrey. And it was thrilling to work with Gerry Arpino, because it was the first time that a choreographer was creating something on me. The first ballet he created with me was *Trinity*. It was a whole new way of working—a whole new ambience. It was a very exciting and marvelous way to return to America. I was twenty, and it was wonderful. Then, Gerry created *Cello Concerto* to music of Vivaldi for Erika Goodman. But Erika suffered a knee injury, and I was taught the role. Shortly afterward, he revived *Sea Shadow*, and that is still one of my favorite *pas de deux*. I do *After Eden* with Dennis Wayne, and it is incredible to dance."

I asked Starr Danias to describe some of her feelings about the Joffrey Ballet.

"It's really a unique company. It is the total opposite of a classical ballet company. I think the best way to describe it is to call it a repertory company. For me, it's the ideal company. I couldn't imagine myself anywhere else—at least, not for the moment. It will soon be three years that I've been part of it—and I have a growing love for the company. I see myself growing as a dancer with the Joffrey—and as a person, as a woman. I wake up in the morning enjoying the fact that I'm a Joffrey dancer. All of us have a unique personality. All the women dancers in the company have been trained in classical ballet. All twenty of us do *pointe* work. Some of the men have been modern dancers. Each one of us has a responsibility and an obligation to a certain role. Each dancer has something to look forward to. The Joffrey brings in new ballets each season, and this inspires us because we might land roles in them."

Miss Danias offers some thoughts on her own dancing:

"I can honestly say that I live and breathe my dancing. It's a *giving* process. I would really call it a love affair. During layoffs, I miss dancing in the way I would miss a person. Some people might consider dancing a form of escape from reality. I don't feel that way. I enjoy every part of being a performer. I love putting on make-up, putting on costumes. I find it all incredibly stimulating. I'm flattered when Arpino approaches me with the idea of creating a new ballet for me, such as *Sacred Grove on Mount Tamalpais*, or *Chabriesque*. To me, it's an incredible thing to be the instrument upon whom someone creates something. Every time Gerry does that, it's as though he were giving me a great, great gift. I just love working with Gerry."

What are Robert Joffrey and Gerald Arpino like as creators and as people?

"Well, the two of them are a riot. I mean, when they're together. I wouldn't call them opposites, because they're both Capricorns. Everyone in the company gets along with them. How to describe Gerald Arpino? I think one has to become personal with Gerry. To me, Gerry is like a second father, or like a best friend, or a big brother, or, at times, a boy friend. It sounds a little strange, but I adore the man. He is like a little boy. He gets so excited and stimulated over, say, a flower. Sometimes he makes me feel like an old woman. He becomes reborn so often—I see it in his eyes. When something works choreographically, he becomes so excited. He's constantly thrilling me. Of course, we fight. Sometimes I'm naughty. It's probably because sometimes his ideas are too overwhelming for the kind of person I am. But then he chides me. He puts me in my place—which I need. I realize that what he may be doing is really in my best interest. I know he loves me.

"Bob Joffrey? Well, I've never known another person with such a fantastic sense of humor. He slays me at times. He's really an 'up.' He's especially funny when the walls come falling in—when there are crises. He'll come out saying the funniest things."

How does Starr Danias get along with her fellow dancers?

"Oh, we *have* to get along. We *must* get along. It's a small company. It's not like the old Ballet Russe. We've all heard stories about *them*! Of course, everyone knows everything about everybody at the Joffrey. People say that many of our dancers are potheads—that they take drugs. Well, let's face it. Ours is a unique company because the ballets that it has created revolve around all sorts of subjects—black magic, rock, sex, drugs, eroticism. Some of that rubs off on the dancers in their personal lives.

"Of course, it was a bit hard when I first began working with Dennis

Wayne. As you know, we do *After Eden* together. Mr. Joffrey feels we're a very good team. Our proportions are complementary. I think *After Eden* is a very good ballet for us, because we look well together. But the beginning of our relationship was not good. We never got along. We just didn't hit it off. Dennis is such a tease. I didn't like it, so I would give it back to him which not many girls do. You know, with his looks, everybody falls at his feet. But the beginning was bad between us. When we began working on Gerry's ballet *Reflections*, Dennis used such language! I was still into my London scene, and I was very shocked. He bothered me so. Everything was *my* fault.

"But, somehow, through the bickering and the differences, we grew together. When *After Eden* came, it was just the right time. We had become fond of each other. Anyway, I respect Dennis very much. He's a marvelous artist. It's very stimulating to work with him. Of course, we never, never see each other outside of the theater."

Starr Danias smiles her pretty smile, sips her tea, and concludes our talk by telling me of her aims:

"I love dramatic roles. All my life, I've wanted to dance the Swan Queen. I know I'm not a great technical dancer—I realize that. I don't know if I could ever do thirty-two *fouettés*. I try to improve my technique every day, but I know I'm not a strong dancer. I know I don't have strong legs. A miracle would have to happen for me to turn into a strong virtuoso dancer. But I try to make the most of what God has given me."

Zachary Freyman

FRANCESCA CORKLE

The adorable Francesca Corkle has been a mainstay of the Joffrey Ballet since 1969, the year she joined the company. Audiences have come to love and respond to her sparkle, her infectious charm, and her extraordinary agility and speed. Any performance of Corkle's assures buoyancy, bravura, and wit. Her impish smile, her short, delicate frame, her fleet legs and feet combine to produce a totally captivating stage presence. Whether dancing in Gerald Arpino's *Viva Vivaldi!*, *Confetti*, and *Chabriesque*, or in Bournonville's *Konservatoriet*, John Cranko's *Pineapple Poll*,

Balanchine's *Square Dance*, or Ashton's *Façade*, Corkle gives audiences a wide range of delights. At the age of twenty-one, she is the Joffrey Company's all-around *Wunderkind*.

If her soubrette qualities have been employed to splendid advantage—if her stunning spins, pirouettes, leaps, and turns have fulfilled the needs of a large part of the Joffrey repertoire—her depth as a dancer did not come totally to the fore until Robert Joffrey created *Remembrances* for her in the fall of 1973. This effusively romantic ballet brought out an entirely new Francesca Corkle. Joffrey had clearly intuited the young dancer's potential as a dramatic actress. In Corkle, he not only had a first-class technician but a dancer able to express the high-flown emotions inherent in the nineteenth-century aesthetics of Richard Wagner. *Remembrances* is set to Wagner's "Album Piano Sonata," his "Five Wesendonck Songs" for soprano and orchestra, and to the "Porazzi Theme" for piano.

Corkle, magnificently partnered by Jonathan Watts, suddenly transformed into a lyric dancer. A subtly yearning quality emerged as she danced the story of a woman recalling her past. With enormous tenderness, she conveyed the poetry of nostalgia, the fleeting agonies of young love, the rapturous and ecstatic nuances of that love's brief fulfillment. Corkle introduced delicacy into the heavier fabric of the music. Shyness, restraint, and a passionate understatement served as exquisite counterpoints to the longing quality of the music. Francesca Corkle triumphed in a role admirably suited to her youth and poignancy.

In the winter of 1973, Francesca Corkle and I talked about her young life. She was born August 2, 1952, in Seattle, Washington. Her father is a physician, her mother, a ballet teacher. Francesca is an only child.

"My mother tells me that when I was first brought home from the hospital, the house was filled with music. At a very early age, I responded to music, and I would dance to it. At that time—I must have been about three years old—I became aware that on certain days of the week, my mother would be upstairs in her studio on the top floor of our house teaching children how to dance. Naturally, as soon as I could, I asked mother to give me lessons, too. She said no. She kept on saying no, until I was four years old. Then, at last, I was permitted to go upstairs and study dancing."

Francesca's mother, Virginia Ryan Corkle, is among Seattle's best-known ballet teachers. As such, she was particularly careful in the instruction of her very young child. Francesca was given preballet lessons, and allowed to develop slowly, within the limits of her capacities. Indeed, Mrs. Corkle did not put Francesca on toe until she reached the age of ten, and did not in any way take advantage of the youngster's precociousness.

"Of course, it would have been easy for Mother to push me—to give me all those extras that a budding dancer could get if her mother happened to be a ballet teacher. But, quite on the contrary, Mother didn't let me get away with anything. She was harder on me than on the other students. She always made it very clear to me that there was a separation between her being my mother and her being my teacher. Actually, between the ages of ten and twelve, I had a bit of a hard time. I felt I was doing things really well in class, maybe better than some. And yet, Mother would never say anything to me. We'd go down to the kitchen, and we'd be sitting at the table, and I'd say, 'I don't understand why you don't tell me that I'm doing well.' She'd say, 'As long as *you* know you're doing well, you don't need anyone else to tell you you're marvelous. If I start telling you things *aren't* being done well, that's the time to worry.' And so it went, until the age of fourteen, which was the time I stopped studying with my mother."

Well before the age of fourteen, Francesca Corkle proved something of a dancing phenomenon. At eight, she improvised a solo, which she performed with the Seattle Symphony Orchestra under Milton Katins. At nine, Robert Joffrey invited her to be part of a production of *Aïda* that he was choreographing for the Seattle World's Fair. At ten, she had the opportunity to audition for Gerd Larsen and Michael Somes, who had come with England's Royal Ballet to perform in Seattle. Miss Larsen and Mr. Somes were so impressed with the youngster that they wired Dame Ninette de Valois to tell her that they had discovered a ten-year-old American girl of extraordinary talent, eminently qualified to continue her studies at the Royal Ballet School. Francesca was invited to go to England.

"I've always kept that invitation as a lovely, lovely memory. But it was one of my first heartbreaks, because my parents felt I was much too young to leave home. Also, had I gotten into the Royal Ballet, I would have had to change my citizenship because they only accept British subjects into the company. But it was a thrilling offer. Still, other wonderful things happened. At thirteen, I danced an improvisation to a waltz from Tchaikovsky's 'Serenade' with the Seattle Symphony. Then, the New York City Ballet came to Seattle, with their production of *A Midsummer Night's Dream*. I was a little fairy in that."

When Francesca Corkle turned fifteen, she became a scholarship student of the Pacific Northwest Ballet Association, at Pacific Lutheran University, just outside Tacoma. Robert Joffrey's company was resident there for several summers, and Corkle had the opportunity of studying with Edna McRae, Una Kai, Michael Maule, and Gloria Newman. She also took classes with Robert Joffrey. She learned various roles, including Luis Fuente's and Robert Blankshine's roles in *Viva Vivaldi!* Following that summer—it was 1968—Robert Joffrey invited the dancer to come to New York to appear in the New York City Opera production of Massenet's *Manon*. Joffrey was staging its choreography, and he chose Corkle to dance the role of Cupid.

"I'll never forget it! Working with the New York City Opera was a marvelous experience. Beverly Sills sang the part of Manon, and she was the most glorious person to work with. I learned what it meant to be a professional. I danced the part of Cupid for three seasons at the City Opera. This was all before I joined the Joffrey Company, although I was taking classes at the Joffrey School.

"One night, I went to a performance given by the company. One of the ballets that evening was *Viva Vivaldi!* Suddenly, Luis Fuente injured his foot. I saw him go down. The next day, I was called for a rehearsal to replace Fuente. Of course, it being a male part, they changed a few things for me. So that was my debut with the Joffrey Company. I was still only fifteen."

Because Corkle had not completed her high-school work in Seattle, she was obliged to return home to finish her sophomore year. Corkle did not, however, graduate from high school. She returned to New York for good. Residency was arranged for her around the corner from the Joffrey School in Greenwich Village.

"I simply couldn't have stayed in Seattle another minute. I needed competition. I needed to get out and see what the *real* world was like. My mother felt she had done all she could for me, in terms of my studies. It was time for someone else to put the finishing touches on. And so, I came back to New York, and for six months learned the Joffrey repertoire. At the school, I studied under Perry Brunson and, later, Meredith Baylis. They were tremendous influences, and very good teachers. In June 1968, I was called into the Joffrey Ballet office to sign my contract with the company. I was shaking. I was ecstatic. I was sixteen."

From the moment that Francesca Corkle joined the company, Robert Joffrey and Gerald Arpino nurtured and made use of her brilliant technical capacities. Throughout her first years with the company, it seemed as though Corkle's bravura technique was being exploited. Audiences came expecting fireworks from a young girl only too eager and willing to produce them. She developed a following, and became known as the Joffrey's "whiz kid."

I asked Miss Corkle whether this sort of exploitation disturbed her.

"Well, look, you don't really think that it would have been right for a teen-ager to be handed dramatic or emotional roles. I don't think I was exploited. Remember, it is extremely difficult for a choreographer to work with a talented child. That's what I was—a talented child, and, as such, I had to be handled very carefully. Joffrey and Arpino were very careful not to give me the kind of things that I couldn't handle emotionally. They developed me slowly—without, however, robbing me of challenge. It was all a matter of time. Personally, I have always felt that the whiz-kid aspect of my career is not really *me*. It never has been. I've always been aware of the fact that technique is only the foundation—the underpinning, the structure. What Joffrey and Arpino did for me was to give me time to mature and to develop. I'm convinced that if Mr. Joffrey had created *Remem-*

brances for me any earlier, I wouldn't have been able to manage it as well.

"Actually, the ballet took about three years to be composed. Mr. Joffrey started work on it with me some two years ago. To begin with, he did tremendous research. Then we worked together. Then he stopped completely. Then he picked it up again a year later. So the work was a slow development. And you could say that I matured *into* the work, gradually."

Corkle talked about working with Robert Joffrey:

"To me, he's the ultimate. He's extremely intelligent, sensitive, creative. He's the most positive person to work for. You always have the feeling that whatever he asks you to do, you'll be able to do it. He always makes you understand the emotions that belong to a particular movement. What's more important, he teaches you how to retain that emotion. When we worked on *Remembrances* together, everything had meaning, and everything was closely related to the music. The work just seemed to flow out. Mr. Joffrey never talked too much during its composition. He would demonstrate, and I would do things the way *he* did them. But Mr. Joffrey has a very bouncy way of moving. Later, I learned how to translate that bounce to make it appropriate to my own movements. I would interpret his way of moving. One thing Joffrey was very careful about during *Remembrances* was never to explain things to me *psychologically*. I did my own research —reading about Wagner's relationship with Mathilde Wesendonck— continually listening to the music, and just drowning myself in the period. I found my own psychology."

What of her work with Gerald Arpino?

"It's always very good to go back to Mr. Arpino. He can be very difficult at times, and hard to understand. But there is truth in every single thing he tells you. You've got to be intelligent to be able to work with him. A number of dancers in our company find they cannot work with him. He gets his points across very differently from Mr. Joffrey. Mr. Joffrey always has things very carefully planned out before he begins work. Mr. Arpino is more tied to improvisation. This makes working with him very demanding. Still, once you understand him and his working methods, you learn a tremendous amount."

On the subject of the Joffrey Company's somewhat liberated ambience —its freewheeling, with-it reputation, Corkle expressed some very definite opinions:

"To tell you the truth, I'm a very old-fashioned girl. Although I'm happily situated in the company, and get along very well with all the dancers, I can't really say I'm *in* the company. Somehow, I feel that if you seek fame, you should remain somewhat mysterious. If you know everything about everybody, illusions are shattered completely. My fellow dancers may find me very antisocial or moody, or what have you. I don't go around accepting invitations to this or that party, and I don't find myself getting involved with the other dancers' problems or complaints. That just distracts me. I mean, I love to observe how one company member relates to another. It's amusing to me. It's fascinating. I'm sure the kids talk about me a lot—favorably or unfavorably. But I'd rather go along in ignorance. Because, to me, ignorance *is* bliss. When we go on tour, the members of the company get very involved with a lot of outside activities. A lot of them are into rock music, which I'm not particularly interested in. They get very hung up on who's doing what to whom. Well, I think that's all unfortunate. I feel a dancer's life is a twenty-four-hour thing. You cannot divide your life. You can't forget about the dance once you leave the rehearsal studio."

Francesca Corkle smiled her pert smile, and told me of her aims as a dancer:

"I have never thought of being anything less than great. I could never relate to remaining in a *corps*—being lost among others. I want to give of myself—beautifully. I want to give of myself with as much love as possible. For me, dancing is the most natural thing in the world. I find it much easier to dance than to do anything else, practically. At the moment, I don't have much of a personal life. I'm still young—at least, that's what I keep telling myself. I don't worry about the future. I enjoy day-to-day living. If I met a guy I fell in love with, it would be wonderful. It would help my dancing. Still, that somebody would have to love me for myself and not for my dancing."

GARY CHRYST

In Gary Chryst, the Joffrey Ballet has a major character dancer. A short, limber, intense dynamo of a man, he gives visceral life to traditional roles that have been associated with the likes of Nijinsky and Massine. The Joffrey revivals of *Petrouchka, Parade, The Three-Cornered Hat, Le Beau Danube*, would be pallid without the presence of Gary Chryst. The twenty-four-year-old dancer, with his puckish good looks, his nervous, restless nature, and his instinctive sense of theater, lends truth and fidelity to the various roles he interprets.

Chryst as Petrouchka displays his strong gifts for pantomime and psychological expressiveness. As the Chinese Conjurer in Massine's *Parade*, he gives stunning credibility to movements that are as bizarre as they are original. As the Dandy in Massine's *Le Beau Danube*, he swaggers and trots with an impish gaiety altogether true to the spirit of the work. Of course, he learned the Massine roles under the careful guidance of Massine himself, but Chryst, with his genius for mimicry and natural theatricality, brings to each role an authentically personal commitment.

By the same token, Chryst goes to the more contemporary Joffrey repertoire with equal zest and fire. In such works as Arpino's *Trinity* or *Confetti*, Ruthanna Boris's *Cakewalk*, Jerome Robbins' *Interplay*, Kurt Jooss's *The Green Table*, Eliot Feld's *Jive*, Ashton's *Façade*, or Joe Layton's *Double Exposure*, Chryst is a fluent, fleet, crystal-clear dancer, who injects a kind of percussive wit into movement and gesture. Not possessed of the most perfect dancer's body—his line cannot be called elegant, and his neck is somewhat short—Chryst makes up for these lacks through technical bravado, control, and sheer exuberance.

It was between rehearsals, in January 1974, that Gary Chryst and I had a brief talk. The young dancer led me into a cubicle of a room at the American Ballet Center, the official school of the Joffrey company. Wearing jeans and a T shirt, and a tiny earring in one pierced ear, Chryst instantly communicated the electric alertness he manifests onstage. A certain contained restlessness became evident as he began to tell me something of his past.

"I was born in La Jolla, California, on November 28, 1949. My mother did various and sundry things. I don't know my real father, but the one I grew up with was a jazz musician. He played the trumpet and the piano with different bands during World War II. But he thought he wasn't going to be the greatest, and so he became a recording engineer.

"When I was about seven, we moved from California to New Jersey. We lived there for two years—my father worked there. Then, we moved to the Bronx. After three years, we came to Manhattan."

When Gary was still a small boy living at home, his parents taught him all the social dances. He learned the lindy, the fox trot, the waltz. When he went to junior high school, he sang in the school chorus, and performed with it at Carnegie Hall. It was his first stage experience. When the family moved to Manhattan, Gary enrolled in the High School of Performing Arts. He studied singing and drama. He also took two classes a week in modern dance.

"I was sold! Cora Cahan came to teach. She was so exuberant. Then, one time, my parents and I went to see some performances given by the American Dance Theatre at the New York State Theater. Lots of great modern dance companies appeared together—José Limón, Doris Humphrey, Anna Sokolow, Alwin Nikolais. That was around 1965. Well, when

I saw these people, I realized I wanted to become a dancer. I was sort of scared to ask my parents if I could do this, because my father was a Mormon, and my mother was a Baptist, and they had very rigid upbringings. But my father said if that was what I wanted to do, I should go ahead and do it."

Chryst graduated from the High School of Performing Arts by the skin of his teeth. At that time, Norman Walker was the head of the Dance Department, and Walker asked Chryst to join his company. During his junior year at Performing Arts, Robert Joffrey came to teach at the school. At one point, he offered Chryst a scholarship to his own school. The young dancer accepted the scholarship, attending classes while also rehearsing and performing with the Walker company. His schedule became so frantic that during his last year in high school, Chryst fell ill. He decided that he could not continue in Walker's company. He concentrated on his studies at the Joffrey school. By the age of sixteen, he was made an apprentice with the Joffrey Ballet. As an apprentice, he danced in the New York City Opera production of *Manon* choreographed by Robert Joffrey. The year was 1967. When Gary Chryst turned eighteen, he was invited by Joffrey to join the Joffrey Ballet.

"Just before I joined the company, I had a big moment of hesitation. I wasn't sure I wanted to be a ballet dancer. Somehow, I knew that I would have to give my life to it, and I was thinking of other options. I wasn't at all sure I wanted to get up at eight in the morning and go to bed at one in the morning, spending all that time in class, at rehearsal, doing performances. It seemed overwhelming.

"Also, I always had the ambition of being an actor. At every opportunity, I would go and see Broadway shows. I'd go to all the musicals. I was fascinated by theater. Anyway, early in 1968 I decided to do some summer stock. I danced in a production of *Guys and Dolls* that starred Betty Grable. Then I did *Milk and Honey* with Molly Picon. I was a solo dancer in it and it was a lot of fun. While I was doing the show, I received a call from Edith d'Addario, who is the secretary of the Joffrey School. She told me that Mr. Joffrey wanted me in his company. I told Molly Picon about it. She's a fantastic woman, Molly. I mean, at the time I worked with her, she was seventy-six. Every morning, she would be jogging in the parking lot. She did cartwheels and somersaults on stage! Well, she urged me to accept the offer. I was still uncertain.

"Also, during that engagement with *Milk and Honey*, my father died. Miss Picon and her husband were going to give me money to go home— we were in Westbury, Connecticut. I called my mother, but she said, 'You don't need to come home. Your father wouldn't want you to miss a performance.' Well, with one thing or another, I decided that maybe I *should* join the Joffrey."

Gary Chryst entered the company in August 1968. Almost immediately, he danced major roles and found his real challenge in discovering the Fokine and Massine classics.

"I think I'm basically a dancer in the Fokine tradition, where it wasn't so much a matter of the steps as the achievement of a totality of feeling. When I danced Petrouchka, I did a tremendous amount of research, and I arrived at some ideas of my own. I looked at all the Nijinsky photographs, and noticed that Nijinsky's make-up gave him a constant look of sadness. I mean, the mouth, in the original make-up, was all crooked. Petrouchka could never smile. He always looked the same. I went to Mr. Joffrey and told him I wanted to change that look of constant pain, and he allowed me to do this. Mr. Joffrey, who is a great stickler for tradition, can be approached on things like that—if your ideas are valid and honest. And so, it was a challenge for me to portray Petrouchka somewhat differently, while still retaining the original concept."

Chryst recounted his experience of working with Léonide Massine on *Parade*:

"It was the weirdest thing. When Massine first came to us to restage *Petrouchka* and *The Three-Cornered Hat*, he was very stand-offish, very distant. Somehow, we couldn't relate to him. Then, when he came to do *Le Beau Danube*, things got better. In *Parade*, he warmed up to us, and I think he really liked me, personally. But when we began work on *Parade*, all the dancers in it felt that Massine was kind of putting us on, with the things he asked us to do. Of course, none of us knew the ballet at all. We had just seen the Picasso décor, and we had heard the Satie music. But we didn't know the movements. Anyway, during rehearsal one day, Massine said to me, 'Cross your eyes! Push out your cheeks! Stick your tongue out! Roll your eyes up in your head! Flex your cheekbones!' I thought, Come on! What is this?! It was wild. I thought he was giving me these things to see how far I could control my face. I mean, it wasn't movement. He did that to all of us, and we started doing it. It all felt very silly, and it continued feeling silly until the first performance. We all thought the ballet would be a bomb. We couldn't 'feel it,' and we couldn't relate to each other as dancers.

"Well, after we worked in costume, we started feeling a little excited. Then came the make-up sessions. That was a thrill, because Massine himself put the make-up on me. Of course, he had danced the Chinese Conjurer himself, back in 1917, when *Parade* was first performed, and he must have had a memory of Picasso's make-up. I remember, we were in the foyer of the theater. Massine came up to me, grabbed my neck, and started to apply the make-up to my face. His hand was shaking . . . he's nearly eighty. But what he did was fabulous. He started these thin lines that then became thicker, and then got thin again. It was very Picasso, the way the curves looked. I've never been able to duplicate the make-up he put on me.

"While Massine was doing this to my face, Claude Picasso, one of the painter's sons, photographed the whole thing. It was all very historical. It was an experience!"

Asked about his relationship with Robert Joffrey, Gary Chryst said that he admired the choreographer's sense of theater. Of Gerald Arpino, he replied, "He tells me I remind him of his younger self—the energy. Mr. Arpino is very hard on me." Asked what he feels during the act of dancing, Chryst replied that when he dances, it is always for someone else. "I think of people. I dance *to* someone. In a sense, when I dance, it is as though I were making love to someone. It's a crazy passion."

What of Gary Chryst's private life?

"I'm not a very private person. Sometimes, I wish I were. It would save me a lot of trouble. What's my life like? I work. But I also play. When I'm off, I do all the things Mr. Joffrey hates his dancers to do. I go water-skiing, surfing, mountain-climbing, bicycle-riding, and horseback-riding. In fact, anything I've never done before, I'll do.

"I live in a little apartment in Greenwich Village. I live in a little apartment with a giant Schnauzer. I like giving little dinners. I think about my life, and about my career. Last year, I wanted to leave the company. I just wanted to do something else. Somehow, I want to do something all my own, because Mr. Joffrey is Mr. Joffrey, and I'm Gary Chryst, and we are two different individuals. I work under Mr. Joffrey, which is not difficult at all. But you want to make your own mark. After all, I've been connected with him since the age of fifteen. On one hand, I never want to leave him. But in order for me to fulfill my own ego, I have to leave. It's in the cards. Maybe it will never happen. Who knows?

"I'd love to choreograph. But that's difficult, too—a young choreographer doesn't have much of a chance, by today's critical standards. The dance critics have killed off all the young choreographers. It's only the ones who are famous that keep on choreographing—and get the attention. So you get intimidated.

"About three years ago, I got fed up with dancing. The reason was simple—I wanted to be a perfect dancer. Well, I finally came to the conclusion that there is no such animal. What a dancer has to remember is that all he can do is to work *toward* perfection. It's a very frustrating thing to do. It's a masochistic thing to do—working for that perfection which will never be."

Looking Ahead

ALVIN AILEY

I am a bachelor, and I am a loner," said Alvin Ailey, as he led me up two flights of stairs to his apartment in mid-town Manhattan. "And nobody ever comes to my place." I had had a difficult time persuading Ailey to allow me to visit him—to allow me to see how he lives. Though a floor-through, the apartment is small, compact. There are no concessions to elegance. In one small room, cardboard boxes are piled in a corner ("I'll have to get around to these one day"). The living room is sunny. There is a couch, a coffee table, a butterfly chair. The curtains consist of a sari-like

Indian silk cloth hanging over a curtain rod. There is a fireplace. On its mantel are many small primitive sculptures—masks, figures, and objects collected in Africa, South America, the Orient. They are not displayed, but piled together pell-mell. Larger pieces—shields, arrows, standing figures—flank the door leading to the bedroom. Here, the bed is unmade. A television set has the image going, but no sound. There is sound from a record player, however, The music is avant-garde jazz. Ailey listens to music constantly. Record albums are piled high: Stravinsky, Britten, Mary Lou Williams, Bach, Medieval chants, Duke Ellington—and more. Facing the bed is a large color reproduction of Hieronymus Bosch's *Garden of Delights.*

Ailey is a tall black man. His burly figure moves with litheness across the rooms. Still, he seems curiously uncomfortable in his own surroundings —the result, no doubt, of my presence. He offers me a glass of pink champagne. "My favorite drink," he says. We drink in silence. Finally, Ailey sits in the butterfly chair. He relaxes into it with a certain weariness. His face is very strong, and rather sad. But in a moment he smiles. "Where do you want to begin?" he asks me. "From the beginning," I tell him.

"I was born in Rogers, Texas, in 1931," he says. "At that time, the town had only a gas station and grocery store. My mother and father separated when I was three. I always lived with my mother. I just recently discovered my father. His name is also Alvin Ailey—so I'm a junior. He's married again, and has several children. My mother remarried when I was fourteen—so I have a stepfather and a stepbrother who is twenty-one.

"What I remember of my childhood is that we lived around with relatives—know what I mean? There was poverty. Those were the Depression years. I went to elementary school in Navasota, Texas, a tacky little town. The school was across the railroad tracks. One of my earliest memories is climbing under the trains to get to school, and, of course, it was a black school. It was only later I learned we were segregated. There were certain parts of town one didn't go to—certain things one didn't do. I just accepted it. So my early life was very rural. The first dances I ever choreographed came out of these early experiences. I call them Blood Memories. I remember the local Dew-Drop-Inn—the Saturday-night place where everybody went, doing the country dances. There were folk singers and guitar players and it all turned me on terribly. And there was the whole experience with the Baptist Church—the baptisms and the gospel shouts— the itinerant folk singers, like Sonnyboy Williamson. So that early black experience colored everything that I did."

During World War II, Alvin Ailey and his mother moved to California. There were jobs available in the aircraft industry, and Mrs. Ailey went to work in a Los Angeles aircraft plant. It was here that Alvin, aged twelve, met his destiny.

"I first became aware of dance by going to the movies, you know, the

Forties musicals. I became very, very impressed with Fred Astaire and Gene Kelly—the glamour of it all. I began to have dreams. I was athletic and musical, I wanted to write the great American novel, and I wrote poetry. I did everything. I played football in high school, and I did gymnastics, which led me to dancing.

"There was a marvelous fat lady living around the corner from us, Loretta Butler, whom I'll never forget. She had a tap-dancing school in her living room. She had these slick shellacked floors—very chic—and she had all these kids doing tap dancing. I decided I had to do this too, and I remember my journey to get my first tap shoes. I did this for a couple of months, not really digging it very much. Then, I remember a friend I had, Ted Crumb. He said he was studying classical ballet, which was unheard of for boys. He said, 'I do ballet.' I said, 'How the hell do you do ballet?' He told me to come and see him perform at the high school, and I did. And that's how I first met Carmen de Lavallade. She and this boy danced together at assembly. She went to the same high school. And she danced on *pointe*. It was beautiful. Later, Ted Crumb asked me to come over to his house, and he started doing these exercises—incredible things that just blew my mind. They were contractions, releases, and falls—crazy things. I'll never forget that day! He said he had seen these things done at the Lester Horton School in Hollywood."

Ailey's face lit up at the recollection of being taken by his friend to the Lester Horton School. Horton, a dancer and choreographer, had begun his career as a designer and stage manager for the Indianapolis Civic Theatre. Later, he became an authority on the dances of the American Indian and also worked with Michio Ito, developing new ideas from the schools of Japanese dance. Lester Horton's approach to modern dance techniques was instrumental in creating wide interest in the genre.

"I was tremendously impressed by Lester Horton," Ailey continued. "There were all kinds of people around him, all kinds of ideas, all kinds of music, painting, sculpture. Lester was the genius of all this. So I enrolled in his school and studied for a month. Then I left. I went to UCLA to study Romance languages. I didn't really see myself as a dancer. I mean, what would I dance? It was 1949. A man didn't just become a dancer. Especially a black man. I mean, you could be a Dunham dancer, or you could be a tap dancer—you know, show business, big swing. Finally, Horton called me back. He thought I should continue studying with him. He put me on scholarship. And so I made the big break. I quit school, left home, and went to live in Hollywood. At Horton's, I mopped the stage and changed the gels; I worked in the costume shop; I painted scenery. To earn money, I worked as a waiter in a nearby restaurant. And I was happy. Lester let us know that we were *all* beautiful. There were Japanese and Mexicans and blacks, whites, greens, and pinks. And it was great. I was very happy being in the milieu of the dancers. I was eighteen."

It may have been a sense of insecurity over his abilities as a dancer that made Ailey decide to quit the Horton school once again. After one year with Horton, he suddenly left for San Francisco, and enrolled at Berkeley University to continue his studies of languages. In order to live, he took a job as a baggage loader with the Greyhound Bus Company. Ailey had studied and worked for about a year in San Francisco when a producer befriended him and offered him a job dancing in a night club—the Champagne Supper Club. On an impulse, Ailey accepted the offer.

"I was enticed to come and dance in this night club, and I did a lot of jazz dancing. It was the time of the last great black chorus line, and it was a marvelous experience. I danced for several months, and learned a great deal. For some reason, the show was invited to come to L.A., and once there I began hearing from friends what Lester Horton was up to. I heard he was doing dances based on pictures by Paul Klee, he was doing Lorca pieces, he was doing music of Ellington and Stravinsky. He was doing Mexican themes. Well, I couldn't resist. I went to the school, and I met with Horton. This time I said, 'This is it!' I quit the club, I quit the University, and I started studying with Horton again. The year was 1953, and I was now twenty-two. Lester had started a children's school at his theater, and I started teaching kids. One time, we were preparing to stage a benefit for the school. While preparing and rehearsing, Lester suffered a heart attack. He died at the end of 1953. It was a terrible thing, but we had our next season to worry about."

Soon after Lester Horton's death, Ailey and the company's business manager decided to keep the school and the company alive.

"I did everything that I thought Lester would do. I designed the costumes, I did Noguchi-type sets, I went to shop for fabrics, the way Lester did. And I began to choreograph dances. I didn't know anything about form and such. I only knew how to imitate Lester. I choreographed a tribute to Lester—*According to St. Francis*, and another work based on themes of Tennessee Williams, which I called *Mourning Morning*.

"Now, the Horton Company had previously been invited to Jacob's Pillow, and Ted Shawn had invited the company back for the summer of 1954. So we went, because we had signed a contract. We drove across the country in a station wagon, with all the costumes and stuff. We presented my two ballets. Well, Ted Shawn was appalled. He wrote a letter to our business manager saying: 'How dare you send this young man with these long ballets that have no form.' And Walter Terry came to review us, and he wrote that my works were 'Kitchen-sink ballets.' I wasn't really hurt. I wanted to make dances."

When Ailey returned to Los Angeles with the Horton dancers—Carmen de Lavallade was among them—he tried, unsuccessfully, to keep the school and company together. Horton was obviously a one-man operation. Ailey and the business manager quarreled, and things came to an impasse.

Ailey left the company upon receiving a telephone call from theatrical producer Saint Subber, who was then in Philadelphia trying out a musical adaptation of Truman Capote's *House of Flowers*.

"The show was in terrible trouble in Philadelphia," Ailey recalled. "George Balanchine had just been let go as choreographer, and Herbert Ross was brought in. It was Herbie who asked for me and for Carmen de Lavallade. He wanted us as the lead dancers for the show, and so we went East. Carmen and I danced in *House of Flowers* for five months. While in the show, I began to study with everybody I could find. I studied with Martha Graham, with Hanya Holm, and composition with Doris Humphrey. When *House of Flowers* closed, I danced with various small companies, including Anna Sokolow's. Even though I starved a lot, I became immersed in the dance world. Then, in 1957, I landed a job in the Lena Horne musical *Jamaica*, and Jack Cole, who choreographed it, became an idol. He blew my mind completely. He was the first man since Lester Horton that completely knocked me over. Anyway, after a while, I decided to give a joint concert at the YMHA— on Ninety-second Street. A friend of mine, Ernest Parham, and I gathered together thirty-five of the most incredible dancers in New York, and we gave eight concerts in March 1958. I did *Blues Suite* and some Latin dances, and a solo dedicated to Lester Horton that I danced myself. So those were our first concerts in New York, and they were very successful. We received very good notices from John Martin of *The New York Times*. Then, I decided the next time I would give a concert on my own—which I did, in 1959, again at the 'Y.' Then I gave two more concerts, and by 1960, I was ready to form my own company."

Ailey went on to say that he had intended his company to be a kind of Brechtian showcase for black music and culture—black America's contribution to music and dance. The company, he said, was very influenced by Katherine Dunham and it was then an all-black company. He installed his group at the Clark Center for the Performing Arts, at Eighth Avenue and Fifty-first Street, where the company took and taught class, and also performed. It remained at this location until 1969, when it was invited to become the resident dance company at the Brooklyn Academy of Music.

Some years earlier, however (in 1961, to be exact), Ailey became briefly involved in acting. He appeared as a straight actor in such plays as *Call Me by My Rightful Name* and *Tiger, Tiger, Burning Bright*. Soon he was back dancing with his own company. The group was invited to appear at Jacob's Pillow (1961), and the following year, the State Department asked the company to tour Southeast Asia. The eight dancers and five musicians making up the company—it was called the American Dance Theatre—toured for several months, dancing works by Ailey, Glen Tetley, John Butler, and Lester Horton. It was the beginning of the company's great popularity. Later under the name of the Lavallade-Ailey American

Dance Company, the group expanded to twelve, and made another Asian tour. In 1965, when the company was traveling in Europe, Alvin Ailey gave up dancing professionally. He would now concentrate exclusively on creating dances.

His output as choreographer had already been impressive. Works such as *Blues Suite, Creation of the World, Revelations, Knoxville: Summer of 1915*, and *Feast of Ashes* (choreographed for the Robert Joffrey Ballet) were receiving wide attention and praise. In 1969, the Ailey company took up residence at the Brooklyn Academy of Music. But Brooklyn proved dissappointing:

"We got disenchanted with Brooklyn. There was a community thing there that I thought should be happening. Harvey Lichtenstein, who runs the place, really wanted to make a Lincoln Center in Brooklyn. Well, he couldn't do that—he had to think about the community he was in. Anyway, Harvey and I didn't see eye to eye, and I said we'd better get the hell out of there—which we did. In 1970 we toured colleges, and the State Department sent us to North Africa and to Russia, where we stayed for six weeks."

Since 1971, the Alvin Ailey Dance Theater has established itself as one of the most potent companies in the world. Its appearances in New York and elsewhere have been received with ovations and unstinting critical praise. By 1973 it had found a home base—the New York City Center— where it gives regular seasons, alternating with the Joffrey Ballet. Ailey continues to choreograph for his own company, as well as for outside companies. His work is marked by the free use of disparate elements of the dance vocabulary. At its best, the Ailey group generates an uncommon exhilaration, achieved by a tumultuous and almost tactile rhythmic pulse. Ailey's own best works are charged with a dazzling and uninhibited movement and life.

The exuberance and poignancy of the black experience are well served in Ailey's splendid *Revelations, Blues Suite*, and *Cry*. But the company's repertory is rich in a wide variety of works that fall outside the ethnic range. Ballets set to music of Samuel Barber, Carlos Surinach, Benjamin Britten, and others, make clear Ailey's interest in enlarging both his repertory and artistic scope. He is greatly aided in this by the presence of a number of superb dancers, each trained in both classical and modern techniques. Judith Jamison, Dudley Williams, Kelvin Rotardier, Linda Kent, John Parks, and Sara Yarborough, among others, form a highly responsive body of remarkably disciplined artists.

Like all choreographers, Ailey has his weak points. Often, he does not carry his choreographic ideas to their logical conclusion. Excessiveness frequently jars the flow and impulse of his dances. In his effort to combine ballet with contemporary movement, he sometimes loses sight of the over-all design and the intent of his dance expression. When attempting pure ballet, he clings to too many elementary movements. Basically, Ailey is a theater man. When he introduces the elements of "show-biz" into his work, things come to life, and the dances become joyous and extroverted.

What does choreographing mean to Alvin Ailey?

"I choreograph because I think dancing is beautiful. I am very involved with people. I love a lot of people, and that's very difficult to do. I suppose I'm looking for love through my work and trying to give love through my work. I am trying to express something that I feel about people, life, the human spirit, the beauty of things. I'm trying to celebrate man's achievements—the beauty of music, of shapes, of form, of color, light, texture. The idea of a person's doing this with his body—the idea of freedom through discipline—is beautiful to me. And so is the idea of people working together."

Ailey has often been criticized by black militants for having integrated his company. White dancers have appeared with him since 1964.

"Yes, I've had flack from black militants," says Ailey. "But it's a question of everybody being human. Look, I'm militant. I'm very much against racism. Don't forget I'm a Texan. I'm a Southerner, and I'm violent about anything racial. But I think that we have to get together—and dance together. I'm very happy when I see an audience in Houston, Texas, applauding my mixed company when they walk down the stage hand in hand. They are applauding human beings doing this thing. I want to make them forget color. I get this business that white kids can't do this or that kind of so-called black movement. Well, the truth is some of the black kids can't do it either. The point is that's not important. I like to celebrate the difference. I mean, people are people. If somebody dances the blues a little differently, well, that's groovy."

How does Ailey assess his own works?

"My own works are like the inside of my head, and if they're going well, then the inside of my head is going well. If they don't go well, then I'm very disturbed. My ballets are all very close to me—they're very personal. I try to do things that relate to me very personally, and to society in general. I think that people come to the theater to look at themselves, to look at the state of things. I try to hold up the mirror, although I try not to be too depressing about it."

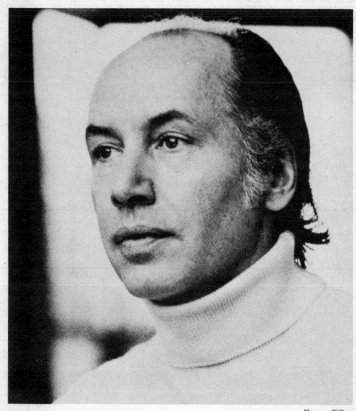

Hannes Kilian

GLEN TETLEY

On a sunny London morning, in July 1972, I made my way to Covent Garden, where I had been invited to attend a run-through performance of Glen Tetley's ballet *Labyrintus*. This was the second major work the American choreographer had been asked to stage for the Royal Ballet—the first having been *Field Figures*, set to a score by Karlheinz Stockhausen. The new ballet, to music of Luciano Berio, was in progress when I arrived at the opera house. Onstage were Royal Ballet dancers Lynn Seymour, Deanne Bergsma, David Wall, and Virgie Derman. They danced an intricate set of abstract variations, forming strange, beautifully composed patterns. The set consisted of two enormous mirrored panels, which were being moved manually by two male dancers. As the mirrored panels were slowly set in motion, the dancers' reflections could be seen shifting along with them, their images at times appearing upside-down in the mirrors. The effect was both startling and spellbinding.

At one point in the ballet, Miss Seymour danced offstage, leaving Mr. Wall and Miss Derman dancing together. As these two completed their variation, Rudolf Nureyev leaped onstage, obviously about to execute a solo. Upon seeing the two dancers behind him, Nureyev stopped cold, and walked off. Clearly, something had gone wrong. Glen Tetley called a halt to the run-through, and everyone took a break.

Later that day Glen Tetley came to visit me, and, during the course of our talk, told me what had happened during the run-through.

"Well, Rudy and I had a fight," Tetley began. "Of course, I know Rudy well enough by now to know that when he gets tired, he has to get his adrenalin up by having a fight. What happened was that he was very concerned about the entrance of his solo. He felt there wasn't enough light, and then, he suddenly saw that parallel to his entrance there was an exit choreographed for David Wall and Virgie Derman, which he had never seen because he had been busy. Well, he walked offstage, and we had a fight about it. He said, 'I don't want that exit in there—I don't want David and Virgie.' And I said, 'Do you want me to change the choreography?' He said, 'I don't see why, when I make my entrance, there should be all that monkey business going on behind me.' I then told him, 'Rudy, I don't want you to make an entrance, nineteenth-century style, for a solo variation.' He answered, 'Well, maybe it's choreographed wrong.' I said, 'No, it's choreographed right, because I have a transition across your entrance, and it's very exciting because you come out of darkness into light, instead of coming on with a battery of spotlights.' He then said, 'I shouldn't be in the ballet at all.' And I said, 'I think it's a little late for that.'

"Anyway, I just started to ignore him, and put my arm around him, saying, 'Rudy, will you trust me?' Of course, he came around, and danced magnificiently. But I also had bad moments with him last year when I did *Field Figures*. Rudy had wanted to be in it, but he was not available for as much rehearsal time as I wanted. So I got Desmond Kelly—and thank God, because Desmond was marvelous to work with. Then Rudolf asked if he could do it, too. He told me the part wasn't very big, and would I put in a solo for him. I said no. I told him that if he wanted to do the work, he had to do it as it stood. He accepted, we began rehearsals, and we worked beautifully together. I remember that at one moment he said, 'I have to work by my eye.' It was a revelation, because he has an incredible eye, and a God-given way of moving. He's really marvelous for contemporary works—fantastic!

"But Rudy did become difficult. I kept telling him, 'You asked to do this.' Finally, we got to the first stage rehearsal of *Field Figures*, and he started dropping people, and kicking people, and carrying on. I told him, 'Rudy, these are people I love, and I won't have you working this way. If anyone's wrong, *you're* wrong. It was made for them, and they know it, and if you would listen, and watch them, they will help you.' Well, he calmed down and he did cooperate, and he was marvelous in all the performances. The point is, I'm not cowed by Rudy, because I don't like that kind of star behavior. There's nothing I want to gain in power in working with Rudy. I really don't feel that way. I like Rudy because he moves well, and because he's a brilliant dancer. But I don't like him if he's going to be a prima donna."

Both *Field Figures* and *Labyrintus* proved very successful with the critics. If audiences were not exactly ecstatic, they nevertheless found these works a fascinating departure from the more or less traditional fare usually offered by the Royal Ballet. Tetley gave them a highly refined combination of ballet and modern dance, fusing elements from both schools in ways that showed each genre to its best advantage. What is more, he proved that dancers trained in the rigid principles of classical ballet could execute steps and movements that were seemingly alien to them. *Labyrintus* and *Field Figures* were studies in psychological penetration, the movements echoing emotional states, sometimes fugitively, sometimes literally expressed. Tetley formed his own style through vast experience in every kind of dancing, and is today considered one of the most forward-looking of choreographers.

Glen Tetley, who, in 1974, succeeded the late John Cranko as director of the Stuttgart Ballet, was born in 1926, in Cleveland, Ohio. When he turned six, he and his family moved to Pittsburgh. At eighteen, he enlisted in the Navy's V-12 program and he entered Franklin and Marshall College, a school in Lancaster, Pennsylvania. It was his hope to become a doctor. He finished his premed training at Franklin and Marshall, then came to New York and enrolled in Columbia's College of Physicians and Surgeons. One night, he attended a performance given by Ballet Theatre. At the evening's end, he knew he wanted to become a dancer.

Among the works he had seen that night was Antony Tudor's *Romeo and Juliet*, performed by Nora Kaye, Hugh Laing, and Alicia Markova. Tetley saw a world he did not know existed, and he immediately wanted to be part of that world.

"I gave up medicine, and lived in New York on practically no money. My family was very much against the idea of my dancing, and there was no financial support. It was 1945, and I was very old to begin a career in dancing. Still, I was determined, and I began to take classes. One day, my money ran out, and I had a friend who was in *On the Town*, which Jerome Robbins had choreographed, and which was just about to go out on tour. I went down to the theater to borrow a couple of dollars from this friend, so I could eat. Jerry Robbins was standing there, and he asked, 'Have you come to audition for the show?' I say no. He said, 'Well, you look very much the type for the show. Would you audition?' Being totally naïve about dancing, I auditioned for him—and got the job!

"Jerry not only gave me a job, but also a solo spot in the show. Then he went away and left me in the hands of an assistant who went out of his mind for two weeks, because I knew nothing about dance. He worked with me, and I had to do this tap dance, and I had never done that. Tap shoes were brought me a half-hour before curtain time, and I had to go on with AllynAnn McLeary, who was the star of the show. I danced, but never made a sound, I was so terrified. Milton Rosenstock was the conductor, and he came back and said, 'Relax, relax!' And Betty Comden was very sweet to me. Everyone tried to calm me down. Then Jerry came back in a blind fury and said, 'You be here tomorrow morning at nine o'clock, and I'll give you something you *can* do!' So, I survived, and I stayed in the show for six months. It really shook my ideas about dancing, and I never got over this original stage fright—this terror. I decided then to go back to medical school. Dancing wasn't for me. We closed in Chicago, and I had my ticket back to New York."

But Tetley did not return to medical school. Jerome Robbins recommended him to his own teacher—Helen Platova. Later, someone suggested that he study with Hanya Holm, who, at the time, had a studio in Greenwich Village Her approach and technique were ideal for Tetley. When Holm offered him a scholarship, Tetley began his studies in earnest. Since he had no money, he lived in Miss Holm's studio, cleaning the place for his keep.

"I loved Hanya. We had a very close relationship. She was Mary Wigman's chief assistant in the Wigman school in Germany. She started the Hanya Holm School, which was based on Wigman technique, but much more technical—much more space-oriented and analytical. Wigman was very brilliant, erratic—and a genius. Hanya was cooler, more theoretical, and a great teacher. I stayed with her for five years.

"The one great advantage of her technique is its discipline and its involvement with the basics of movement. When this dance movement started in Germany, Wigman and Kreutzberg and Laban and Holm got together, wanting to find a technique for dance that would underlie all forms of dance. What was a basic *plié*? What was a basic *relevé*? What was the hip placement for extension? They worked out a very basic language for all of these movements. And, like Martha Graham, they took many things from the Oriental dance. One reason I liked all this so much was that I had gone to medical school, where everything was analytical and anatomical. The beauty of Hanya's technique was its absolutely sound basis, anatomically, physiologically, and every way."

Eventually, Glen Tetley became Hanya Holm's assistant, often traveling with her to Colorado, where she ran a summer school. In the early Fifties, when Miss Holm began to choreograph musicals, Tetley again assisted her. He worked with her on *Kiss Me Kate* and *Out of This World*, and he danced in both shows as well. During this period, Tetley began study with Martha Graham, Antony Tudor, and Margaret Craske. With Hanya Holm's technique under his belt, he found it much easier to approach classical dance. Things began to go quickly for him, and he was seldom out of a job.

Tetley danced on many early television shows, and for five seasons was lead dancer with the New York City Opera. He was in the original NBC production of Menotti's *Amahl and the Night Visitors*. He danced in concert with Pearl Lang and José Limón. He toured Europe with a small company formed by John Butler. He was in Robert Joffrey's first company, dancing the classical repertoire. In 1958, Tetley, together with Carmen de Lavallade and Buzz Miller, danced at the first Festival of Two Worlds, in Spoleto.

When he returned from Spoleto, Agnes de Mille asked Tetley to go into the musical *Juno*, which she was choreographing. She created a special dance for him, called a "Slip-Jig." It came at the finale of the first act and stopped the show. Glen Tetley became an overnight sensation.

"On the basis of that performance," Tetley recalled, "Two marvelous things came to me: Martha Graham gave me some sound advice, and Lucia Chase asked me to join her company—American Ballet Theatre. I remember Martha Graham coming backstage opening night. You know, she's Scotch-Irish from Pittsburgh, and I am Scotch-Irish from Pittsburgh. Anyway, she came back and said, 'I want to talk to you.' She took me back to her house. I had been studying with her for some time, and she said, 'Now I want to tell you a few secrets of my career, because I think people are going to be asking things from you, and I want to prepare you.' And so, from eleven that night until seven the next morning, she talked to me. I was mesmerized by her. She said that she had to be careful of people using her or treating her as just a performer. She told me how she had once been invited to Newport by society people to come and dance. They told her where the back door was. She said 'Oh, no. I come in the front door!' And she told me, 'I'll tell you the three most important things in life. When you're asked to do something, your first question must be: How much money do I get? The second question you ask is: What will my billing be? And the third question, which you don't really have to ask, is: What am I going to do?'

"Martha then asked me to come into her company, and I was in something of a dilemma, because of Lucia Chase, who had also asked me. Well, I decided to join Martha. Martha made *Embattled Garden* for me. I danced the Serpent in it. And during that year she made *Clytemnestra* and made the role of Apollo for me. To work with Martha, to be close to her, to know her as a friend, was one of the greatest experiences in my life. She taught me so much! By this time I had become quite a strong technician, and Martha taught me to re-examine everything—not intellectually but emotionally. She wanted me to open up, and take everything out of the mind, and to let the emotional quality take control of the movement. She opened up a whole world of performance for me. She incredibly enriched the way I feel about movement, about theater."

Lucia Chase, of American Ballet Theatre, did not give up on Glen Tetley. She waited out his period with Martha Graham, then approached him again with an offer to join ABT.

"I had many reasons for going to Ballet Theatre," said Tetley. "For one thing, I needed money. We did not get paid at Martha's. But more than that, Lucia said she'd give me Tudor ballets. I would dance in *Lilac Garden* and in *Pillar of Fire*. These were fantastic ballets, and I would be dancing them with Nora Kaye, which was like a dream come true. I remember the first night I went on in *Pillar of Fire*, Nora, on whom it was made, and who breathed and lived it, did not want to rehearse it. I was terribly nervous, and we never did it on *pointe*. So, there we were on the Met stage, all walking around, and Nora came to me and said, 'What's the matter? You nervous?' Well, I was terrified, and even furious that she would ask that. Just before we went on, she came in the wings and grabbed me by the balls, which was Nora's 'Good-luck' sign, and that made me laugh. I relaxed and said, 'Okay. I'm with you.' We did the ballet, and I loved performing with her."

Tetley joined American Ballet Theatre in 1960, dancing Tudor works, and doing roles such as Jean, in Birgit Cullberg's *Miss Julie*, the Husband in Cullberg's *Lady from the Sea*. And he danced in *Billy the Kid*. When the company toured Russia, he danced the title role in Fokine's last ballet, *Bluebeard*. When he returned to the States, Jerome Robbins asked Tetley to join his year-old company, Ballets: U.S.A.

"Jerry offered me his *Afternoon of a Faun*, *The Cage*, *The Concert*, *Moves*, and *Opus Jazz*. He also said he'd do a new ballet for me (which became *Events*) and I accepted, because it sounded like the greatest repertory anybody could ever have. And so I stayed with him for that entire year. It was great to come back and dance for Jerry. And it was great working with him. Now, Jerry changes diametrically when he walks in that stage door—because he's a sweetheart offstage. I mean, socially, he's a dream. Of course, what I loved about Jerry was his absolute precision—about everything. I've never known anyone who gave directions in such specifics. If you have lived through that, you've really passed through something. He wears you out completely. But his were great ballets, and I was determined to do the very best job for Jerry."

But the relationship between Glen Tetley and Jerome Robbins did not

THE PRIVATE WORLD OF BALLET   430

end well. There was a falling-out between them over billing, and when the year was over, Tetley decided to leave Ballets: U.S.A., and take a year off. He refused many offers to perform, and began thinking of choreographing on his own. With the financial help of a friend he began preparing four original works, each to be danced by himself, Linda Hodes, and Robert Powell. He commissioned three composers to write original scores, and used Schönberg's *Pierrot Lunaire* for his initial choreographic effort. Carlos Surinach, Harold Shapero, and Peter Hartman wrote new scores, Rouben Ter-Arutunian, Willa Kim, Beni Montresor, and Peter Harvey designed sets, and within a year's time, he was ready to present his work at the Fashion Institute of Technology. When critic Walter Terry saw the four new ballets, he wrote: "Mr. Tetley has been a brilliant dancer, but he obviously has no talent whatsoever as a choreographer."

"Well, it was the kiss of death," Tetley recalled. "I sort of took to my couch. But ten days later, in the Sunday *New York Times*, John Martin wrote a three-column review about my *Pierrot Lunaire*. It was absolutely fantastic. Now, one shouldn't live or die by reviews, but they do things to you. Anyway, that Martin review really launched my career as a choreographer."

On the basis of *Pierrot Lunaire*, the Netherlands Dance Theater invited Tetley to join them as guest artist, and asked him to mount *Pierrot* for them. While in The Hague, he composed several new ballets for the Dutch company, including *Sargasso*, later performed at American Ballet Theatre, with Sallie Wilson and Bruce Marks in the principal roles. For ABT he also composed *Ricercare*, with music by Mordecai Seter and sets by Rouben Ter-Arutunian, danced by Mary Hinkson and Scott Douglas, which proved an enormous success. Tetley then returned to the Netherlands Dance Theater, composed more ballets, danced and toured with it. When the company appeared in England, Marie Rambert saw Tetley's work and invited him to come to her company, which was then reorganizing itself. Rambert wanted to re-form her company, somewhat in the image of the Netherlands Dance Theater, and Tetley seemed the man to do it. He went with Rambert, and staged four new ballets for them, plus *Pierrot Lunaire* and *Ricercare*.

In 1969 Glen Tetley returned to New York with the intention of restarting a company of his own. He secured a large grant from the National Endowment, and pulled together a company of twelve dancers. They danced several new ballets, as well as older Tetley works, and began to tour in America and in Europe. During the company's European tour, Tetley was again approached by the Netherlands Dance Theater—this time, with the offer that he be the company's artistic director. Tetley accepted, and with Scott Douglas as his ballet master and teacher, began to reshape the company.

"I thought, with the Netherlands, I am going to be a really good artistic director," Tetley said. "Whatever I see that's wrong or false, I'll change. I decided to speak the truth—which nobody wanted to hear. I immediately started in on such aspects as underpaid choreographers, underpaid royalties, low-level teaching, and a rather stagnant repertoire. Hans van Manen, my codirector, agreed with me completely. But I only succeeded in stirring up a lot of mess in the company. After I'd been there four months, I suddenly witnessed these terrible feuds among the people in the company. The upshot was that the board of directors came to me and said, 'There is great turmoil in the company, and I want to hear your problems.' I told them that most of the problems pointed to the business director of the company, who was overworking the company, and who wasn't letting the artistic directors do their job. And so, the dancers came and said, 'Would you take the company over yourself?' I told them I couldn't possibly do that, since I knew nothing of the structure of Dutch contracts, etc. Finally, I resigned.

"I was there for the year of 1970, and during that year I did a tremendous amount of work. I repolished my repertoire, I did several new ballets, including *Mutations*, which was a huge success for them. Anyway, I've been on my own for the past few years, and I've been very, very happy. I live in Spoleto now. Of course, one of the happiest periods of my life—and one of the most terrifying—was when the Royal Ballet asked me to come and do a new work for them. This was *Field Figures*, which I did two years ago. And now, I've come back to do *Labyrintus*."

Glen Tetley, who was subsequently made the head of the Stuttgart Ballet, spoke to me for several hours that afternoon in London, answering my every question with thought and consideration. To conclude our interview, I asked Tetley if he could describe his choreographic methods—his aims in dance.

"One of the hardest things in the world is to put dance into words, because it exists on a level that is preword. Well, I can start out by saying what many people have said about my work. They have said that I make a synthesis of classical ballet and American modern dance—which, consciously, I have never tried to do. You see, to survive I had to learn to do everything, from Broadway musicals to television to concert dance to Martha Graham to classical ballet. To get the job, I had to do it all perfectly. For me, there was never any difference between these things. It was all part of the equipment. When I first began to choreograph, I said to myself that I would never put in any movements that I thought were false—false to the theme I wanted to do.

"I've been choreographing twelve years, and only now have I learned that the best preparation for working on a ballet is to do *no* movement preparation before you go into the studio. It's taken a lot of courage for me to do that. When I'm working in a studio, I find a total loss of identity and ego. I don't know who I am or why I am. I'm lost in the work. It's like falling in love. I become immersed in the other person—in the dancer. I have to work physically. I feel choreography is a supremely physical act. It's the subliminal, tiny things about the choreographer himself that is transferred to the dancers. It's all about the way the choreographer himself moves—the way Tudor moves, or Robbins or Balanchine or Agnes or Martha. That's the hallmark of their choreographic style. It's the tiniest difference that is the great difference.

"So, when I work with dancers, I work in a very physical way, and I've learned not to prejudice myself—not to prepare myself in movement. I know the music, but I don't immerse myself in it at the beginning. For me, first come the movements. All right, I begin through my own body, but immediately I want to see how the dancer will transform that, and I try to pick up all the little accidentals *they* do. And I like for things to stay as open as possible. I like the possibility of change. Actually, there is no great philosophical thing I can say about choreography. I mean, when I choreographed *Field Figures*, it sort of spinned itself out. I remember the first day I walked in on the dancers. They were all standing there, and I was really terrified. They were in one corner, and I was at the opposite corner. I said, 'I think we should get closer together.' And I said, 'I know you're all waiting. But let me tell you something: There's no story, and there are no steps. We're going to have to make them together.' "

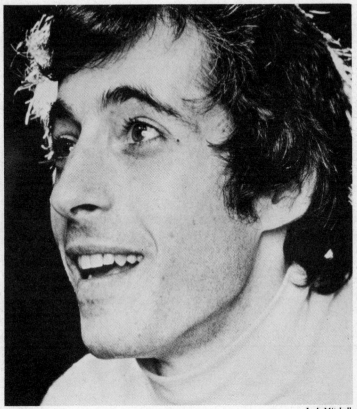

Jack Mitchell

ELIOT FELD

Slouching on a sofa and smoking a cigarette in his West Side New York apartment, Eliot Feld gives the impression of an awkward teen-ager, restlessly wondering what he's going to do with his life. His large hazel eyes, in a sensitively modeled face, continually register surprise—as though the world were one long, crazy spectacle to be looked at, but not necessarily to take part in. An innocence clings to Feld—a little-boy-lost look that is at once endearing and oddly irritating.

In point of fact, Eliot Feld is in his early thirties, and a dancer and choreographer of extraordinary talent and temperament. It has been suggested that his personality is in total contrast to his appearance, that his angelic looks hide a stubborn, difficult, truculent man. Be that as it may, he has produced ballets of lyricism, wit, and charm. And he was nothing if not charming and witty during our talk.

"I was born in Brooklyn, on July 5, 1942, and I went to Yeshiva until the fourth grade," Eliot Feld began. "Then, I was kicked out of Yeshiva for bad behavior. Then I went to public school. When I was about eleven, I started studying at Mr. Balanchine's school—the School of American Ballet. I was the Little Prince in the first production of the *Nutcracker*. I was a prince at eleven, and it's been downhill ever since."

Eliot's father died when he was six. His mother, a travel agent, remarried when the boy was ten. His new father was an attorney. Eliot remembers his grandfather, who had come from Russia, and who loved to recite Shakespeare in Yiddish. He also remembers that as a very young boy he kept dancing around the house, so much so, that his mother, some years later, decided to enroll him in the School of American Ballet. At the school, the boy studied with Antonina Tumkovsky, Ruthanna Boris, and Muriel Stuart. One of his most vivid memories was working on the role of the Little Prince with George Balanchine.

"I was really the understudy, and in the second cast of *Nutcracker*, although I did it in the first season and the second season. Rusty Nichols was the original Prince. I remember particularly working with Mr. Balanchine on the pantomime in the second act. To this day I remember the words. He wrote the words down on a piece of paper so that I would remember the sequence of the story. I can, to this day, sing the words on that music. We worked in the wardrobe room, and he was a very gracious, natural man—not at all frightening. In fact, I think Balanchine is the most civilized man I've ever met.

"I recently had a conversation with him, about my doing a Haydn ballet for his company. Well, Mr. Balanchine has the most gracious way of saying no. Like, 'Maybe this time isn't the right moment,' or 'Oh, that work. Well, I don't know . . . we've just done a Haydn ballet last season.' I said that they had more than one Tchaikovsky ballet, and he said that Tchaikovsky is different. He suggested that I use the music of a modern giant, and I asked him . . . like, who? He said Stravinsky. I said, 'Or . . .' He said, 'Or, or . . .' I said, 'Or Stravinsky?' He said, 'Yes, yes. That's right!' So we both screamed with laughter. That's the kind of encounter I've had with him as an adult."

Feld remained at the School of American Ballet for about two years. He then decided he wanted to become a modern dancer, and began study with Donald McKayle, and briefly danced in Pearl Lang's company. He also enrolled in the High School of Performing Arts, shifting back and forth from the ballet department to the modern department. Now fifteen, Feld could not make up his mind which course of study to pursue. One day, Feld and a girl friend were walking down Seventh Avenue. They came to the Winter Garden Theatre, where *West Side Story* had just opened. Impulsively, the girl dared Feld to sign up as a replacement. Feld accepted the challenge, walked into the theater, and said he'd like to audition. He was told to return at a certain date. When he did, Jerome Robbins, Leonard Bernstein, and Stephen Sondheim, creators of the show, auditioned Feld and accepted him as a member of the *corps* for the London company, which they were just casting. Elated, Feld rushed home to his parents to give them the good news. They were totally against the idea. He was only fifteen, he hadn't finished school, and he was not ready to be on his own. Feld made terrible scenes about it, but finally told Hal Prince, the producer of *West Side Story*, that his parents would not let him go to London. On the next day, Prince told the young dancer that he could join the Broadway company. He danced as a member of the Sharks. A few months later, when the role of Baby John became available, Eliot Feld stepped into the part. He remained with the show for a year, toured with it for six months, and then participated in the filming of it. During this period, he also received his high-school diplomas from Performing Arts and Professional Children's School.

When Feld left *West Side Story*, he felt at sea. "I didn't know what I wanted to do, whether I wanted to act or dance or what. I guess I went through a kind of adolescent confusion. I tried to act, and it was a disaster. When I got to be eighteen I went into analysis. But what I did mostly was play Ping-pong. There was a Ping-pong parlor on Ninety-sixth Street and Broadway. Some people spend time in poolrooms. I spent time in Ping-pong parlors. Anyway, that was the seedy part of my life. And that's what I did from eighteen to twenty-one—played Ping-pong, read a lot, and talked a lot to my analyst—except that she wasn't sensitive to what my needs were. But it was a good experience for me. I'm happy I did it. It kept me alive, and that's what was important. It was like a life preserver at a very difficult time.

"At the age of twenty, I was so bored that I decided I'd start studying ballet again. I discovered a teacher, Richard Thomas, who was then teaching at the June Taylor School, and he became a very important person in my life. I don't know how he saw that I had talent as a dancer, because I had very little facility for ballet dancing. I didn't have pointed feet or dainty legs, and I was so out of condition that I could hardly do a *grand plié* without getting cramps in my legs. But Thomas sensed a talent. I, instead, felt I couldn't do anything. I used to have tantrums and cry in class. I was really, in a way, asking to be kicked out. But he held on to me, and one day he told me that ABT was having auditions, and he wanted me to go. I told him he was crazy. It had never occurred to me that I would be in a ballet company. So I went, and was rejected. They took some boy who couldn't dance a step. He had pretty little feet; he was just perfect, like an etching—but he couldn't get from his right foot to his left. It was just incredible. So that really got me angry. I knew I was a better dancer. It was then I thought, Hell, I'm going to do this. Six months later they again held auditions, and this time they took me into the company."

Eliot Feld entered the *corps* of American Ballet Theatre in 1963. He was now twenty-one, and life had a purpose.

"We did endless one-night-stands, and I had a great time. Being in the *corps de ballet* on a tour was fantastic, because you'd get up in the morning at seven, and at eight you were on a bus. I used to make a bed in the luggage rack, on top, so my face was about an inch from the top of the bus—I'd sleep there. You'd get into a city at three in the afternoon, have something to eat, then you'd go to the theater and do your work. When that was over, you'd come back to the hotel. We used to play cards a lot, or play around in other ways. Then, in the morning, you'd get up again, and back into the bus. You just kind of floated. In the bus someone would tell you when to urinate. 'Okay, five-minute piss break!' So, your whole life was organized. You didn't have to worry about a thing. I remember all that very fondly. I liked that. Possibly also because it was the last period in my life where I had no responsibility—or, rather, whatever responsibility I had I could meet very easily."

Dancing in the *corps* gave Feld the experience and discipline he needed. And watching principal dancers, like Royes Fernandez, Lupe Serrano, Toni Lander, Bruce Marks, or Sallie Wilson, proved invaluable. Feld danced in most of the repertoire, from *La Sylphide* to *Billy the Kid* to *Theme and Variations* to *Giselle*. But he was restless:

"I didn't like being a peasant in *Giselle*. I mean, we were in South America maybe nine months after I joined the company, and there I was, a peasant, wearing orange tights and a straw hat and some fucking grapes on my back. I thought, What am I doing here? I thought of myself as some angry young man, and here I was, dressed in this goddam peasant outfit!"

Soon Feld would get the opportunity of dancing in something more challenging. Jerome Robbins came to Ballet Theatre to stage Stravinsky's *Les Noces*. Feld had, of course, danced under Robbins during *West Side Story*—a period not noted for any friendliness between them.

"I was an ornery kid when I first met Robbins. I had a difficult time accepting corrections from him. I was recalcitrant, and he was sensitive to it. It was really an unfortunate experience for me. And it was probably a great deal my fault. When Jerry came to ABT we got along very well. I worked much better for him, and I think he was pleased, because as *Les Noces* went on, I got more and more to do in it. I loved working for him; he demands your full attention, your full abilities. He exercises your mind, especially in a ballet like *Les Noces*, which is so complicated rhythmically."

The experience with Robbins may have stirred creative impulses in Eliot Feld, for soon after *Les Noces* he felt the need to choreograph. "I heard a piece of music—Prokofiev's Fifth Piano Concerto—and there was a toccata in it, a very fast movement, which was about two minutes long, and I just saw this dance for two people, a kind of chase. So I started working. But what I wanted was impossible physically. I worked on it for two months, and finally it came out the way I had pictured it. Then I got an idea for another movement—a trio for two boys and a girl. When I finished that, I spoke to Jerry and asked him to come and look at it. He came, and he was really very impressed. It was so nice to see Jerry as spontaneous as he was at that moment. He told me I should do something with the work. And so, I asked him to speak to Lucia Chase and ask her to produce it on his recommendation. He said he would—absolutely. And he did. Ballet Theatre then asked me to mount this ballet for them. I called it *Harbinger*, and it was my first work, ever."

The critics hailed *Harbinger* as something less than a masterpiece—and so, by 1966 Eliot Feld had launched his career as one of the most exciting young choreographers in the country. He instantly began working on a new ballet—*At Midnight*, to songs of Mahler—a rather lugubrious work, which, nevertheless, found favor with critics and public alike.

"The success was very strange. I really ignored it to a large extent. The thing is I had no craft. It was all instinct. I didn't know how I'd done the first ballet, and I didn't know how I was going to do the second one. I mean, I went into a room full of people and I had an idea in my head, but that was all. There were no mechanics that I could grab onto. With my first ballet, I knew I wasn't a choreographer, so it was frightening—I knew that whatever I did was more than what was expected of me. But with my second one, I had been hailed as the bright new thing, and I had no technique of any sort. I still don't. Now, of course, I know that nobody really does, so it's all right. But I didn't know it then."

In 1968 Eliot Feld left American Ballet Theatre ("The company just wasn't responsive to my needs. I knew it was a destructive situation for me to be in"). He went to Canada to stage a new ballet—*Meadowlark*—for the Royal Winnipeg Ballet. Toward the end of 1968, Feld gathered together a company of fifteen dancers, including Christine Sarry, John Sowinski, Elisabeth Lee, and Olga Janke, and began rehearsing them in a program of six ballets which would be performed during the summer, at the Festival of Two World in Spoleto. For the occasion, Feld created *Intermezzo*, to music of Brahms, and *Cortège Burlesque*, to music of Chabrier. These, together with *Harbinger, At Midnight, Meadowlark*, and Herbert Ross's *Los Caprichos*, constituted the program. The company called itself the American Ballet Company. Prior to departing for Spoleto, Feld spoke to

Harvey Lichtenstein, who had just then been appointed director of the Brooklyn Academy of Music, and it was agreed that after Spoleto the company would take up residence in Brooklyn.

Eliot Feld's American Ballet Company danced at the Brooklyn Academy for a year and a half. But money ran short, travel bookings were minimal, and the company finally disbanded in 1971. Looking back on that period, Feld fell into a certain gloom:

"To form and run a ballet company you need gobs of money. You have to be able to absorb tremendous losses during performing periods, especially in the beginning when your company has not developed an audience or a reputation. Well, people just didn't come. You see, we were presenting something different in dancing. What we were presenting had to find an audience that related to what we did. Joffrey has found an audience, as has the New York City Ballet, as has American Ballet Theatre. But it has taken years for these companies to develop those audiences. That's what we had to do. Perhaps I didn't have the patience.

"Anyway, it was a fantastically productive time for me—and not only that, but having my own company really permitted me complete freedom to discover what I wanted to do. It allowed me to discover who I was as a choreographer. Also, we developed a sense of values—and an aesthetic. We lived by that aesthetic. We knew when something was good."

In February 1974, Feld's dream for re-forming his own company came true. With the support of The Rockefeller Foundation, he created the Eliot Feld Ballet. Joseph Papp offered the young choreographer rehearsal space at the Vivian Beaumont Theater at Lincoln Center and performance space at Papp's downtown Public Theater. A spokesman for The Rockefeller Foundation announced in the press that Eliot Feld "is the most important artist we have in dance, along with Balanchine and Robbins. . . . Feld is a great American artist, one who must work in the context of his own company."

What is Eliot Feld's choreography about?

"I don't know. I know that it's about dancing to the music. That's what it's about more than anything. I hear a piece of music, and ideas begin crystallizing out of it. When I choreograph, I try not to talk. The best thing is to dance. To talk is just a last resort. I try to discover the movement. That's where I really missed having my own company, because after working with the same people—people who related to you—things began to happen. We looked for movements together. When I choreograph, I don't walk into a room with a bag of tricks. I really look and try to search for what this ballet is about. It's only tantalizing when you have dancers who enjoy that treasure hunt with you."

While he was without a company of his own, Feld accepted invitations to compose new ballets for other companies. He choreographed *Winter's Court*, to Renaissance music, for the Royal Danish Ballet, and two works to Stravinsky—*A Soldier's Tale* and *Eccentrique*—for American Ballet Theatre. In 1973, he composed a new ballet, *Jive*, to music by Morton Gould, for the Joffrey Ballet. It was a work of spunky charm and inventiveness, but the critics compared it to Jerome Robbins' 1945 ballet *Interplay*, which also employed a Gould score.

"I really didn't intend to do any nostalgia piece—or Fifties piece—when I did *Jive*. I was interested in slang, and giving form to slang. I was interested in my reaction to that music, here, in 1973. So it's irritating that people feel the need to compare the work to Jerry's. It's also irritating that Jerry always comes out better. But it's unimportant—such trivial nonsense. The work will stand or it won't stand."

Eliot Feld, a rebel *with* a cause, dislikes talking about himself on personal terms:

"I'd rather not discuss myself, because it's not important. I'm not important. It's only the work that's important. I really feel that what makes me different from a chimpanzee is that I'm able to do good work. We can all eat, sleep, and make love, and I'm very lucky to have found something that I do well, because it gives me some value. Otherwise, I would just be taking up space."

Martha Swope

ARTHUR MITCHELL

To start a ballet company takes money, time, and public support. To start a black ballet company takes money, time, public support, and daring. Arthur Mitchell, long associated as a principal dancer with the New York City Ballet, has taken that daring step. Four years ago, he formed the Dance Theatre of Harlem, a company of some thirty dancers. What is more, the company has its own school and rehearsal space, with a staff that includes Mitchell, Karel Shook, and Tanaquil LeClercq.

Why a black ballet company?

When I visited the school and talked to Arthur Mitchell and Karel Shook, the answers came flying. Said Shook:

"Let me say that neither Arthur nor I wanted to prove that black people can do ballet. We know they can, although the myth is that they can't. People say that their backs are built the wrong way or that their behinds are too big. Black people *can* do ballet. Ballet is nonethnic. So we didn't want to prove that it *could* happen, we just *wanted* it to happen. Another reason was to have something of our own. I don't mean a possession. It's hard to explain. But we wanted to do it our own way."

Said Arthur Mitchell:

"It's not that I woke up one morning and got this great emotional feeling and said, 'I'm going to start a company.' What *did* happen was that about five years ago, I was off in Brazil forming a Brazilian ballet company. I had been invited to do this. Then on the last day I commuted to Brazil, Martin Luther King was assassinated. I got very upset. I said to myself, This is silly. Why am I making these nine-hour trips, going around the world, building ballet companies. I should be doing this at home."

For years, Arthur Mitchell was the only black dancer with the New York City Ballet. A product of the High School of Performing Arts and the School of American Ballet, the forty-year-old, New York-born dancer began his professional career performing in musicals and with various modern dance groups. In 1956, he joined the New York City Ballet, easily moving to the rank of principal. He appeared in such ballets as *Western Symphony, Interplay, Agon, Ebony Concerto, A Midsummer Night's Dream*, among many others. His brilliant, quicksilver technique, and tempestuous good looks made him a favorite with the public, and with George Balanchine, who had carefully and lovingly nurtured his career.

When Mitchell's Dance Theatre of Harlem had been in existence for only two years, Balanchine invited the company to come and perform on the same stage with the New York City Ballet in a benefit gala performance of a work jointly choreographed by Balanchine and Arthur Mitchell. The event, held at the New York State Theater in May 1971, was an odd one.

On the surface it appeared to be an exhilarating exercise in largess on the part of Balanchine. It was, after all, a gesture of generosity that prompted him to invite a relatively unprofessional group of dancers to come and share an experience that by his own consummate high standards might very well have turned out to be a study in technical contrast. The brilliant balletic refinements of the tautly trained white company might, more than likely, be seen to advantage over the younger and less experienced black group. As it turned out, this joint choreographic effort of Balanchine and Mitchell, based on *Concerto for Jazz Band and Orchestra* by the Swiss composer Rolf Liebermann, proved an erratic venture, in which neither company came out looking well. The nature of the music, with its clearly differentiated rhythmic sections, found the Harlem dancers engaging in boogiewoogie, mambos, blues, while the City Ballet dancers performed the more recherché, abstract passages.

What the event *did* prove was that integrated ballet dancing could be the most natural thing in the world. Indeed, Clive Barnes, dance critic of *The New York Times*, wrote an impassioned review in which he practically commanded the New York City Ballet to clear the way for integration in its own ranks. He wanted to see more "black faces" among the Balanchine dancers.

Discussing the event, Karel Shook was somewhat less than thrilled:

"What was so awful was that the public had never seen our company dance before. Balanchine should have allowed us to dance, say, his *Concerto Barocco* or his *Suite No. 3*. If the two companies were brought together after that, it would have been wonderful. But our dancers were presented as the cliché idea of all-black dancers—All they can do is jazz. However, I thought that our dancers showed up to wonderful advantage. They danced with much more energy, they were better trained. All those New York City girls, with fat behinds and fat legs! I really was quite shocked."

Arthur Mitchell's view of the evening was far more tempered: "It's very easy for people to say, 'Well, I don't like that.' But, you see, they forget that it's the first time it's ever been done. First of all, the score used was the kind on which you couldn't force another style. Also, one must remember that we were working with a man who is a genius—a genius who comes out of another era. So you have a boogiewoogie in the score. Well, a boogiewoogie is a boogiewoogie. Also, I felt that my kids learned a great deal by working with the New York City Ballet. You can't buy what one can learn from Mr. B. He is *the* master craftsman. Of course, it was fantastic for me, because it was the first time I worked with Balanchine in another capacity. I'd always worked with him as a dancer. Anyway, just the association of the two companies established The Dance Theatre of Harlem."

Be that as it may, the point to be made is that in the world of classical ballet, the black dancer has received scant attention. Mitchell has been one of the exceptions. But he claims to have had a special attitude about it:

"I'm a fighter. I will fight for everything. Also, I'm an optimist. I do not look at the bad side of things. I have always believed that there is nothing that a human being can't do if he equips himself with technical knowledge. Of course, there are people whose breaking point is different. There have been many, many black dancers who have tried to go into classical ballet, but whose breaking point or stamina was less than mine. As I said, I'm a fighter. Look, the School of American Ballet has always been open to black kids. The trouble is that many ghetto kids don't go downtown. And

Balanchine isn't going to bring his school up to Harlem. Anyway, the majority of schools throughout the country tell the black kids to go into jazz or modern dancing. That's a fallacy, of course. And that's what we're trying to correct."

An interesting glimpse into the knotty problem of integrated ballet companies came when I visited George Balanchine a few days after the gala performance held at the New York State Theater. Balanchine was furious upon reading Clive Barnes's admonition that he integrate the New York City Ballet:

"He says he would like to see more black faces in the company. Well, I can answer that. I would like to see a lot of black people writing his articles. Why not? Are they so bad? Can't they write ballet criticism? As you know, I started as a choreographer many years ago. And many years ago, I wanted to have very-well-trained black people dancing. You must understand that Negro blood or Japanese blood or Russian blood doesn't mean a thing to me. I don't take people because they are black or white. I take exquisite people—people who are made to dance certain types of dancing, which for me is mainly classical dancing. You have to have a certain kind of build, because otherwise you will suffer. The fact is, we have black children in our school. But they don't stay in the school long enough. It's always like that, with whites or blacks. Mothers would come to me and ask how long it will take her child of eight to become a ballerina. I say it takes about eight to ten years. Then it takes another ten years. So, it's about twenty years' work, and that, of course, only if God blesses these ballerinas to really become first class. Well, the mothers say, 'Oh, no, that's too long.' Then they take their children away.

"Years ago Arthur Mitchell and I made a big campaign. We went to Harlem to find children. We offered them scholarships. But you see, they didn't want to stay. It took too long. Now Mr. Barnes says we should integrate. Why? Just because we have a white company? It is as if you would ask a black theater company doing *Emperor Jones*, to take *me* to play the Emperor Jones. No? Are you against me? Is it because I'm Russian? They would say, 'No, it's because you don't look like the Emperor Jones!'

"You will say, 'What about Arthur Mitchell?' Well, Arthur stayed and he learned classical dancing. I have helped Arthur, and I have helped his company, even before foundations came along with grants. Eventually, his company will learn to dance very well. They are now dancing only certain things well. What is difficult is that they are doing classical dancing and it's hard to become the most exquisite classical dance company in the world. It took me since 1934, and only *now* is it really something. I would say that it will take Arthur about twenty years to develop his company along classical lines. These young people he has now, they will eventually leave, get married, just as my people did. So, it's a slow process. You have to train the children."

Balanchine, who is a Board Member and a Vice-President of the Dance Theatre of Harlem, went on to say that he wishes the company great good fortune, and that he would continue to help them in any way that he can. As for the gala benefit in which both companies joined forces, his attitude was one of consternation: "If people were offended by the benefit, let *them* sponsor a benefit, and let *them* do what they want. It's nothing but talk. Why don't *they* give a million dollars to Arthur Mitchell so that he can build a theater? But nobody will do that. They will only talk. I don't talk. I *do*."

Again, Balanchine turned to the question of integration:

"If I had a beautiful black dancer who was only adequate, I would not take him. Should I take a black dancer just because he is black? No. It's not right. Because I take only the best. If I found a fantastic black dancer I would take him immediately. I wouldn't want anyone else to get him. But I cannot accommodate dancers just because they are black. My life is about deciding who is worthy or good enough to be a first dancer. I decide. Nobody is going to tell me what to do.

"When I took Arthur there were many objections. People said, 'What are you going to do with him? He is black.' I said, 'He will dance.' Finally, he became integrated, not in a black sense but in a whole sense. He danced for many years in the *corps*. Then I started to give him other things to do. I don't want to see two Japanese girls in my *Swan Lake*. It's not right. It's not done for them. It's like making an American blonde into a geisha. It's a question of certain arts being things unto themselves. Japanese art is one thing; Chinese art is another. You cannot change what's inherent in a particular art form. As for my critics, these people . . . it's not their business to dictate to other people. They can say when a ballet is terrible, they can say that a dancer is no good, but they cannot tell me what I should do."

The Dance Theatre of Harlem is *not* an integrated company. Its dancers are all black. The school, however, is totally integrated. As Karel Shook put it:

"What people neglect to remember is that children living in ghettos and underprivileged areas are not necessarily black. It's very difficult to reach the poor child, whether he is black or white. The parents are not interested, and the schools are not interested. So, we go out and get the children, or they wander in by themselves. We have a wonderful staff. We are particularly proud of Tanaquil LeClercq, who, as you know, was one of the great dancers with the City Ballet, and is now confined to a wheel chair with polio. I must say, we had to convince her to come and teach here. She and Arthur are very close friends. He danced his first leading role with her, and she danced her last performance with him. I've known her since she was a little girl. So we asked her, and she said, 'No, I couldn't do it. I don't want to have anything to do with it.' At last, we persuaded her. So on the first day she came in and we gave her a demonstration. She used to write her lessons down, but she doesn't do that any more. She was one of the first to put our girls on toe. She is the most spontaneous teacher, and everybody loves her."

Other teachers at the school include Netti Spanardi, Tommy Jonsen, Marie Brooks, Kathryn Grant, and Ann Tyus. Arthur Mitchell does not do a great deal of teaching at the school. He likes administrative work, but when he goes on the road to do lecture-demonstrations with his company, he teaches company class.

Arthur Mitchell continues to dance with the New York City Ballet, although he has curtailed his activities so that he can guide his company and school. Summing up his life in the dance, he says:

"I feel dance is the mother of all the art forms. Before a child is even out of the womb, it kicks—and kicking is dancing. The state that the world is in today, and all the preaching that's going on, makes movement take on a different value. The aesthetics of dance—the beauty of it, the line of it, the physicality of it—that's communication . . . that's freedom."

Louis Peres

LAR LUBOVITCH

When Lar Lubovitch's ballet *Scherzo for Massah Jack* was premiered at the American Ballet Theatre on January 17, 1973, the critical reception was not entirely favorable. It was a ballet that left the critics puzzled. Its content was vaguely reminiscent of the ante-bellum South, with figures in crinolines and ruffled shirts moving amidst dancers dressed in costumes that resembled striped tops—figures that seemed to represent abstract whirling shapes, serving as mysterious symbols of . . . what? The music employed was a trio for violin, cello, and piano by Charles Ives.

The critics were puzzled, but the audience seemed to make contact with this odd work and its emphasis on speed, jagged gesture, surprising counterpoint, and lyric line. The evocation of the South was treated in almost dreamlike fashion—fugitive moments of realism emerged from a maze of abstract movement. What shone forth was Lubovitch's treatment of time. He filled each moment with the sort of fresh exuberance that should be the hallmark of every young choreographer. Lubovitch's work always has about it a nervous, tensile thrust. It is as if the going from one place to another is charged with enormous impatience. The dancers, whether in close formation or spread out, seem always to leave an area of space charged with energy. Very quickly they return to the space they have just abandoned, needing to recapture that energy point.

Scherzo for Massah Jack, the American Ballet Theatre's 100th commissioned work, was evidence of the company's vast range of repertoire and its interest in giving opportunities to young choreographers to create.

Lar Lubovitch arrived at my apartment wearing khaki overalls and heavy workshoes. He wore large green eyeglasses that cast a subtle shadow on his turbulently handsome face. His eyes are green, his hair brown, curly, and worn long. His short, compact build exudes nervousness. During our talk he was extremely fidgety, and when he answered questions the words came in a staccato rush.

"I'm twenty-eight years old. I was born in Chicago. My father was in business with his brothers in a small department store. All my grandparents had come over from Russia. I have an older sister and a younger sister and brother. They are all very creative. We started in a sort of slum area in Chicago. There was a block of Greeks, a block of Mexicans, a block of Jews. But it was predominantly black. I grew up there until we moved to a slightly better economic location. As a little boy I always danced. There wasn't a time when I didn't dance. Of course, I never knew that dancing was something you could do with your life. I was never exposed to professional dancing. That only came when I was eighteen and going to college at the State University of Iowa in Iowa City. Before that, I never knew that the ballet existed. It was an advantage for me because I didn't have millions of lessons to unlearn."

Lubovitch initially wanted to become a painter. He took art courses at the University of Iowa, but soon abandoned art. Visiting the university was the José Limón company, which proved a revelation to the young student. Limón presented, among others, his *Moor's Pavane* and *Emperor Jones*, and the spectacle of these works ignited Lubovitch's imagination to such an extent that he left Iowa (he had been there only a year and a half) and enrolled in Connecticut College for a summer semester in the dance department. When the summer was over, he moved to New York and was given a full scholarship in the dance department of the Juilliard School of Music. To support himself, he took a job as a waiter.

"My first teachers at Juilliard were strokes of incredible luck. They were: Antony Tudor, Louis Horst, Lucas Hoving, and Anna Sokolow. There were also people from the Martha Graham company, really fine teachers like Bertram Ross and Ethel Winter. I was completely overwhelmed. Of course, Tudor was just fantastic. Tudor choreographed phrases in his class which were so exquisite to dance that the whole sense of dancing them was, in itself, having mastered the technique. Just being in his class was a glorious dance. That was certainly my first classical dancing. I didn't know a step. I didn't know a single French dance expression. I didn't know anything. But I was able to copy the phrases Tudor was demonstrating. He would demonstrate with such a sublime kind of poetry that it was my first glimpse of what inspiration looks like. His classes were eloquent. He would come in and give us a traditional *barre*. These were very organic phrases, so it didn't jostle or disturb the body. Then we would come to the center, which was very exciting for everyone, because anything could happen. Tudor had a tremendous rapport with his pianist, Betty Sawyer. She could immediately translate into music what was right for the phrase he was requesting, and she knew very obscure music, which was wonderful to dance to. I just sort of rode on what he was saying. I didn't formulate questions until some years later.

"I was immediately able to do everything. My body was built for it. I was able to sit down with my legs stretched far to the side. My feet had acceptable arches, and my back was straight. The only question I did ask Tudor about dancing was how long he thought it would take me to really dance and have a technique. He said it would take ten years. I was very upset at the prospect, but now, ten years later, I would tell anyone the same thing. It *does* take ten years."

Lubovitch trained in both modern and classical dance. Soon after he entered Julliard, he began dancing professionally in Pearl Lang's dance company. He also performed with Donald McKayle's company. In addition, he danced with John Butler and Sophie Maslow. The initial dancing experience was not altogether easy for Lubovitch.

"At that time dancing on the stage was a very nervous thing for me. I didn't adapt to it in a relaxed way. I took it as a test and it wasn't working at all. I was much too approval-oriented. If you're bent on proving, you're not really *doing*. It took me awhile to learn this. Of course, that may be the same trip for everybody. So I continued to dance and was a member of the Manhattan Festival Ballet and later went to the Santa Fe Opera for two summers. At Sante Fe I did my first choreographing. I put together peasant dances for *Don Giovanni, The Marriage of Figaro,* and *Carmen,* which was a perfectly lovely experience. I didn't mind it at all. After that, I joined Glen Tetley's company. Tetley is a wonderful choreographer. You watch what he's doing very closely because he has a particular presence of creativity. I found myself momentarily at home in his style of movement."

In 1965 Lar Lubovitch became a member of the Harkness Ballet. At the time, the company was undergoing various directorial changes, and Lubovitch danced under such artistic directors as George Skibine, Donald Saddler, Brian Macdonald, Lawrence Rhodes, and Benjamin Harkarvy. Lubovitch's appearance being somewhat less than that of a *danseur noble*, he was assigned character roles—"monsters, ogres, rapists"—and he would dance in works that bore modern influences.

"They couldn't make me look classical, which was all right, but I had from the beginning felt that the spirit behind the company was not very creative. I made my protests known. I was a bit of a renegade. At one point, I wanted to choreograph for them because the works they were doing were just so many vegetables. We would do seasons of the most horrible repertory you can imagine. It was humiliating appearing in these works. That was the kind of atmosphere. The thing is the company had some absolutely terrific dancers. There was Larry Rhodes, Helgi Tomasson, Elisabeth Carroll, Lone Isaksen, Brunilda Ruiz, Dennis Wayne. Wonderful artists. The company was not lacking in artistry. So I asked them if I could choreograph, but they said I had no experience. I asked for a three-month leave of absence, which they gave me. During those three months I got some dancers together, and I began choreographing. That's how I came to give my first concert in New York. I used electronic music, some Buddhist temple chants, and the concert was a success. I went back to Harkness, but again they would not let me choreograph.

"On the advice of Ben Harkarvy, who by the way was a wonderful director, I left. It was very, very painful for me to leave. I was crushed because I believed in all the dancers, and I believed in my capacity to help the company to be more creative. But nobody believed in me. I was constantly being put down for expressing myself."

The break with Harkness was obviously traumatic for Lubovitch. He went through a hellish period, although he continued to give small concerts of his own work in New York. At one point he quit dancing.

"I tried a couple of different kinds of therapies. Mostly, I read a great deal on my own—a great deal of Freud and R. D. Laing. I once tried a purely Freudian analysis, but I found that totally dissatisfying. What's more, I found it ignorant. For me, it was damaging because all the negative possibilities are exploited at once. Then I got into R. D. Laing, who just devastated me. That made a tremendous alteration in my whole thinking process. When he said 'think,' he gave you methods. He was amazing. Then, I ran into the work of Eric Berne. That just simplified the thing so much. Laing for me was like a map of the nervous system—it was an enormous, cosmic thing. Then, Berne uncosmified it, and suddenly I began to see everything just as plain as pie. So I have been with a therapist who follows a more or less Berne-ian concept."

In 1971 Lar Lubovitch formed his present company. It consists of some sixteen dancers, a number of whom came from the Harkness company. But he also hired dancers who had been Graham-trained and others who had studied with a variety of modern and classical teachers. It is a mixed group.

"All of my dancers come from a wide variety of backgrounds and none of them resembles each other in technique. The important thing is that they're all incredibly fine dancers. That's where I start from as a choreographer. For me, it's *dancing* first. I don't call it modern and I don't call it classical. I like dancing to be an experience. It is not a test, it is not a message, but simply an experience to be had. It doesn't matter what it means. People are so conditioned for 'A' is for Apple and 'B' is for Boy. They want an answer to What does it mean? That's not what I'm after. What I'm after is: Did *your* body experience a sensation at the sight of this dancing? Dance is a physical and emotional experience. It's not something cerebral. It's not something artistic. It's something that's essential to every human being."

Lar Lubovitch is one of the few choreographers who involves himself totally in the production of his ballets. He invariably designs his own sets and costumes and does the lighting. He has done this for most of the eighteen ballets he has choreographed so far.

"The sets, the lighting, the costumes are usually known to me before I begin to choreograph any work. The palette of the work is clear to me from the outset. It never occurs to me to work in any other way."

Turning to the method of his choreography, Lubovitch is equally precise:

"I work first from a purely structural standpoint, where I'm really just working on shape. That's where it all begins for me. I begin to build shapes, separate from the music, separate from the ego states that the dancers or myself bring in at that moment. I just work on pure visual shape. Then, from that shape, I begin to build motive. After that, I work it to the music to find out how it correlates. I search for the relationship between my shape and the music. I like to think that I build dance *within* the same time of the music, sharing the same time capsule, not necessarily extorting that time identically, but in a correlative way. Then, the combination of the shape, emotional suggestion, and musical correlation is the finished phrase."

This visual and musical relationship is very apparent in such Lubovitch ballets as *Whirligigs, Knots, Tangles, and Confusion, Joy of Man's Desiring*, the oddly titled, *Some of the Reactions of Some of the People Some of the Time on Hearing Reports on the Coming of the Messiah, The Time Before the Time After After the Time Before*, and the recent *Three Essays*, to music of Ives.

I asked Lubovitch to describe the kind of music that propels him into choreography.

"I think that I'm attached to musical works that are supported by a particular motor rhythm, one that creates a kinesthetic compulsion in my muscles. It must be music that moves me physically, not intellectually. I must be set in motion by this music. Having found such a piece of music, I can then attach my imagination to it, and see what I can do with it physically.

"Actually, I think that choreographers are mainly self-taught. I don't believe that one can study choreography. And I don't necessarily believe that you can learn too much from the work of other choreographers. All *that* does is to give you an insight into how other works are put together. I think something that is very important for anyone who is going to create something out of nowhere is to come to that thing as stripped bare as possible. In that way, you bring your most intimate expression to your work. There's an automatic kind of individuality in doing that—because every person is so uniquely different from every other person. Also, it is terribly important not to be swayed by the opinions of others.

"I believe an artist has to throw out a great deal of what he creates. I think you have to be willing to do that—to throw away and not hang onto the creative moments in your life. These moments have to be by-passed in order to make room for the next step. You mustn't stand still at a point in your work where you receive the approval of a great many people. I see a lot of choreographers doing this. They're very creative, and they hit a moment when everyone says, 'Yes! That's it!' Then, they'll take that moment, and for the rest of their creative career they'll hang onto the characteristics of that widely accepted moment."

Young, energetic, tense, and decidedly gifted, Lar Lubovitch looks to the future with optimism, and a minimum of self-doubt:

"I have great confidence in myself as a choreographer. When I expressed that to someone, he said, 'Maybe you'll find some humility in the future.' That was just bullshit. I mean, some people think you're not supposed to have confidence—that it means something's wrong. Well, I *do* have confidence. I know my work is good, and I'm not afraid to stand on that.

"I know that for me dancing is the deepest, the most personal expression of myself. Someone once asked me what I would do if I knew that the world would end in a few hours. I knew immediately that I would do a wild dance. I would dance and continue dancing until I didn't have anything left to dance on."

PHOTOGRAPH CREDITS

The author and the publishers wish to thank the following for their kind permission to reproduce the photographs which appear on the pages noted: Anthony, PAGE 3; Julian Braunsweg, PAGE 52; Anthony Crickmay, PAGE 153; The Dance Collection, New York Public Library, PAGES 3, 15, 31, 47, 52, 53, 63, 71, 75; Frank Derbas, PAGE 83; Dominic, PAGE 125; Kenn Duncan, PAGES 117, 202, 410, 417; Zachary Freyman, PAGE 404; Hughes, PAGE 31; Hannes Kilian, PAGES 169, 424 (© 1970 copyright by Hannes Kilian, Stuttgart); Bil Leidersdorf, PAGES 227, 232, 237, 244, 254; Richard Lescsak, PAGE 365; Dina Makarova, PAGES 207, 216; Jack Mitchell, PAGES 359, 433; I. Momauw, PAGE 15; The Music Collection, New York Public Library, PAGE 10; The New York City Ballet, PAGES 287, 312, 325, 332, 344, 353; Louis Peres, PAGES 23, 29, 36, 43, 67, 101, 109, 147, 176, 221, 258, 349, 378, 385, 390, 394, 446; Roy Round, PAGES 131, 136, 142, 157, 162; Maurice Seymour, PAGE 52; Bert Stern, PAGE 319; Norma McLain Stoop, PAGE 187; Muriel Stuart, PAGE 39; The Stuttgart Ballet, PAGES 169, 424; Martha Swope, PAGES 25, 91, 190, 196, 268, 278, 295, 304, 338, 371, 440.

INDEX